MOTIVATION
OF
PERSONNEL

MOTIVATION
OF
PERSONNEL

A. Dale Timpe

Series Editor
The Art & Science of
Business Management

Facts On File Publications
New York, New York ● Oxford, England

This is volume one in Facts On File's series "The Art and Science of Business Management," each volume of which provides a broad selection of articles on an important business topic of our time.

Motivation of Personnel

Copyright © 1986 by KEND Publishing

Library of Congress Cataloging-in-Publication Data

Motivation of personnel.
    (The Art and science of business management)
    Bibliography: p.
    Includes index.
    1. Employee motivation—Addresses, essays,
lectures. I. Timpe, Dale.
HF5549.5.M63M67 1986   658.3'14   86-2099
ISBN 0-8160-1460-4

Composition by Facts On File/Maxwell Photographics
Printed in the United States of America

10 9 8 7 6 5 4 3 2 1

CONTENTS

Preface ix

Acknowledgments x

PART I: MOTIVATION—A PRACTICAL PERSPECTIVE

1. Diagnosing and Treating Managerial Malaise
   by Sigmund G. Ginsburg 2
2. Motivation: Good Theory—Poor Application
   by Joel K. Leidecker and James J. Hall 9
3. How Managers Motivate
   by James McMahon 17
4. How to Motivate Your Employees
   by John F. Collins 21
5. Modern Motivation
   by Roy W. Walters 24
6. The Causes and Consequences of High Morale
   by Jan Berkhout 27
7. An Omission in the Planning Process
   by Andre Nelson 32
8. Job Loyalty: Not the Virtue It Seems
   by Jeanne Dorin McDowell 35
9. If You're Really Serious about Employee Motivation...
   by Smith W. Brookhart III 41

PART II: MOTIVATION, MONEY AND REWARDS

10. Can Money Motivate?
    by Stephen C. Bushardt, Roberto Toso and M. E. Schnake ... 50
11. The Power of Pay
    by Robert W. Braid 54
12. Compensation and Benefits: Today's Dilemma in Motivation
    by Stephen C. Bushardt and Aubrey R. Fowler 58
13. Motivating Without Money—Easier Than It Seems
    by Lin Grensing 65

14. Pay Policies
    by Linda Gail Christie 70
15. Money May No Longer Motivate Some Employees
    by Carol Cain 72
16. If Employees Perform, Then Reward 'Em
    by Kevin Francella 75

PART III: THE ENVIRONMENT OF MOTIVATION

17. How to Create a Motivating Work Climate
    by George Lynn 80
18. Constraints to Effective Motivation
    by John Nirenberg 83
19. Getting Motivated Employees to Perform
    by Dennis C. Kinlaw 88
20. On Fish Tanks and Expectations
    by John H. Zenger and Jean E. Edwards 93
21. A Critical Reevaluation of Motivation, Management, and Productivity
    by Erwin S. Stanton 96
22. Corporate Esprit de Corps Languishes
    by Margaret Price 106
23. Motivation Management
    by L. Ed Berry 109
24. Fulfilling Employee Needs—The Key to Motivation
    by Randal D. Naylin 113
25. Implementing the Open-Planned Office Concept
    by Harold L. Airson III 118
26. Low Productivity? Try Improving the Social Environment
    by Keith Davis 125
27. Managerial Risk Taking
    by Suzanne Sisson 128
28. The Trickle Down Theory: Motivation Starts at the Top
    by Frank C. Drazan 135
29. Bosses: Don't Be Nasty (And Other Tips for Reviewing
    a Worker's Performance)
    by Carol Hymowitz 138

PART IV: MOTIVATION RESEARCH, MODELS AND CONSTRUCTS

30. Motivating by Strategy
    by Warren Lamb 142
31. Toward a Theory of Career Motivation
    by Manuel London 149

32. Let's Put the Work Ethic to Work
     by Daniel Yankelovich and John Immerwahr 171
33. Motivation: New Directions for Theory, Research, and Practice
     by Terence R. Mitchell 178
34. Five Steps to Improving Employee Performance
     by Michael Smith and Jan Wing 194

PART V: MOTIVATION—SYSTEMATIC APPROACHES

35. A Coordinated Approach to Motivation Can Increase Productivity
     by James M. McFillen and Philip M. Podsakoff 202
36. Tracking Motivation
     by Kenneth A. Kovach 216
37. Performance Coaching: Hitting the Bull's-Eye
     by Ellen J. Wallach 221
38. A Five-role System for Motivating Improved Performance
     by Robert E. McCreight 225
39. Activation Theory and Job Design: A Usable
     Motivational Tool for Small Business Managers
     by Gene Milbourn, Jr. 229
40. It's Smart to Get Your People to Work Smart
     by Ian Rolland 236
41. Motivate!
     by Don Caruth and Robert M. Noe III 238
42. Management Guidelines: Understanding Needs
     by George Miller 241
43. Coaching...A Management Tool for a More Effective Work Performance
     by G. Eric Allenbaugh 250
44. Motivating Employees in an Automated Office
     by Edward D. Garten and Frances J. Garten 259

PART VI: THE THEORY OF MOTIVATION

45. Why Employee Motivation Has Declined in America
     by Philip C. Grant 262
46. Maslow, Motivation and the Manager
     by J. B. Gayle and F. R. Searle 270
47. In Search of Motivation
     by Michael E. Cavanagh 275
48. How Good Is Values Analysis?
     by Niles Howard 283
49. Getting Down to the Brass Tacks on Employee Motivation
     by Martin J. Kilduff and Douglas D. Baker 290

50. Help Employees Motivate Themselves
      by Leonard Ackerman and Joseph P. Grunenwald 298
51. Integrating Major Motivational Theories
      by Brian H. Kleiner 303
52. How to Uncover a Hidden Corporate Asset
      by Carlton P. McNamara 310

PART VII: MOTIVATION AND JOB FOCUS

53. Motivate the Older Employee
      by Richard F. Tyler 316
54. Mid-Career Block
      by Richard A. Payne 320
55. Motivating the Modern Employee
      by Robert W. Goddard 331
56. Boring Jobs? Redesign Them!
      by Roy W. Walters 336
57. Motivating Your R&D Staff
      by George E. Manners, Jr., Joseph A. Steger,
      and Thomas W. Zimmerer 339
58. Finding Out Why a Good Performer Went Bad
      by Steve Buckman 348
59. To Improve Performance, Try a Little 'Psychological Touching'
      by Herbert E. Brown and Thomas D. Dovel 352

Motivation Bibliography 357

Index 362

PREFACE

People and performance: Two major areas of concern in every business. Management must establish a harmonious environment wherein these two factors complement each other, but often conflict develops instead, because of the inherent disparities between them. Management has to maximize the individual's effectiveness when at any moment the individual's attention may be directed primarily to personal considerations. Success in motivating personnel depends on aligning organizational and personal interests.

Devising appropriate strategies means determining how to get each individual within the organization to make a personal commitment to its planned objectives. This requires attention to a diversity of factors relating to human needs. First, the heightened focus in contemporary society on the rights of the individual has introduced new considerations and demands that have made the task of managing and motivating subordinates more challenging. The employee's quest for fulfillment and satisfaction is no longer job-centered. In addition, wage demands and employee-benefit programs have escalated labor costs. These factors are further compounded by the prevalent corporate takeover and merger activity and the emerging service economy that is creating major dislocation for both white- and blue-collar employees.

Loyalty and employee commitment are now much more difficult to achieve. Management as a result is forced to examine new techniques for motivating employees to improve performance. Furthermore, the growth in office jobs, that now comprise over 50 percent of the work force and over 70 percent of the payroll, has focused management attention on white-collar productivity. These developments have prompted publication of this book, a primary resource tool for those charged with managing employees in today's increasingly complex work environment. The entire management hierarchy must come to grips, and quickly, with the challenge of declining performance.

The articles assembled here provide access to a broad spectrum of practical knowledge, research and theory relating to employee motivation. The objective is to provide a diversity of insights from practical experience together with a conceptual framework for understanding that experience more fully. The sources represent a wide range of professional publications, including a number not readily available to most business managers. This volume is thus a unique compendium of information and opinion on the subject, providing an overview not available in other, more narrow treatments of the issues involved. An awareness of a wide variety of perspectives provides the executive a broader sense of options, a clearer view of potential or actual problems, and a more defined understanding of the interrelationships in each case.

For those wanting a more detailed discussion on a particular aspect of the problem, the Motivation Bibliography provides a valuable resource aid.

A. Dale Timpe, Series Editor
The Art & Science of
Business Management

ACKNOWLEDGMENTS

The articles presented in this volume are reprinted with permission of the respective copyright holders, and all rights are reserved.

Leonard Ackerman, Joseph P. Grunenwald. "Help Employees Motivate Themselves" by permission of *Personnel Journal,* © 1984.

Harold L. Airson III. "Implementing the Open-planned Office Concept" by permission of the *Journal of Systems Management,* © 1983.

G. E. Allenbaugh. "Coaching. . .a Management Tool for a More Effective Work Performance" from *Management Review* by permission of AMA Membership Publication Division, American Management Association, © 1983.

Jan Berkhout. "The Causes and Consequences of High Morale" by permission of *Personnel Journal,* © 1982.

L. Ed Berry. "Motivation Management" by permission of the *Journal of System Management,* © 1979.

Robert W. Braid. "The Power of Pay" from *Management World* by permission of the Administrative Management Society, © 1984.

Smith W. Brookhart III. "If You're Really Serious about Employee Motivation" from *Bank Marketing* by permission of Bank Marketing Association, © 1984.

Herbert E. Brown, Thomas D. Dovel. "To Improve Performance, Try a Little 'Psychological Touching'" by permission from *Sales & Marketing Management,* © 1981.

Steve Buckman. "Finding Out Why a Good Performer Went Bad" from *Supervisory Management* by permission of the author, © 1984.

Stephen C. Bushardt, Aubrey R. Fowler. "Compensation and Benefits: Today's Dilemma in Motivation" from *Personnel Administrator* by permission of The American Society for Personnel Administration, © 1982.

Stephen C. Bushardt, Roberto Toso, M. E. Schnake. "Can Money Motivate?" from *Management World* by permission of Administrative Management Society, © 1981.

Carol Cain. "Money May No Longer Motivate Some Employees" from *Business Insurance* by permission of Crain Communications, Inc., © 1982.

Don Caruth, Robert M. Noe, III. "Motivate!" from *Management World* by permission of the Administrative Management Society, © 1984.

Michael E. Cavanagh. "In Search of Motivation" by permission of *Personnel Journal*, © 1984.

Linda Gail Christie. "Pay Policies" from *Office Administration and Automation* by permission of Beyer-McAlister Publications, Inc, © 1984.

John F. Collins. "How to Motivate Your Employees" from *Nation's Business* by permission of the U.S. Chamber of Commerce, © 1982.

Keith Davis. "Low Productivity? Try Improving the Social Environment" from *Business Horizons* by permission of the Foundation for the School of Business at Indiana University, © 1980.

Frank C. Drazan. "The Trickle Down Theory: Motivation Starts at the Top" by permission of *The American Printer*, © 1984.

Kevin Francella. "If Employees Perform Then Reward 'Em" from *Data Management* by permission of Data Processing Management Association, © 1983.

Edward D. Garten, Frances J. Garten. "Motivating Employees in an Automated Office" from *Supervisory Management* by permission of AMACOM, a division of The American Management Association, © 1983.

J. B. Gayle, F. R. Searle. "Maslow, Motivation and the Manager" from *Management World* by permission of the Administrative Management Society, © 1980.

Sigmund S. Ginsburg. "Diagnosing and Treating Managerial Malaise" from *Personnel*, adapted from the book "Ropes for Management Success" by permission of Prentice-Hall, Inc., © 1984.

Robert W. Goddard. "Motivating the Modern Employee" from *Management World* by permission of the Administrative Management Society, © 1984.

Philip C. Grant. "Why Employee Motivation Has Declined in America" by permission of *Personnel Journal,* © 1982.

Lin Grensing. "Motivating Without Money—Easier Than It Seems" from *Supervision* by permission to The National Research Bureau, Inc., © 1983.

Niles Howard. "How Good Is Values Analysis" from *Dun's Business Month* (formerly *Dun's Review*) by permission from Dun & Bradstreet Publications Corporation, © 1981.

Carol Hymowitz. "Bosses: Don't Be Nasty (and Other Tips for Reviewing a Worker's Performance)" from *The Wall Street Journal* by permission of Dow Jones & Co., © 1985.

Martin J. Kilduff, Douglas D. Baker. "Getting Down to the Brass Tacks on Employee Motivation" from *Management Review* by permission of AMA Membership Publication Division, a division of The American Management Association, © 1984.

Dennis C. Kinlaw. "Getting Motivated Employees to Perform" from *Supervisory Management* by permission of Periodicals Division, a division of The American Management Association, © 1983.

Brian H. Kleiner. "Integrating Major Motivational Theories" by permission of the *Journal of Systems Management,* © 1983.

Kenneth A. Kovach. "Tracking Motivation" from *Management World* by permission of the Administrative Management Society, © 1983.

Warren Lamb. "Motivating by Strategy" by permission from *Management Today,* © 1984.

Joel D. Leidecker, James J. Hall. "Motivation: Good Theory—Poor Application" from *Training and Development Journal* by permission of the American Society of Training & Development, © 1981.

Manuel London. "Toward a Theory of Career Motivation" from the *Academy of Management Review* by permission of the author, © 1983.

George Lynn. "How to Create a Motivating Work Climate" from *Supervision* by permission of The National Research Bureau, Inc., © 1983.

George E. Manners, Jr., Joseph A. Steger, Thomas W. Zimmer. "Motivating Your R&D Staff" from *Research Management* by permission of the Industrial Research Institute, Inc., © 1983.

Robert E. McCreight. "A Five-role System for Motivating Improved Performance" by permission of *Personnel Journal*, © 1983.

Jeanne Dorin McDowell. "Job Loyalty: Not the Virtue It Seems" from *The New York Times* by The New York Times Company, © 1985.

James M. McFillen, Philip M. Podsakoff. "A Coordinated Approach to Motivation Can Increase Productivity" from *Personnel Administrator* by permission of The American Society for Personnel Administration, © 1983.

James McMahon. "How Managers Motivate" from *Supervision* by permission of The National Research Bureau, Inc., © 1983.

Carlton P. McNamara. "How to Uncover a Hidden Corporate Asset" from *Management Review* by permission of AMACOM, a division of The American Management Association, © 1979.

Gene Milbourn, Jr. "Activation Theory & Job Design: a Usable Motivational Tool for Small Business Managers" from *American Journal of Small Business* by permission of University of Baltimore, © 1984.

George Miller. "Management Guidelines: Understanding Needs" from *Supervisory Management* by permission of AMACOM, a division of American Management Association, © 1981.

Terence R. Mitchell. "Motivation: New Directions for Theory, Research, and Practice" by permission of the author and the Academy of Management Review, © 1982.

Randal D. Naylin. "Fulfilling Employee Needs—the Key to Motivation" from *Supervision* by permission of The National Research Bureau, Inc., © 1982.

Andre Nelson. "An Omission in the Planning Process" from *Supervision* by permission of The National Research Bureau, Inc., © 1984.

John Nirenberg. "Constraints to Effective Motivation" from *Supervisory Management* by permission of AMACOM, a division of the American Management Association, © 1981.

Richard A Payne. "Mid-Career Block" by permission of *Personnel Journal*, © 1984.

Margaret Price. "Corporate Esprit de Corps Languishes" by permission of *Industry Week*, © 1983.

Ian Rolland. "It's Smart to Get Your People to Work Smart" from *Industry Week* by permission of Penton/IPC, Inc., © 1983.

Suzanne Sisson. "Managerial Risk Taking" from *Training and Development Journal* by permission of The American Society of Training Development, © 1985, all rights reserved.

Michael Smith, Jan Wing. "Five Steps to Improving Employee Performance" from *Supervisory Management* by permission of the author, © 1983.

Erwin S. Stanton. "A Critical Reevaluation of Motivation, Management and Productivity" by permission of *Personnel Journal*, © 1983.

Richard F. Tyler. "Motivate the Older Employee" by permission of *Personnel Journal* © 1984.

Ellen J. Wallach. "Performance Coaching: Hitting the Bull's Eye" from *Supervisory Management* by permission of the author, Ellen Wallach, Career Development Consultant, © 1983, The American Management Association.

Roy W. Walters. "Boring Jobs? Redesign Them" from *Data Management* by permission of Data Processing Management Association, © 1982.

Roy W. Walters. "Modern Motivation" from *Management World* by permission of the Administrative Management Society, © 1983.

Daniel Yankelovich, John Immerwahr. "Let's Put the Work Ethic to Work" from *Industry Week* by permission of Penton/IPC, Inc., © 1983.

John H. Zenger, Jean E. Edwards. "On Fish Tanks and Expectations" from *Training* by permission of Lakewood Publications, Inc., © 1984.

Part 1
MOTIVATION— A PRACTICAL PERSPECTIVE

1.

DIAGNOSING AND TREATING MANAGERIAL MALAISE

Sigmund G. Ginsburg

Unchecked, an insidious malady that strikes managers can lead to employee dissatisfaction, lower productivity, and falling profits. Fortunately, there are solutions.

Human resources professionals are used to dealing with the "blahs" problems associated with assembly line and repetitive clerical work: the "blue-collar blues" and the "white-collar woes." Increasingly, however, they are facing a problem that is often difficult to identify and even harder to treat: the problem of previously productive managers who begin to plateau or burn out—those who, in other words, get a bad case of "managerial malaise." This article will help human resources professionals identify those who are prone to or have the "disease" and discuss ways to avoid and overcome it. To identify those who have or may get manager's malaise (which can strike good managers—particularly the high achievers and fact trackers), the following quiz will be helpful. Each question should be answered with a number that corresponds with one of the following responses: 0 = very rarely or never, 1 = rarely, 2 = sometimes, 3 = fairly often, 4 = frequently, 5 = very frequently or always.

1. Are you bored with your assignment at work?
2. Are you unexcited with what lies ahead in your career?
3. Do you suffer from headaches, stomach distress, rashes, or other ailments that occur frequently and tend to linger?
4. Have you been taking more time off for illness?
5. Are you overeating (or undereating), smoking more, or drinking more?
6. Do you regard lunch as the best part of your day?
7. Are you constantly watching the clock to see how close it is to quitting time?
8. Do you find it harder to get out of bed in the morning than you used to?
9. Do you live for the weekend?

10. Do you suffer from headaches, depression, or irritability on Sundays?
11. Is it hard for you to go back to work on Mondays?
12. Do you argue with people on and off the job?
13. Are you lethargic when you are away from work?
14. Are you hyperactive when you are away from work?
15. Are you lethargic at work?
16. Are you hyperactive at work?
17. Do you feel depressed at work?
18. Do you feel depressed at home?
19. Do you go from extreme highs to extreme lows in your feelings about work or life in general?
20. Do you find that you are taking more time to accomplish less than you used to?
21. Do you increasingly evaluate your performance in terms of creating a good atmosphere and good human relations rather than specific, concrete job achievements?
22. Are you spending less time at work (leaving early, coming in late, taking longer lunch hours, and so on)?
23. Do you hate to come back from vacation?
24. Do you have a feeling of not wanting to accomplish anything important next week, next month, next year?
25. Do you have a sense that your work is not particularly worthwhile or challenging?
26. Do you feel that much of what you do is trivial and could by done by almost anyone?
27. Does it seem much of what you do is simply filling up time—paying too much attention to detail, being too finicky, scheduling unnecessary meetings, or prolonging meetings unnecessarily?
28. Do you measure success in terms of how little went wrong instead of how much went right?

Total the score. The manager whose score is 100 or more has a very severe case of managerial malaise; unless immediate action is taken the disease can annihilate his or her career and psychological health. A score of 70-99 indicates a serious case; quick action is necessary to prevent the manager from reaching extremis. Managers whose scores are in the 40-69 range are showing signs of the malady and steps to prevent worsening are indicated. A score in the 20-39 range shows that the manager is healthy but susceptible. And a manager who scores below 20 is in the pink.

MANAGERIAL MALAISE: WHAT IS IT?

The manifestations of this malaise are captured in many of the 28 questions above. Managerial malaise is a feeling of not being as productive as possible, a feeling of not being sufficiently challenged by current projects or excited by the prospects of future ones. It is a belief that one's creativity and potential are not being tapped as fully and as frequently as possible; that one's efforts—and those of the organization—do not matter very much and are not done with distinc- tion or style; that the organization and its employees are really second rate; and that one is losing drive, ambition, and dreams of high achievement.

CAUSES OF MANAGERIAL MALAISE

Successful managers are motivated by a variety of factors. These include a broad range of responsibilities, challenge, positive impact on the organization, recognition, compensation, good relationships with superiors and others, freedom to innovate, being their own boss, the pace of the organization, the quality of the organization and its people, and the future possibilities for both individual and organization.

In addition, the successful manager is concerned with continued learning and growth on the job. Talented people remain motivated and highly creative when they feel what they are doing today or this year is significantly better and more challenging than what they did last year.

High achievers continually want to acquire, improve upon, and demonstrate new abilities, skills and knowledge. They want to feel they've advanced in terms of knowledge and performance. Executives invest so much of their egos in their jobs that when they find themselves running in place rather than climbing higher, they become frustrated and disappointed. If the high achiever reaches a plateau, he or she is likely to become bored.

Both the individual and the organization should continually ask, "What have I (or he, or she) accomplished this year that is significantly better than last year, that demonstrates significant growth in my (or his, or her) ability to deal with this particular area and that indicates a solid base for further learning and skills contribution to the organization and my (or his, or her) self-esteem?"

But many things can disrupt this growth process. A manager can be going through a "mid-life crisis" in which he or she begins to question life, career, goals, and marital relationship. Another frequent cause of malaise is the job or organizational environment. There may be economic stagnation or recession (and thus fewer opportunities for growth, innovation, mergers, acquisitions); increased foreign and domestic competition; smaller profits resulting in decrease (or no) compensation increase for the manager and his or her staff; high turnover in the company; greater responsibilities because of staff cuts; more regulations and red tape; concern about job security; and so on.

Often, a combination of pressure in climbing the executive ladder or dealing with years of stress will cause a manager to burn out. A manager can also "top out" when he or she reaches an earnings or position peak—because of personal limitations and/or conditions in the organization that are beyond his or her control—which, given current economic conditions or compensation, may preclude him or her from getting as good a job elsewhere.

THE BIG PICTURE

Managerial malaise may be simply one aspect of an overall malaise. We are tired of hearing the litany of nostrums for America's economic and management problems; lower taxes and create incentives for business and individuals; encourage savings by individuals and capital investments by business; reindustrialize and deregulate American business; emphasize productivity and motivations (quality circles, quality of life issues); look to high technology, computerization and robots, and so on.

But what is often overlooked is the need to emphasize entrepreneurship, risk-taking, enthusiasm for outstanding management, and high standards and aspirations. We seem to be jogging, holding ourselves in, advancing slowly. We should be running all out to achieve immediate creativity, innovation, and success. We should also be prepared for running the marathon: looking far ahead, planning and advancing for the long haul and setting objectives for accomplishment five, ten, or more years down the road. Too often as managers we fall prey to being lazy and content with merely getting by. This, coupled with our demand for instant gratification, has led to a deemphasis of the need for excellence in what we do. The value of standards, hard work, praise, and recognition has been debased, and this devaluation has permeated not only our organizations but our educational systems as well. Our society has become too permissive, too "laid back," and this influences each individual from kindergarten through graduate school through the upper levels of management.

American business has been too concerned with short-term profits and dividends and too little concerned with the future and with employees' motivation, job satisfaction, and ideas. We overemphasize numbers, computers, and quantitative analysis. Too many executives and recent MBA graduates have lost (or maybe never had) the entrepreneurial spirit and zest for making tough decisions and taking significant risks. Wrapped up in financial analysis and management information system reports, they have become too remote from the heart of the enterprise they manage and from the concerns of customers and employees, the markets and technology of today and tomorrow.

More and more, we accept with a shrug that pervasive lack of pride in craftsmanship and quality of work and service. Our society is turning out, more than ever before, people who expect praise, a promotion, a bonus, a gratuity, a large increase—for inadequate or merely satisfactory performance. That ought not to be enough for ourselves, our staffs, our organizations, our corporate and national leaders, our nation as a whole.

POSSIBLE REMEDIES

For each manager and organization, the cure for managerial malaise will be different. Of course, in some cases, it might be best for the organization and the individual if he or she found a new job or career. However, before a manager takes such a major step, some alternatives are worth trying. Both the organization and the manager must understand the potential seriousness of the situation and the necessity of careful planning and action to cure the symptoms and underlying causes of the malaise. (The individual should also have a thorough physical check-up, some physical or physiological problem may be the major or a contributing cause of malaise.) From the organization's point of view, there must be a greater concern for people within the organization, the effect of the corporate culture, and how things can be improved to meet the needs of people while meeting corporate goals. People's needs should be a major corporate goal.

SPECIFIC ACTIONS

- Change the breadth, depth, and type of assignment and expand the manager's scope of responsibility.
- Assign special projects.
- Make mobility assignments among staff and line functions and units.
- Vary the manager's assignments; exercise his or her ability to undertake supervisory, staff, line, and planning responsibilities.
- Encourage new knowledge through education, training, seminars, and conferences.
- Expose the manager to public and community activities; give him or her opportunities to develop speaking and writing abilities.
- Offer opportunities to serve with and lead inter- and intraorganizational committees and task forces.
- Offer opportunities for short- or long-term travel or relocation.
- Encourage new interest in hobbies and recreational activities.
- Encourage regular exercise.
- Encourage closer contact with family and friends.
- Encourage discussion of frustrations with spouse, trusted friends, supervisor, or someone else in the organization (if this does not carry a significant risk of hurting a career). Suggest professional counseling if necessary.
- Offer exposure to the newest techniques and technology in the manager's field, related fields, and potential areas of responsibility.
- Help the manager set ambitious personal and professional goals and strive to attain them; emphasize a concern for creativity and innovation, planning,

implementation, control, communication, evaluation, and staff development.

- Help the manager set ambitious professional goals for his/her staff and strive to attain them; emphasize the recognition of individual needs and ambitions and the possibility of malaise.
- Encourage the manager to change or modify his or her work habits and work schedule, to intersperse interesting topics, meetings, and problems with more humdrum ones to break up the day; to learn to recognize important items and to treat trivia trivially.
- Help the manager practice time management and stress management techniques, recognizing that the goal of time management is to make time available for important efforts.
- Advocate the use of lunch time, on occasion, solely for relaxation.

PREVENTIVE MEDICINE

From kindergarten through graduate school, from the first day in an organization to the last, we should enforce high standards. Whatever an individual's position, we must develop the organizational structure, environment, and concern that encourages, demands, and rewards the individual's best effort. We should assist the individual—provide opportunities, challenges, resources, training, incentives, and rewards—but the goal should always be consistent, outstanding performance. We should emphasize talent, enthusiasm, hard work, and the quest for true distinction. We must seek to improve each individual's ability and satisfaction. In addition to technical knowledge, the successful executive needs to have the power and influence of good interpersonal skills, drive, empathy and zest.

As managers and executives, we are rightfully concerned about success and material comfort for ourselves and all who help the organization achieve its objectives. However, man lives by more than bread and conspicuous consumption. Increasingly, an important aspect of motivation, satisfaction and productivity is "psychic income," that is, recognition, challenge, learning, growth, maximum utilization of one's abilities, high standards, a sense of mission, accomplishment, and team effort. Such income can be realized through an organization's concern and an emphasis on human needs and aspirations.

Good management can be exciting and stimulating. Managerial tasks should be approached with enthusiasm. As managers we tend to be too calm, cool, and collected. While this is valuable, we need more fire, more passion and concern as we strive to achieve our goals. There is both science and art to successful management. The successful executive combines some of the characteristics of the salesman, dreamer, artist, planner, philosopher, counselor, preacher, warrior, and diplomat. He or she is a boss, colleague, peer, subordinate, student, teacher, mentor, and role model.

The challenge for executives at all levels is to reach beyond their grasp, to strive for true excellence; to set ambitious and challenging goals for themselves, their units, and their organizations. Complacency and acceptance must give way to challenge and a healthy dissatisfaction with the status quo. The result can be a great exhilaration in meeting great expectations. A well-managed organization that is concerned both with outstanding results and optimum job satisfaction and personal growth for its staff exemplifies both the art and science of management.

The organization that fails to deal with the problems that result when individuals fall prey to the manager's malaise is failing to maximize the effectiveness and contribution of its most precious resource: the talented individual. The individual, in turn, who does not look objectively at the possibility of being a victim of manager's malaise may well end up performing well below potential and feeling trapped and unfulfilled.

The goals set forth are indeed tough, requiring the best that we can offer as individuals and as organization members. We will need a renewed passion to succeed—to make our particular organization more productive, challenging, and satisfying. We will need to emphasize a new attitude that will involve not only renewed effectiveness and efficiency, but also learning, growth, pride, progress, purpose, and a concern for quality, craftsmanship, and high standards of production and service. Our credo might well be taken from Theodore Roosevelt's statement, *To the Man in the Arena*:

> It is not the critic that counts nor the man who points out how the strong man stumbled or where the doer of deeds could have done them better. The credit belongs to the man who is actually in the arena; whose face is marred by dust and sweat and blood; who strives valiantly . . .; who knows the great enthusiasms, the great devotions, and spends himself in a worthy cause; who, at his best, knows the triumph of high achievement; and who, at his worst, if he fails, at least fails while daring greatly, so that his place shall never be with those cold and timid souls who know neither victory nor defeat.

Sigmund G. Ginsburg is vice-president for finance, treasurer, adjunct professor of business administration, and adjunct professor of higher education administration at the University of Cincinnati. Mr. Ginsburg is author of Ropes for Management Success: Climb Higher, Faster, *published by Prentice-Hall, Inc. He has written more than 60 articles.*

2.
MOTIVATION: GOOD THEORY— POOR APPLICATION

Joel K. Leidecker
James J. Hall

> Lack of success is often due to a misunderstanding of the theories or to a poor application of good motivational concepts.

Many of us have difficulty in motivating ourselves. It comes as no surprise that the task of motivating others is a difficult, complex one. To increase the probability of success in this task, behavioral scientists have expended considerable effort to provide us with greater understanding of the dynamics of motivation.

Vast amounts have been written concerning the motivation of organizational members; several related theories are reviewed in this article. When these theories are applied in the "real world," the results are often negative, or, at best, neutral. Management practitioners are then quick to point out that the theory is not workable, or irrelevant. They may try to lower the theorist's defenses by saying, "It's a good theory, but it doesn't work." The theorist realizes, however, that there is no such thing as a good theory that doesn't work. Or is there?

We seem to have two options: either we have a bad theory that naturally doesn't work, or we have a good theory that is not being properly applied.

The authors choose the latter option and, in this article, attempt to support their choice. In the first part of the article, several motivational theories will be examined, and their contributions and implications for management will be discussed. In the second part of the article, the authors, based on their own observations, a review of literature, and discussions with management practitioners, will make a case for their contention: "Not Bad Theory—Just Poor Application."

The intent of the article is not to degrade management or eulogize theoreticians, but to stimulate managerial and academic thinking as to how we can more effectively transfer conceptual knowledge into practice.

PATH-GOAL FRAMEWORK[1]

Most motivation theory is based on the premise that human energy is due to internal tensions or needs. The objective of most behavior is the reduction of these tensions. Human action or behavior is thus seen as a means of reducing these tensions by attempting to attain goals that can satisfy the activated needs.

The path-goal framework suggests persons will behave in a manner which will lead to the attainment of a goal which they value, and which they expect they can achieve. This framework identifies, for the manager, three criteria which are important for the motivational process (tension reduction):

1. *Goal availability.* For example, within an organization, some goals may not be perceived as available to the employee.
2. *Goal value.* How likely is it that the reward offered by the organization provides the means to satisfy a goal valued by the employee?
3. *Perceived effort-reward probability.* How likely is it that a given amount of effort will result in the attainment of a valued goal? Does the organization consistently reward the behavior it desires?

The remainder of this section on theory will focus on the second criterion: *goal value.* The goal an individual selects is dependent on the need that is activated. We could conceivably identify hundreds of needs or tensions; such information, however, would be difficult to use. What is needed is a framework which can give us a "handle" to identify, examine and understand the particular needs that cause goal-directed behavior. Two important frameworks are those developed by Maslow[2] and Herzberg.[3]

MASLOW'S NEED HIERARCHY

Maslow's framework first groups all needs into five categories (that are now familiar to most managers): (1) physiological, (2) safety, (3) social, (4) esteem, (5) self-actualization. These categories, Maslow suggests, are related to each other in the form of an orderly hierarchy in which one category of needs becomes activated only after the lower level is relatively satisfied. (The lowest level in the hierarchy is the physiological and the highest is the self-actualization.)

HERZBERG'S DUAL FACTOR THEORY

This framework makes two important contributions to the manager's skill in motivating others. First, it is more explicit than Maslow's as to the link between certain needs and job performance. That is, this framework specifies the needs which can be satisfied by high job performance.

Secondly, the framework generates an application model, job enrichment, which helps the manager to use the theory.

The Dual Factor Theory identifies two basic job dimensions:

1. *The conditions surrounding*, or extrinsic to, *the task.* These would include administrative policy, shop cleanliness, interpersonal relations, fringe benefits, and cost of living pay increase. Herzberg calls these conditions hygiene factors because, although they may be important prerequisites to job satisfactions, they do not themselves generate high performance. Hygiene factors operate to remove obstacles in the work environment rather than being directly related to motivation on the job.

2. *The task itself.* Does it provide a sense of achievement (and recognition for that achievement)? Is the task an interesting one, one that you like to think about after work? Does the task provide you with a challenge that can lead to a sense of growth? Task conditions are called motivator factors because it is their presence or absence that largely determines whether or not individuals will be motivated toward high performance.

In general, the needs concerning hygiene factors consist of the lower levels of the Maslow need hierarchy: physiological, safety, and social. The needs concerning motivator factors consist of the higher levels: esteem and self-actualization.

The critical point for the manager to understand is that the satisfaction of higher level needs is far more likely to lead to high performance than is the satisfaction of lower level needs. There are two implications for the manager. First, he or she must create a climate in which the individual is able to satisfy the lower level needs so that the higher level needs can become active. If the manager creates a threatening climate, or blocks social relationships, the subordinate is likely to stay at the lower level need levels (safety and social, respectively).

Second, the manager must be sure that the task is sufficiently challenging and interesting so that it can serve as a means to the satisfaction of higher level needs. Otherwise, the worker whose higher level needs are active will have to look elsewhere (generally off the job) for satisfaction. One approach to this second responsibility of the manager is known as job enrichment. The objective of job enrichment is to redesign the task so that performance leads to satisfaction of the higher level needs.[4]

SUMMARY OF THEORY

This section first described a general framework for understanding the interaction between needs and goals; we called this the path-goal framework. Secondly, the section examined frameworks which provide the manager with an effective way of looking at needs, and of understanding their relationship to job performance. These frameworks consisted of Maslow's Need Hierarchy and Herzberg's Dual Factor Theory.

POOR APPLICATION

Successful implementation of these motivational concepts requires that the manager focus on several areas which, unfortunately, often are neglected.

This section identifies three areas in which management has failed to fully understand either the motivational concepts themselves or their implications for action:

1. The nature of rewards and their relationship to goals.
2. The importance of performance evaluation and feedback.
3. Enrichment of job content.

The authors describe situations in which the motivational concepts' messages are poorly implemented if, indeed, they are really applied at all. If the authors are correct, the role of the manager will change, and traditional training programs should be altered.

Path-Goal theory stresses the importance of the linkage among motivation, performance, and goal attainment. According to this theory, two important variables in the motivation process are:

- The availability of the rewards perceived as important by the employee (do the rewards in fact exist and/or has management shown they do exist?)
- The probability of achieving these rewards through prescribed behavior (high performance linked to rewards such as promotion and salary increase).

The authors believe that management in many organizations has not done a good job in the two areas outlined above. This belief is based on observations of our own, discussion with professional and non-professional employees and reviews of the management literature.

1. The companies who are lax in the area of *availability of rewards* are characterized as follows.

a. Many organizations have failed to apply the messages of Maslow and Herzberg. In these organizations, rewards are still focused on lower-level needs (hygiene factors) rather than providing employees with opportunities to satisfy higher level needs (Herzberg's "Motivators"). Thus, many rewards necessary to ensure employee goal-fulfillment do not exist. Since research has established the relationship between goal-fulfillment and performance, managers must spend more time identifying employee needs and their job related goals.

b.   Besides the identification of the employee's needs and goals, managers should spend considerable effort identifying the rewards at their disposal and determining how they can best use them.

Eventually, through the linkage of an employee's goals and the rewards offered, the manager attempts to motivate high levels of performance. Thus reward identification and usage, as well as goal identification, become important prerequisites in the process of motivation. Having identified rewards, managers must then be sure that they convey to all employees what rewards are available, and that they clearly identify the means (path) to achieve such rewards.

The availability of rewards is a necessary condition of motivation, but the most important aspect of availability is not what management says is available, but what each and every employee *perceives* as available.

2.   The means or method for achieving rewards leads us into the second implication of the path-goal framework: that is the linkage between performance in an organization and the attainment of the desired rewards.

So many companies, or managers within the companies, fail in this area, and then the employee sees a low probability of achieving a desired reward even though it is available. An example of this failure in organizations is that valued characteristics are not the rewarded characteristics. Management generally has a stated policy that good performers will receive the bulk of the extrinsic rewards offered by the company (salary, promotion, status symbols).

In so many organizations this policy is not carried out. Other criteria, usually not stated, may influence who receives the rewards. When a pattern of inconsistency develops, and a high performer perceives that his or her chances of achieving a particular extrinsic reward are no better than that of the moderate or low performer, management may have created a motivational problem. This inconsistency (rewarding low performers) will most likely reduce performance-related behavior because it is not rewarded, or because other behavior is rewarded more often.

The importance of the relationship between employee goals, availability of rewards and probability of employee achievement is emphasized in motivational theory. This section has identified how companies and managers have been less than successful in heeding the lessons of theory.

PERFORMANCE EVALUATION

Achievement motivation has been alluded to in the concepts of both Maslow and Herzberg. Maslow suggests it is one of the higher level needs to which more and more individuals are aspiring, and Herzberg states that achievement is one of the "motivators" that must be fulfilled if management desires to motivate employees to higher levels of performance. Other researchers[5] also have done extensive work on achievement motivations, and the results provide two interesting lessons for managers:

- It is important to have work situations in which concrete feedback is available as to how one is doing.
- It is important to establish well-defined, as well as achievable, task objectives. These may be mutually agreed upon or, in some instances, set by management.

The concepts of Maslow, Herzberg, McClelland and others concerning the higher level needs such as achievement, provide guidelines to action for management personnel in the area of performance evaluation and feedback.

The provision of identifiable task objectives, and feedback as to performance toward these objectives, is lacking in many organizations. The following observations are examples of poor application of good concepts:

1. Managers, for whatever reasons, are not providing accurate, open feedback as to an individual's performance. Listen to this comment: "Jim is O.K. as a person, but you never know where you stand. I'm not sure what is expected of me, or where I fit in, and I get very little information as to how I am doing."

Statements by subordinates, similar to the one preceding, imply a failure on the part of the supervisor. We know that two important elements in the motivational process are missing: well-defined, achievable task objectives, and specific feedback as to the accomplishment of the objectives. Managers have a responsibility to minimize the climate characterized by the employee's quote.

2. Identifying group task objectives and linking them to task responsibilities of individual members is a time-consuming operation. Many managers place a low priority on this task. Therefore task-oriented goal-setting never gets accomplished, and, consequently, one of the prerequisites to achievement motivation may not exist.

3. Mutual goal setting, the sharing of the goal setting task with the employee, is avoided by some managers because they believe this is an infringement upon management prerogatives. The employees of a supervisor with this set of beliefs are likely to be denied the opportunity to fulfill higher level needs.

4. In many cases task objectives are identified, performance is evaluated, and the results are conveyed to the employee. Yet, the employee remains unsure of management's view of his or her accomplishments in terms of preestablished objectives. This situation occurs because the manager's conveyance is replete with generalizations, due in part to inadequate effort in his evaluation of the employee. The manager has again failed to effectively apply a good concept.

In summary, it appears many managers and company managements have failed to recognize the importance of establishing objectives and performance feedback as motivational tools.

ENRICHING WORK CONTENT

Some of the most controversial motivational programs being adopted throughout the nation are those based on Herzberg's "job enrichment" model, or similar plans stressing the motivational possibilities intrinsic to the task or work itself.

Job enrichment and similar programs, if implemented by people who fully understand the purpose, and done in a well-planned manner, have tremendous potential for solving many of the "motivational" problems that exist in industry today. However, practitioners either have seen job enrichment-type programs as a remedy for all motivational problems, or have not expended the effort necessary to bring about the programs' success.

The observations that follow are offered as examples of our contention:

1. The director of personnel or company executive, who, after being in a management development program or listening to a speech by an exponent of enrichment, decides to implement the program in his or her company. The manager calls a meeting of the staff, tells them what he or she knows, assigns some enrichment material to be read, and then embarks on a company-wide program. Don't laugh! We have seen some almost this bad. The purpose is not to berate, but to have to ask yourself these questions: "Have I, as a manager, expended enough effort to give a program of this nature a chance?" "Do I know what is necessary to implement a job enrichment program, and have I done it?"

2. Motivation through enrichment involves adding meaningful tasks and removing tasks that may cause boredom. The implementation of a program of this nature requires a changing emphasis in the manager's role. Some managers will resist because they see a usurpation of management prerogatives. The manager who is inflexible, who cannot see that enrichment frees him or her to become involved in aspects of the job that need more of his or her attention, has to alter thinking. If he or she doesn't, he or she becomes a deterrent to the program, and his or her contribution will diminish in the reorganized work place.

3. Many training departments that thoroughly understand a program of job enrichment, and offer good classes as to purpose, background, and content, fail to provide the most important ingredient. Managers need *skill development* as to how to "enrich" a job; they need practice and experience. Good, intellectualized learning does not guarantee successful implementation. What does your company provide along these lines?

4. In addition to skill development, another important ingredient is commitment and support from top management. Enrichment-type programs take time and considerable amounts of effort on the part of the individual implementing the program. What kind of support does your top management provide (budget overruns, rewards for extra effort and successful completion, etc.)?

In short, many of the problems and failures that have been experienced with job enrichment-type programs result from an application breakdown.

SUMMARY

Recognizing that motivational theories are often unsuccessful in practice, this article asks why. Are the theories wrong, inadequate, or irrelevant? Or, is the problem to be found in the implementation stage? The authors contend that the lack of success is often due to a misunderstanding of the theories or poor application of good motivational concepts.

After briefly reviewing several related motivation theories, the authors describe the ways in which the concepts are often poorly applied—if, indeed, more than "lip service" is paid to the concepts. The implications for managerial actions along three dimensions are discussed: problems concerning the nature of rewards and their relationship to goals; weakness exhibited in the relationships among performance, evaluation, and feedback; and misinterpretations concerning the process of job enrichment content.

The authors hope that the ideas expressed in this article will stimulate thought and dialogue concerning the appropriateness of your organization's motivational philosophy and action program.

REFERENCES

1. For a discussion of the path-goal model, see Martin T. Evans, "Managing the Managers," *Personnel Administration* (May-June 1971), pp. 31-38.

2. Maslow, A. H., "A Theory of Motivation," *Psychological Review* (Vol. 50, 1973), pp. 370-396.

3. Herzberg, Frederick, "One More Time: How Do You Motivate Employees?" *Harvard Business Review* (January-February 1968), pp. 53-62.

4. For descriptions of job enrichment programs, see M. Scoot Meyers, *Every Employee A Manager* (New York: McGraw-Hill, Inc., 1970), pp. 69-75; and The Conference Board Record, *Job Design for Motivation,* Report No. 515 (1971).

5. See Saul W. Gellerman, *Motivation and Productivity* (New York: American Management Association, 1963); and David C. McClelland, "That Urge to Achieve," *Think* (Nov.-Dec. 1966), pp. 19-23.

Joel K. Leidecker is an associate professor and chairman with the management department at the University of Santa Clara, Santa Clara, California. James L. Hall is an associate professor with the management department at the University of Santa Clara, Santa Clara, California.

3.
HOW MANAGERS MOTIVATE

James McMahon

Employees need challenging assignments, the need to feel they are part of the action. A manager can fulfill these needs through delegation.

"Of all the resources available to management—money, materials, equipment and people—the vital resource is *people*," says one management consultant. "Unlike other resources, people have a remarkable potential for growth and development. This consideration makes employee motivation a most important and most challenging aspect of management."

You can increase your management effectiveness by helping your employees realize their potential and by inspiring them to give the best of their energies and talents in meeting organizational objectives.

"My effectiveness as a manager," says one successful department head, "is measured by the group's progress in accomplishing organizational goals. It's no secret who heads the department."

Motivation begins with your attitude as a manager. Do you see your role as that of adopting a management style which will satisfy employees' needs, while at the same time accomplishing company goals?

As a manager, your perception of your role in regard to your people, your understanding of their needs and your skill in aligning their personal goals with the goals of the organization will determine your success in motivating employees.

Motivation is not a part-time activity. It's not something a manager adds after the organization has been set up and is in operation. It involves basic relationships that are built into the organizational structure. In setting up an organization, keep layers of management to a minimum. Provide for logical divisions of functions. Good organization helps to clarify duties and responsibilities, makes for clear-cut decisions and more effective communication—factors affecting motivation.

Situations sometimes arise that require temporary modifications of organizational structure. For example, the need to lighten the load of an older employee, or to take care of a personality problem in a particular unit. Guard against letting these temporary changes become permanent. As soon as the need for the change has passed, get back to the more logical division of functions.

Today's employees need challenging assignments. They need to feel they are part of the action. You, as the manager, can fulfill these needs through effective delegation.

"In this company, management gives you a job to do," says one satisfied middle manager, "and as long as you get results, you're free to do it your own way."

In effect, delegation provides employees with continuous on-the-job training programs with opportunities to learn and grow. To take full advantage of such programs, the delegation-minded manager pushes authority and responsibility down to the lowest practical level.

Effective delegators also delegate most decisionmaking. Although decisions about some matters (policymaking, high-level promotions, decisions affecting more than one unit) must be made by top management, most decisions can best be made at lower levels where more complete information is available and where lower-level managers have a better understanding of the problem.

Some managers—with a reputation for motivation—delegate as much as 90 percent of all decisionmaking to their subordinates. They see it as part of their job as managers to develop decisionmaking capability at all organizational levels.

A county highway department which ranked high on the motivation scale had a tradition of sound organization and clear-cut delegation of authority and responsibility. However, as a result of a change in top management, such delegation was withdrawn, followed by continual reassignment of middle managers.

"Now nobody knows for sure what they're supposed to be doing," says one confused manager. "We seem to be kept continuously off balance.

Everything is in a state of flux." The effect on members of the organization was evidenced by a substantial increase in resignations and early retirements.

Motivated employees know what their jobs are. They know how their jobs relate to company goals and objectives, what results are expected of them—and they know they're free to accomplish results in their own way.

The tendency of newly promoted managers to "bring their old jobs with them" can create problems in maintaining clear-cut delegation. Ken Smith was promoted to assistant general manager after 10 years in production. As with many capable men promoted into top management, Ken found it difficult to adapt to his new role and was inclined to drift back into his old environment in production, where he felt more comfortable.

"I wish he'd stay out of my office," confided the new production manager. "I even find him out of line giving detailed instructions to my people. How do you tell your boss to let go of his old job?"

Psychologists tell us that deep within us is a desire for recognition. Employees respond to a boss who instinctively treats subordinates with dignity and respect. Such recognition builds self-esteem and encourages the employee to live up to the confidence shown by the manager.

Some managers make a habit of explaining to subordinates why their jobs are important and how their work fits into the total operation. Such explanations do more than keep the employees well-informed. They bring the employees into your confidence and recognize them as important people in the organization.

A word from the boss about something new that's coming up or about a recent incident affecting the company's future makes the employee feel like an "insider," an important factor in motivation.

If there's one element of magic in motivating employees, it's calling people by name. For most managers, this involves intensive and continual effort (card files, notes, pictures), yet nothing is as effective in improving personal relationships. Nothing fills our need for recognition so much as hearing someone is interested enough in us to remember who we are.

"The new manager called me by name," says a 27-year-old San Francisco junior executive, "it makes me feel like a member of the team."

In Los Angeles, a newly appointed middle manager wanted to make a change in one of the letters he had dictated a few minutes before. "Will you ask that stenographer who was taking my dictation to step back into my office," he says over the intercom to the head of the steno pool. "That stenographer" has a name—and would feel more kindly toward the manager if he'd learn what it is.

Another form of recognition is listening to what employees have to say. When you give an employee your sincere attention, you recognize that employee as an important person, a person whose ideas and opinions interest you. As a good listener, you can show by your very posture your readiness to hear the speaker out. A good listener stops all activity, looks the speaker in the eye and concentrates on what the speaker has to say. By satisfying the speaker's basic need to be recognized, you establish a deeper, more lasting personal relationship.

"I don't always agree with the new manager's decisions," says a hospital attendant, "but before she decides what to do, she listens to what her people have to say." Knowing that the manager really understands their point of view may be all employees need, to feel right about something that's bothering them.

Most managers find that a genuine word of praise for work well done can be much more effective than criticizing an employee's shortcomings. The production department of an East Coast furniture company was having trouble meeting production schedules. The head of the company assigned a vice president to investigate the problem. In talking to the first-line supervisors, the vice president sensed a complete lack of motivation. As one of the more vocal supervisors summed it up: "The production manager has yet to say word one in praise of a job well done. It's not that we expect to be complimented every time we do something right, but when a tough job has been especially well done, we'd like to know that he's aware of it."

Later an opportunity came to assign a people-oriented manager to the production department. Within a month, a noticeable improvement took place in the department's ability to meet production schedules.

High on the list of motivating factors is a manager's habit of decisiveness. Nothing wastes employees' time more than a manager's requests for additional studies, endless meetings, more reports, long after the point where a judgment should have been made and the problem resolved. Timely decisions motivate employees by inspiring confidence in management.

In the press of day-to-day problems, managers tend to lose sight of the importance of two-way communication at all organizational levels. They're inclined to limit their communication to a smaller and smaller group until they seldom talk with anyone except their immediate staff.

"I make it a point," says one executive, "to periodically break out of this tightening circle and get out among the rank and file. Just stopping by a person's workplace and talking about whatever happens to be going on at the moment provides an opportunity to discuss any ideas the employee might like to bring up. What we talk about isn't as important as that feeling of partnership shared by the employee and myself. Employees are individuals. They are most effectively motivated on a one-to-one basis."

4.
HOW TO MOTIVATE
YOUR EMPLOYEES

John F. Collins

Here is a primer—on hiring, on promoting, on paying and on listening—for the
small business that wants to improve productivity.

In the daily crush of problems and challenges, many owners and operators of
small businesses deal with personnel matters in terms of the immediate task at
hand. They believe that human resources management is the concern of big
companies with specialists and budgets for such activities.

The fact is, however, that sufficient attention to employee motivation and
involvement can be a major factor in helping small business achieve the
productivity increases necessary for improved profits. Small businesses may
have to make some adjustments in present attitudes to receive the rewards
possible from proper management of human resources.

Some fundamental concepts should be understood from the outset.

To be motivated and productive, employees must feel a high degree of interest in their jobs and derive a large amount of satisfaction from them. Motivated
and productive employees must believe that their salaries, benefits, working
conditions, and job security are reasonable and that they are being treated
fairly by their immediate managers and by management generally.

Beyond that, if employees are to be maximally productive, they must be
given the opportunity to work in an atmosphere in which all employees are
conscientious and cooperative.

The function of human resources management is the implementation of
these concepts through employment decisions, wage and salary administration, management training, and communications.

Here are specifics in each area for improving productivity through improved
personnel policies:

Employment. Recruitment and selection of employees is the most important
factor in building and maintaining a productive work force. A company must
treat employees fairly, provide reasonable compensation and benefits and
develop a positive work atmosphere if it is to achieve a reputation as an excellent place to work and thereby attract above-average applicants. In too

many instances, recruitment and selection of employees is not recognized as an important function, and the individual responsible for hiring does not have the necessary knowledge and experience.

To provide sufficient time for the recruitment process, personnel needs should be anticipated as far in advance as possible. Selection mistakes occur under pressure to fill openings quickly and through failure to identify the key personal and technical qualifications for successful job performance.

Except for positions calling for highly specialized knowledge or skills, an applicant's personal characteristics are more important than his technical qualifications. Such characteristics are positive attitude, conscientiousness and interest in the work to be performed.

When qualified applicants have been selected, an appropriate amount of time and effort should be devoted to training the newly hired employees so that they become productive as soon as possible. Managers should show a continuing interest in new employees' progress and encourage them to ask questions. The first few weeks of employment are critical, and frequent communication with new employees is essential.

Management training. When an opening develops for a department manager, the employee with the best technical qualifications is generally promoted. The employee selected might not have the necessary interest and aptitude for becoming an effective manager but invariably will accept the promotion. Newly appointed managers often do too much work themselves. They tend not to delegate effectively and to interfere in their employees' work. Employees should be given a general outline of how their work is to be performed, should not be over-supervised and should have the opportunity to solve most of their work-related problems.

Newly appointed managers need specialized training in many areas: the nature of management responsibilities and management style; keys to employee motivation and productivity; employee selection, orientation and training; salary administration and performance appraisal; employee communication; administration of personnel policies and practices; and handling of employee problems.

Wage and salary administration. The primary purpose of an effective wage and salary program is attracting and retaining the type and caliber of employee required to attain the company's goals rather than motivating and increasing employee productivity. Such a program is essential to ensure that employees are treated fairly in salary matters. Managers should understand the company's salary objectives and policies so that they can answer employees' questions about salaries.

Salary ranges should be established for positions based on their duties and responsibilities, their relative value in the salary market and salaries paid elsewhere for similar positions. Salaries should be administered on a rate-range basis. The salary structure should be reviewed annually and adjusted according to external trends and the company's experience in attracting and retaining employees.

Flexibility is one of the most significant aspects of an effective wage and salary program. Employees should move through their respective rate ranges based on performance and potential for promotion.

Management should review employees for salary increases throughout the year rather than reviewing all employees at the same time each year.

Generally, employees should be reviewed for salary increase on an annual basis after their initial salary review. Employees whose performance is not satisfactory should not be granted a salary increase until their performance improves. Employees whose performance is outstanding should be rewarded by granting them relatively larger salary increases at shorter than normal intervals. Employees must understand that salary increases are granted for performance, not the passage of time.

Employees are motivated by the satisfaction they get from doing their work and from improving their performance and skills. Managers are responsible for getting work done by employees, for motivating them and for helping them improve their performance. The necessity for a well-designed performance appraisal plan is clear. It serves as a basis for evaluating and rewarding employee performance, for improving performance and for assisting employee development.

Essential elements of the plan include self-appraisal by the employee, appraisal of the employee's performance by the manager and joint development of plans to improve that performance in the future.

Communication. Effective communication between managers and employees is essential for employee motivation. The manager's attitude, feedback and listening are essential for good communication. The manager must be willing to negotiate rather than give a directive and to let employees discuss and modify messages so that they are more understandable and acceptable.

Employees who work in a receptive, positive work environment are more likely to listen.

Information about the company, its history, operating philosophy, employment policies and practices, and employee benefits should be communicated in an employee manual that is concise and factual and written in a positive tone. Employee benefits and employment policies and practices should be formulated carefully to meet their objectives, be uncomplicated and be administered consistently so that employees know they are being treated fairly.

For the human resources program to be effective, a company's resources specialist must have the knowledge and ability to gain the trust and respect of its executives and managers. The specialist's primary responsibility is to ensure that employees are treated fairly and consistently and to assist executives and managers in handling their people responsibilities.

John F. Collins is president of J. F. Collins Associates, a consulting firm on human resources management, of Flossmoor, Illinois.

5.
MODERN MOTIVATION

Roy W. Walters

Employees respond to challenge, not chiding.

It is people's roles and relationships to the organization that are key to motivation and productivity. Business, industry, and government are finally beginning to realize that new strategies are required in managing people.

Traditional approaches to the motivation problem appear outdated today. Productivity by coercion is out of the question. Authoritarianism in the workplace reinforces alienation and can lead to problems with workers, ranging from high turnover to indifference to quality of work, to workers restricting output, and even to sabotage. Moreover, excessive pressure from the top tends to stifle ideas and constructive criticism.

Similarly, managers who try to instill fear and anxiety in their subordinates miss the mark. The adage, "If they don't worry, they don't work," fails to take account of the way employees' needs evolve, and the way their motivation increases as they achieve higher levels of satisfaction from their jobs. Furthermore, anxiety in managerial ranks can easily induce risk-aversion behavior and information manipulation, neither of which aids the quality of an organization's performance.

Some managers try a more subtle approach. They beseech, they implore, they invoke loyalty "to the team." They cajole and act like "one of the guys," and they may even try to inflict a "sense of participation." At best, these tactics succeed only in the short run, and then workers begin to feel duped and resentful. When this kind of exhortation fails, managers will often say they have a "communication problem" in an effort to convince themselves and others that the problem is not the message itself, but only the way it was received.

Use of incentives is another gambit still used by many managers. This ploy is just a continuation of the old "carrot-and-stick" management philosophy. Naturally, employees get enthusiastic when they receive their first bonus award or color television. But do we want people getting their kicks from winning awards and prizes, or do we want them to get their kicks by realizing that they are becoming increasingly competent in what they do?

Any good manager's objective in trying to improve performance should be a long-range one: to help people develop their competence by giving them added responsibilities and opportunities for new learning. These are psychological reinforcements, measures to employees that they are growing and developing.

Granted, there seems to be no limit to the human appetite for wanting more of the good things in life. But that's all the more reason to think twice about rewarding good performance with bonus payments and merchandise.

It is important to ask, "What behavior do we want to reinforce?" Some organizations give habitual absentees an extra dollar for each day they show up on the job. I don't want to reinforce that. I expect them to be there. One crucial problem with the incentives is that they tend to treat symptoms without correcting the problem. For example, a "buck-a-day" incentive scheme may appear to curb absenteeism. However, absenteeism is rarely the real problem. Rather absenteeism, lateness, turn-over, sabotage, thumping drums for unions, submitting unwarranted grievances, and so forth are merely manifestations of a person's deep dissatisfaction with his or her work. This is a problem that bonus money and merchandise awards, no matter how valuable, will hardly solve.

Many managers make the mistake of assuming that incentive and motivation are one and the same. Since this is far from being the case, incentive programs often have disappointing outcomes. Motivation is an internal psychological process, while incentive devices are external to the worker.

Most people are born with the innate drive to grow, both physically and psychologically. There is little we can do to stop or stunt physical growth. But much can be done to inhibit psychological growth. Creating parental dependency, reinforcing societal badges—report card marks, merit badges, cash bonuses, TV sets, etc.—rather than the achievements themselves, all the while keeping people in non-learning situations, have dramatic effects on a person's growth drive.

At work, the only way people can demonstrate motivation is to have a motivating job. No pressure from bosses to do more, move faster, or create more can cause motivation. These pressures cause movement. Movement is external, while motivation is internal.

All of us learn much at the subconscious level. We learned, but we were never aware that we learned. It required no energy, no effort. We didn't set out to learn. We just did.

Certainly employees can be pressured into doing more. Threats, stated or implied, will make them do more. But, doing more is not the same as being motivated.

Managers must remember this differentiation, and also remember that our responsibilities are to unlock employees' motivational potential.

All of us want to progress, to be more and better tomorrow than we are today. So, employers must provide such an opportunity to get the best work from employees. This means creating an atmosphere that is conducive to growth.

Employers shouldn't be constrained by narrow, rigid definitions of jobs and responsibilities. Instead, they should view subordinates' jobs as flexible and dynamic.

The implications of this motivation concept are vast. Both staffing and organization structures will be affected. As people's motivation is unleashed there will be clear evidence that fewer people are needed for the current amount of work. This is the payoff both for the organization and the individual.

6.
THE CAUSES AND CONSEQUENCES OF HIGH MORALE

Jan Berkhout

The term "morale" is used rather loosely in industrial psychology, sometimes equivalent to the term "motivation" and sometimes equivalent to "satisfaction."

N.R.F. Maier proposed that the term motivation should be restricted to individuals and not applied to groups, and that the term morale be reserved for descriptions of group behavior.[1]

High morale, then, is a term used to describe a group that appears to have an unusually high level of satisfaction associated with both membership in the group and the performance of its functions. It is possible to observe naturally occurring high-morale groups in either military, industrial, or competitive athletic situations. Such groups have a number of features in common.

Size. The largest high-morale groups seem to be limited to 40 or 50 individuals. This is the size of the largest athletic teams, military tactical units and industrial shop crews. This is the largest size of a functional group in which all members are doing more or less the same thing in the same place and time, and are affected alike by external events. Since couples and triads seem to have their own over-riding social dynamics, the smallest observable high-morale group is likely to number four or five.

Structure. All members of a high-morale group are likely to be known to each other, with few if any sociometrically isolated individuals. Any particular type of group decision-making mechanisms may be present, from the most democratic to the most authoritarian, but a high morale situation is not likely to persist if this mechanism is not accepted as legitimate by all the group members. A high-morale group will typically have a mechanism for replacing critical decision-making personnel who are absent or incapacitated. Again, any kind of mechanism is tolerable if it is generally perceived as legitimate.

It seems to be crucial for high morale that all members of the group are perceived as contributing positively to the total effort, no matter now minimal their actual input may be. The group accepts any effort as worth more than no effort at all, and does not compare individuals to the group average or to the possible contribution of a potential replacement, and thus find some individuals wanting.

GOAL ORIENTATION

High-morale groups are always associated with some tangible goal. In a military context the goal may be the capture of territory, the destruction of a certain number of enemy units, or the completion of a certain number of missions. In desperate situations the goal may simply be to hold a position for a certain number of days. In competitive athletics the goal is typically a championship or record, but may also be merely the bettering of some previous status. In industrial contexts, goals are generally production or sales totals, but may also be efficiency targets such as cost control, or energy use reduction, or even such intangibles as market share. Whatever the situation, these goals will have certain features in common:

1. The goals are universally perceived as both attainable and worthwhile. An occasional scoffer can be rejected from the group, but reservations about worth and attainability by more than a very few will effectively destroy the high morale situation.

2. The group perceives progress towards the goal as being both steady and tangible.

3. The attainment of the goal cannot be too far in the future. In competitive athletics a term of six months is about the maximum interval over which a high morale situation can be sustained. The high morale episodes in military campaigns are typically somewhat shorter. High morale campaigns in industrial settings vary from a few weeks to a few months, but not longer. There seems to be some natural term to a high morale situation, and few seem to last beyond half a year.

The need for steady and tangible progress implies that some form of feedback or communication system is available by which the group can monitor its progress. Lack of perceived progress extending more than a few days is harmful to morale, and progress should ideally be visible on a daily basis. Even a failing or lost cause can generate progress.

OPERATING CHARACTERISTICS

High morale groups are typically resistant to performance decrements due to stress. In both military and athletic settings, such groups will continue to function effectively after sustaining high casualties, and industrial members will continue to perform when injured or otherwise incapacitated. In industrial settings, high-morale groups tolerate low or delayed pay, in some cases working without pay at all. Absenteeism in high morale groups is low to nonexistent. Members willingly fill in for absent or incapacitated colleagues. A high-morale group will also tolerate very poor working conditions, such as noise, heat, cold, bad lighting and even physical danger without complaint.

It does not follow that high-morale groups are particularly efficient. All persons are perceived as contributing to progress towards the shared goal, including some whose contribution is in reality minimal. The group's attention is focused on the goal and on progress towards it, not on cost effectiveness (except in those rare cases where operating efficiency itself can be made a plausible goal, in which case total output may fall). The group operates to protect its individual members from criticism, and its decision-making and authority structure from interference.

CREATING A HIGH-MORALE GROUP

From a somewhat cynical management point of view, a high-morale situation is something that can be deliberately created. The group has to be given some tokens of autonomy. If the group is created from scratch, some time must elapse so that the members can become familiar with each other.

The group authority structure must then be legitimated. This is a sensitive operation requiring subtlety and experience. A group can be asked to elect a leader, but this may not seem to be a legitimate procedure to some members, particularly if the choice is contested and a formal opposition develops. An authoritarian leadership can be imposed on the group, but this has obvious pitfalls. Informal authority rotating among a subgroup of salient personalities offers another possibility. In any case, once a leadership has been accepted, the group will defend it against further changes, so the initial choice has to be well thought out.

A goal must be selected conforming to the criteria mentioned before. The time frame of the goal will be one to six months in the future, and care must be taken to be sure the goal is worthwhile to the members and seen as attainable. The goal can actually be directly negotiated with the group in most cases without compromising the mystical target quality it will acquire in operation. If the goal is set too low, it will be reached in too short a time and high morale will dissipate prematurely. If it is set too high, morale will dissipate as soon as it becomes clear the goal is unattainable.

Every military commander seeking to inspire his troops is aware of the trade-offs involved in this sort of compromise, and these trade-offs will be found in the industrial setting as well. Unfortunately, a prematurely filled goal cannot be followed immediately with another, higher target.

High morale almost never survives that process. One of the most important decisions to be made when creating a high-morale group is the nature of the feedback to be provided. Daily information is best. In an industrial setting it can consist of output and production information presented publicly in some graphic way. Hourly communication is impractical, and even daily feedback is undesirable if short-term fluctuations in progress tend to dominate the daily variations.

The impression desired is one of steady and reliable progress, but the measure should be sensitive enough to reflect short-term bursts or extreme effort as these are made. The units to use, and the update intervals presented, are critical choices also, because the group's perception of progress will be closely tied to the units used and will not be easily shifted or modified.

PROBLEMS WITH HIGH-MORALE GROUPS

Deliberately creating a high-morale group is not without risks. The primary danger is that morale will suddenly evaporate, leaving a highly frustrated and contentious group of people whose productivity may well be lower than if the high morale situation had never existed. To some extent this happens even when the goal is successfully reached on schedule. Managers should plan for this eventuality.

Since the appearance of progress is essential to the maintenance of morale, there is a great temptation to falsify progress in the daily feedback. On a day-by-day basis this course of action will always seem attractive to middle-level managers who must implement such lies, since it is they who must otherwise deal first-hand with the collapse of morale which must otherwise follow. If high morale can be maintained, the lie may come true. If morale collapses, all hope of reaching the goal may be lost.

Another problem with high-morale groups is that management may lose effective control of them. It may prove impossible to replace weak or unproductive members, change leadership, and in extreme cases it may even become impossible to offer instructions or advice. Management can become an adversary of the group—a stress factor to be ignored or overcome. The implementation of novel production strategies is difficult, since high-morale groups are inherently quite conservative about changing their operating habits. If progress is satisfactory, morale will be maintained, but greater progress will not seem worth the taking of unknown risks.

Consequently, high-morale groups should be set up only if a satisfactory production process or tactical doctrine is already in place. High morale groups should not be combined with any other types of innovation or reorganization.

High morale is called for only when a fixed period of high stress or unpleasant working conditions or financial exigency is predicted. High morale is incompatible with many other management goals. Safety in particular is not amenable to high-morale treatment. A high-morale group will also tend to ignore cost considerations, maintenance problems, theft prevention, fairness, equal opportunity, record keeping, and due-process generally.

A PEAK EXPERIENCE

High-morale groups are inherently transient. When a short-term period of stress can be foreseen it may be wise to create one. When a particular production goal is of overriding importance to an organization, high morale may be the optimum way to achieve it. But it must always be kept in mind that morale must eventually drop, and will probably drop below baseline levels. Creating high morale is a trap for inexperienced managers who do not plan for the inevitable letdown, and who create high morale in the hope that everything will get better and stay that way. Any organization that relies on a permanent state of high morale is misguided.

Finally, it should be noted that being part of a high-morale group is a peak experience for most of those involved. The effervescent giddiness of participation in a shared and successful group action seems to provide a lasting satisfaction quite independent of the specific project being undertaken. Fortunate individuals may have many such experiences in a lifetime, and most people have at least a few, but it is an event that defies conversion into a steady state.

REFERENCES

1. Maier, N.R.F.., *Psychology in Industrial Organizations* (Boston: Houghton-Mifflin, 1973).

Jan Berkhout holds a doctorate in psychology from the University of Chicago. He is a consultant in the field of industrial psychology, and a member of the Human Factors Society.

7.
AN OMISSION IN THE PLANNING PROCESS

Andre Nelson

> If you have run out of ideas, let your employees add their comments. Make them feel
> as if they are an important cog in the wheel.

The hi-tech industry in the Silicon Valley in northern California and in its overseas facilities is experiencing a period of mushrooming growth and increasingly intense competition for the market of the future. Among the problems this competition brings into sharp focus are: should some of the organizations involved turn toward more decentralization or more centralization; is now the time to pay less attention to engineering and more to marketing; and how may greater efficiency in production be obtained?

A manager who is in charge of a production plant overseas for an American computer manufacturer was discussing this latter problem and stated: "I have been called back here to meet with headquarters. The purpose of the meeting is to discuss some of the problems facing the administrative staff in their forecasting and planning for future marketing needs. Whatever the plan regarding computer related needs for the future as they visualize it, whether it be office automation equipment or personal computers, I know that my department will be expected to become even more efficient. I don't see how my supervisors or I can possibly come up with any more plans toward that objective. We are just about 'tapped' out."

ARE YOU TAPPED OUT?

Possibly he and his supervisors were "tapped out" as he put it or had run out of ideas. However, I pointed out that as he tries to develop a plan for increased production, there is a resource which he and the average manager and supervisor tend to overlook: that is the employees themselves.

Purposeful planning on the part of the manager, or his or her staff, consists of many things. The major ones are obvious: having an objective, communicating it, identifying assumptions (in the case of top management, will desk computers or minicomputers be the hot item of the future?), selection of a method to use in reaching the objective, and finally setting up standards so you know if the objective is being reached. Almost all managers, consciously or unconsciously, go through these steps, with the exception of one. We often fail to communicate the planning objective to the employees who will be affected. Their input to the planning process is not asked for. The concept that you and I too often hold is that we are the managers, we are the ones paid to do the thinking and planning. Besides, what could the people on the line doing the work add to our planning process which would be worthwhile?

WHAT YOU NEED IS A FRESH VIEWPOINT

The answer is...a fresh viewpoint! Remember they are the ones who are doing the job. If there is any person who knows the shortcuts to getting more production and also the things which are standing in the way of more efficiency, it is the individual running the punch press or mill, or working on the assembly line. As an example, one of the largest steel mills in California was about to shut down because the plant was losing money. The employees asked that the plans for closing the plant be delayed for a short time so they could come up with a plan by which production costs might be reduced. This was done. The workers submitted many plans which if followed would put the plant on a profitable basis once again. One proposed plan suggested investing in a new machine to shear the metal—the cost in wasted scrap could be cut by over 50 percent. This was an obvious need which the manager and supervisors should have picked up on in the past. The employees operating the equipment were aware of it, but did not bring it to the attention of management. They felt if management was not concerned about it, why should they as hourly workers be? The end of this vignette is that management did accept the results of the workers' participation in the planning. The plant remained open and operating at a profit.

At Ford's Louisville assembly plant, which made trucks and LTDs, managerial staff was concerned with improving the quality rating the corporate auditors were giving their product. With this goal in mind, management set about planning how they could achieve it. One source they turned to was the hourly workers. These employees were asked to contribute ideas, the ideas were listened to and the workers felt involved in the planning. As a result of this strategy, changes were put into effect. Now the trucks made in that plant get the highest quality scores by Ford. There are those who believe that the trucks now made at that plant by the same workers as before may be as defect-free as any being produced in our domestic market. Much of the credit for this improvement is due to the workers who were involved in the planning, the new "employee involvement program" as it is termed by Ford, and those who contributed several hundred proposals for improvement, the majority of which were put into effect by managerial staff. However, managers of organizations do not have to wait for a crisis prior to involving employees in the planning. On the other hand, involving them early in the planning, if the result of the planning is going to impact on them at the job site, may well help avert a crisis.

You and I, and those we work with, tend to value and be concerned about physical objects and planned objectives, according to the amount of effort we have spent in their development. As a boy, I lived on the coast of Maine. One summer, I bought a canoe and spent several weeks carefully sanding it down and applying innumerable coats of varnish to its hull. It gleamed like glass and I was inordinately proud of it. I treated it with great care when using it so it would not get a scratch on it. Towards the end of the summer, a friend asked if he could use it to travel to an off-shore island. With much reluctance, I let him use it. I shall never forget how it looked when he returned it to me. He had not used any care when he grounded the canoe on a shore; he simply dragged it up over the shale and rocks. Needless to say, the varnished surface I had been so proud of was now gouged, cracked and peeling. However, that meant nothing to the person who had borrowed the craft. He had nothing invested in it; he had not spent endless hours sanding and painting, in the end to have a product of which he was proud and protective.

A similar analogy applies when you, as a manager, develop a plan which is going to affect the workers on the job but do not let them play any part in the development of that plan. The employees will read the directions for the new program, listen to you explain the plan and then put it into operation probably with little or no enthusiasm. The thought in their minds may often be, "If it fails, it will be no reflection on me. I have nothing invested in its success. However, if they had asked me, I probably could have pointed out ways to prevent it from failing."

Assuming the employees had been involved, directly or indirectly, in the planning, it then becomes a part of them, just as that canoe, over which I had spent countless hours of effort, became a part of me. Being involved to some degree in the planning, the employees have a stake, an investment, in ensuring that they do all they can to make it succeed, otherwise it reflects unfavorably on their own ability. As a result, they will do all they can to see that "their" plan does work.

In conclusion, that is what I discussed with the young manager who was concerned with finding some new approaches to improving productivity and at the same time getting the support of the employees for his plan. As I pointed out to him, my experience has been that often your task can be made so much easier and your planning far more effective by your letting the person who does the job participate in the planning, assuming it is feasible. Draw on the skills and support your workers will give you when you ask or permit them to become involved to some degree in planning. They must have something to contribute. After all, many of us, now managers, came from their ranks!

8.

JOB LOYALTY: NOT THE VIRTUE IT SEEMS

Jeanne Dorin McDowell

Veteran employees provide continuity. But all too often they are insecure, dull and dependent.

Not long ago a psychologically oriented consulting firm was hired to help a billion-dollar bank set up a succession plan. As consultants typically would in such cases, the firm, Rohrer, Hibler & Replogle, asked the bank's chief executive officer to pick potential successors from his 10 top executives.

They were all staunchly loyal; the shortest time any of them had worked for the bank was 15 years. Yet the C.E.O. could not in good conscience suggest promoting any of the men. Not one had shown initiative or leadership potential in his long tenure with the company. In fact, the C.E.O., by nature a paternal man, had been covering up each of his manager's mistakes and, at times, actually doing their work for them.

The C.E.O. retired in despair and his successor was hired from outside. Within a year the new boss fired seven out of the 10 top executives.

"They were managerial pygmies," recalled John Sauer, head of the consulting firm's New York office. "They had a lot of loyalty but none of the skills to compete."

The virtues of loyalty are well chronicled: it keeps down the cost of turnover, now estimated as high as $85,000 per departing middle manager, and provides the continuity needed to put long-term plans into effect. But management psychologists and more than a handful of corporate executives are starting to recognize that loyalty can be highly overrated. They increasingly view the company soldier who blindly follows orders year after year as dull, dependent, and a drag on corporate dynamism.

"The sleepy solid citizen who stays with the company for 30 years isn't loyal," said Rosabeth Moss Kanter, professor of organizational management at the Yale Graduate School of Management. "He is simply viewed as having nowhere else to go."

Indeed, a growing number of corporate thinkers are now saying that the compliantly loyal individual simply cannot contribute much in a business environment characterized by fierce global competition and rapid-fire changes in technology—in other words, the environment of the 1980s. Instead, many chief executives seek underlings who may be short in commitment but long in talent and willingness to take risks.

"I want spirited managers who will challenge the system," says John Teets, chief executive officer of the Greyhound Corporation. "I don't want lukewarm employees. They breed mediocrity and a womb-to-tomb attitude."

To be sure, the question of loyalty's worth may be moot these days. Loyal employees are a vanishing breed (see Figure 1). "If I were in the seniority pin business, I would be out of a job today," said James Cabrera, president of Drake Beam Morin Inc., a New York firm that specializes in outplacement for executives.

Figure 1
New Values Spawn: THE DEMISE OF LOYALTY

Loyal employees, whether they are boon or bane, are increasingly hard to find these days. The last recession, the slew of takeovers, and the push in many corporations to cut costs have claimed almost 450,000 managerial, executive, and administrative jobs since 1979, according to the Bureau of Labor Statistics.

Companies may have wound up with trimmer, more efficient staffs, but they have also wound up with a huge cadre of managers who no longer believe that their corporate employers will return their loyalty in hard times. And, psychologists warn, just as loyalty begets loyalty, perceived betrayal begets cynicism and self-interest.

"Loyalty has always centered around the notion that 'the company will take care of me,'" said James Cabrera, president of Drake Beam Morin Inc, an outplacement firm. But now, said Steven Temlock, president of Organization Consultants, "The myth that institutions will take care of us has been shattered."

The new disloyalty has a ripple effect. Employees who feel betrayed by the company they had pledged allegiance to usually assume a once-burned-twice-shy attitude to their next employer. Says a marketing vice president who recently started a new job after losing his previous one in a takeover: "I'm loyal to the extent that I do the best job I can, but loyalty doesn't extend into my personal feelings anymore."

Corporate loyalty, apparently, is being replaced by loyalty to family and friends. For example, more and more managers are refusing to take jobs that require relocation. Although in many cases the reason stems from unwillingness to jeopardize the income of a working spouse, psychologists say that loyalty is at play too; executives are growing more reluctant to ask spouses or children to move when they do not wish to do so.

But while many executives bemoan the demise of loyalty, psychologists say that corporations are often better off without it. Consultants at Rohrer, Hibler & Replogle, for example, paint a picture of the overly loyal employee as someone who is averse to taking risks, is task-oriented rather than a strategic thinker, requires structure, defers to leadership, refrains from expressing himself for fear of jeopardizing his job, and follows corporate policies even if they lead to deleterious results. Here are two examples the consultants offer of the damage misguided loyalty can do:

- A small toy-manufacturing company circulated a pro forma memo encouraging its staff to reduce costs. One veteran manager took the memo so literally that he almost ruined the product. He replaced strong metal hinges with plastic ones and eliminated some parts. The products broke down and the company's reputation for quality was seriously damaged.
- The chief counsel of a large electronics company, believing that loyalty meant giving the boss what he wanted, did not discourage a highly litigious C.E.O. from filing frivolous lawsuits and refusing to settle them out of court. By the time an outside consultant was called in to assess the situation, the company had paid out millions of dollars in unnecessary legal fees and court costs.

During a business downturn, the problems that such blind loyalty cause can be even more insidious. Many loyal employees, psychologists say, believe that if they give a company solid, steady, and continuously reliable performance, it will respond with job security and regular promotions.

But, warns psychologist Peter McGinnon, when such employees see a chink in that security armor—for example, if they are passed over for promotion, or see equally loyal colleagues laid off during a cost-cutting push—their reliability evaporates. Fearful of demonstrating their anger or fear, they consciously or subconsciously try to subvert the system indirectly. They submit reports late, forget to schedule meetings, and cannot be found when a quick decision has to be made. They bring up irrelevant issues at meetings, yet withhold important information. Only when confronted outright by the change in behavior do they become outwardly belligerent.

This syndrome is particularly noticeable in companies that are facing new types of competition, regulatory upheaval, or both. A prime example is the American Telephone and Telegraph Company, where the slogan "the spirit of service" rallied generations of telephone workers. The 1983 breakup of the company, and the 9,000 layoffs that ensued, left employees feeling demoralized at best, panicky at worst.

"The breakup caused a lot of pain," said Douglas Bray, a renowned management psychologist who ran the human resources function for AT&T until his retirement a few years ago. "Many of the people had grown up during the Depression and had heard stories of the telephone company's loyalty to its workers. There was a pride in being part of the world's largest corporation. There is much more insecurity now."

Less dramatic, but nonetheless similar, scenarios are being played out at other companies that were once thought of as bastions of job security. Insurance companies, banks, and public utilities increasingly are dangling promises of bonuses or other plums before their employees' eyes. Their hope is to infuse the troops with a competitive spirit, a desire to innovate, and a willingness to take risks in order to reap rewards. But they are meeting resistance from employees who prefer the security that the salary structure of old seemed to provide.

"I get a call a day from senior executives in insurance companies who want me to design an incentive program for managers," said Michael Cooper, president of the Hay Group, a Philadelphia compensation consultant firm. "But these people are security-oriented. If you offer them incentive compensation rather than a fixed salary, they become frustrated." The result can be what psychologists call "passive aggressive" behavior—the type of belligerence typical of a dependently loyal employee who suddenly feels betrayed.

Of course, no one says that all long-time employees are more trouble than they are worth. Healthily loyal employees, psychologists say, stay with a company because they agree with its methods and philosophies, and because their jobs are personally satisfying. "There is a difference between someone whose attachment to a company comes from a positive sense of himself and someone who stays because he is afraid of separating," says Michele Berdy, a clinical psychologist.

The second type of employee is more often found in advertising, high technology, and other industries where high turnover is commonplace. Bob Robbins, vice president/management supervisor at Geers Gross, a New York advertising agency, is a typical example of the healthily loyal employee in these types of positions. Mr. Robbins is in his 30s, and this is his fifth job. He has been with Geers Gross for less than a year. He expresses no intention of leaving, but laughs at the idea that a sense of commitment would make him stay if he felt dissatisfied. "The common thread through all of my job moves has been that I have left when I felt my skills can no longer be tested," he said. "I'm committed to an organization as long as I am challenged."

A few companies have learned to get the best of both possible worlds: employee longevity and employee independence. The International Business Machines Corporation, for one, incorporates the beneficial aspects of loyalty without encouraging the drawbacks. I.B.M. employees receive job security and extraordinary benefits in exchange for their devotion to the I.B.M. way. The turnover rate is extraordinarily low, yet the company has not fallen victim to the stodginess that can accompany a staff that has been around too long. The reason: I.B.M. has made it clear, through its policy of awards and through whom it promotes, that its definition of loyalty includes constant innovation and attention to customer service, not just rigid conformity to dress codes and other rules. "The common denominator among our employees is that they are achievement oriented, and we reward them for it," said W. E. Burdick, vice president of personnel.

A similar reward system is working at the Hewlett-Packard Company, which, despite recent setbacks in its product lines, has not suffered any mass departure of people. "If you have a good idea, the company wants you to try it, and that inspires my loyalty," said Kim Wisckol, who was recently named manager of office productivity after she devised a plan to automate office procedures.

Perhaps the only type of loyalty that cannot be explained in terms of reward systems and corporate cultures is the loyalty inspired by particularly charismatic leaders. Often, psychologists say, that loyalty stems from a desire on the employee's part to be like that leader.

For example, An Wang, the 65-year-old founder and head of Wang Laboratories in Boston, "represents the American dream," said Thomas Martin, Wang's manager of human resources development. "He started in a small lab above a garage in Roxbury, and today is the owner of a multinational corporation." Similarly, Lee A. Iacocca has made a name as a hard hitter who made good without being born to it. "Executives who work for Lee Iacocca acquire his mannerisms," said Roderick Gilkey, associate professor of management at Emory University. "They dress like him and speak like him, but without being aware that they are doing it."

That sort of conformity, however, may not be all good. For one thing, it breeds a tendency to agree with everything the revered leader says, not necessarily for fear of losing a job, but out of blind belief that the leader is always right. Moreover, if the leader retires or resigns, the executives left behind may take a long time to develop an allegiance to his replacement. Often, they never do, and the corporation suffers.

Companies may not learn how much—or what type of—loyalty they have inspired in their work forces until a time of crisis. For example, a recent report by an independent consultant noted an "impressive reserve of loyalty among people who had been through so much" at the Bethlehem Steel Corporation. Although the company has laid off or eliminated the jobs of thousands of people since 1981, the consultant notes that remaining employees felt Bethlehem was only responding to an economic decline in steel that was beyond its control.

The company's handling of the layoffs—for example, its willingness to pay for outplacement services for fired employees who wanted them—also lessened the feeling of abandonment, Bethlehem executives say. And the employees who stayed, they claim, did not in general manifest belligerent behavior. Instead, they displayed healthy loyalty—that is, joined with top management to try to help the company survive.

Delta Air Lines, too, is a case of loyalty helping in a time of crisis. The company demonstrated its own loyalty to employees when the 1973 oil embargo forced it to curtail flights. While many other airlines laid off excess on-flight workers, Delta reassigned them. In 1982, employees said thanks by chipping in and buying a $30 million Boeing 767 for the airline. Seven thousand employees turned out to christen the plane "The Spirit of Delta."

It was as much gratitude as loyalty, employees now say. "When I needed it the most, Delta wrapped itself around me like a warm blanket, and I'll never forget it," said James Ewing, director of national media relations and a 24-year Delta veteran. "I don't even have a resume."

9.

IF YOU'RE REALLY SERIOUS ABOUT EMPLOYEE MOTIVATION . . .

Smith W. Brookhart III

Participative management can help take the mystery out of developing human resources.

At the heart of Centerre Bank's employee motivation program is the no-gimmicks, day-in, day-out practice of participative management. The management of human resources, generally agreed to be key to a bank's success, often gets no more than lip service. How many managers—at the top, not to mention at the middle level—make a conscious, consistent effort to motivate their subordinates?

A test: Do you personally spend six hours a week supervising and counseling those who report directly to you? Do you solve problems for your subordinates or coach them through solving their own?

Briefly put, participative management is a multi-step process whose most important, and most difficult, steps are the selection and development of people in their jobs. Starting at the top, the management team should be comprised of people whom you can trust, and must represent the major divisions of the bank. They are not necessarily the most competent technicians in the bank, but they must seek and accept responsibility, demonstrate leadership, and be active supervisors.

Individual development plans should be worked out for each member of the team. At Centerre we start literally with a blank piece of paper and, to each member of the management team, say, in effect: What does the bank need from your position? And what authority do you need to get the job done? From such a session, we can look at strengths and weaknesses of an individual and help fill any gaps so that we can help them become better managers.

```
                        POSITION DESCRIPTION FORM

Position Title:  VP - Marketing and Personnel        Location:  Main Bank

Department:  Marketing                             Prepared by:  (name)

Function:

    Administrative Marketing and Personnel Department
    _____
    _____


Reportability:

Reports To:      Smith W. Brookhart, President & CEO

Supervises:      Personnel Officer, Personal Banker and Investment Officer


Authorities:

a.    Allocate money for advertising and public relations and promotional programs.

b.    Approve MC and Visa merchants and set discount rates.

c.    Direct Personnel function, Personal Banker, and Investment Consultant.


Reponsibilities:

a. Advertising and public relations activities of the bank.

b. Supervise maintenance of payroll, benefits program, and personnel records.

c. Insure that the personnel function is in compliance with bank policy and
   Federal State regulations.
d. Director training program for banks.
```

PEOPLE-SKILLED SUPERVISORS

Next is finding people-skilled supervisors. To do that right from the start, develop a position description rather than a job description. Generally job descriptions are not worth the paper they are written on because they are task-oriented and quickly outdated.

A position description identifies responsibilities, authorities, and other basic parts of the position (see sample form): (1) What is the function of the job overall? (2) Who does the person report to? (3) Who reports to the person? (4) What authorities does the particular supervisor have? (5) What are his/her specific responsibilities? (Centerre writes individual position descriptions for all employees of the bank.)

Another part of the process of selecting and developing people-skilled supervisors that Centerre has found effective, yet simple, is job modeling.

Under the standard process of selecting people to do something that they have not done before, the chances of their being successful—whether they are from within the organization or outside—are about 35 to 40 percent. Through the process of job modeling, we have brought that success ratio up to over 80 percent.

JOB MODELING

Starting with a blank form, a group of people who would work with the person to be chosen for a particular position get involved in developing the model, keeping in mind the needs of the position. We gather, say, four people

APPLICANT REVIEW

POSITION: _Bookkeeper_ NAME: _____

Weight	Score 1-10	Total	Want Characteristics
8	7	56	Friendly
9	7	63	Team Player
7	8	56	Detail Person
8	8	64	Accurate
8	8	64	Tactful
7	6	42	Trainable
8	9	72	Responsible
9	9	81	Dependable
10	0	0	Confidential
7	8	56	Self-Starter
5	6	30	Appearance
6	7	42	Speed
6	8	48	Self-Development
7	7	49	Communication Skills
7	6	42	Comfortable with office machines
5	7	35	Works well under pressure
117	170	800	

Comments: _____

together who are affected by a given job and we pose the question: "What do you think the person for that position would look like if he or she were perfect?" "What behavioral characteristics would we want him or her to possess?" That goes for new hires, promotions, or lateral transfers.

The job model for a bookkeeper, for example, was prepared by the bookkeeping supervisor, her first assistant, the personnel officer, and one teller. (See sample on opposite page.)

Next, the job modeling group rates the characteristics listed on a scale of 1 to 10 depending on importance, then each of the characteristics is multiplied by weights on a scale of 1 to 5. This gives us a measurement of how a person fits specific behavioral characteristics.

The job model forms also can be used to rate and standardize information on resumes. I once went through 210 resumes on loan officer applicants in three hours and scored them using the model sheets.

We go one step beyond the initial job modeling exercise. We remodel the job and set it up on the basis of negotiable characteristics: those we are willing to contend with and those we are not. Through this step we come up with questions to ask in an interview and areas to focus on in a reference check.

By the time we get through the modeling process, we have established in a systematic fashion what we are looking for in a person to fill a position. Most of the time, we are looking for behavioral characteristics that will allow a person to succeed in our organization, not technical competence other than the basic skills required for a job.

ONCE YOU FIND THEM . . .

After the selection process is completed, the next step is to develop goals and action plans to ensure that our folks are successful. We make the goal-setting step simple and not terribly time-consuming.

Who sets the goal? Normally the supervisor, along with input from the individual. I start the process by going through bank goals for the year, working with the management team. Then my goals come out of that. Five goals are enough to give you the significant things you should do—and be able to remember what they are!

Once the goals are established, each one is listed on the top of a sheet divided into four sections: one for each quarter. These sheets then become the action plans. We see on paper actions that will be taken in each quarter to achieve the stated goal.

The supervisor checks the progress of the actions listed through the technique of coaching. In our bank, coaching is the most significant contribution that we ask our supervisors to make, that we train them to do.

Coaching is not a performance appraisal. It's an informal visit during work hours to talk about problems, follow-ups, progress and achievement. It's a

GOAL/ACTION PLANS

Name: (marketing officer)

Goal: Increase deposits by 15 percent

Action Plans: * denotes "on-going"

1st Quarter	2nd Quarter
1. Maintain Newcomer Program. 2. Work with Al on Newcomer prospects. 3. Maintain weekly survey of competition and offer competitive, profitable pricing of products, services. 4. Use media to introduce/promote products/services. 5. Personalize ads with photos of employees and facilities to introduce specialized products.	1. Introduce Valued Customer card to customer with banking relationship over $50,000 by April 30. 2. Business Man's seminar, May, 1984. 3. Training session for cross-sell program "How to sell a new customer on our Bank"
3rd Quarter	**4th Quarter**
1. Direct mail letter to professionals and business owners (customers and non-customers) offering Sue's expertise in investing seasonal cash flow. Include new brochure on investments available. July, 1984.	1. Monitor results and weep or rejoice.

Evaluation: _____

Rating period-from _____ to _____

regular quarterly check-up on the goals, again, not formal, but a talk that begins with, "How are we coming with such a project that was supposed to be started. Did it get off the ground?"

We have a standard procedure in dealing with problem resolution: Employees who come to a senior manager with a problem must also bring three possible solutions. The manager is not solving the problem, but rather helping them, with his better "data bank," to pick the best alternative, thus allowing the employee to expand and learn how to solve problems. When employees can solve problems that arise, they are motivated.

A good coach in a management position is just like a coach in an athletic situation. If you really want your team to win, you can't play for them, but you can direct them how to do it, and then help them learn the techniques which will let them be winners.

Performance appraisals—we do those too; we all have to do them. At Centerre they come at year-end for all the people who are measuring personal goals against bank goals. For those who are not, the performance appraisals are on employment anniversaries. We do not talk salaries at these sessions; that topic follows about 30 days after the appraisal session. Once salary is given we start a new round of goals.

Bonuses are important at Centerre. We pay for performance and we differentiate. The bonus pool depends on the bank's net earnings based on a formula and can be anywhere from two to eight percent. We've been known to stretch, even double, that eight percent for outstanding performance. We do not allow across-the-board department bonuses.

Individual development plans also are part of Centerre's effort to strengthen the skills of our supervisors. Basically we operate from the position that we cannot change people's personalities and behavior weaknesses, and, therefore, we strive to place people in jobs where their strengths are needed.

Our bank develops non-supervisory employees much the same way we develop supervisors: through position descriptions, goals/action plans, individual development plans, and the use of bonuses and incentives. Last year we spent in excess of $50,000 in training—more than $1,000 per employee. All of our 48 employees were in some kind of training-in-bank sessions, outside seminars, workshops, or schools. Also, Centerre pays complete tuition for college-level night school courses, if they will help employees become better managers.

A simple cross-sell program that our marketing director put together in just four months involved almost everyone in the bank. It is based on the approach that everyone who comes in or calls the bank is a prospect for a cross-sell by any employee. All personnel were given calling cards which are used to record the sales and contacts. We told employees that for every product they cross-sold we would give them $5, and for every new customer, the employee would receive $15.

Between January 15 and March 30, we had 315 cross-sells that added about one-half million dollars in new deposits. Thirty employees, three directors, and one director's wife have received bonus payments.

THE CEMENT OF MOTIVATION

If you are willing to go as far as we have described to make employee motivation a living, day-to-day commitment, then in our experience you must go that extra mile with internal communication—because that is the cement that holds together a motivated organization.

Centerre solidifies that accomplishment by utilizing at least seven communications techniques:

1. MBWA—Management By Walking Around

One of my primary responsibilities is making myself visible, letting people talk to me—to complain about work or to tell me about something that has happened in their personal lives. This lets employees feel they have a boss who is concerned about them and who knows what is going on in their departments; that someone cares enough to show concern about an employee, not just about bank customers. All of our supervisors practice MBWA.

2. Management Team Meetings

The management team meets once a week from one to three hours to go over any topics that need to be discussed. The agenda of all the items brought up is published and given to the officers, so they know what goes on in those meetings. Then if the officers have questions about a discussion or decision that took place in the management team meeting, they have the opportunity to ask.

3. Communication Meeting

The people who interplay on a daily basis from different departments come together bi-weekly for an hour or hour-and-a-half. They publish the minutes of what they talk about, and all officers get to see those.

4. Staff Meetings

Once a month all staff meet in the morning before the bank opens. General topics are covered in these sessions. We might bring in an economist to project what's going to happen in the tourist season or the FBI to talk about robberies or a psychologist to discuss stress—any topic to provide general information to the staff.

5. Department Meetings

Monthly, the staffs of each department get together to review the information from the management meeting agendas, communications meeting agendas, and the staff meetings. Then this group covers the normal gripes and discusses problems and innovations.

6. Officer Meetings

Nine or 10 times a year for up to three hours, officers meet to discuss anything that went on in the management meetings and communication meetings on which they want discussion. I review overall bank performance, we go through the marketing plan for the upcoming month, plus we discuss any items an officer wants to put on the agenda.

7. In-house Newsletter

The monthly in-house newsletter produced by the marketing department includes typical gossip (new babies, new grandmothers), jokes and cartoons (we pay $1 to an employee who brings in one that is published), a calendar of events, and a spotlight of an employee and a director.

Centerre's approach to motivation can be summed up this way: We've come to believe that motivation is not a one-time program; it's the day-to-day operational handling of people. It's meeting people's needs.

Does it work? Is all this worth it? We think the answer is an unqualified yes.

Centerre Bank of Branson is a high performance bank because of quality and motivated people.

Part II
MOTIVATION, MONEY AND REWARDS

10.
CAN MONEY MOTIVATE?

Stephen C. Bushardt
Roberto Toso
M. E. Schnake

While money is one of the most powerful motivational tools, its use must be tailored
to each employee's values.

Can money motivate? By all indications, it seems that organizations which
rely on financial rewards to improve their employees' performances do not
achieve noticeable results.

While there are many explanations for the lack of success in using money as
a motivator, they all too often focus on a comparison with other reward systems
without analyzing the mechanics of the money system. What is needed is a
greater understanding of financial motivators, an understanding which would
enable organizations to determine if they should use money motivations or
adopt another type of reward system.

Not all organizations meet the requirements for establishing a money
system, as we will show later. On the other hand, those organizations that can
use money as a motivator have one of the most powerful motivational tools
available.

New insights into the use of money as a motivator are provided in the
"expectancy theory of motivation." This theory dictates that in order for an
individual to be highly motivated, he or she must have a high drive in effort
and performance, along with a strong overall desire for the end rewards, a
desire which overshadows negative factors. In the event that one of these positive factors is low, the level of motivation will tend to be low.

CONDITIONS TO MOTIVATE

In order for a monetary reward system to motivate greater performance,
three conditions must be met. First, the employee must have a high net

preference for money. By "net preference," we refer not only to the desire for money, but to other outcomes associated with performance as well. In essence, net preference is the average desire for all outcomes associated with performance. The achievement of a positive outcome such as money can have negative aspects such as more hours of work per week or higher standards of performance. Depending on the weight each employee gives to each type of outcome, an employee with a high desire for money may have a low net preference for the total outcomes associated with performance.

Most employees have a high preference for money. In using monetary rewards to motivate greater performance, it may be necessary to remove the negatives, thereby increasing the overall net preference. Yet, in other cases it may be possible to raise the net preference by adding additional positive effects to support the desire for money. These include promotions, praise, higher responsibilities, or a new position that enjoys visibility or social status. In other words, even if money is generally accepted as being a highly desirable outcome, its motivating effects can be reinforced to produce a high net preference by removing undesirable conditions and adding highly desirable ones.

The second condition necessary for monetary reward systems to motivate greater performance is that the employee perceives that money is tied to performance. In other words, a direct relationship exists between the level of performance and the amount of money. As performance increases, the level of remuneration increases, and as performance declines the level of remuneration declines.

The third condition is that the employee perceive that effort leads to performance. He or she should perceive that as his or her efforts increase, his or her performance will increase accordingly.

The first condition for money to be a motivator is a high net preference. It used to be fashionable to downgrade one's desire for money.

This appears to be changing as many studies report employees are ranking money as one of the most important factors in their job. One only needs a preference for the things money can buy to have a high preference for money.

While most employees have a strong preference for earning more money, they often do not want the stigma that tends to be associated with earning more money. Employees who earn more money by performing better may often be snubbed by their fellow employees. We have repeatedly observed that the highest performer is ostracized from the group. Thus, many employees who could be high performers and receive more money opt not to do so because group membership is valued more than the additional money.

Other employees who can be motivated by money believe that if they earn more money through higher performance, management will raise the work standards. It does not matter if management will change the standards or not, only that he or she perceives that management will change them.

Still other employees may have a preference for more money, but figure that it is not worth the effort. Many employees will say, "Why should I put forth a great deal of effort when what little extra I earn the government will take?" Other employees feel that the extra effort for the monetary rewards is not worth giving up the time spent in socializing either on or off the job.

In using money as a reward, managers must be aware of the "real" and "nonreal" implications. With the cost of living constantly going up, an employee will perceive only "real" money as a reward. That is, only monetary rewards in excess of the cost of living are regarded as a gain, and smaller increases as staying even or falling behind. If an employee is given a pay raise for high performance which is less than the inflation rate, he or she may perceive that he or she is being punished instead of rewarded. The cost of living increase is considered an automatic part of showing up for work every day.

These are but a few of the common reasons why some employees' preference for money is low. The negative attitude about monetary rewards varies from individual to individual.

TYING MONEY TO PERFORMANCE

The second condition for money to be a motivator is that the employee is well aware that if he or she performs well, he or she will be paid well. Money cannot motivate unless employees perceive that money is tied to performance.

Even if management were to tie money directly to performance, many employees would still not perceive the relationship. If the money reward comes in the form of an annual merit raise in December, it is unlikely that he or she will see the connection between the raise and his or her performance the previous January.

If management were to tie money to performance and eliminate the time lag between performance and the reward, many employees still might not believe that money is tied to performance. Management has often failed in past attempts to tie rewards to performance for many reasons. To begin with, management may not have defined performance. Some jobs change rapidly, making performance requirements obsolete.

In other cases, the performance requirements are so varied as to be difficult or impossible to measure. In many jobs, performance can be accurately measured through time-study methods. In many others, various instruments are used to assess performance. Unfortunately, the validity of these performance-appraisal techniques is in serious question, as many studies show that employees do not feel that the performance appraisal is very accurate. Hence, it is doubtful that performance appraisal techniques can increase the employees' perception that rewards are tied to performance.

In other cases where management can measure performance, they are often reluctant to actually tie rewards to performance. A major reason is the fear of a discrimination suit. If a minority, female, or older employee happens to be a lower performer and receives less money, he or she may initiate a lawsuit. Of course, if the difference in pay is due to performance, the disgruntled employee does not have a strong case. But management, in an effort to avoid negative publicity and the cost of legal defense, often opts not to pay on the basis of performance.

Another problem associated with tying money to performance is the inflexible nature of monetary rewards. That is, as performance declines, seldom is the salary reduced accordingly.

Another difficulty is employee self-esteem. Many people do not perceive a relationship between their effort and performance because they lack confidence in themselves. Sometimes the employee just doesn't believe he or she can be a high performer. When this occurs, it does not matter if he or she perceives a strong relationship between performance and pay and has a strong desire for money. He or she will just not be motivated.

An employee may lack confidence because he or she lacks skills or believes that is so. If the individual does lack skills, he or she should be trained in the appropriate skills or transferred to a job he or she can do. In the latter case, confidence-building by the supervisor may suffice.

A company implementing a monetary reward system needs to consider costs and benefits. The benefits of higher performance are highly desirable but the costs can be exorbitant. The decision to use money as a motivator should be made only after a thorough analysis of both costs and benefits.

These will vary depending on the industry, company, task, and individual employee. Only a few companies are able to use money as a motivator. Is yours one of them?

Stephen C. Bushardt is an assistant professor of management at the University of Southern Mississippi. Roberto Toso is a doctoral student in economics at Mississippi State University. M.E. Schnake is a doctoral student in management at Mississippi State University.

11.
THE POWER OF PAY

Robert W. Braid

The paycheck motivates—if used properly.

No organization can revitalize its work force or increase productivity if it doesn't have a realistic compensation system. Pay motivates, if it is properly used.

In recent times, the contribution of an equitable compensation program has been underemphasized. Current motivational theories tend to pass over the role that financial rewards play in motivating the work force. The most skepticism comes from the low value management experts attribute to the motivational effect of wages.

Money may not motivate all of the people all of the time, but we must not forget that employees must be rewarded financially for productive performance if it is to continue. To employees, wages are a means of satisfying their needs and wants. Some see their income as a means of providing a very basic subsistence for themselves and their family. Others see it as a vehicle for providing some degree of security. These employees usually put some portion of their income in the bank for future purposes.

They see money providing an element of independence, and don't want to lose everything if they change or lose their jobs. Or, it can provide a nest egg for their old age.

Still others see income as a means to provide their families or others with some of the nicer things of life, such as vacations, presents or a night on the town. And there are those who see their salary as a status symbol, a measure of achievement. They convey their accomplishment through their houses, their neighborhoods, their cars and clothes. In many cases wages satisfy two or more of these psychological needs. But, no matter how you cut the cake, money does have a strong influence on the behavior of most people.

An organization is undermining its ability to motivate its employees if its compensation program evolves in a haphazard fashion. Compensation systems should be reviewed periodically to ensure that they are competitive when compared with similar industries and other companies in the community.

Wages should also be equitable when compared with other internal groups of employees.

Employees do not live in a vacuum. They expect to get paid as much as others for doing the same kind of work in the same organization and in other companies in the same locality. If they perform tasks requiring greater skills, experience, and education than other tasks, they expect to get paid more.

In many organizations, compensation programs have grown over the years through additions, deletions, and trial and error without an overall master plan. Although there are many other factors that impact on employee job performance, a sound compensation program that is perceived as equitable is critical to morale. Poor pay promotes poor morale, fosters complaints, and encourages turnover and union activity.

Developing and administering an effective compensation program is a highly complex and specialized field. However, every manager should be familiar with the basic tenets of a sound compensation system. This will put him or her in a better position to evaluate the adverse consequences an inadequate program may have on his or her ability to improve job performance.

There are three characteristics to a sound compensation program.

1. *Competitive.* Salary levels and benefits must be high enough to attract competent people. The ability to acquire qualified employees is critical to the success of every organization. You can't get a $10-per-hour technician for $4.50. If a company does, it's probably because of temporary economic conditions. Then it's a pretty sure bet that when the economy changes, so will the employee. By the same token, in a tight labor market, companies have been known to pay more for employees than they are worth and, even though the economy changes, they can never get rid of them.

In recent years, much emphasis has been placed on training and development of employees. Your first concern is to get people who are willing and capable of performing, learning and growing.

Competition for competent and motivated employees will always be keen. And a trial-and-error philosophy is becoming increasingly risky. Legal and social pressures are making it progressively difficult to correct recruiting and selection errors through arbitrary firing and layoffs. And one of the major considerations in attracting good employees is how much you are willing to pay.

2. *Rational.* Individual employee salaries must be in proportion to the measured importance of the job and salaries must be comparable to similar jobs. Consideration should also be given to the level of performance and the length of service.

Job analysis is critical to a rational compensation program. This consists of developing a job description and a job evaluation.

A job description describes why a job exists. It describes the specific tasks, duties and responsibilities of the job. It also identifies working conditions, equipment used and relationships with other positions in the organization.

Job evaluation is a systematic approach for determining the relative value of a job within the organization. Job evaluations rate the value of the job, not the employee filling the position. It is an attempt to establish equal pay for equal work. Developing an equitable compensation system is a difficult task, and should be done by knowledgeable and experienced people. Job evaluations also serve as a basis for external comparisons of jobs to ensure that your pay scale is competitive in the community.

3. *Performance Based.* To be effective, a compensation program must induce and reward improved performance. Ideally, salary increases should recognize an employee's recent contribution to the company. Automatic pay raises have little or no motivational value.

Virtually every manager in North America agrees that pay increases should be granted on the basis of performance. However, evidence seems to suggest that, in reality, age and length of service count more than proficiency.

This is because, in practice, most organizations use the payroll more as a means of satisfying employees than motivating them. A company may give a top performer a $1,000 raise, then turn around and give a marginal employee $700. It doesn't take the top performer long to figure out that the difference of $5.77 a week isn't worth the extra effort. All employees soon conclude that, regardless of effort, pay increases are basically across the board.

Administering the payroll is a complex job. Many companies rely on specialists to develop rates and set policies—an important and legitimate function. Unfortunately, many tend to emphasize equity at the expense of motivation. These specialists often develop narrow pay ranges and inflexible policies on the frequency and amount of pay increments. Another problem companies have to deal with is inflation and changes in the availability of certain skills, often requiring across-the-board increases.

If the budget is tight, there may not be much left for increases based on performance.

All these problems notwithstanding, experts agree that pay can be a motivator if tied to performance. Here are some points to consider when evaluating the effectiveness of pay increases based on performance.

- The increase should be large in relation to a person's base pay. For someone making $20,000, a raise of $1,000—or $19.23 a week—won't do it, especially if nonperformers are getting a $10-a-week raise. Some experts suggest that, for impact, the absolute minimum increase should be 15 percent.
- The increase must be clearly tied to objective standards. If you can't measure the individual's contribution objectively, then merit increases are of questionable value.
- The employee must be able to exercise control over his or her output.

- The employee must recognize and accept the cause/effect relationship of his or her additional effort and initiative. Those employees who deserve increases should get them, and those who don't should not.

WAGE COMPRESSION

For the last ten years, managers have been watching the compensation gap between themselves and their subordinates become smaller and smaller. There are cases where hourly workers, in many cases unionized, with an incentive plan or with overtime (and in some cases with neither) make more than their supervisors. The resulting wage compression is a problem for many organizations.

These same pressures have also had an effect on the availability of funds for merit increases. A survey conducted by the American Management Associations indicates that the inability of merit increases to keep pace with inflation is a very sensitive issue and, according to the respondents, likely to disrupt employee morale and increase turnover.

There are no easy answers to this dilemma. In periods of economic uncertainty, it is difficult for companies to solve this costly problem. Under tremendous pressure from international competition, some key industries have been taking a tough line with respect to wages and salaries. They have also been forced to purge white-collar positions. As economic conditions pick up, these now leaner, more productive industries will be in a better position to use the paycheck as an integral part of their motivation program.

Robert W. Braid is professor of management at Atlantic Community College, Mays Landing, New Jersey. This article is excerpted from his book Introduction to Management.

12.

COMPENSATION AND BENEFITS: TODAY'S DILEMMA IN MOTIVATION

Stephen C. Bushardt
Aubrey R. Fowler

The authors present suggestions for redesigning the compensation package to improve productivity.

Is your organization faced with continually increasing employee compensation costs while productivity and individual performance fail to keep pace with those increases? Do you find that satisfactory employees frequently leave your organization, necessitating unwanted hiring and training expenses? Looking back, do you feel that your present employees are less motivated towards excellence in performance and more inclined towards transience than were employees of many years ago? Many managers would answer yes to the above questions and then berate today's work force while lamenting its disinterest in the work ethic that made this country great. Unfortunately, in many instances, the root cause of the problems mentioned lies not within the employees but, rather, reflects weaknesses in the organization's pay and benefits system and its relevance to employee needs.[4]

An understanding of the impact of rewards on employee motivation is necessary. Such an understanding will facilitate the redesign of the organization's wage and benefits package to motivate improvements in performance while encouraging higher employee retention.

REWARD AND MOTIVATION

The wage and benefits package is intended to provide rewards to employees in exchange for their contribution to organizational goals. Of fundamental importance to that exchange is the degree to which the individual employee values the "reward" offered.[1] If, in fact, the offered reward is highly valued by the employee, its impact would be to motivate behavior consistent with a continued reception of the reward. If the reward is valued lightly or not at all, its impact on motivating desired performance is negligible or non-existent. Unfortunately, in too many cases today the reward offered falls into the second category and employers find themselves paying for expensive compensation packages without achieving the levels or types of employee behavior desired.

Further complicating the evaluation of the effectiveness of an organization's compensation package is the fact that rewards can be differentiated into two distinct categories, system rewards and individual rewards, in accordance with the two distinct types of behavior sought.[4] System rewards are those granted to all members of an organization, contingent only on continued membership in the organization. Such rewards impact morale and rate of retention to the extent that employees value them, but they do not motivate individual performance above the minimum level necessary to ensure continued membership.

Individual rewards are those that are separately determined for each employee based on the level of performance exhibited by that employee. If the reward offered is valued by the employee; if the employee recognizes that the reward is contingent upon a given level of performance; and if the employee feels that the desired performance is within his or her capabilities, then the employee is motivated to engage in behavior necessary to achieve the performance desired by the organization.[7]

Assuming that a primary goal of an organization's wage and benefit system is to induce its employees to exhibit the highest level of performance of which they are capable, the typical system of today fails in two important ways. First, most rewards offered fall into the systems category, thereby motivating membership rather than performance. Second, many of the rewards offered fail even to motivate continued membership because they are not highly valued by the employees to which they are offered.[3] This failure to motivate employee performance or membership creates a dilemma for those responsible for designing and administering the organization's compensation package: the dilemma of constantly increasing costs without a requisite increase in productivity. This dilemma has important ramifications within the organization itself and, in a broader sense, within the nation's economy as productivity declines impact on inflationary pressures and the competitiveness of U.S. goods on world markets.

DILEMMA DEVELOPMENT AND CAUSE

In earlier times, the compensation package was heavily weighted towards individual rewards with a resultant high level of individual performance. However, employees were not tied to the organization by system rewards and were, therefore, inclined to move on whenever they saw an opportunity elsewhere for higher individual rewards. As system rewards became more prevalent, employees developed a greater tendency towards longevity and employers found that the administration of system rewards required less effort than did individual rewards since individual performance measurement is not necessary. This trend towards systems rewards has been accelerated by organizational acquiescence to union demands for conformity within compensation systems for their members, by the growing proportion of white-collar and service jobs within the economy (areas where individual performance is difficult to measure), and by the impact of federal and state legislation requiring that certain benefits, i.e., unemployment compensation and social security, be provided to all employees.[3] Government impact is also felt in the application of the income tax system and its exemption from taxation, both to employer and employee, of the costs of many of the employee benefits that are by nature system rewards.

Of these various factors acting to promote the expansion of system rewards the single most important is the reluctance or inability of management to measure individual performance in an equitable manner and to administer individual rewards without resorting to factors such as nepotism, organizational politics, and cronyism. This failure on the part of management, this inability to provide individual rewards necessary to the motivation of excellence in performance, is at the foundation of the decline or stagnation in productivity affecting organizations today.

The impact of management's failure is heightened when the rewards that are provided do not even motivate continued membership. This leads to problems associated with turnover to compound those associated with a lack of individual effort above minimum standards. This failure to motivate membership results when the rewards being offered are not valued sufficiently by individual employees so as to induce a desire to continue belonging to the organization offering reward. Common examples of such non-motivators would be the offering of dental insurance to an employee without dependent children, the offering of attractive pension benefits to employees in their early 20s, the offering of excellent maternity benefits to single employees or those who have chosen to forgo raising a family, or the offering of company products at reduced costs where those products have limited appeal to the employees. This problem, also, is exacerbated by governmental intervention, since government regulations, which require a new universal availability of many system rewards (i.e., worker's compensation), regardless of the particular organization to which one belongs, and the transportability of others (i.e., pension benefits under ERISA), tend to blunt any tendency for these rewards to motivate membership in any particular organization.

These factors, an increased tendency to provide system rather than individual rewards and the failure of intended system rewards to motivate membership, have created today's dilemma. They also give insight into the means by which the dilemma might be solved.

A NEW DIRECTION

Of primary importance to a solution of the productivity problem is to reemphasize the offering of individual rewards.[1] To do so, effort must first be expended in designing a system that accurately and impartially measures the performance level of all affected employees and then ties specific and desirable rewards to given levels of performance. Secondly, the system must be communicated to employees in a manner that clearly states the rewards offered and the performance necessary to achieve those rewards. Next, the organization must provide all employees the opportunity to fairly compete for the rewards offered without hindrances from a lack of necessary training, improper or inefficient allocation of resources, or prejudicial treatment based on factors other than performance. Finally, the organization must follow through in implementing the system, measuring and rewarding levels of performance in accordance with the standards set by the system.

In designing the individual rewards system, care must be taken to ensure that the performance measures selected are accurate reflections of the behavior desired, exhibiting both reliability and vaility, and are, in fact, a measure of observable behavior rather than an immeasurable personal attribute such as attitude or initiative.[5] Furthermore, and frequently overlooked, steps must be taken to ensure that those responsible for measuring performance have both the knowledge and the opportunity necessary to make a fair and accurate evaluation of the behavior being measured.

If an organization can successfully initiate a system of individual rewards, it should benefit from the changes in behavior motivated by the rewards offered, i.e., the organization can expect increased productivity. In addition, the availability of individual rewards will increase the effectiveness of system rewards as they lead to improved morale and recognition for individual contributions to organizational goals.

Two additional thoughts regarding individual rewards are that oftentimes it is very difficult to provide individual rewards within the formal compensation benefits package. Furthermore, system rewards are frequently mistakenly offered under the guise of individual rewards.

Whenever the formal package doesn't allow for individual rewards, it is important to recognize that individuals still need motivation of performance to reach desired levels. In this situation one can rely on rewards outside the formal package, such as praise for a job well done or providing an opportunity for advancement to those exhibiting excellence in performance to provide the motivation not generated by the formal compensation package. To avoid the mistake of offering system rewards as individual rewards, an examination of the rewards given to a top performer compared with that given a low level performer will indicate the degree of individual reward. If there is little or no difference attributed to longevity, then the reward is not an individual reward.

The most frequent misconception confusing system and individual rewards involves salary. In this area the quick test of comparability between high/low performers is particularly applicable in indicating either a need to redesign the system to involve performance differentials, or to discontinue expectations of motivation resulting from the offering of more money when that offer is not tied to performance. Furthermore, many studies indicate that the quick test will often result in findings that low performers are paid at higher levels than high performers, indicating that some factor other than performance is being rewarded.[2,6]

Of primary importance to the effectiveness with which system rewards motivate membership is the degree to which they are valued by the employees to whom they are offered.[8,10] Unlike individual rewards which will generally be reflected in the employee's pay, system rewards are usually offered as part of the benefits package. There are examples in each category contrary to those generalities: a $50 Christmas bonus given all employees as a system reward or an extra day off for the employee of the month as an individual reward. But for the most part, the generality holds. Due to the package nature of most employee benefit plans, it is almost certain that there are some benefits offered that do not motivate all employees, resulting in the partial ineffectiveness of those packages in motivating employee retention. In fact, it is entirely possible that some of the benefits offered actually motivate no one to remain with the organization and are, therefore, a waste of the organization's resources.

PROVIDING APPROPRIATE BENEFITS

The important thing then is to take steps to ensure that system rewards are offered in such a way as to provide each employee with a set of benefits appropriate to his or her needs and desires. Two basic methods suitable for achieving that goal are the cafeteria approach to benefits allocation and the multi-package approach. The cafeteria approach involves the allocation to each employee of a dollar amount of compensation and then allowing the employee to choose the mixture of cash and benefits desired.[9] This method best answers employee satisfaction with the organization's compensation offer. However, it can be difficult to administer and will likely involve higher costs than other compensation plans.

The second method, the multi-package approach, solves the problems associated with the cafeteria approach while retaining, in part, its opportunity for individual choice. Requisite to the design of a multi-package plan is the gathering of information regarding the preferences of employees. This information, most readily generated by use of an employee survey, can then be used to develop a number of separate compensation packages, each designed to appeal to a different group of employees in accordance with similarities in their expressed preferences. This allows employees some choice in benefits received and, by limiting the number of packages offered to a manageable number, reduces administrative difficulty and costs.

A third option regarding the allowing of individual choice in compensation selection is to combine the two methods. Offer a limited number of plans involving different mixtures of the basic compensation elements, *i.e.*, pay, vacation, retirement and medical insurance, and along with them offer a variety of options to be selected by individual choice. This simplifies the design of the various standard packages and allows a greater opportunity for each employee to satisfy his or her individual preferences.

In many instances, declining performance and turnover problems are related to weaknesses in the organization's compensation and benefits package. Those weaknesses, primarily the lack of individual rewards and the ineffectiveness of system rewards, may be addressed by the organization through a reevaluation and redesign of the organization's pay and benefits package. The expected results of such a redesign include improved morale, increased productivity and a higher retention of satisfactory employees. These changes solve the dilemma associated with increased compensation costs not balanced by productivity improvements. They also require more attention to employee behavior and a greater sensitivity on the part of management to the needs of its employees in order to effectively motivate desired levels of performance.

In particular, the rising cost associated with compensation and benefits places an increasing responsibility on the personnel administrator to provide new and innovative ways to deal with employee performance and turnover.

REFERENCES

1. Belcher, David W., *Compensation Administration* (Englewood Cliffs, N.J.: Prentice-Hall, Inc., 1975).

2. Evans, William A., "Pay for Performance: Fact or Fable," *Personnel Journal* (Vol. 49, No. 9, Sept. 1970), pp. 726-731.

3. Glueck, William F., *Personnel: A Diagnostic Approach*, revised edition (Dallas: Business Publications, Inc., 1978).

4. Katz, Daniel and Kahn, Robert L., "System Rewards and Individual Rewards," in Henry L. Tosi and W. Clay Hammer (eds.), *Organizational Behavior and Management: A Contingency Approach* (Chicago: St. Clair Press, 1976).

5. Kearney, William J., "Performance Appraisal: Which Way to Go," *MSU Business Topic* (Winter 1977), pp. 58-64.

6. Meyer, Herbert H., "The Pay-for-performance Dilemma," *Organizational Dynamics* (Vol. 3, No. 3, Winter 1975), pp. 39-65.

7. Porter, Lyman and Lawler, Edward, III, *Managerial Attitudes and Performance* (Homewood, Ill: Irwin, Inc., 1968).

8. Shea, James H., "Cautions about Cafeteria-style Benefit Plans," *Personnel Journal* (Vol. 60, No. 1, January 1981), pp. 37-41.

9. Tavernser, Gerald, "How American Can Manages Its Flexible Benefits Program," *Management Review* (Vol. 69, No. 8, August 1980), pp. 8-13.

10. White, William L. and Becker, James W., "Increasing the Motivational Impact of Employee Benefits," *Personnel* (Vol. 57, No. 1, Jan.-Feb. 1980), pp. 32-37.

Dr. Stephen C. Bushardt and Aubrey R. Fowler are both assistant professors of management at the University of Southern Mississippi, Hattiesburg, Mississippi.

13.

MOTIVATING WITHOUT MONEY— EASIER THAN IT SEEMS

Lin Grensing

Job redesign can consist of both job enlargement and job restructuring.

Today's economy has made it increasingly difficult for many organizations, large and small, to give their employees what most of them want: a raise. Fortunately, some recent studies have shown that money isn't everything. Sometimes non-monetary incentives can do just as much to motivate an employee and, in fact, some researchers have suggested that money is actually a dismotivator in that its presence does not necessarily guarantee job satisfaction.

When we speak about motivation, we are talking about the "why" of behavior or performance. In effect, the carrot on a stick that makes an employee want to continue in a position and strive to do the best job possible. We're talking more about the desire to do something than the ability. Many employees may have the ability to do a job but just may not be functioning at their full potential because they are not being adequately motivated.

THEORETICAL BACKGROUND

Several researchers have suggested theories of motivation which have widespread application in organizational structures. A.H. Maslow devised a hierarchy of needs in 1943 and although it was primarily a psychological model, it was reinterpreted for organizational settings in 1960 by Douglas McGregor. There are five basic needs as defined by Maslow. They are physiological, safety, social, self-esteem, self-actualization.

According to Maslow, once a need has been satisfied, we move further up the hierarchy in an attempt to satisfy the next highest need. He also suggests that once we have satisfied a need, we will no longer be motivated to satisfy it further. McGregor expands on this concept by suggesting that in the organizational structure of our society, most Americans have essentially satisfied their physiological and safety needs. Therefore, since money and job security satisfy the lower order needs, increasing these rewards generally does not motivate employees to greater organizational effort.

McGregor is also widely known for his formulation of the Theory X and Theory Y theories of management. Theory X is regarded as a "conventional" approach and assumes that human beings are inherently lazy, that people must be controlled and motivated by the fear of punishment and that they try to avoid responsibility as much as possible. On the other hand, Theory Y management, known as the "behavioral" approach, assumes that physical and mental effort is as natural in a work setting as it is at play and at rest, that the threat of punishment is not a viable means of inducing people to work, that a commitment to objectives is a reward in itself and that the average human being learns to seek responsibility rather than avoid it.

More recently, a new technique of management has been proposed: Theory Z. Theory Z style of management is a Japanese approach which stresses employee participation and input into organizational structure by making use of a form of participation known as Quality Circles. Japanese management has become increasingly popular in the United States in recent years due to an interest and fascination with Japan's overall productive efficiency and worker satisfaction.

Herzberg (1966) identified 16 factors which he classified as either intrinsic or extrinsic to the job. Intrinsic factors are associated directly with performing the task, while extrinsic factors "surround" the job and serve no motivational function. These factors are as follows:

INTRINSIC	**EXTRINSIC**
Recognition	Salary
Achievement	Relationships with co-workers
Possibility for growth	Technical supervision
Advancement	Company policy and administration
Work itself	Working conditions
	Status
	Factors in personal life
	Job security

Note: As a qualifier to this study, however, Schwab, DeVitt and Cummings (1971) have found that extrinsic factors may also be instrumental in motivating high performance.

Individual differences are very important in determining what will motivate an employee. While some employees may feel that more money would make their jobs more enjoyable, others may opt for increased vacation days or more input into managerial decisions.

Cafeteria style benefits have recently become quite popular, primarily because of the recognition of variations in the nature and individual desires of employees. Even so, there is considerable evidence that employees' performance can be substantially increased without the use of monetary rewards.

How then can you as an employer increase your employees' job satisfaction and motivate performance?

There will, of course, be limits to what you can reasonably expect to accomplish depending on your own position in the organization and more importantly on your willingness to experiment and perhaps upset the stability or status quo in your company.

It might be helpful to first look at some of the major innovative techniques that are becoming increasingly popular in organizations across the country.

JOB ENRICHMENT

Job enrichment techniques are means of motivating employees by making their work more interesting and making the workplace a more challenging and satisfying place to be.

Job enrichment techniques can be broken down into team efforts, increased participation, job rotation and job redesign. These techniques are designed to alter the job, often by increasing the employee's self-dependence and allowing for a greater role in participative decision making. Employees may be asked to join operating or management teams, groups of supervisory and management personnel that will work together to deal with operational problems. By allowing employees a chance for increased participation in goal setting, they begin to feel more a part of the organization. Studies have shown that these types of procedures encourage employees to work as a group to solve certain specific problems while at the same time motivating performance on the job.

Job rotation provides employees with an opportunity to experience different jobs regularly. Rotation can occur within a department or between departments. Job redesign, on the other hand, takes an employee's existing position and makes changes to encompass greater responsibilities, greater control, more frequent feedback, and more varied job responsibilities. Job redesign can consist of both job enlargement and job restructuring.

MANAGEMENT BY OBJECTIVES

The term Management by Objectives was coined in 1954 by Peter Drucker and has grown increasingly popular in its application. A Management by

Objectives or MBO program is a comprehensive series of specific goals and objectives set up for all levels and groups of employees within an organization.

The program itself involves participation at all levels and includes an extensive training program to familiarize everyone in the organization with the steps involved.

The first phase of the program usually takes from two to six months and includes the setting of goals by top management and an introductory training program for the supervisory personnel. Following this step, training continues throughout the organization until all hierarchical levels have been familiarized with every aspect of the program. Within the next two years, all management components are integrated into the MBO system.

Advantages of this approach are that it forces results and a clarification of the organizational structure. In addition, it elicits commitment from employees toward the good of the company and helps develop effective control systems. Since employees themselves are directly involved in the program and in goal setting, it is felt that Management by Objectives increases motivation among employees and contributes to a feeling of belonging in the organization.

SIMPLIFYING THE PROCESS

The procedures we have discussed thus far require a great deal of organization rearrangement and a substantial time investment. There are, however, several other ways of motivating employees that may not require as much time but that can be just as effective.

Recognition is an important aspect of employee motivation. This can range from a simple pat on the back for a job well-done to testimonial dinners, citations and special awards.

Task systems which require the specification of activities required for a day's work allow employees to leave as soon as their assigned tasks are completed, even though they will be paid for a full eight hours.

Variations in working hours can give employees some control over their schedules and experience indicates that this type of program can be effectively dealt with interdepartmentally. Working hours can be scheduled by expanding the workday, staggered hours or flex-time, variable hours and perhaps by special arrangements during vacation seasons to provide for optimum use of daylight hours.

Career development can serve not only an employee's interests by allowing the pursuit of educational interests but can also benefit the employer—due to his employee's increased knowledge and resultant increase in self-esteem.

Participation, mentioned previously, is an important aspect of on-the-job motivation and one which need not require an exceptional amount of time. Employees can be encouraged to make suggestions for improvement of procedures or changes in the organization. They may be invited to join committees and offered the opportunity to attend meetings of higher management in order to allow them a chance to voice their objections and express opinions.

Perhaps one of the most overlooked and yet one of the most important aspects of employee motivation is working conditions themselves. Physical surroundings have a great deal of effect on a person's psychological well-being and studies have shown that colors and office arrangements can greatly contribute to what may be unconscious determinants of job satisfaction. Often, simple things such as allowing employees the freedom to have coffee or cigarettes at their desks, or to keep personal possessions on desks, or to decorate with plants or pictures, etc., can make the workplace more enjoyable and more conducive to a good attitude among employees.

Sometimes, the simple things are what really count. Small gestures—an interest in the employee's well-being, a willingness to listen to personal and company-related problems, a flexibility of company policies when appropriate, the ability to offer praise when deserved—all of these can prove effective in motivating your employees to perform more efficiently.

All non-monetary, all effective. What more could you ask?

14.
PAY POLICIES

Linda Gail Christie

To motivate employees, managers must have more say in payroll decisions, instead of just following personnel department directives.

Administrators want to get more mileage from employees and keep them happy without sacrificing the bottom line. However, salary practices tend to thwart a manager's ability to get the best out of people.

Managers rely on the personnel department to develop innovative and competitive pay plans. However, wage and salary departments recommend pay policies based on the *competition's* practices. Each company, therefore, reinforces and perpetuates sameness and mediocrity.

Take, for example, a typical case involving a manager whose assistant has quit. The personnel department tells the manager that the starting pay for the replacement cannot exceed $300 per week.

After two weeks of interviewing, the manager finds a perfect candidate. But there's one hitch: the candidate already makes $300 and wants a 10 percent increase to change jobs. Personnel says, "No." The applicant says, "No." And the manager must continue interviewing or hire someone who requires more training.

Personnel seeks to control salary costs and preserve internal equity. The manager says the right person saves time and money with higher quality output. Let's examine the above case further. The savings of $30 per week for the assistant not hired amounts to an annual payroll and benefits savings of $2,200. If the manager makes $1,200 per week, including benefits, four weeks of interviewing for one-fourth of each day costs the company $1,200. During this time, the manager also performs the assistant's job—costing an additional $1,500 (one-third of his monthly wage).

Add up the manager's $1,200 for interviewing time, plus $1,500 for performing the assistant's job. This equals $2,700—in just one month. Unless the manager puts in quite a bit of overtime, the company may also suffer reduced services and production output, delayed decisions, and fall behind on any number of important duties. Hidden costs may be quite high.

Managers also may be restricted by merit increase and budget constraints. For example, seven percent of payroll may be available for both cost-of-living and merit raises. But what if the department employs all "outstanding" or all "average" performance employees? How does the manager distribute the money? If the bell-shaped curve doesn't fit, the manager and the profit-producers are out of luck.

Often a manager also must adhere to a rigorous merit increase schedule: every three months, every six months, once a year, etc. Why? If an employee is worth more after two weeks on the job, the manager should be able to reward the effort with a raise. Also, contrary to many personnel department policies, merit increases should not be divorced from performance appraisals. Money should be tied as closely as possible to performance.

The wage and salary department should not have pay-approval and hiring rate authority over a manager's decisions. Making money through the labor of others is a manager's responsibility.

When managers lose the power and authority to compensate and reward employees as they see fit, their ability to lead and produce profits is diminished. Therefore managers should tell the Human Resources Department what *they* need to do their job, not vice versa.

Linda Gail Christie is president of Christie Speciality Productions, a management consulting firm based in Tulsa, Oklahoma. She is the author of Human Resources: A Hidden Profit Center, *published by Prentice-Hall, Englewood Cliffs, New Jersey, 1983.*

15.
MONEY MAY NO LONGER MOTIVATE SOME EMPLOYEES

Carol Cain

Profit sharing can motivate employees even though many of them are not necessarily motivated by money.

Money has long been considered a primary motivator in the workplace. However, researchers are saying that since the workplace and employee attitudes are changing, so are the motivators.

"Money does motivate people who still don't have enough," said Bert Metzger, president, Profit Sharing Research Foundation, Evanston, Ill. But there are other motivating forces as well, he says.

"(Motivators) vary from person to person. . . . Some are interested in money and security, others in challenge and commitment," said Donald Nightingale, a professor at the Queen's University School of Business, Kingston, Ontario.

Both Mr. Metzger and Mr. Nightingale presented the findings of their research into motivation at the 35th annual conference of the Profit Sharing Council of America.

They told conference participants that profit sharing can motivate employees, even though many of them are not necessarily motivated by money.

Business should be interested in motivational research because of the general principle that "the motivational pattern of employees results from interplay of personal motivators and the environment in which the employee works," Mr. Nightingale said.

"The best management can do is create a sharing climate, a motivational environment," Mr. Metzger said.

A first step in creating this environment is to understand the workforce, both men said.

There are basically two groups of workers: traditional and non-traditional, said Mr. Nightingale, citing research done by Daniel Yankelovich of Yankelovich, Skelly & White Inc., the New York-based polling firm.

About 56 percent of the American workforce falls in the traditional category, he said, where money and status still are important motivators. These workers are usually older, blue-collar employees whose work is a habit, although some conservative white-collar workers and some younger workers are included in this group.

The non-traditionalists are almost all younger than 35. They include not only poorly educated and impoverished people, but also bright young people who have turned to leisure activities for motivation because they couldn't find a challenge in the workplace.

The definition of success is changing along with workplace motivators. "(Success) is no longer measured in job status," Mr. Nightingale said. Many employees measure success as a product of self-realization and fulfillment, he said.

"There is a lessening fear of economic insecurity and a growing psychology of entitlement," Mr. Nighingale said, listing other changes.

That's why, on the whole, employee benefits offer no motivation to a person that works harder than another, he said. "They're generally seen as rights of office, not rewards for harder work."

Knowing the demographics of the workforce can help managers develop a motivational environment, keeping in mind that "there is no single program to meet the diverse needs of the people," Mr. Metzger said.

Increased employee participation and changes in supervisory styles can be employee motivators. Research suggests that more employee participation, involvement and communication are among criteria to be considered in designing an effective workplace in the 1980s, Mr. Nightingale said.

"Communication is the lifeblood of employee motivation. No one can turn themselves on unless they do so in terms of perceived benefits," which requires communication, Mr. Metzger said.

Although money may not be a motivating factor to some people in today's workforce, "people's fortunes go up and down during a lifetime," Mr. Metzger said, noting that money may be important later.

That's where a profit-sharing plan can be a motivator, he said. "Profit sharing is more than just money sharing. It's the creation of a corporate partnership."

Profit sharing can be used to fit the changing needs of the American worker, Mr. Metzger said. Through communication, profit sharing can be equated with dignity, recognition, involvement, concern, caring, and self-fulfillment.

Profit sharing must "be recognized in terms meaningful to the employees," he said, again citing the need for communication.

Mr. Metzger told a story about how an early profit-sharing plan was communicated in one company in France.

The story involves Edmond Jean LeClaire, often recognized as the father of profit sharing. Motivated by comments from a friend, Mr. LeClaire shunned the management philosophy of the times and designed a profit-sharing system, with the objective to increase the efficiency of his house-painting operations sufficiently to justify making profit-sharing payments to his employees.

"Would it not be wiser to earn 50 francs and give half to an employee, than to earn 25 francs and keep them all?" Mr. LeClaire reasoned. To answer his question and the skeptical notions of others, Mr. LeClaire decided to start a profit-sharing program and judge the results.

The program was announced in 1942. One year later, he assembled the 44 eligible workers around a table and in the center dropped 12,266 francs (then about $2,000), which was labor's share of the profits. The company would not have made the extra money had it not been for the profit-sharing program.

The workers left the table knowing they were no longer mere journeymen who acted like machines—they had all become partners, said Mr. Metzger.

"Does your profit-sharing plan come through to employees (like that)?" asked Mr. Metzger.

Profit sharing will not motivate employees if it is rigid in structure, Mr. Metzger said, nor will it motivate workers if it is not based on trust, not perceived by the employees as their fair share of the company and, most importantly, not properly communicated.

The complete story of Edmond Jean LeClaire is included in the book Profit Sharing: A Natural for Today's Changing Work Force/Economy. *The book is available from the Profit Sharing Research Foundation, 1718 Sherman Ave., Evanston, Ill. 60201.*

16.

IF EMPLOYEES PERFORM, THEN REWARD 'EM

Kevin Francella

> The popular phrase "money talks" is taking a back seat to the manager who talks—positively—to employees.

Employee morale in your department has been low for the past couple of months, though you haven't realized it. You've noticed that a few employees have missed project completion dates, but you figure it's a letdown after a recent series of tough deadlines.

The problem did not come into focus until the day the coffee break banter spilled into the DP department. You overheard a conversation between two of your employees in which each lamented that they were not being recognized or rewarded for the quality and effort of their work. Moreover, they said *you* only emphasize the negative things they do and rarely tell them when they are doing a good job.

How will this attitude affect your employees' performance? Should you be more conscious of praising employee performance, instead of focusing only on shortcomings? And how should you best reward employee performance?

While criticism for a poor job is not given a second thought by a manager or supervisor whose job it is to get the most out of his or her employees, praise and recognition for a job well done rarely hold a front-and-center position in a manager's psyche. Criticism, at times, can act to motivate an employee to do a better job and increase productivity, yet it can easily get to the point where it will turn off more employees than it will help.

Reward—praise and recognition—have become hot topics for organizational psychologists looking to optimize employee satisfaction, and thereby increase productivity.

What, then, is the best way to let an employee know he or she is doing a good job?

"Passing the buck"—monetary rewards, whether a hike in salary or performance perks—still remains the most popular tool for optimizing employees' satisfaction and motivating them to do a better job. The reasoning is simple: The more money you offer someone, the harder he or she will work. And most employers and managers believe money alone is enough to expect happiness and high performance from their employees.

Money as a motivational tool for spurring production first gained widespread acceptance in this country at the turn of the century in the wake of the studies of Frederick Taylor, the so-called "father" of scientific management. Scientific management is based essentially on the assumption that workers will put forth extra effort on the job to maximize their economic gains. Most of the research during this period was centered in industrial America and focused on piece-rate incentives systems.

But for the next several decades, organizational psychologists have been demonstrating that money alone isn't as potent a motivating force as theory and common sense suggest it ought to be. Elton Mayo's historic work at General Electric in 1922 showed that incentive payment schemes had not succeeded in increasing work or decreasing turnover in a department where the jobs were particularly monotonous and/or fatiguing. When employees were able to structure the work themselves, Mayo found productivity increased dramatically. Monetary rewards proved less effective than psychic rewards.

Organizational psychologists today rely more on the "social man" concept of employee satisfaction and motivation, which contends that people in work settings are generally motivated by group forces: group pressure, social relations, and organizational structure.

Today, the popular phrase "money talks" is taking a back seat to the manager who talks, positively, to employees. The manager who creates a positive "organizational climate" with monetary rewards, a compelling work structure, and positive feedback, gets the most from his or her employees, psychologists contend.

Yet, in spite of the many textbook theories on employee rewards and praise, no clear methods exist for delivering them in every work environment. As the individuals in the work group and the individual managers vary, so do the ways of creating positive climates.

According to organizational psychologist David S. McClelland, a manager must understand himself or herself well enough to know what he or she can or should do in a given organizational situation. "A manager may discover," McClelland says, "that while his staff wants and needs many signs of approval and friendship, he is rather aloof, priding himself that he got where he is today by not wasting time with 'the boys.'" With this new insight, McClelland says, the manager can create a positive climate for his or her employees, even if he is not personally inclined to openly show approval.

The manager who wants to keep his or her employees satisfied and motivated to give their best every day, shouldn't let monetary factors allay an effort to meet psychological needs.

Get in the habit of complimenting employees sincerely for a job well done. A personal thank-you offered face-to-face is all it may take to make an employee hustle; a note of congratulation on the completion of a special project is positive encouragement for the employee to give his or her best.

Whatever the situation, make the compliment personal and sincere. And the process need not be a drawn-out affair; brevity can be potent and may go a long way in lessening the potential of resentment from those employees who have not deserved the accolades.

Remember, these occasional pats-on-the-back shouldn't have all the meaning twisted out from overuse. Don't dwell on them in the fear they will turn off employees rather than motivate them. Pick your spots and make them meaningful.

While overuse of accolades may backfire, there are other ways of overdoing it. Buying employees flowers, lunch, or drinks after work may be perceived as too "buddy-buddy" by some employees and especially by your superiors, not to mention that such well-meaning practices get expensive.

Keep in mind, you're not trying to get employees to like you, you are trying to get them to work for you.

Part III
THE
ENVIRONMENT
OF MOTIVATION

17.
HOW TO CREATE A
MOTIVATING WORK CLIMATE

George Lynn

> Reward and punishment strategies don't work for people because, unlike animals, people have established sets of goals and values that are particular to each individual.

As a supervisor, how often have you said: "My people are under-motivated—they don't care about their job. How can I motivate them to get the work out?"

Well, if morale is low and people don't seem motivated, forget about trying to motivate them. You can't do it! Relax!

Does this last statement sound ridiculous? It should, because it goes contrary to what most supervisors have been taught for years: The standard principles of management are, "Organize," "Coordinate," "Motivate." Whatever the management course, the message was always the same: "To get people to work for you, you have to stimulate them." This was usually called "motivating" them and involved some variation of the reward or punishment strategy. This sounds simple enough. The problem is that these reward/punishment approaches rarely work. They may work for pigeons and dogs, but people aren't pigeons or dogs.

Reward and punishment strategies rely on providing *extrinsic stimulation* on a correct schedule for their effectiveness. They don't work for people because people, unlike animals, have established goals and values that are particular to each individual. Extrinsic stimulation does not take these intrinsic factors into account.

DETERMINE WORK PAYOFFS

When we talk about motivating people, we need to shift our perspective a bit. An operating theory of human motivation is offered here. It is built on three principles:

1.   People do things that have some intrinsic payoff for them. Everybody wants different things in life. Abraham Maslow talked about five different types of payoffs (he called them "needs") that people have, from the need to survive (the payoff is money) to the need for "self-actualization" (the payoff is personal growth from the work itself). Maslow said that once lower order needs are met (survival, safety), people naturally become concerned with meeting higher order needs (social, status, self-actualization). The important point here is that no two people have the same payoffs; no two are motivated the same.

2.   People won't work harder or better unless the work itself has some intrinsic payoff for them. Frederick Herzberg suggested that work can be made more satisfying by what he called "vertical job loading." This involves increasing a jobholder's autonomy on the job by providing him/her with more information and more complex work and by decreasing controls as appropriate. Herzberg also pointed out that giving people more money does not increase their productivity. If working conditions are oppressive or pay is inadequate, people will work less. But giving them more money (once an adequate reimbursement is decided) will not make them work harder.

3.   To build productivity and motivation, the supervisor must do two things: Find out what each person's individual work payoff is and help the person achieve his/her work related payoffs in such a way that both individual and organizational needs are met.

STRIVE FOR AGREEMENT AMONG EQUALS

Here are two ways to accomplish this.

1.   *Determine work payoffs.* Take a close look at each person that you supervise and the job that he/she is doing. Get an idea of the particular strengths of the person and how you can build on these strengths. Then have a conversation with the person. Ask: "What's in the job for you? Are you in it for the money and benefits (this is perfectly legitimate) or for something else? Is there some aspect of the job that you find particularly interesting? What problems are you running into?" Together, devise ways to build more interesting elements into the job and decrease problems. Have this conversation once every couple of months or as the situation requires it.

2.   *Help the person attain his/her goals as the person works toward the organization's goals.* Once you have pinpointed your employee's job payoff, you are in a position to spell out *your* payoff in terms of what you want the other to do for you. To do this in such a way that both of you get what you want, do the following:

a.   Set clear goals and give frequent feedback. Tell the person exactly what you expect from him/her, when you want the results, and by what standard. Let your people know how they're doing. Acknowledge success.

b.   Get out of the way and let each person do his/her job as he/she sees fit. Insist on open and honest communication. Good communication is not a "soft management" value but an absolute essential to error detection and timely exploitation of opportunity. Be willing to negotiate work objectives and time lines with your staff.

c.   Expect great things and know that your staff will deliver. Show them by what you say and do that you have full confidence in them and will do what you can to represent their interests in the organization.

As you integrate these three practices into your supervisory style, you create a work environment characterized by mutual support and the expectation of success. Each of your staff knows where he/she stands with you and knows what the conditions are for mutual goal attainment. Once this happens a feeling of "agreement among equals" results. This kind of feeling is what effective supervision/motivation is all about. It is easily sensed in high performance organizations. If it could be put in words, it might go as follows: "We are all in this together and we are all responsible for the outcome!"

George Lynn, M.A., M.P.A., is an organization development consultant and human relations trainer in Seattle, Washington.

18.
CONSTRAINTS TO EFFECTIVE MOTIVATION

John Nirenberg

Any one of four constraints can interfere with a supervisor's efforts to increase motivation.

When managers think about motivation, they are thinking about increasing productivity; they are thinking that there must be some way to reduce tardiness, absenteeism, and turnover while increasing the productivity of their subordinates. All motivational programs begin at this point: that something needs to be done to increase employee output. But plunging into a motivational program without first assessing the current motivational environment often leads to disappointing results as managers have found. No matter what kind of program is instituted, if managers don't first look at the prevailing constraints to effective motivation, then their efforts to motivate subordinates will ultimately be ineffective.

The constraints to motivation can come from subordinate attitudes and managerial style. Sometimes they are also the results of environmental factors. Here are four frequently found constraints.

THE WRONG ATTITUDE

The first constraint is related to an attitude that many managers share—unfortunately.

Because one is "the boss," there is an almost irresistible tendency to believe that one is by nature superior to those being supervised. There are two reasons for this. First, in the hierarchical structure of the workplace as represented by the organization chart, a functionally superior role suggests that one is not only organizationally superior but by definition more capable. After all, why would one hold a superior position if one were not more capable?

Second, since a person is believed to be promoted on the basis of merit from a competitive field of candidates (peers often become subordinates of a newly appointed manager), such an individual naturally assumes that he or she is the most capable and begins what becomes a continual process of proving that in fact he or she is more capable. Should the manager falter or occasionally slip, then defensiveness replaces confidence.

This phenomenon is, of course, worse among younger managers who, due to lack of experience, are afraid of failing and have not yet developed methods of concealing their fear. No one ever overcomes this fear entirely.

But as managers become older and more experienced, they develop more sophisticated ways of emphasizing that they are the most capable persons available to hold the position.

If derived solely from role pressure or fear, this attitude is destructive because in one's attempt to prove he or she is the most capable one must inevitably undermine the performance of his or her subordinates or simply fail to recognize their good work. Thus, motivating these employees becomes a double-edged sword. One must encourage and recognize the good work and capabilities of subordinates to motivate them but doing so seems to suggest to some managers that their own abilities are not up to par. The encouragement and recognition given employees are seen by these managers as loss of power or stature in the eyes of their subordinates.

The irony is that a manager who suddenly changes his or her behavior, loosens up, and no longer perceives performance improvements in subordinates as personal failure, risks being viewed as manipulative. Change must come slowly and be genuine. A manager must first recognize that he or she need not devote so much supervisory time to self-aggrandizement. Rather, the person must begin the process of recognizing others' ability to improve and do superior work. Then, the manager must begin to show his or her subordinates that their capabilities and potential will be recognized. In this manner the supervisor must work to win their respect. Over time, he or she can eliminate the first constraint to improved motivation.

THE TREADMILL

Constraint number two is the belief that one can never do enough, that there is always room for improvement.

The industrial ethic states that "an organization must grow or die." There is no middle ground; the forces of change and competition require a company to grow to survive. This attitude is so much a part of our conventional thinking that it is easy to understand how such thinking has come to be applied to employees. At worst, it is thought that they must improve performance, increase output, and develop new skills, or be replaced. At best, it is believed that everyone can improve and has the responsibility to do so. Thus, working has become a source of great stress. Over time one may come to believe that nothing is good enough, that one's work is not valued or appreciated. This attitude becomes a constraint to motivation when motivational efforts are perceived as manipulative tools to increase output and not as programs to increase performance while also satisfying subordinates' needs.

There is also the very real danger that employees will be asked to increase productivity beyond a level of which they are capable.

Most work groups are made up of a variety of abilities. A goal to improve performance by 10 percent will be relatively easier for a person performing at 60 percent of ability than for one performing at 90 percent of ability. Then again, because of different capacities and beliefs among subordinates about their ability to improve and the value of such improvements, it may be as difficult for the person performing at 60 percent ability to improve 10 percent as it would be for the one performing at 90 percent ability to do so.

So, as managers begin a motivational program, it is essential that they know the real capacities of employees and have realistic performance expectations.

It is vital for managers to know exactly what performance is possible and sustainable given actual work requirements. Once this is known, management will not be tempted to create the treadmill effect. During those few times a year when extraordinary effort is required, there should be no problem in motivating employees to meet the unusual demands because they will understand that it is a short-term necessity, not a new standard. Everyone is capable of a short-term burst of energy that exceeds the daily pace. But no one can be expected to perform that way every day.

A person who runs a four-minute mile cannot be expected to run 40 miles at the same pace.

Motivational Sabotage

Any of the following four factors can interfere with a supervisor's efforts to increase motivation:

Constraint 1: A supervisory attitude that tells employees that the supervisor is much more capable than they are.

Constraint 2: An organizational belief about increasing performance that makes employees feel they are on a treadmill.

Constraint 3: Supervisory behavior that is influenced by the supervisor's view of the nature of mankind and by personal biases and prejudices.

Constraint 4: Rules and practices within the organization that compartmentalize employees and are seen by them as demeaning.

Employees who are not faced with the treadmill are more amenable to special effort when the occasion calls for it, provided a proper motivational climate exists.

BIAS

The third constraint involves the generalized view of people which influences one's behavior and attitude toward others. A manager's view influences the way he or she relates to others and reacts in a given situation. This view of mankind is based on the person's experiences, training, the cultural environment in which he or she was raised, and so forth. If the manager views others as being lazy, incompetent, reluctant to accept responsibility, and only interested in a paycheck, he or she will often treat subordinates with distrust, suspicion, and little respect, and practice a form of supervision where fault finding, blaming, and reprimands are frequent. If a manager sees people as generally creative, seeking fulfillment at work, wanting responsibility, and committed to the job, he or she is likely to trust subordinates, delegate challenging and responsible tasks to them, and supervise at a distance, offering compliments as well as constructive criticism.

Since motivational programs ultimately succeed or fail according to how subordinates respond, the message managers communicate to their subordinates about their view of people is a vital determinant of the employee's response to motivational effort. Managers commit motivational sabotage when they transmit an attitude of distrust and little respect for employees while going through the motions of implementing a motivational program. Further, a manager who has low regard for his or her subordinates is almost certain to design the wrong kind of tangible rewards, such as money, in the belief that they are all that is important to subordinates, when in fact subordinates may be more interested in increasing their responsibilities and earning the organization's respect.

When employees are respected and treated as genuinely important, integral parts of the organization, motivational programs stand a better chance to succeed and are more likely to reflect the real needs of subordinates.

To deal with our biases, the third constraint to effective motivational efforts, we need to focus on specific subordinate behavior. This will enable us to isolate our prejudices and preconceived expectations from day-to-day interactions. Understanding our view of people and our prejudices, the message we then send to subordinates, and the way we are perceived by them, will help us overcome the third constraint. We must develop interpersonal skills that make our treatment of others more compatible with their needs and that make it likely that our perceptions of them and ourselves will be as accurate as possible. Over time, we will begin to interact with individual subordinates in a goal-directed, objective manner. We will become better able to design a motivational strategy that reflects the real requirements of our particular workplace, not our imagined view of the nature of mankind.

THE ENVIRONMENT

Besides these attitudinal problems, there is a fourth constraint—environmental factors—that can contribute to motivational sabotage.

Formal organizations by their very nature are highly controlled systems. Generally designed for the purpose of providing a product or service at the lowest possible cost, they tend to treat employees as a group as a necessary evil. The structure of organizations encourages compartmentalization and passive, dependent, subordinate behavior on the part of employees. This is contrary to mankind's nature, a fact that can be proven simply by pointing to life's experiences. Outside of work, the typical employee strives for an active, independent life where he or she is capable of behaving in many ways and developing diverse and intense interests and relationships.

Thus organizations may unwittingly block an individual's growth on the job, committing motivational sabotage. How can one be expected to work harder or be more productive for an organization that stifles natural impulses?

Since so much of what happens at work is taken for granted, it is difficult to identify the often subtle forces that discourage an employee from putting forth that additional effort, from becoming self-motivated. For example, while control is an essential factor in all organizations, the manner in which it is exercised often unknowingly contributes to motivational sabotage. Take the requirement that employees bring in a doctor's note to verify an illness, which suggests that one is not trusted. Or consider the rule that employees must line up for their paychecks. This is also frequently perceived as demeaning since the checks could easily be delivered to the employees. Demanding that employees ask permission to go to the restroom and allowing only five minutes' absence from the work station are other dehumanizing practices.

There are many more equally disturbing practices. Each manager should seek them out and try to remove them. One simple way to find these trouble spots is to ask yourself why you wouldn't want to change places with your subordinates and why you would want to change places with your superiors. The answers will provide clues to the areas in need of improvement.

In any motivational effort, it is not enough to understand the principles of motivation. First we must remove the barriers to motivation created by the four constraints mentioned here. Minimizing the effects of these constraints reduces their disruptive effect upon a program designed to increase employee motivation and performance.

John Nirenberg is associate professor at San Francisco State University.

19.
GETTING MOTIVATED
EMPLOYEES TO PERFORM

Dennis C. Kinlaw

> Managers and supervisors are too quick to conclude that poor employee
> performance is due to motivational problems.

Don Wallop, a manager in an aerospace company, recently told me about a problem he had with one of his engineers. "When I hired him," he said, "I was convinced he was the person we needed. He's bright and has the perfect skill mix. I know that he could do the job if he wanted to. But he hasn't produced. He doesn't seem to want to run with the ball and only does what I tell him. His technical reports and evaluations never suggest new directions or give the customer any more than he or she asks for. I've talked to him several times but nothing has changed. I think I'm going to have to tell him to start looking elsewhere. He isn't motivated to do what the job requires."

Pat Keller is in charge of 15 clerks in the central mailroom of a large insurance firm. She was pleased with her promotion to the job a month ago, but now she's not so sure about the job. The problem is her employees. "They don't care," she said. "They flat out tell me that they don't care. They abuse their sick leave and are late to work. If I'm not right here at the end of the day, half of them leave early. Not one of them keeps the authorized lunch period. They don't want to do their jobs, and I'm powerless to make them."

Don and Pat hold one belief in common. This belief amounts to a serious misconception or myth that keeps them (and many supervisors like them) from managing the performance of their subordinates as well as they might. The myth: If their employees don't perform, they're not motivated.

Don said about his engineer, "He isn't motivated to do what the job requires." Pat said about her clerks, "They don't care." Both Don and Pat have concluded that they have a problem in motivating their employees. This conclusion is based on opinion and not on much fact. Don is convinced that his engineer has the credentials and the right skill mix. He knows that the person could do the job if he wanted to do it. Pat has observed that her people are absent and late and take unauthorized time for lunch. She has concluded that they don't want to do their jobs. But Don and Pat really don't know what is keeping their employees from performing.

I've listened to stories like Don's and Pat's often enough to know that they have probably jumped the gun in diagnosing the cause of the performance problems. What I have found in dealing with a great variety of performance problems in many different organizations is that motivation is most likely to be the least significant contributing cause of poor performance.

There are four factors that contribute to performance:

1. The employee has a clear understanding of what is expected.
2. The employee has the competency to perform what is expected.
3. The employee is supported by a facilitating work environment.
4. The employee is motivated to perform.

Motivation—that is, the desire to perform up to expectations—is only one of the four factors that determine performance.

If we accepted at face value the complaints of supervisors like Don and Pat, we would be left with the bizarre image of thousands of workers greeting each new day with the affirmation that they would not do their best at their jobs, that they would strive to be mediocre, or that they might make a special day of it by completely failing as often as possible. This image is too fantastic to believe, and we need not believe it because it doesn't fit the facts. When employees don't perform, it is usually a problem in expectations, competency, or environment—not motivation.

CLEAR EXPECTATIONS

The first step in managing performance is to ensure that people know what is expected of them, that is, that they know what they are to do and how well they are to do it.

Defining expectations, or standards, is both a formal and an informal process. The formal designation of standards occurs through the organization's performance appraisal system. The informal development of standards occurs through the ongoing activities of assigning work, reviewing progress, and giving feedback.

Performance expectations have the more direct impact on performance when:

- Expectations are specific and concrete.
- Subordinates are involved in the process of developing their expectations.
- Expectations are challenging but achievable.
- Expectations describe measurable results.

- Expectations describe a "whole" or identifiable piece of work for which the employee is largely responsible.
- Expectations are meaningful to the employee.

Establishing expectations has an impact on the three other factors in performance: competency, a facilitating work environment, and motivation. Employees can only be judged competent or incompetent if the expectations of the job have been clearly defined. The competency of employees can only be efficiently modified through formal and informal training if we have first identified what is to be done and what knowledge and skills are required to do it.

Clear expectations are also related to building a facilitating work environment. Some of the elements in such an environment are regular feedback, coaching, and counseling. These activities can only be useful when they are focused on clear performance expectations.

Expectations also influence motivation. One consistent finding is that employees are energized—their willingness to perform is aroused—when they know what their performance goals are.

COMPETENCY

Competency is a second factor in managing performance. Competency is a complex characteristic consisting of natural ability, confidence, knowledge, and the skills needed to do the job. Employees who do not have the competency cannot perform. Competency can be lacking because the employee never had the competency or the employee has lost the competency.

Employees may never have had the necessary competency because they were hired for the wrong job and do not have the natural ability to develop the required knowledge and skill. Here the problem is one of staffing, and no amount of training or increased motivation is going to solve the problem. The obvious strategy is to move the person to another job.

Modifying the job to meet the employee's competencies is another, often neglected strategy.

Employees who have the ability but lack the knowledge and skill are candidates for training.

Loss of competency can occur because the requirements of the job have changed or because the employee has changed. In the first instance, the employee has yet to demonstrate the competency to perform the job. In the second instance, the employee demonstrated at one time the competency to perform the job but no longer demonstrates that competence.

To identify all the reasons that cause changes in jobs and employees is beyond the scope of this article. There is, however, an underlying cause to many of the problems in loss of competence. This is loss of competency that results from the loss of ability to learn.

People lose the ability to learn sometimes because they learn their jobs too well. Others lose the ability to learn because they have learned that it is safer not to learn. There are no rewards—only punishment—from failing to learn fast enough in the environment for learning.

One message to management should be clear. Providing training and education activities to employees doesn't pay off only in updating knowledge and skill. The most important payoff from training and education may be the maintenance and development of the ability to learn.

Competency has already been related to job expectations. It is also related to motivation. Motivation tends to decline if there is such a serious deficit in competence that the employee has less than a 50 percent chance of performing or there is so much competency to perform the job that the employee is 100 percent sure of performing the job well.

When jobs are not structured to ensure that employees keep learning, we prepare them for a loss of competency to perform because we discourage the competency to learn.

FACILITATING WORK ENVIRONMENT

The third factor related to performance is a facilitating work environment. This factor refers to all the external conditions of the job, that is, the resources that exist to do the job and the obstacles that keep the job from being done. Resources may be time, facilities, money, technology, equipment, and people. We have all been in the position from time to time of knowing what was expected and of having the competency to perform, but lacking the resources to perform. Our self-competency affects our perception of resources. The lower our self-perceived competency, the greater our perceived need for resources.

Environmental blocks to good performance frequently have their source in poor management practices and the general work environment. Some common environmental blocks are:

- Excessive competitiveness
- Procedural bottlenecks
- Inaccessible information
- No tolerance for risk
- Company rituals

Some common management practices that create blocks are:

- Inadequate feedback
- Failure to use line of responsibility
- Failure to give personal support
- Failure to make decisions
- Failure to be accessible

Of these, perhaps the one most tied to managing performance is feedback.

Feedback reinforces performance that is desirable and helps adjust performance that is not desirable. It should be given not just when performance is not acceptable but regularly. Reinforcement is most useful when it is immediate. Negative feedback also shouldn't be saved up and delivered in large doses.

Most of all, feedback should be concrete. When it is negative, it should never focus on traits or characteristics. There is no positive value in telling people that they lack depth or are not creative, committed, motivated, or reliable.

IN SUMMARY

Managers and supervisors are too quick to conclude that poor employee performance is due to motivational problems. There is, of course, something very attractive about such a conclusion because it allows one to abdicate responsibility for performance. When, for example, we conclude that employees are not motivated, it is an easy mental step to the deduction that it's the employees' fault, and, from this state of ineffectiveness to conclude, "If it's their fault, then I can't do anything about it."

Before we conclude that our people are not motivated, that is, that they don't want to work up to our expectations, we would be well advised to determine if the other factors essential for performance are in place. We must be certain, first, that our subordinates understand what is expected; second, that they are able to do what is expected; and third, that they have a work environment that supports their doing what is expected.

Our problem very often in managing performance is that we keep asking the wrong questions. We keep asking, "How can we motivate employees?" We can become a lot more effective if we start asking, "How can we get motivated employees to perform?"

Dennis C. Kinlaw, Ed.D., is president, Commonwealth Training Associates, Inc., Norfolk, Virginia.

20.
ON FISH TANKS
AND EXPECTATIONS

John H. Zenger
Jean E. Edwards

The time has come for a profound change in our expectations of people in the work place.

As any ichthyologist and most petshop owners could tell you, big tanks make big fish. If a fish that has been in a small bowl is moved to a larger tank, it begins to grow even if it is fed exactly the same amount of food and treated in the same manner as before. The larger tank somehow signals the fish to grow, while a small bowl telegraphs "stay small."

Managers consistently create "small bowls" for their subordinates and then wonder why those employees seem to unplug their brains as soon as they arrive at work. They don't make decisions, they don't exercise good judgment, and they don't seem to care much about their jobs or the company.

In the small-bowl environment, everyone loses. Employers get less than they're paying for, and employees remain headless and heartless on the job.

We communicate minimal expectations to employees by telling them exactly what to do and when to do it. We control them with time clocks, buzzers, bells, and coffee breaks. We hold few meetings with employees, carefully separating the work "planners" from the work "doers." We communicate as little information as possible about the organization, its financial health, its position in the marketplace and its competitors. Employees receive little specialized training to help them become proficient in their jobs. We give them little positive reinforcement or recognition for average or above-average performance.

All of this is tantamount to placing the employee in a small, tight tank. The underlying message is that we don't expect much in the way of performance or growth. Since people have a habit of doing what they believe they are expected to do (see J. Sterling Livingston, "Pygmalion in Management," *Harvard Business Review,* August 1969), these practices are self-defeating all the way around.

The problems created by low expectations and small-bowl treatment shouldn't come as news to anyone. What is intriguing, however, is the fact that some organizations obtain superlative results from essentially the same type of workers as their mediocre counterparts employ. What are these organizations doing right?

According to researchers at the Public Agenda Foundation, workers are motivated to work hard when:

- Their tasks are interesting and varied and involve some learning, challenge and responsibility.
- They have enough information, support, and authority to get the job done.
- They help make decisions that affect jobs (because bosses recognize that the workers know their jobs best).
- They understand how their own work fits into the larger picture.
- They are treated as individuals who are personally important to the company.

To return to our fishy metaphor, excellent companies place employees in larger tanks. When the whole person is *expected* to be on the job, employees rise to the occasion and grow to meet greater expectations.

We believe three things must be set into motion in order to create an innovative, large-tank environment.

Expectations. First, we need to create a whole new set of expectations, both about employees and on the part of employees. Employees must come to expect new things not only from management, but also from themselves. They must be willing to accept new roles and responsibilities inside their organizations. Management must let employees know that they are expected to come to work with their hearts and heads well connected to their hands.

Skills. Secondly, we must teach people the *skills of being a good employee* not just the technical skills of a job. Such technical skills are vitally important, but we believe there are "employee skills" just as there are general management skills.

These skills cover four broad areas. Employees must learn how to learn a job and what is expected of them; how to be an effective team player, including how to offer and receive help from co-workers and how to become a contributing member of any work-team meeting; how to build a stronger relationship with one's immediate boss, including an ability to confront difficult situations with him or her; and how to work inside a large organization with policies that must cover large numbers of people.

Combining expectations and skills. Finally, we must change expectations and teach these employees skills simultaneously. Doing one or the other is not sufficient; it is akin to treating a symptom instead of the disease.

For the last few decades, companies have been treating the symptoms of employee dissatisfaction. Remedies have ranged from bowling leagues to bonuses to company beer busts. But the illness cannot be treated with such superficial curatives.

The time has come for a profound change in our expectations of people in the work place. We need to invest in training that will allow them to be fully effective and to grow to their full potential. Otherwise we will never cure the disease that develops, as Studs Terkel put it, "when peoples' work is too small for their souls."

John H. Zenger and Jean E. Edwards are president and product manager, respectively, of Zenger-Miller, Inc., of Cupertino, Calif., a supplier of training programs and services.

21.
A CRITICAL REEVALUATION OF MOTIVATION, MANAGEMENT, AND PRODUCTIVITY

Erwin S. Stanton

We must take a more realistic look at how employees are managed.

The problem of declining productivity and work performance started slowly—perhaps almost imperceptibly—several years ago, and many thought that it was only temporary and would soon disappear. However, the problem did not vanish and, if anything, it worsened to the point that it is currently causing ever-increasing concern to companies, the government, and to most responsible Americans.

Indeed, the long-standing belief and assumption that U.S. business and industry was invincible and that no other country could ever approach us, much less surpass our technological superiority and leadership, was virtually taken for granted. It was assumed that the nation's industrial machine would continue just as it had in the past, making periodic improvements as it went along and, in so doing, advance our ever-rising standard of living. As such, a pattern of expectations was established in the minds of most people that better things—for many, even affluence—lay ahead.

But something has drastically gone wrong and it has been long in the making. The American industrial machine is currently ailing and clearly is not the vaunted and unchallenged mechanism that it has been for such a long time. Furthermore, our traditional technological superiority is being increasingly challenged by overseas competitors. In addition, our national productivity is declining, while our labor costs keep rising. Over the course of the past years, American employees have demanded, and generally received, higher wages and benefits that have unquestionably enhanced their standard of living. At the same time, however, productivity has failed to keep pace with rising labor costs, causing business and industry to lose much of its traditional and long-standing competitive advantage. During the past decade, wages have increased at an annual rate of 8.2 percent, while productivity growth has been limited to only 1.3 percent. The end result is that many American products are being outpriced, both at home and abroad.

THE JAPANESE CHALLENGE

The effect of this disastrous slippage in our industrial vitality is evident all around us. By now most Americans are clearly aware of the powerful challenge that has been posed by the Japanese auto industry, which is competing very successfully against U.S.-built cars, not only in our own country but also in the international market. But the nation's competitive decline is hardly limited to the automobile market, although that market probably has received the greatest amount of publicity and attention. Actually, the list of industries in which foreign competition has become a formidable and threatening factor is ever growing, and now includes industries in which the U.S. has long been the leader, such as steel, textiles, footwear, and consumer electronics

Business Week estimates that the loss of competitiveness by American industry in recent years equals $125 billion in lost production and some two million lost jobs. As a result, not only is the nation's standard of living being threatened, but also the profitability, viability, and even the very survival of numerous U.S. companies is likely to be in future jeopardy. In addition, the decline of the U.S. industrial machine could have serious implications for America's standing, power, and world role in these turbulent times.

WHY HAS PRODUCTIVITY DECLINED?

It is much easier to document the decline in productivity growth than to offer a truly satisfactory explanation as to why it is occurring in the first place. While there is no universal agreement as to the cause of the decline in productivity growth, most observers concur that the reasons are numerous, complex, and interrelated. However, a recently emerged consensus agrees that the following factors bear major responsibility:

- a decline in research and investment in new capital equipment
- a decline in research and development expenditures
- an increase in the cost and burden of government regulations
- the effects of inflation
- a rise in energy costs
- a decline in employee motivation and in commitment to high quality work performance

MOTIVATION AND PRODUCTIVITY

I fully recognize and respect the widely held belief that the drop in productivity growth unquestionably is the result of multiple factors and causes. Nevertheless, I believe that the decline in employee motivation and in commitment to work are two of the major causes of the slowdown in productivity.

To be sure, many employees are motivated to work productively; they take hold of the job, and they do contribute to their organization. However, every manager has encountered employees who, despite the company's best efforts, do not really care about either the company or the job. Such employees are a drain on their departments and they simply do not earn their keep. Similarly, as consumers, we have all encountered personnel whose work is shoddy and of poor quality and whose application and interest appears to be almost totally lacking.

On the other hand, some people take a drastically different view in assessing the relationship between employee motivation and productivity.

These individuals, who may be referred to as the Motivational School, seriously challenge the above explanation of the decline in business productivity. Armed with numerous research studies, they contend that most people want to work and are both interested in and capable of making a significant contribution to their company.

Furthermore, they argue, people seek personal fulfillment and self-actualization through their work. If employee productivity is unsatisfactory, they contend, then the fault lies with management and its failure to pay proper heed to these research findings and to appropriately implement the recommendations suggested by the behavioral scientists.

Which is the correct answer? Do people *really* want to work? Are they, in fact, self-motivated and self-directed? Or is the opposite more typically the case? Which factors, conditions, and situations affect the relationship between employee behavior and productivity? What specific recommendations can help managers direct the activities of their employee and achieve the goals and objectives of their companies?

THEORIES OF WORK MOTIVATION

For the past 20 years, numerous studies, research reports, and well-formulated theories have attempted to explain the complex behavior of people at work and, more importantly, to gain for the practicing manager some rather specific prescriptions as to the best way to manage employees for optimized productivity. Indeed, the influence of such applied psychologists as Maslow, McGregor, Herzberg, Likert, and Argyris on the management of human resources has been quite formidable. It is most unlikely that there is a manager today who, at one time or another, has not been exposed to some of the ideas and people management suggestions offered by these behavioral scientists.

The 1960s, when these theories were first proposed, were fruitful years for the formulation and development of psychological concepts designed to make a contribution to the world of work. In order to more clearly understand these theories, one must consider the time frame during which their formulations were developed, as well as some of the more significant economic, political, and sociological factors which influenced their thinking.

Essentially, the conceptual underpinnings of the various motivational principles put forth by the psychologists were predicated on the fact that America had a powerful, impressive, and magnificent industrial machine that offered the prospect of considerable prosperity for all of its citizens. At the same time, these psychologists believed that people had within themselves the ability, talent, and potential to enable the industrial machine to function in the best possible manner and, consequently, to virtually guarantee economic prosperity and an ever-higher national standard of living.

In this context, the vast majority of employees have an almost inherent desire and motivation to work productively and to contribute substantially to the progress of their companies. Furthermore, the motivational psychologists asserted, most people want to and indeed are capable of participating actively with management in decision-making as it affects their jobs. As a result, if management wants to fully utilize its human resources, a participative leadership approach should contribute substantially to reaching this objective.

HOW WELL HAVE THESE THEORIES HELD UP?

Many seasoned managers—including those who have been exposed to the popular work motivation theories in the course of their training and development sessions—become quite uncomfortable whenever they hear these principles so enthusiastically and universally proclaimed by ardent supporters. To seasoned managers, the concepts sound very good in theory, but their own experiences tell them that the principles do not always work as well as they have been heralded—and frequently they do not work at all.

Many managers see a paradoxical inconsistency between the theories and recommendations so convincingly put forth by the motivationalists and the stark reality of the practical world of work in which the managers function every day. Indeed, on numerous occasions these managers have personally encountered many employees who simply are not committed to high quality work and who consistently fail to perform at a satisfactory level, despite management's best efforts to implement the motivationalists' recommendations.

In the final analysis, then, how valid, realistic, and practical are these highly acclaimed motivational theories? Do they really hold up under critical scrutiny? Or are we merely dealing with the utopian and ultrahumanistic theories of idealists, rather than looking at reality?

AN EQUIVOCAL ANSWER

In my opinion, the answer is an equivocal one. Yes, at times the motivational theories do work; they work quite well with interested and committed employees deriving considerable satisfaction from their work while contributing to the effectiveness of their companies. And no, at times the motivational principles do not hold up in practice, and, as a result, many managers who have attempted to implement the theories have become disappointed and sadly disillusioned. Why, then, the paradox and the dramatic inconsistency in the results?

I would suggest that the many discrepancies are the result of the motivationalists' claim of the virtual universality of their findings and of the general applicability of their recommendations for the management of human resources. The motivationalists appear to have minimized the complexity and diversity of the motivational process and the influence and effects of numerous situational and contingency factors and circumstances in the workplace.

Essentially, three factors explain why some employees are indeed motivated to work while others are not:

1. The motivation to work varies widely in people.
2. In the past decade, there has been a significant change in many employees' attitudes toward work.
3. The increase in various government social support programs has contributed significantly to the decline in work motivation in many people.

DIFFERENT WORK ETHICS

It is true that many people are strongly motivated toward work and that they seek to fulfill themselves through the job. Frequently, work serves as the main focus of a person's life. However, to be motivated toward work is not a universal human phenomenon inherent in every individual. Actually, the importance of work varies tremendously and, for many, work is simply not the most essential part of their lives. In fact, it may not even be all that important in the first place.

To some people, since work provides income, it serves predominantly as a means to an end, that end frequently being off-the-job, leisure, and family activities. Of course, this does not mean that a person does not want a pleasant, interesting, and generally agreeable job; these are subjective qualifications that will vary with each individual. However, many people do not seek, or even expect to find, self-fulfillment through work, but rather seek it through nonwork activities. Nor does this mean that these individuals are dissatisfied with their work, as many behavioral scientists and journalists would have us believe. Essentially, people want different things from life.

Similarly, the motivationalists have stressed that most people have a strong need to plan, organize, and control their work, and to have more of a participative input in matters that directly affect them on the job. (Note, for example, the current fascination with quality circles, an idea imported from Japan.) However, as many managers have learned from first-hand experience, not everyone has the ability, intelligence, or experience—or, for that matter, the desire—to engage in such functions.

To categorically expect all employees to engage in participative management is completely unrealistic and may even invite chaos in the workplace. While many employees do want to participate, and indeed may come up with some useful ideas that can be implemented, others require a more structured, clearly defined, and nonambiguous work environment in which management provides precise instructions on how the job is to be done and what is expected of them. Indeed, many employees find such a work atmosphere most-supportive psychologically, and report that they perform at their best under these very conditions.

CHANGING ATTITUDES TOWARD WORK

One of the major factors contributing to the decline in productivity is a very profound change in the attitude toward work. Historically, Americans have been taught to work hard and to put their shoulder firmly to the wheel. Indeed, the work ethic has long been an integral part of the American way of life and of our cultural heritage.

In recent years, however, disturbing evidence has indicated that many people simply do not want to work too hard any longer. Indeed, it would seem that the relative affluence that our country has enjoyed for many years has given rise to a preoccupation with the self, a dramatic rise in self-indulgence, and an increased emphasis on instant gratification and the pursuit of pleasure-seeking activities—accompanied by a decline in commitment to work.

Some observers have linked this change in work attitude to the rising phenomenon currently referred to as the "psychology of entitlement."

Succinctly put, this attitude is the widespread expectation that everyone deserves certain benefits, privileges, and rights without necessarily having to expend a whole lot of effort—not because they have earned them, but rather because they are entitled to them by virtue of living in today's world. Put another way, they feel that society basically "owes" them certain privileges: a good, comfortable job and a high income, for starters.

Undoubtedly, the vast number of government social support programs currently available has encouraged the changing attitude toward work. At one time, being unemployed was a personal catastrophe. Today, losing one's job may still be a major problem, but the event is considerably cushioned by liberal unemployment benefits, which are often supplemented by food stamps and other forms of government assistance. While ordinarily these programs serve a most useful purpose, in many cases they have been abused by people and have resulted in a weakening of employee motivation and a lessening of the will to work.

In short, I believe that many people have become fat, lazy, and complacent. And, while I would not go so far as to declare the work ethic dead, it would certainly seem that it is currently ailing and needs a good dose of revitalization.

REALITY-CENTERED MANAGEMENT

In my opinion, if we are to get productivity growth moving again, we must take a fresh and more realistic look at how we manage employees. In any organization, one will find many very different kinds of jobs being carried out. These jobs call for a wide range of abilities, interests, and talents, and accordingly make very different demands on the people holding them.

At the same time, a wide diversity exists among employees. For example, a given person may be well suited to one job but clearly unsatisfactory in another. Effective management calls for a more realistic evaluation of the type of individual who is right for a given assignment, as well as for the most appropriate leadership style. Consequently, there is no one correct management style that will fit all employees and all situations.

Reality-centered management recognizes that some employees will want to express themselves and will seek maximum self-fulfillment through their work and will, as a result, be quite eager to participate with management in decision-making activities. At the same time, however, other employees in the very same department will not attach such meaning to work and will, consequently, look to management for clear and explicit direction and supportive supervision.

FLEXIBLE LEADERSHIP

To be effective, therefore, managers need a more flexible leadership style that will allow them to be more participative with certain employees, while taking on a much more directive and supportive posture in their approach with other employees.

Reality-centered management advocates a leadership style that ranges anywhere from being highly directive to notably participative. As such, it should not be viewed as a dichotomous model. It is most unlikely that any management will fall at either extreme end of the scale. Rather, a manager's customary leadership style and manner of directing employees tends to gravitate toward either the directive or the participative side.

However, I wish to emphasize that effective managers need to be flexible in their approach to managing employees.

How does the manager know which is the correct or most appropriate leadership style to use in any specific situation? To respond to this very strategic question, let's take a look at some of the factors that would suggest that a manager's style should lean either toward the directive or the participative end of the continuum. Here are some appropriate guidelines.

FACTORS SUGGESTING A MORE DIRECTIVE MANAGEMENT STYLE

The employee tends to be more leisure-oriented, rather than seeking fulfillment through work.

The employee's job experience is such that he or she lacks the requisite qualifications to take on greater responsibilities.

The employee's educational or skill level is relatively modest.

The employee has a personal reluctance to take on additional job responsibilities.

The employee requires a relatively structured, clearly defined, and essentially nonambiguous work environment in order to perform well.

The employee needs fairly close and supportive supervision.

The employee does not express a personal interest in becoming involved in decision-making activities.

The employee fails to identify sufficiently with the goals and objectives of the organization.

FACTORS SUGGESTING A MORE PARTICIPATIVE MANAGEMENT STYLE

The employee seeks to fulfill many of his or her ego and psychological needs through expression at work.

The employee has the necessary intelligence, education, and experience to take on additional responsibilities.

The employee is interested in having more of a say in matters that affect him or her on the job, and wants to participate in decision-making with management.

The employee does not feel anxious, uncomfortable, or insecure when faced with relatively unstructured and ill-defined work situations.

The employee is sufficiently self-reliant and self-confident to not need close and supportive supervision from his or her superior.

The employee identifies with the goals and objectives of the organization.

GET BACK TO BASICS

In addition to managing employees in a more realistic manner, organizations should get back to some of the management basics that seem to have been neglected in recent years. Specifically, we need to revitalize the following essentials of sound management:

Recruitment and selection. Extra attention should be given to initial personnel recruitment and selection so that truly qualified individuals who are inherently more motivated and capable of contributing to the company will be hired.

Training and development. Appropriate training and development should be given to employees so that they will become more productive on the job.

In part, such training should instill a positive attitude in employees and an acceptance of the concept of mutual obligation. Unquestionably the company has certain obligations to the employee, but the employee also has a reciprocal responsibility to the company, which includes a high level of excellence in work performance.

Performance appraisals. A fair, objective, and accurate employee performance appraisal program should be developed which will provide factual information with respect to a person's current work and which will clearly indicate the specific areas where future improvement is required.

Supervision. Effective, ongoing supervision and direction of employees by qualified and properly trained managers is necessary if a satisfactory degree of productivity is to be attained. As part of such a strategy, managers should set high standards of work performance that stress excellence and insist that these standards be met.

Compensation. An organization must have an equitable and attractive reward and compensation system that clearly and tangibly recognizes the achievements and contributions of employees.

The above five strategies may not constitute a true breakthrough in management practice. Indeed, these strategies have been around for some time, but inadequate attention has been given to them. It is time to return to proven management basics if we are to regain our competitive edge. Fortunately, American business and industry is still strong and powerful—in fact, it remains as the undisputed world leader. In addition, our potential for yet greater growth is exceedingly promising. Clearly, the hour is late, but there is still time if vigorous and decisive steps are taken promptly.

REFERENCES

Argyris, Chris, *Integrating the Individual and the Organization* (New York: John Wiley & Sons, 1964).

Herzberg, Frederick, *Work and the Nature of Man* (Cleveland: World Publishing Company, 1966).

Likert, Rensis, *The Human Organization* (New York: McGraw-Hill, 1957).

Maslow, A. H., *Motivation and Personality*, 2nd ed. (New York: Harper & Row, 1970).

McGregor, Douglas, *The Human Side of Enterprise* (New York: McGraw-Hill, 1960).

"The Reindustrialization of America," *Business Week* (June 30, 1980), pp. 56-142.

Yankelovich, Daniel, "We Need New Motivational Tools," *Industry Week* (August 6, 1979), pp. 61-68.

Erwin S. Stanton holds a doctorate in personnel psychology from Columbia University. In addition to his consulting work, he is a professor of management at the Graduate School of Business Administration, St. John's University, New York. Dr. Stanton has written several books, including Successful Personal Recruiting and Selection; Reality-Centered People Management: Key to Improved Productivity; *and* The Manager's Guide to Equal Employment Opportunity Requirements. *This article is based on the author's book,* Reality-Centered People Management: Key to Improved Productivity *(New York: AMACOM, 1982).*

22.
CORPORATE ESPRIT DE CORPS LANGUISHES

Margaret Price

But faster-growing firms often net high worker morale.

"Working 9-to-5, what a way to make a living," go the lyrics of a popular song, entitled "9-to-5." And, at least in spirit, many American workers today seem to embrace that down-in-the-mouth sentiment.

Generally speaking, employee morale is nothing to cheer about. Recent data from the Hay Group, a Philadelphia-based consulting firm, show that employees today are less happy with their companies than at any time since 1975. Information drawn from 1,200 organizations and 250,000 employees also shows that:

- Over 79 percent of professional, clerical, and hourly workers are dissatisfied with their company's internal communications.
- Under 30 percent of professionals, clerical, and hourly workers see adequate advancement opportunities.
- Over 55 percent of professionals in growing fields plan to leave their current place of employment.

"We predict that as we move out of the recession (1983), [professionals such as] engineers and data-processing systems analysts will start to [leave] in such large numbers that the turnover problems companies had with these groups before the recession will look small in comparison with what they'll encounter after the recession," says Dr. Michael Cooper, partner and national director at the Hay Group.

The reasons for worker malaise vary. The harsh recession affected a wide range of concerns, from wages to job security to advancement opportunities. In addition, absorbed with bottom-line financial results, managers may not have been addressing employees' most important concerns: challenges and advancement opportunities. Furthermore, observers point out, the baby-boom generation, reaching its mid-30s, heightened competition for jobs.

Obvious? All the while, apparently, human-resources managers apparently haven't been heeding the ominous signs. For instance, in a "mini" survey this summer the Hay Group found that despite widespread champing at the bit by disgruntled workers, only seven percent of human resources officials expect to place a high priority on the professional-turnover issue in the coming year. In contrast, 50 percent expect productivity to be a top priority concern in human resources management. (The second- and third-highest priorities—43 percent each—should be communications and compensation, respondents said.)

"Turnover isn't the concern it was three or four years ago," adds Dr. James W. Walker, vice president of the New York consulting firm, Tower, Perrin, Forster & Crosby. "I think companies [right now] are more concerned with cost-relating to people, utilization of people, [and] whether they have the right skills to help their company [seize opportunities] in the recovery." And to the manager's advantage, he notes, the labor market "is still not tight in many job categories."

But the morale scene is by no means entirely bleak. Indeed, at least one survey by the Merit Report, entitled "Women and Work, An In-Depth Survey," finds that 45 percent of both sexes report being "very happy" with their jobs. (However, older women are more apt to be "very happy" with their jobs than younger women, while the opposite is true of men, the survey reports.) And, the Hay Group reports, morale is considerably higher in fast-growth than in slow-growth companies. Indeed, on the latter point the Hay Group detects what Dr. Cooper calls "two Americas"—of slow- and of fast-growing companies. Significantly, the latter type apparently is more able to accommodate what its employees value most: challenges for professionals and advancement opportunities for managers.

RXS FOR MORALE PROBLEMS

What should companies do to fight worker apathy? Some organizations have already instituted programs designed for a variety of reasons, including morale boosting. These efforts include instituting dual career ladders and quality circle programs, undertaking employee-attitude surveys, generally decentralizing operations, and changing the corporate culture.

Exemplifying the last point is Bethlehem Steel Corp. Even before the latest recession struck, this troubled company in 1980 decided to change from "what some describe as autocratic to much more participatory," reports Tim Demma, a special assistant supporting the implementation of the Quality of Work Life program in Bethlehem's sales function.

The steelmaker now has "many separate efforts going on with the same goal: enhancing productivity through employee participation." For instance, employee-participation groups in each location and department serve as vehicles for supplying input into decision-making. And, among other things, a program has been set up to identify and resolve quality-related problems in plants and in the home office. One major success: office productivity gains through automation.

Bethlehem Steel is still closing plants and laying off workers. And such uncertainties mean that "morale is still low here. But it would probably be lower if people weren't involved with trying to make things better," says Mr. Denna.

While Bethlehem's program was designed to improve productivity, morale is obviously a key to any productivity gains.

Low morale "would show up as low commitment to the goals of an organization," sums up J. Richard Wible, technical services director, American Society for Personnel Administration, Berea, Ohio. Thus, he suggests ways of measuring this important concern: Undertaking attitude surveys about a variety of working conditions and then responding one way or another: and perhaps conducting a confidential exit interview, complete with questionnaire, just before employees leave a company.

23.
MOTIVATION MANAGEMENT

L. Ed Berry

A list of rules for providing a good employee motivation climate.

The management of motivation is to get people to do what you want done, when you want it done, how you want it done, because the people want to do it.

To start, the manager should ask himself how much he really knows about the individuals in his department. There is no supervisor who has so many people reporting directly to him that he cannot make it his business to find out with respect to each individual the significant factors about family background, racial origin, special personal obligations, ambitions and drive, all of which will have a distinct bearing on the way that particular human beings will be expected to interact with the others in the department. This information frequently is available in personnel files; it also can be covertly obtained over a period of time from the people themselves. Such knowledge will often provide a key to actions that might otherwise appear stubborn and irrational.

Once the manager knows the background of the people reporting to him, he can easily see that no two people are exactly alike and that their needs will vary in type and intensity. For one man, his economic and social needs may be satisfied rather readily but he has an almost insatiable need for recognition, prestige, and status. For another, the overwhelming driving force, at least for the present, may be economic needs and consequently the desire for more money. In a third case, the need to belong and be an accepted and important part of the group may be primary. The difficult task which the manager faces is to translate what he knows about needs in general to each specific individual. In essence, the manager must determine where each individual stands in the needs hierarchy and what incentives can provide the opportunity to satisfy those needs.

It should also be recognized that usually the social, psychological, and, in some cases, the self-fulfillment needs are not outwardly expressed, at least in a direct sense. It is not socially acceptable to ask for a feeling of belonging and a sense of importance. The manager, however, must be sensitive to when his people are seeking, in indirect ways, these satisfactions. He must be able to sense whether or not they feel that their work has purpose, meaning, and direction, whether they are properly challenged, when new experiences are desired, when accomplishment and recognition are being sought, and when growth and advancement are important. Once the manager is aware of and sensitive to these needs, he has taken the important first step on the road to effective management.

One of the biggest challenges which a manager faces is that of creating a favorable job climate which is conducive to individual and group motivation. Before such a climate can be created, the more basic needs of man—the physiological and safety needs—must be at least partially satisfied. Most of these needs are met through wages, fringe benefits, physical working conditions, and overall company policy and administration.

Often these factors cannot be controlled by the individual manager, especially in larger companies where the benefits program, the major company policies, and the wages paid to employees are dictated by someone at the company's headquarters. In almost all cases, there are company policies concerning salary review dates, wage and salary structures to be complied with, and a limit of some sort with respect to the general level of wages paid. If these company policies are insufficient to fulfill the individual's basic needs, then the factors are present which can cause job dissatisfaction. To a certain degree, some of these weaknesses can be offset by good leadership.

THE MOTIVATION CLIMATE

How can the manager develop within his department the climate necessary to spawn motivation? There are two aspects of creating the proper motivation climate. First is the manager's personal approach to leadership as it reflects his day-to-day contact with his subordinates. Second is the general structure of the job climate he creates.

The Personal Approach. I was once told that if you want to get the best work possible from someone, you must treat him as a person, not as some inanimate object. The whole idea of personal leadership may be summed up in the statement, "a manager must treat people as people." An effective manager must have personal involvement with his subordinates. This does not necessarily mean socializing with them. Rather, it means that a manager must develop a genuine interest in his subordinates in terms of things that are important to them. Perhaps this point can best be illustrated by an example. Most of us have had the experience of meeting someone for the first time and walking away with a very favorable impression. In analyzing why that person impressed us we very often find it was because he showed sincere and keen interest in us. In short, our ego received a boost. Employees are no different.

It should be emphasized that the manager must be genuine and sincere in his interest in his subordinates. People will always be able to see through an artificial or insincere expression of interest. They may be fooled for a while but very soon they are able to sense the phoniness and develop a feeling that the manager is trying to "take them for a ride." However, when an employee feels that his boss is sincerely interested in him, his problems, his future, and his well-being, he is more likely to be a high producer.

Another aspect of the personal approach to leadership is that the manager must realize that he sets the pace as far as ultimate accomplishment of results is concerned. By his action or lack of action, his decision or lack of decision, the manager daily sets the standards by which his subordinates will work. The level of accomplishment he gets from his people will, to a large degree, be a reflection of what he expects and what he demands. If he expects the worst, the chances are he will get just that. If he is satisfied with a medium level of performance, the chances are equally good that that is what most of his people will give him. By the same token, the manager who has consistently high expectations of subordinates, usually ends up with higher overall performance.

Creating Job Climate. In recent years, I have visited in several business offices. Two of these offices stand out in my memory. In one of the offices, I observed that the employees were careless and sloppy in their work, they performed their tasks begrudgingly, and their main interest seemed to be the hour hand on the clock. In the other office, I was impressed with the attention to details exhibited by the employees, their apparent happiness in their work, and the almost electrifying excitement of the tasks to be performed. In one office there was much hustle and bustle; in the other, an almost dead silence—in spite of the fact that both companies were involved in the same type of work. What was the difference in the two offices? The difference was in the job climates which had been created by the management of the two offices. It was evident that in one office the people were totally involved in their work. In the other office, it was equally evident that the only involvement the employees had was the monthly paycheck!

One of the most important factors in creating a good job climate is enthusiasm. Enthusiasm in a business is very contagious. Once it catches hold, it is difficult to stop. The individual manager can do much toward building a favorable climate for maximum results by establishing a good "mental set" himself. If he is excited and interested, the chances are good that his people will adopt the same mental attitude.

The fact that a man is performing various tasks in the course of doing his job means that he is physically involved in that job, but this is not enough to trigger his initiative. Someplace along the line he must become mentally and emotionally involved. That is, he must feel that there is more to his job than just physical activity and a paycheck. In order to accomplish this, the manager must see to it that the objectives of the organization are integrated and blended with the needs of the individual. This blending of objectives may be accomplished in several ways:

1.   Each individual should know where the department fits into the total operation of the company, how this job fits into the department, and why his

job is important. This will help him feel that he is making a worthwhile contribution to the company.

2.   There must be a clear understanding between the manager and
employee as to what is expected from the employee. Unless the manager has
clearly outlined for the employee what he expects and the specific standards by
which he will be judged, it is not reasonable for the manager to expect any
more than he gets. Letting the employee know what is expected (it must be
explicit) gives him something to work for. It gives direction to his efforts, and
he can see tangible results in terms of accomplishments.

3.   The manager must take special care to be sure that each individual in
his department knows exactly where he stands. If the employee has done a good
job on a project, he should be recognized by the manager. By the same token, if
the employee has done a poor job, he should be told how it could have been
done better. The relationship between the manager and the employee in terms
of what is being accomplished must be a continuing one.

4.   The employee should be encouraged to voice his opinions and to
present his ideas and suggestions to management. He must feel that any contribution he makes will be taken into consideration by management. In this
way, he will become both mentally and emotionally involved in the affairs of
the company.

5.   The manager should assign tasks such that individuals will be
challenged. One of the strongest needs people have is for a sense of
achievement. If there is not a challenge, this need cannot be satisfied.
However, it should be cautioned that the challenge should be reasonable and
represent attainable goals.

6.   Man's highest goal is self-fulfillment. This can be satisfied only when he
is given the opportunity for growth and advancement. If these opportunities
are not forthcoming in his present job, he will most certainly look elsewhere.

7.   The manager should delegate duties and responsibilities whenever
possible. This will relieve the manager of some of his work and at the same time
make the employee's job more meaningful. This shows respect for the
employee's judgment, fosters his initiative and confidence, and makes him feel
more important.

CONCLUSION

Thus we see that by being aware of and attending to the needs of the individuals working for him and in so doing creating a job climate in which these
needs can be satisfied, a manager can create an environment in which the
employees will want to do the best possible job, and do it when the manager
wants it done.

*L. Ed Berry is the director, Information Systems, for the Zapata Corporation of
Houston, Texas. Mr. Berry has 15 years experience in the data processing field, with
over 12 years experience in supervisory and management positions.*

24.
FULFILLING EMPLOYEE NEEDS— THE KEY TO MOTIVATION

Randal D. Naylin

What is your motivational style? Does it need changing?

What is the most serious problem in business today? If you are like most businesspeople, you will say "personnel." This is what a Presidential Task Force found when looking into the problems of small business. Of the many personnel problems, the ones involving motivation are often the most serious. Motivating employees is perhaps the most difficult task you as a supervisor can ever attempt to accomplish.

How can you decide what to do? There seem to be as many ways to motivate people as there are people trying to motivate. I will not attempt to solve every problem but will try to encourage you to think about your motivational style and perhaps how you can change it.

As a supervisor, you cannot attempt to fulfill all of an employee's needs and desires. It would be far too expensive and impractical to even try this. But by identifying these needs and desires, you can begin to understand the things you can control.

A. H. Maslow, past president of the American Psychological Association, has said man's needs can be ranked in order of their importance. As man fulfills each need, he is then free to concentrate on the next. Knowing what these needs are will help you to understand what employees hope to gain from their jobs.

MASLOW'S NEED-HIERARCHY THEORY

1. Physiological needs—food, water, sleep, etc.
2. Safety needs—physical and psychological safety and security
3. Social needs—attention, belonging and acceptance
4. Ego needs—respect, recognition and achievement
5. Self-actualization—desire to reach one's full potential

113

As man is able to and actually does achieve each need, he then tries to fulfill other needs.

I conducted a survey and found there are many wants and desires businesspeople believe can be influenced. The non-fulfillment of these wants and desires has produced many problems within organizations. Many of these will be problems you might be experiencing right now. As you recognize them, you can then begin to eliminate them from your organization.

EMPLOYEE WANTS AND DESIRES

1. Employees want praise and recognition. They feel they get noticed only for the things they do wrong and not for the things they do right.

2. Employees want job security. They want to know if they can depend on their jobs.

3. Employees want the opportunity to advance and gain new experiences.

4. Employees want communication. They want to know where they stand in the eyes of their employers, what they are doing right or wrong.

5. Employees want to feel involved in the company. They want to take part in making decisions, so they know where the company is going.

6. Employees want to be treated fairly. This applies especially where pay is concerned.

The employees of today expect more from their jobs and employers than ever before. They are better educated, better informed and more knowledgeable than any group of people ever have been. This makes your job even more difficult. You must be concerned with and aware of the "people problems" present in your organization. Most importantly, you must want to act upon these problems. Ignoring them will not make them go away; it will only make them grow.

WHAT CAN YOU DO TO SOLVE THESE PROBLEMS?

There is no swift and easy answer to this question. The answer depends upon several things, such as the size of your organization, the type of your organization and the type of employees you have.

PRAISE AND RECOGNITION

Most employees say praise and recognition are some of the things that are most effective in motivation. Most managers do use praise to some extent, but not enough. In the survey I took, I found 70 percent said they used praise only "sometimes." Most said they used reprimands more than praise in motivating people.

To effectively motivate by praise and recognition, you must always be on the lookout for work well done. Take the time to write down the things your employees do right and communicate your thanks and praise to them. To be effective, this praise and recognition must be communicated to the employee immediately. DON'T PUT IT OFF! Make it a habit to take time every day to do this.

Many companies have established formal recognition programs. Some have, for example, an "employee of the week." They recognize superior performance by an employee each week. You might try using certificates for recognition. Give one for some single special performance.

Remember to make your praise and recognition special. Don't let it become mechanical. Do it sincerely, and do it often.

JOB SECURITY IS A MUST

In today's erratic economy, many people are concerned their jobs are not safe, that they could lose them. If they feel this way, they won't work as they should. They will lack enthusiasm.

To overcome this problem, make sure your employees understand the guidelines for dismissal in your organization. If you don't have any, make them. Let them know how they stand in relation to those guidelines. This could be accomplished in the job evaluation interview I will discuss later on. Help them to feel secure. Many of the employees you least suspect may be frightened by the prospect of losing their jobs.

ADVANCEMENT AND GROWTH

Today's employee wants more out of his job than just money; he or she wants the chance to advance and gain new experiences.

An employee should be able to see what he or she must do to advance in an organization and should be given the opportunity whenever possible. Some organizations bring in personnel from outside to fill positions. Give your own employees the opportunity to show what they can do.

Your employees have experience and knowledge in many different areas. Let them participate in determining their own job duties. As much as possible and as much as they want to, let them gain experience in many areas.

JOB EVALUATION INTERVIEWS

The job evaluation interview can be a key to solving several problems in organizations. In the survey I conducted, I found less than twenty percent of small businesses are using some type of employee evaluation program. Those using evaluations feel they are very effective as a motivational tool.

There are many things an evaluation interview can and should accomplish:

1. You can learn about an employee's personal goals, desires and attitudes. Having a general idea of these will allow you to determine what your motivational approach should be.

2. You will have the opportunity to set goals with the employee regarding his work performance. Goal-setting should be participative. To reach a goal, an employee should help set it.

3. Previously-set goals and performance can be evaluated. After setting a goal, there must be reporting and evaluating of progress in relation to the goals.

4. The interview will give you the opportunity to praise and recognize or to punish if necessary. Keep a file on each employee and take notes so this can be accomplished in the interview. Remember, a carrot motivates much better than a stick.

5. The interview will allow you and the employee the opportunity to communicate. The employee should be informed of organizational goals and developments. You can also find out what the employee feels would improve the organization.

There is no "right" way to conduct an evaluation interview. It must be tailored to each specific business and job. But there are several guidelines that should be followed in conducting these interviews:

1. Keep it impersonal. Don't indulge in personal attacks; take the opportunity to give positive reinforcement.

2. Plan in advance the objectives you want to accomplish, but don't keep it so structured as to stop free discussion.

3. Let the employee talk! Let him express his thoughts and let him participate in goal-setting and evaluation.

PARTICIPATIVE MANAGEMENT

The degree to which supervisors normally allow their employees to participate depends upon the basic leadership philosophy of the supervisor. Douglas McGregor, a leader in motivational theory development, has said participation can become a farce if it is used as a gimmick or for kidding people into thinking they are important. He feels if management has a basically low opinion of employees, participation will not work.

There are several reasons and benefits for allowing employees to participate in decision making:

1. It has been proven that when a decision is made by a group, it is usually of much higher quality than that made by an individual. If high quality is a concern, then participation is an advantage.

2. If a decision must be completely accepted by a group to be effective, then participation should be used. People feel much more inclined to follow a decision they have helped make and feel responsible for.

3. Employees will feel closer to the company and job satisfaction will increase if they feel they have really helped to form company policy.

FAIRNESS AND PAY

Nothing can cause more contention in an organization than perceived unfairness in pay. Many companies try to keep pay levels secret to avoid this problem, but it is well-known that this is almost impossible to do. Where money is concerned, people always seem able to get information.

To eliminate this perceived unfairness, many companies have a published wage scale. They have shown employees how pay is established and how the particular employee is paid. It's also a good idea to make clear the steps necessary to increase pay. Though many pay structures may be fair, problems often occur when employees don't know specifically how standards are established.

Money can be used as an important motivator. Of the businesses surveyed, I found over 70 percent used some type of commission system, and most of these have some other type of monetary motivation program. They feel money is important, but that it must be used as a part of a total motivational program to be effective.

CONCLUSION

In talking with and surveying business supervisors, I have found that most want to improve the way they motivate. They know they should but they don't take the time. This article discusses goal-setting with employees, but you should also take time and set goals for yourself. Decide what personnel problems your organization has and plan how to overcome them. There are few things in your organization that need your attention as badly.

We have come a long way in recognizing the needs of employees, but obviously we can go further. If we do, production will increase and running our businesses will become easier.

25.
IMPLEMENTING THE OPEN-PLANNED OFFICE CONCEPT

Harold L. Airson III

The author explodes the myth that improved office landscapes alone will motivate employees.

Organizations need to know more about the process of changing offices before they spend thousands of dollars that may lock them into a design that doesn't work for them. After all, the effectiveness of decisions, supervision, communications, and interaction can be significantly influenced by the degree to which the design of the office meets the needs and work requirements of the organization. In other words, a properly designed office can have a positive effect on employee productivity and job satisfaction.

Before one decides to modify an office environment then, one must realize that doing so is more than just an exercise in aesthetics. A change in office configuration is, in reality, a significant organizational change intervention. And the effectiveness of any new office design is dependent on the manner in which visual change is integrated with the behavior change perspective so that the result is an improvement in employee satisfaction and productivity. Open, planned offices are not for everyone.

OPEN-OFFICE LANDSCAPE

In an open-office landscape, the physical environment (mainly lighting, climate control, and acoustics) creates an atmosphere in which work is pleasant for all employees. Background noise is continuous (because it is the sum of many "random" noises), yet soft and diffuse (due to acoustic features) and thus not distracting. Specially designed desks and files maximize space utilization and minimize effort in their use. The relative positioning of desks provides optimum work flow in terms of the time required to process a unit of information and the quality of information output. Visually the "free" arrangement also creates a "random background" which provides fewer distractions than a more "orderly" arrangement. The spatial layout facilitates informal, face-to-face communication and should obviate certain formalities, such as excessive meetings and written communications, and reduce the time spent on the telephone. The sight of others performing their work as part of the general atmosphere is stimulating and makes work more compelling, thus increasing motivation and efficiency. The fact that organization members see more of each other than in conventional offices reduces intrigue and preconceptions among fellow workers and between boss and subordinate. This increases cooperation and improves relationships. Awareness of the total organization reduces "group egoism" and increases teamwork and cooperation, while strengthening identification and involvement with total department objectives and activities.

The open, planned design is founded on two principles: Flexibility and cost savings. It's flexible in that movable partitions are used in conjunction with modularized furniture. An extensive use of plants, special lighting, and masking around utility systems, frequently accompanies the open planned design and provides additional flexibility. From a cost perspective, money is saved in construction and physical rearrangements.

Besides space flexibility and cost savings, the anticipated results are a potentially more effective organization. Unfortunately, few studies have been conducted that have conclusively shown solid improvements in productivity or job satisfaction. If anything, the results of open planned office changes have been anything but consistently positive.

How does the open-office plan compare with the "traditional" office? Koehn describes the typical, conventional office: too many are the result of considering how many average-sized humans can be placed in a given quantity of space. Too many offices have been designed to fit the space they have been forced to occupy. The result is a series of featureless, drab containers of squashed-together cubicles. All too often, office design criteria are based solely upon rank and the presumed prestige or the current status of the inhabitant. Furthermore, if the user's needs are even considered, those doing the considering are frequently outsiders who know little or nothing about the business operation of the organization. They see the organization as consisting of a quantity of so many executives, managers, secretaries, typists, and clerks.

Of all the studies that have been conducted concerning the benefits/shortcomings of the open-office design, the findings of Young and Berry are typical. They investigated the impact of the environment (to include office landscaping) on the expressed productivity of office workers engaged in decision-making, design, and/or creative work. Regarding open offices their findings substantiated those of others; namely, positive attitudes were expressed on job satisfaction, communication, effectiveness, and productivity, but negative attitudes were expressed on lack of visual and auditory privacy, lack of confidential communication, lack of territory definition, and lack of freedom.

Often the new, landscaped office looks better but is generally judged to work no better than the old, conventional one! There is no reason to ascribe either positive or negative characteristics to one or the other on the basis of available data. Often there is no evidence to suggest that workers take advantage of the design to adapt their workspace to their work. Instead, workspace layout seems to be controlled by supervisors and supervisory policy.

Before Brookes and Kaplan initiated their study, proponents of the open-office concept often assumed that an office is primarily an information processing center and that office architecture can directly affect the efficiency of that processing. These innovators then proposed a rationale for office planning based upon the need to structure the office environment about the organizational processes which are to be accomplished within it.

This was done by departing from the traditional design of long-corridor, cubicle, fixed-wall row of small private offices together with bull pens of rows of desks in clerical areas—and by substituting scattered work groups in a large open-office plan. (The geometry of the layout was supposed to reflect the pattern of work groups rather than being a superimposed rectilinear plan.)

Among the many advantages claimed for the open-landscape approach to planning were that group cohesiveness would be enhanced by the admixture of executives, management, supervisors, and clerical staff, and that productivity would also be enhanced.

Three important points about the concept of office landscape are:

1.   All levels of staff will participate in the open landscape (not just clerical workers and a few supervisors).

2.   Psychological needs for privacy, etc., will be accommodated by providing work stations whereby anyone seeking to avoid interruptions will be able to turn his back on the traffic stream.

3.   Since the design will have no fixed partitions, no fixed wall, no fixed bank screens, it is possible for work groups to change and adapt their work areas to the changing needs of their business.

The result was that noise, visual bustle, lack of privacy, and loss of personal space seem to be a problem in open-office landscaping. In no published reports have the claims of increased office productivity been substantiated! Moreover, functional efficiency decreased, if anything.

The most-liked quality of landscaping according to the employees surveyed was the improved psychological climate: such things as color, attractiveness, and atmosphere. The most frequent criticism was that the landscape was too public. Overall reactions to the office landscape were favorable and employees felt they were communicating more effectively.

Other surveys found that the significant *motivational* asset that the open-office landscape concept possessed has been all but ignored in most discussions of the subject. Despite extreme change in physical environment—from a very bad conventional office to a rather good landscape office—*attitudinal* changes about the work itself, the nature of the job, and the role of the individual with respect to his job, changed only *minimally.* It is clear that the physical design of the office, whether landscaped or not, cannot motivate the work force. The truth is that office landscaping is a mere hygiene factor. Even if there were dissatisfactions initially, a positive change in the office environment would only result in a condition of no dissatisfaction.

ISSUES BEYOND OFFICE LANDSCAPE

Before considering implementation of the open-office plan, three factors that significantly influence design effectiveness must be carefully considered:

1. The state of employee morale
2. Work flow requirements
3. Individual job characteristics

Regarding employee morale, remember that the state of morale establishes the foundation for the reaction to the new open office. High employee morale will enhance employee design receptivity; low morale will hinder receptivity. For example, Szilagyi found that when significant levels of pay dissatisfaction existed, the open office was perceived as an additional threat to the employees' security. Also, employees in boring, mundane, and dissatisfying jobs such as secretarial and clerical positions generally viewed office design changes as an ineffective mechanism to reduce their dissatisfaction. On the other hand, employees in challenging, complex jobs viewed the office's freedom and adaptability features in a positive manner. Interestingly, when poor supervisory relations existed, subordinates viewed the open concept as just another managerial ploy to reduce their freedom of interaction and to allow supervisors to better "keep an eye" on workers.

With respect to work flow requirements, three additional considerations should be evaluated: (1) What are the visual and verbal communications requirements among employees? Partitions may prohibit needed communications and interfere with employee-dependance relationships. (2) Social density, or the map of the possible physical accessibility of a worker to his colleagues, is also important in that it is strongly related to the type of work being done. For example, employees in the product planning and new business department of a large petroleum company who experienced a significant social density increase, experienced less conflict, greater job clarity, and increased job satisfaction. On the other hand, social density decreases caused a dramatic drop in morale for telephone operators. The new, open office has eliminated their value-added factor of social interaction! (3) Privacy is also very often needed by employees to perform day-to-day activities. The openness associated with partitions can have a negative effect when delicate and confidential discussions are conducted in "individual" offices.

Lastly, regarding job characteristics (variety, autonomy, performance feedback, and challenge), changing the office design may unknowingly enhance or retard motivation, morale, and/or productivity.

STEPS TO FOLLOW

Szilagyi, Holland, and Oliver developed these steps from the experience of managers, and from the studies reported here on the open, planned design made the following recommendations:

1. Set definite goals for the office. For example, one goal should be to improve or at least hold the present level of organizational morale, motivation, and performance.

2. Put the right people in charge of the office change. Both the interior architect and the company's "move coordinator" must work as a team to ensure that the goals of the move are met with the greatest efficiency and the least disruption of organizational life.

3. Conduct an organizational diagnosis prior to the design of the new office space. Consider the overall morale level and organizational climate characteristics, and identify the inevitable pockets of resistance.

4. Evaluate the level of importance that status symbols are given by employees.

5. Examine the work-flow requirements, communications patterns, and worker interdependencies in the old and new office designs for their impact on performance. Consider especially physical and social densities.

6. Carefully evaluate the impact of the office design change on the individual worker's job so that the motivating potential of the job is not seriously damaged.

7. Forecast your future manpower and office equipment needs/trends so that the right amount of flexibility can be part of the office design.

8. Encourage participation of functional managers and subordinates in both the design and implementation stages of the new office change. Successful participation in a change process increases the probability of employee commitment to the design change.

In addition to these "keys to success," insist on the need for a total systems approach to office design, one not limited to communications and operations research but one which can respond to the following questions and optimize the trade-offs involved.

1. What type of staff can learn to live in what style of office?

2. What changes in work, goals, or supervision can be made to enhance office productivity?

3. Does the style of the office environment serve to self-select those who will work in it?

4. What are the meaningful indices of office productivity for management?

5. What are the meaningful indices of corporate goals, reflected at group and individual levels?

6. What are the meaningful indices of status, cohesiveness, etc.?

7. Which is the more cost-effective in the long run: an office with low maintenance and re-set up costs and lower performance, or a conventional office with less noise and interruptions and higher performance?

Pragmatically, Wicker proposes that ecological psychologists (and systems managers!) must *continue* to develop a technology for deliberately intervening in behavior settings (the basic environmental unit in ecological psychology) to improve setting functioning and to increase the satisfaction, productivity, and well-being of the people who occupy them.

REFERENCES

Fadel, R., "The Interaction between Physical Environment and Affiliative Behavior," *Dissertation Abstracts International* (Vol. 39, No. 3), p. 1163.

Koehn, H., "Forget the Black Boxes," *Journal of Systems Management* (Vol. 14, No. 4), pp. 32-34.

Morgan, M., "Office of the Future: Is Management Ready?" *Journal of Systems Management* (Vol. 14, No. 3), pp. 28-32.

Oborne, D. & Heath, T., "The Role of Social Space Requirements in Ergonomics," *Applied Ergonomics* (Vol. 10, No. 2), pp. 99-103.

Penrose, J. "The Effect of Open Office Landscaping on Communication," *Dissertation Abstracts International* (Vol. 39, No. 4), p. 1927.

Sundstrom, E., Burt, R., and Kamp, D., "Privacy at Work: Architectural Correlates of Job Satisfaction and Job Performance," *Academy of Management Journal* (Vol. 23, No. 1), pp. 101-117.

Szilagyi, A., Holland, W., and Oliver, C., "Keys to Success with Open Planned Offices," *Management Review* (Vol. 68, No. 8), pp. 26-41.

Turney, J. and Cohen, S., "The Development of a Work Environment Questionnaire for the Identification of Organizational Problem Areas in Specific Army Work Settings," Technical Paper 275 (U.S. Army Research Institute for the Behavioral and Social Studies, 1976).

Wicker, A., "Ecological Psychology: Some Recent and Prospective Developments," *American Psychologist* (Vol. 34, No. 9), pp. 755-765.

Worchel, S. and Teddlie, C., "The Experience of Crowding: a Two-factor Theory," *Journal of Personality and Social Psychology* (Vol. 34, No. 1), pp. 30-40.

Worchel, S. and Teddlie, C. "The Role of Attribution in the Experience of Crowding," *Journal of Experimental Social Psychology* (Vol. 15, 1979), pp. 91-104.

Young, H. and Berry, G. "The Impact of Environment on the Productivity of Intellectually Challenged Office Workers," *Human Factors* (Vol. 21, No. 4), pp. 399-407.

Capt. Harold L. Airson III is currently assigned as chief, Analysis Branch, Office of Modernization and Planning, 1st Personnel Command, Schwetzingen, West Germany. He holds a B.S. degree in general engineering from the U.S. Military Academy, an M.S. degree in Systems Management from the University of Southern California, and has pursued graduate studies at the Georgia Institute of Technology and Harvard University.

26.
LOW PRODUCTIVITY? TRY IMPROVING THE SOCIAL ENVIRONMENT

Keith Davis

Conditions outside the company affect job motivation, too.

Advanced technology and the high quality of life in the United States should encourage higher productivity; in fact, productivity has inched up rather slowly, and at times even declined, during the last two decades. Our productivity gains, compared with those of other advanced nations, are among the lowest. There are several reasons for our low gains in productivity. I want to focus on an important—and usually neglected—one.

A major cause of low productivity is that society does not provide a rewarding environment *outside the company* for motivation within the company. Motivating employees by building better job environments and improving the quality of work life is important, but by focusing only on the job, we are focusing on only half of the motivational problem. We are overlooking the other half: the social environment outside the company. We are putting all our efforts into the superstructure of motivation and ignoring the foundation.

There are two types of motivation. Micromotivation, which we will call Type A, relates to the conditions on the job and within a single company. Macromotivation, which we will call Type B, relates to conditions in the social environment outside the company that may influence motivation on the job.

In order to improve Type A motivation, managers have tried new incentive plans, supervisory training, quality assurance campaigns, organizational development, and other such programs. They have brought in experts in motivation, who also emphasize Type A motivation because they were employed to do so. These efforts usually bring about some improvement, but often the results are not as good as expected. Both management and the experts may walk away muttering to themselves, "Do we really understand motivation? I wonder if we are overlooking something."

Neither managers nor experts can be faulted for continuing to work on Type

A motivation. It is beneficial and it is the type that management can do a good deal to control. But more attention needs to be paid to Type B motivation.

TYPE B MOTIVATION

Type B motivation is vital to job motivation because it strongly influences employee responses to both the job and its rewards. The employees' social environment determines their attitudes toward work, their feelings about working conditions, their response to incentives, their expectations about supervision, and most of their other job responses. This conditioning also determines whether or not the rewards that management offers will be perceived by employees as rewards. Without a suitable Type B environment, the chances for high job motivation are weak.

Some employees, for example, reject a promotion to a supervisory position because the rewards are not worth the necessary extra effort. Other employees refuse to work very diligently because they prefer leisure; they want to earn just enough to live on while they enjoy other pursuits. The social environment is weakening job motivations in these and other ways, none of which management can control. Examples are as follows.

A *declining work ethic.* According to surveys, the work ethic has been declining for years in the United States. It is giving way to a leisure ethic and other alternatives, so that a number of today's employees come to work without the strong motivation that employees had in the past.

Lower status for work. Some people who still operate under the work ethic are regarded favorably by the social system, but others, especially those in business, are likely to be condemned as grubby money chasers. Still others are labeled workaholics by their children and accused of being out of step with modern times. People with a strong work ethic are rarely our modern heroes.

Inflation. Employees who still insist on hard work will find that their paychecks and savings are eaten away by inflation. The net reward for hard work is low, hardly worth the cost to employees and their families.

A *tax system* that penalizes hard work and success. Those who work to improve themselves are taxed at a higher rate as they earn more pay. This clearly is a penalty for improved performance. And the progressive tax brackets are not indexed to inflation, so that even those workers who receive no increase in real income are being pushed steadily by inflation into higher tax brackets. This is a penalty for merely continuing to work.

As a typical employee earns more, the *payments made into social security* increase faster than potential benefits. Again, a penalty exists.

According to surveys, many employees work hard to build an estate for retirement and for their families after their deaths. But *progressive income and estate taxes along with inflation* leave many employees who have worked hard and saved for a comfortable retirement with only a subsistence living.

These are only six examples from a multitude of social penalties for hard work. These problems seem to have been overlooked or ignored by most politicians, intellectuals, motivation specialists, and managers. I have worked in the area of motivation for 30 years, and rarely have I heard Type B motivation even mentioned at professional meetings. Perhaps we need to change our priorities for managing motivation. Or perhaps we need to go back to the drawing board and build more of Type B motivation into our models. As long as the Type B foundation is weak, the Type A superstructure will remain shaky.

It is true that if job conditions are unrewarding, motivation is likely to be weak no matter how supportive the external environment is. However, the reverse also applies. If environmental conditions do not support better job performance, motivation tends to be weak, even when conditions on the job are favorable. Both Type A and Type B motivation need to be improved if productivity is to increase at a higher rate. But this is not a job management can do alone. Social attitudes and the social environment must also be changed.

Keith Davis is a professor of management at Arizona State University, the author of numerous books and articles, a consultant on management matters, and an instructor in a number of management development courses.

27.
MANAGERIAL RISK TAKING

Suzanne Sisson

A healthy, productive work environment depends on individuals for whom growth, development, and taking risks are a way of life. The author explains how more people, both managers and subordinates, can overcome the fears that stifle risk-taking behavior.

"We've got to take more risks in this organization!" "We want managers who have an entrepreneurial style!" Increasingly, American businesses are responding to intense competition and generally tighter markets by encouraging risk taking. Consequently, managers are under new pressure to be more daring and to facilitate the same qualities in their subordinates.

The question is how? How does a manager change his or her own risk-taking behavior and help other to change? What are the underlying principles of risk taking?

THE NATURE OF RISK TAKING

What makes risk taking risky is the potential for losing something. The more there is to lose, the bigger the risk. Understandably, the reason we avoid risks is that we focus on what we might lose rather than what we might gain. We either take the risk with tremendous anxiety or we do not take the risk at all. When there is more to lose than to gain, we wisely choose not to risk. At other times we have virtually nothing to lose and much to gain, yet we unwisely choose not to risk.

People take risks based on their ability to predict success from past experiences. Risk taking becomes a habit that contributes to confidence. We can choose to increase or decrease the frequency of risk-taking behavior. Getting ourselves and others to take risks is difficult at best. Fear is the biggest obstacle.

THE ULTIMATE FEAR

Most of the fears that inhibit risk taking lead ultimately to a subconscious fear that people will emotionally or physically withdraw from us. As a consequence of taking a risk we imagine: "If I'm a failure, no one will love me"; "If I succeed, I'll be alone at the top"; or, "If others don't think well of me, they'll leave."

Few of us work in places that encourage talking about such fears, which helps to keep them repressed, although the subconscious fears continue influencing our attitudes and actions. An organization's interest in increasing risk taking is easier to articulate than to implement. Managers can encourage risk taking by understanding some common fears and learning how to overcome them.

ABANDONMENT FEARS

The abandonment fear is manifested in superficial ways unique to each individual. I, for instance, am not a "car person," so the fear of losing my Honda, though inconvenient, is not foremost in my mind. I do not lock my car nor, unfortunately, do I wash it much. You, on the other hand, might care a lot about cars, evidenced by the fact that you drive a Porsche. You have your car, dripping with accessories, washed and waxed and you always lock it. The thought of anything that increases the risk of losing the vehicle makes your stomach churn. Even if our cars are of equal value and we decide to bet them on something, the risk would be different for each of us.

Richard E. Byrd, in his book, *Guide to Personal Risk Taking*, addresses four types of fear that keep us from taking risks: fear of failure, fear of success (related to fear of failure), fear of what others will think, and fear of uncertainty. While it is clear that these fears are real, one can ask, "So what if you do fail or if others don't approve of you?" The fear of being cast aside or becoming somehow invisible can leave a person feeling psychologically immobilized. Taking a closer look at these typical risk-taking personalities and how a manager might coach them helps foster healthy risk-taking behavior.

FEAR OF FAILURE

Picture Carl, the overly careful manager known for his steady, if not static, approach to his work. He likes to keep a low organizational profile which results in little organizational influence for either himself or his work group. He is routinely turned down on requests for additions to staff, development and capital expense monies or raises. He doesn't ask much anymore.

Carl's focus is on his people, and he becomes too involved in their work, rather than associating with his peers and supervisors. His response to problem solving is maintaining the status quo. He prides himself on treating everyone equally, according to the rules, without taking the risk of interpreting rules to make room for individual differences or motivational needs.

If Carl is criticized or confronted by anyone for his lack of vision or leadership in the organization, he reacts defensively, exhibits hostility and, ultimately, becomes depressed. Consequently, people don't criticize Carl much.

Carl is afraid of failure. Opportunities present themselves constantly for personal risk taking and Carl retreats to what he feels he does well.

None of us like to fail, but some people have an excessive fear of failure that all but immobilizes them. Such a person is a perfectionist who internalizes failure and believes that the source of failure comes from within the self. The results are brutal self-punishment and severe limitations on the kinds of risks taken. Risk-taking opportunities are perceived as sources of anxiety instead of interesting, if not exciting, challenges.

FEAR OF SUCCESS

Joan has done very well as a middle manager. She is a young, fast-track performer who started with the company five years ago upon completion of her MBA. Within two years, she was promoted to the position she now holds because she was bright, dynamic, creative, and had excellent leadership skills. She started a new management function and gave it visibility and credibility. In her three years in the position, Joan added three staff people and pulled them together as a strong credible team.

Now Joan is poised on the brink of applying for a job that would be a big break into top management. Suddenly, however, she feels ambivalent and full of self-doubt. She postpones revamping her resume and begins to fantasize about a dream given up long ago to be an interior designer.

Chances are Joan is experiencing some fear of success and is engaging in avoidance behavior. Paradoxically, fear of success is the flip side of fear of failure. The difference is that the more successful one is, the more visibility one has. Success, while seductive and attractive, tends to isolate people. The successful person is set apart. Putting people on a pedestal is unfortunate for two reasons: it's a long way to fall and it creates the opportunity for many people to watch the fall.

FEAR OF WHAT OTHERS WILL THINK

Jim is the picture of ambition, a bright young executive whose entire life is consumed with being promoted and working himself up the organizational ladder. What others think is extraordinarily important.

Therefore, organizational norms are followed exactly. Jim works Saturday mornings and Wednesday evenings voluntarily because his boss works extra hours at that time. His pin-striped suits and tasteful ties are appropriately conservative and corporate. He displays all the proper journals prominently so that people entering his office will note them.

Jim is careful to tell people what he thinks they want to hear. He suggests pragmatic solutions to problems that seem obvious to most people, and his suggestions lack creativity.

We all like to have others think well of us. For some of us, however, what others think becomes what we think of ourselves. The risk of losing the favor or approval of others can be threatening and, if not a major crisis, at least an identity crisis of sorts.

FEAR OF UNCERTAINTY

Miriam has everything under control at work and she wants no surprises. She needs to know at all times that her staff is productive and follows the rules, so she discreetly checks the attendance log and disciplines lack of punctuality. Miriam prides herself on how much she delegates. Her method is to assign a lot of work and then make all decisions with her staff on their assignments. This helps her monitor the staff and keep her involved. She prefers to work with concrete issues.

Miriam is vaguely discontent in her position, which she has had for ten years. She has not sought another position because she feels comfortable and secure, even though a little bored at times. She will continue, as so many others, to use institutionalized norms (policy and procedures, bureaucratic channels, etc.) to feel safe in rejecting anything that might hint of change and, thus, a need to take a risk. Her dominant fear is not so much failure as it is being unsure of outcomes. Hence, anything that suggests an unknown creates intense anxiety because it presents the possibility of lessened control.

It has been said that it is not change we fear as much as the loss of control associated with change. When we lose control and feel we cannot manage our lives, we react with anxiety, depression, loss of confidence and a host of other equally uncomfortable feelings. Taking a chance on something means that the outcome is ambiguous and not completely known. We are leaving familiar territory and crossing a bridge to a new place.

For some, ambiguity is so intolerably painful that fear inhibits approaching bridges. Others do approach and shake and quiver as they cross. People like Miriam, who cannot tolerate ambiguity, will have difficulty taking risks.

Telling employees that you are going to take risks encourages them to do the same. It is imperative that they understand what you are doing so your behavior change doesn't trigger paranoia. Begin by identifying smaller, less threatening risks, then work up to larger ones.

MODELING

Numerous studies show the strong impact of managerial modeling on subordinate behavior. Subordinates take cues from their peers; from subordinates, if they have any; and, most importantly, from their bosses. If a manager wishes to increase risk taking among subordinates, the place to start is by demonstrating consistent risk-taking behavior and an attitude acceptance of personal failures.

Visualization is an effective way to model behavior. As a manager, it is important to demonstrate that you prepare yourself for successful risks by focusing on the positive outcomes of what you want. You may want to suggest that subordinates concentrate intensely on the desired end product.

Try to imagine yourself giving that speech to the vice presidents in a poised and confident manner, with all the facts at your disposal. Urge subordinates to use this vision as a meditation exercise several times a day. The goal is to help the fearful risk taker focus on positive results rather than on self-defeating, negative results.

ENCOURAGING THE POSITIVE

For Carl, whose risk-taking initiative is impeded by fear of failure, suggest that he raise his profile, make better working alliances with peers and reduce involvement with subordinates. Carl might be resistant and need to talk through his fears and concerns at first. Encourage him to do so.

When he is through, begin focusing on the positive results that would come from a new assignment. The objective is for Carl to begin realizing what can be gained rather than lost. This activity may need to be repeated over and over again.

It is crucially important for Carl's manager to be patient and understanding while continuing to draw out the benefits to be gained from new endeavors.

ACCEPTING MISTAKES AND FEARS

A manager should avoid tapping fear of failure, concern over what others think, and uncertainty. Once a subordinate is encouraged to take a risk, be supportive and available without hovering.

With Joan and her fear of success, identifying and defusing fears are important. The manager should also empathize and remind her that, no matter what happens, she is supported. "Joan, you're a very capable professional and I know you're going to do well in that position. But, let's play out the worst that could happen.

"If you didn't do so well, that would be no reflection on you as a person and I'd still think you were the greatest. I'm here for you in whatever way will be helpful." This encourages Joan, articulates the worst possibility and lets her know that she will not be abandoned. Joan's manager should follow up by helping her to focus on the positive.

PROVIDING A NON-PUNITIVE ENVIRONMENT

The environment that encourages risk taking is non-punitive; mistakes are acceptable and not punished. When mistakes are punished or there is the threat of punishment, risk taking is minimal. Jim, who fears what others will think, is extremely vulnerable to the displeasure of others and will go to any length to avoid it. This, of course, robs him of his creativity and individuality. Jim's manager needs to encourage Jim to express his own opinions and to begin trusting himself to take risks rather than parroting what he thinks people want to hear. The manager needs to be accepting of Jim's actions, praising what he has done right and minimizing what he has done wrong. This does not mean that Jim's mistakes will be ignored. Rather, the emphasis will be on what he did right.

The manager who wishes to encourage risk-taking behavior needs to be non-punitive in both behavior and attitude. Attitudinally, the manager needs to accept that the risks subordinates have been encouraged to take might not turn out successfully. Applaud the attempt and do not focus on the failure. This means that managers' fears and anxieties about failure, which might include how subordinates' failures will reflect on him or her, must be defused so they do not extend into the relationship with subordinates.

In essence, it is important for the manager to demonstrate trust in the subordinate while helping the employee take risks appropriate to his abilities and organizational realities. Clearly, some will adamantly resist any attempt at encouraging risk taking. Refusal must be evaluated in the broad context of individual performance, and either be accepted or pursued with further action.

If some form of abandonment is an overriding fear, it seems important for those who are taking risks to develop a support system within the environment where the risk is being taken. Managers have a primary relationship with subordinates and the opportunity for enormous impact in changing behavior. However, the managerial relationship is not enough. The individual needs to create an environment where these changes and challenges will be supported. The objective is to prove to ourselves that we will not be alone in our venture, nor will people disappear when things don't work out.

PLACE YOUR BETS

When attempting to increase risk-taking ability, ask, "What do you stand to lose?" A house, a car, a job, a loved one, your pride, certainty?

Or you might stand to lose more than you could gain and decide not to risk. The biggest fear is usually the fear itself, the result of a lifetime habit of letting fear get too big and being controlled by it. The fears may never go away but they can be accepted, managed and defused by understanding them and learning to work through them.

Learning to take appropriate risks is a complex behavior related to self-esteem, confidence, the ability to make good choices and to personal philosophies and values. These and other components form a system reflecting socio-emotional health. Interestingly enough, like any system, it can be changed by changing one of its parts. By focusing on risk taking, people can be encouraged to engage in behaviors that increase self-confidence, self-esteem and require changing some attitudes about themselves and others in order to become healthier and more productive.

Taking risks is synonymous with life and growth. It is by taking risks that we learn to test ourselves and come to understand what we can do. Most of us grow and develop by reaching further than we thought we could. The job that once seemed overwhelming now seems routine; the peer whose behavior we confronted is now our closest ally; the challenging financial goals we set for ourselves, we met. These risks forced us to try new behavior and allowed us to discover more about ourselves.

Some people naturally take risks more freely because their self-confidence helps them perceive risks as challenges. Others need to be pushed and supported to develop the confidence for accepting risks more easily.

The manager as a mentor and coach can play a unique role in encouraging and supporting risk taking. Managers can use the knowledge gained from understanding abandonment fears and how they influence behavior to model desired behavior, to help subordinates identify fears and to provide support and guidance as the employee begins to experiment with new, risk-taking behaviors.

Suzanne Sisson is an organizational consultant in Minneapolis, Minnesota.

28.
THE TRICKLE DOWN THEORY: MOTIVATION STARTS AT THE TOP

Frank C. Drazan

> Motivation in the minds of some of the gurus of modern psychology shows an inverted pyramid with the top focused down, bringing forces to bear to motivate Mr. or Ms. Producing Worker

Motivation is the hottest topic in management today and has been for the last 10 years. At a conference that I attended recently, the main speaker was a doctor of psychology who spoke on people motivation. I listened to the usual party line: togetherness, keep the dialog open, communicate, etc., etc.—all of those great things that will work wonders with reluctant workers who are non-producing cogs in the machine.

WHO NEEDS MOTIVATING?

The most interesting aspect of the usual talk on motivation is that the direction is always down to the lowest-level employee. Rarely is the unmotivated manager mentioned. A basic assumption is made that all managers become totally motivated when they assume the role of boss or director or whatever. Nothing is further from the truth. Unmotivated, stick-in-the-mud, don't-rock-the-boat managers are legion in industry.

Anyone who has observed the scene in management for the last 10 to 20 years is aware that the most popular, upwardly mobile managers are those who carry the mantle of authority but exercise their options rarely, if ever, and tend to go along with existing procedures. The catchphrase for promotions is "don't make waves." One of the most prevalent concepts subscribed to by the current crop of MBAs is to "play the game"; tell them what they want to hear and move up the ladder. Gamesmanship is a most highly prized talent.

That being the case, if the majority of these upwardly mobile types are in place, stagnation of any company is assured. The logical solution, then, is often sought in the area of people motivation. What is universally overlooked is that workers are not unproductive because of a lack of motivation; they are unproductive because of uninvolved leadership, non-productive conditions, unresponsive managers, poorly maintained equipment, poor or no instructions, unrealistic goals, obsolete tools and machines, poor working conditions, hostile environments, poor raw materials, and an incongruous job mix with unqualified people doing the jobs.

Some may argue that many of these are motivational problems, and indeed they are, but a major factor here is that each of these problem areas is the responsibility of a manager, requiring management actions and reactions. None of these problems are within the control of the worker.

THE BUCK PASSES HERE

The real question here is how do we raise productivity and quality? It's really quite simple: managers must quit searching for a fall guy to take the blame and start doing the job of managing. In its simplest terms, the basic duty of any manager at any level is to provide the means to get the job done. This includes providing tools, training, materials, methods and environments to get the job done. Along with those basics the manager must provide goals, standards, and targets to be met.

Often a worker is put into the position of pounding a one-pound nail with a two-ounce hammer . . . and being pushed to increase productivity.

The core questions a manager must ask himself or herself include: What's wrong with the system, or machine, or method, or training, or facilities that prevents maximum efficiency? Having identified the problem areas, the next step is correction. That's where the rub is. If the first line manager initiates actions to make improvements, the dollar signs go up and more often than not our new hero finds himself rocking the boat. Unfortunately, the boat will frequently continue to rock until the entire operation goes down the tube.

The dilemma a first line manager faces is three-dimensional. His first challenge is to monitor and expedite the administrative and personnel functions of supervision. His task is to develop methods and procedures needed to improve the operation; and he or she must fit into the existing managerial structure without creating problems.

Creating problems covers a multitude of areas. You create problems by asking for money for improvements. You create problems by identifying flaws in existing conditions. The simple concept of change creates problems in many areas.

Motivation in the minds of some of the gurus of modern psychology shows an inverted pyramid with the top focused down, bringing forces to bear to motivate Mr. or Ms. Producing Worker. Actually, the pyramid should be righted, putting the worker on top with all of the forces of management in a supporting role. Having done that, your motivation problems should be over. If in doubt, see Lee Iacocca at Ford Motor Co.

Consider this: In Chrysler's case, one motivated manager on top reshaped an entire company. Isn't it easier to motivate one person than a thousand? Finally, one must realize that motivation and productivity are not man-on-the-line problems. They are man-on-top problems.

Frank C. Drazan is print quality specialist, Graphic Systems Division, Rockwell International Corporation.

29.
BOSSES: DON'T BE NASTY (AND OTHER TIPS FOR REVIEWING A WORKER'S PERFORMANCE)

Carol Hymowitz

> A majority of employees believe their bosses botch reviews of their work, if they give them at all.

Richard Dugan has learned a lot about appraising an employee's performance since a staff member broke down in tears under his criticism. "I've really botched this," he recalls thinking.

Mr. Dugan, managing partner of Arthur Young & Co.'s Pittsburgh office, says it took a long time for him to learn how to give "helpful criticism without being nasty." Now he says he isn't afraid to tell an unsatisfactory performer, "'You'll have to do this and this to succeed here or you should perhaps consider another kind of work.' It's my obligation to give guidance. And most employees don't want a nice guy, they want to know where they stand."

A majority of employees believe their bosses botch appraisals of their work, if they give reviews at all. Psychological Associates, Inc., of St. Louis, surveying 4,000 employees at 190 companies recently, found that 70 percent believed review sessions hadn't given a clear picture of what was expected of them on the job or to where they could advance in the company. Only half said their bosses helped them set job objectives, and only one in five said reviews were followed up during the ensuing year.

HANDLING FEAR

"It's a tough job, the equivalent of walking up to a person and saying, 'Here's what I think of your baby,'" says Robert Lefton, president of Psychological Associates, a consulting company that has provided training—on how to give reviews—to over 100 large companies. "It requires knowing how to handle fear and anger and a gamut of other emotions, which a lot of managers aren't comfortable with," he adds.

Increasingly managers must do a better job of appraising employees, not only to help employees mature but also to increase productivity and company loyalty. Comprehensive performance reviews also reduce the chance that a fired employee who has been warned of unsatisfactory performance will sue the company.

Employees have a right to expect a performance review at least once a year, personnel experts say. A manager should listen to an employee's self-appraisal before offering his own evaluation, then give a balanced picture of the employee's strengths and weaknesses, discuss differences and offer specific suggestions on how to improve. And he or she should work with the employee to develop goals.

These guidelines are simple enough and yet often forgotten by managers in the thick of a review. Mr. Lefton of Psychological Associates recalls observing a chief executive who talked nonstop for three hours to a senior manager during a review. Then he turned to Mr. Lefton and said, "Aren't we having a great exchange?"

Before doing reviews, managers must analyze their styles of confrontation, Mr. Lefton believes. Some managers take a "let me tell you" approach, imposing their own ideas without regard to subordinates. Others mechanically go through the paces of a review but their underlying message is that discussing performance can't make a difference and they offer no solid information to employees. And then there are managers who say, "Gee, everything is great," and avoid all problems.

Bosses admit they are often reluctant to criticize an employee's work. "You don't want to inflict pain," says an executive of a Midwestern manufacturing company. She agonized for weeks about what to say to one employee who was "technically excellent but threw temper tantrums and was obnoxious to work with."

Anxious to avoid a fight, she finally gave the employee a choice. "I told him 'You will have to change the way you behave, or, if that's difficult for you or you don't want to change, I'll give you a severance package.'" He chose the severance.

Other managers must tackle employees who won't listen to criticism. When Bob Reass, manager of strategic operations in sales at Monsanto Co., told an employee to better manage his own subordinates, the employee became angry and the review session turned into a screaming match.

Mr. Reass suggested a "cooling-off period," which proved the best solution. When he reconvened the review session several days later, the disgruntled employee apologized.

Marilyn Moats Kennedy, managing partner of Career Strategies, a management-consulting company in Wilmette, Ill., says it's important to critique the behavior of an employee, not the employee himself.

"If you bark, 'You have a bad attitude,' to your receptionist, for example, you'll likely find yourself facing a very defensive employee. You'll probably get better results if you say, 'When someone steps up to your desk, I'd like them to get the distinct impression that you're delighted to see them.'"

Of the outstanding employee who has one minor flaw, such as repeatedly missing staff meetings, experts say don't ignore the problem. Instead, they say, confront the employee in a positive way ("I'm concerned about this"), state the consequences ("The group isn't getting your views"), and then ask for help ("What can we do about this?").

Reviews shouldn't contain many surprises, such as springing new standards on employees, says Jerome Abarbanel, manager of organization and management development at General Electric Co.'s Credit Corp. unit. A GE manager in one case planned to give an employee who did outstanding work only a satisfactory performance rating because he asked too many questions. But Mr. Abarbanel says that rating would be unfair unless the employee knew in advance how much his boss valued independence.

Personnel experts also have tips for what not to do during a review: don't try to become a therapist to employees with marital, drinking, or other personal problems. Instead, refer those employees to programs within the company or to outside help.

It's also best not to discuss salaries during reviews, they say. For one thing, whether or not an employee gets a raise often depends not only on his performance but also on the financial condition of the company, on the economy, and on wages paid by competitors.

When Monsanto Co., years ago, tied compensation to a structured review process in which employees set their own goals, "We found it didn't work," says Mr. Reass. Employees, afraid to set goals they couldn't meet, instead set easy-to-reach goals. "We found we were sealing our own mediocrity," he says.

Often the most helpful advice an employee can receive during a performance appraisal has to do with his personal standing in the company. Mr. Reass at Monsanto says he is still grateful to a boss who criticized his style of speech. A native New Yorker, Mr. Reass says he has "a Brooklyn accent that comes on strong when I'm under pressure or am tired." His boss told him: "Watch that accent of yours. It doesn't go across well in this Midwestern company."

Carol Hymowitz is a staff reporter for The Wall Street Journal.

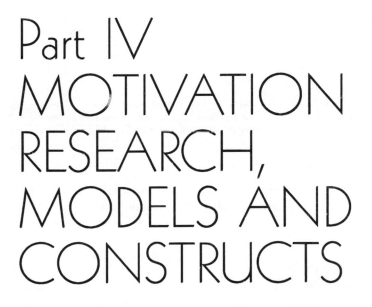

Part IV
MOTIVATION RESEARCH, MODELS AND CONSTRUCTS

30.
MOTIVATING BY STRATEGY

Warren Lamb

The top management personality affects both company strategy and its implementation. Managers may be oriented toward either "attending", "intending," or "committing": the personality orientation must work for the strategy, not against it.

Corporate culture and the nature of the environment have emerged as key issues in today's management of strategy. Culture is usually defined as some form of shared values, beliefs, and behavior, and diagnosing and understanding culture in a company should logically be an essential prerequisite to formulating strategy. How to do this remains vague, however; little has been published on the dynamics of culture creation.

Any corporate culture must have been created by people; and it will be nurtured, developed, and changed by those most intimately bound up with the company's character. Naturally enough, the greatest influences are likely to be the top executives, more particularly the chief executive. A culture, however deep its roots in tradition, is not something fixed. It has its own changing individuality, which to a great extent can be molded by a powerful man at the top.

One way of understanding the personal influence which a strong chief executive can exert on the formulation of strategy and, more important, on its implementation, is to examine how he acts. This means observing what initiatives he actually takes, as distinct from the actions he talks about.

There is probably no need to make out a case for suggesting that what an executive says he will do and what he actually does are two different things, even if he is completely sincere.

Suppose it were possible to follow an executive around for, say, six months and log all the initiatives he took. Matching them to a simple decision-making model would reveal that he took more of one type of initiative than another. A scheme like that used for "action profiling" would be suitable. It would postulate that decision-making requires initiative to act in three distinct stages. The first is the initiative of "attending": *e.g.*, let's define what we mean, let's survey, analyze, study, research. The second is the initiative of "intending": *e.g.*, let's make happen what we want to happen, let's have control, discipline, purpose.

Finally, there is "committing": *e.g.*, go/no go, take the opportunity, buy/sell, sign, spend the money.

Finding any one individual who takes equal initiative at all three stages of the decision-making process must be rare. In most cases, there is a definite orientation towards one of the three stages. Take three chief executives, A, B, and C, oriented, respectively, toward attending, intending and committing. Their differing influence might work like this.

A, the "attending" manager, will formulate strategies tending to take the company into new fields for which no precedent exists; in implementing these strategies, he will be remorselessly thorough in following plans, and always ready to respond to research findings. On the other hand, the "intending" executive will wish to build strategically on what is already most strongly established in company activity. In the implementation stage, his strong sense of mission will show through in a disciplined adherence to basic beliefs, together with a refusal to give up. The "committing" manager C, however, will draw up strategies for exploiting opportunities indicated by available resources. His aim in putting these strategies into practice will be to set the pace in order to be ahead of the competition.

Such influences are not, of course, the sole factor; many other variables have to be taken into account. But few realize the extent to which A, B, and C will influence strategy formulation and implementation because of their personal orientation—as distinct from their background, experience, or application of professionally applied procedures for strategic planning.

When tackled on the subject, A, B, and C are likely to retort that their initiatives are dictated by circumstances. This is only partly true. The scope available to a powerful chief executive to make his personal reading of the circumstances is immense. To a great extent, he is the creator of the environment, the setting in which the economic, financial, and social circumstances of the company are read. A, B, and C, as chief executives, will create different environments. The same circumstances will be read differently by each.

The following example is typical of many experiments which appear to show that executives are highly predictable in their personal readings of circumstances. A group of 12 hotel executives, irrespective of their roles, were divided into three groups of four according to their most obvious motivational characteristic. Each group was asked to "appoint a group leader to report back on initiatives which your company can take for an improved strategy on security."

The report of group A, the "attending" managers, included 27 definitions of different kinds and types of security and of the company's responsibility. Through the spokesman, the group recommended that the company set up a research group to go into the topic thoroughly and report back after three months.

On behalf of the "intending" group B, the spokesman immediately declared one main conclusion: A security manager should be appointed forthwith at each of the company's hotels. He went on to define the function and its authority, noting down the points of disagreement.

Group C offered two recommendations. In line with its "committing" orientation, both could be put into immediate effect. It suggested that a new, recently introduced staff training scheme should include measures to educate all staff on how to handle security needs; and that the current building and conversion program be reviewed with the aim of introducing improved protection measures wherever possible.

Clearly, the strategy for handling security will differ notably, depending on the composition of each group. Irrespective of their roles, backgrounds, intelligence, or capabilities, the three groups created distinctly different environments which affected the kind of strategy selected. So, too, top executives are to some extent the makers of the circumstances in which they operate, particularly in the private sector.

EFFECT OF PERSONALITY

Professor Abraham Zaleznik has reportedly caused some consternation among colleagues teaching business strategy at Harvard Business School by claiming, contrary to the main thrust of current teaching wisdom, that a company's success is determined more by the personality of its executives than by its organization. He goes on to stress that "The person in charge is the instrument through which loyalties build and morale gets created and people are motivated."

Top executives and consultants who use action profiling have now built up many years of experience in using the concept of a three-stage, decision-making process to understand that aspect of personality which is relevant to business planning. Executives are profiled not just for their attending, intending, and committing orientation, but for the total pattern-making of their initiatives. The concept can be refined *ad infinitum*. The first grade of refinement isolates two inter-relating initiatives at each of the stages in decision-making, from which it is possible to show what happens when some initiatives are emphasized at the cost of others.

Thus, at the attending stage, the *investigating* initiative deals with the question, "Have we sufficiently probed and analyzed the information currently available to make a valid contribution to the planning process?" while the *exploring* initiative asks: "Have we looked at alternatives, ideas, diversifications, new discoveries, to gain a full appreciation of the scope available?"

At the intending phase, the inter-related initiatives are *determining*: "Are we sufficiently controlled and strong-willed to do what we say we are going to do or make happen what we want to happen?" and *evaluating*: "Have we crystallized what is important to us for the company's future well-being and what our needs really are?"

Finally, at the committing stage, there is the *timing* initiative: "Are we able to set the pace of competition, tactically seize opportunities, and succeed by operational flair?" and the *anticipating* initiative: "Do we conceive strategy as readiness to take decisions as an outcome of existing trends and according to a plan which is constantly being updated?"

So far as it is possible for an ordinary member of the public to judge, Margaret Thatcher appears to lean heavily towards the *evaluating* type of initiatives, taking many more of them than any of the others. She is starkly black/white about what she believes right/wrong, good/bad, realistic/fanciful. Lord Wilson, to use a contrasting example, appeared to take fewer such initiatives when Prime Minister. He either left them to others or preferred to maintain a "shades of grey" approach, permitting him some flexibility in applying the preeminent tactical *timing* initiative for which he became well known.

One feature of the Thatcher Government, however, is a fairly high measure of consistency between how ministers act and the strategies which they claim to be following. This has not always been the case, nor is it true of many industrial companies. For example, in 1969 Hoover announced a strategy of diversification out of the domestic appliance market, within which it had leading positions in many parts of the world. The initiatives appropriate to acquiring companies in new fields, with little precedent in existing businesses, are *investigating* and *exploring*. Although top executives clearly had the ability to take such initiatives, they were oriented towards *determining*, *timing* and *anticipating*. Basically, this translates into the formula, "Let's apply our will and tactical operating flair to making the best of what we have got, setting objectives along the line of existing trends."

This subliminal conflict resulted in the company rejecting scores of acquisition propositions. In 1974, it was locked into the domestic appliance market quite as tightly as it had been in 1969. In view of the problems which then overtook the company, its executives might well have wished they had truly accomplished the diversification exercise.

The point, again, is not the correctness of the strategy as such, but the initiatives taken either to formulate or implement it. In the Hoover case, someone presumably persuaded the board to agree to a diversification strategy; but, predictably, the readiness to take the initiatives necessary to implement the strategy was not there. Around this period, other companies plunged into undisciplined diversification—perhaps they had an excess of exploring initiative—and suffered. Hoover might have been better off in the end by having failed to implement its strategy. Who knows?

But to declare a strategy and then act in a contradictory way is certainly bad leadership, working against the establishment of an environment within which (in Zaleznik's words), "loyalties build and morale gets created and people are motivated."

The strength of a top executive's motivation to act according to his inherent individual pattern of initiatives is much greater than is currently assumed. For example, a person who characteristically tends toward exploring initiatives will, if he or she has power, interpret, select, or perhaps distort available data to support a strategy of diversification going into unprecedented areas, experimentation, imaginative pursuits. If colleagues offer counter-arguments, they will be argued round. Even if the business climate is against such a policy, the explorer will still find ways and means to build in his predilections.

INHERENT CONTRADICTIONS

Clearly, the provision of finance, the agreement of colleagues and the availability of supporting technical advice are factors which will influence the top exploring executive. He may genuinely agree to a strategy of consolidation for a period. But very soon he will be taking initiatives of an exploratory nature. He finds no difficulty in justifying his initiatives on the grounds that new conditions have arisen. Market researchers are briefed to look for new avenues of investment, product developers are asked to be innovative, new people with new types of skills are taken on, all the time under a strategy of consolidation, which the manager still sincerely believes that he is implementing. Such contradictory leadership has damaging effects. The top executives cannot help but follow his action motivation, but he demotivates his people because of the inherent contradiction, which may be exacerbated by his very sincerity.

More than 10,000 action profiles have been drawn up over the past 30 years. While people change temperamentally, physically, attitudinally (and these changes can have a big influence), it does seem that the pattern of preferred initiatives remains fairly constant. The results are confirmed by the separately conducted research of J.W. Lorsch, another Harvard Business School professor, who claims that through all the vicissitudes of a person's career, "a pattern of enduring features" is maintained.

In another experiment, 12 top executives of a multinational company were divided into three groups according to action motivation. Group A consisted of three "attending" managers, whose preferred initiatives tended to be of an *investigating* and *exploring* nature. Group B, the four "intending" executives, showed, relatively, a lot of *determining* and *evaluating* initiative. In the five-strong Group C, in line with "committing orientation," *timing* and *anticipating* initiatives were at the fore. The groups were asked to "appoint a group leader to report on initiatives for improving inter-company transfers of personnel." In response, group A reported an unfinished discussion on the principles involved in moving people around the world, often into strange cultures, and with strain upon the family. Group B declared emphatically what should and should not be done, primarily the latter, and instanced transfers which it believed to be wrong. Group C came out with 33 quick-fire recommendations for steps to make inter-company transfers more acceptable, *e.g.*, serving food of different cultures in company canteens. Clearly, again, the composition of the group, irrespective of each executive's role, capability, training, or experience, greatly influences interpretation of responsibility and the action to be taken.

Another factor is at work whenever executives meet together. In both the hotel group and the multinational company, there was a strong incidence of readiness to share the respective initiatives. When this happens, people will reciprocate each other's initiatives, irrespective of their roles or whether they like each other. Individuals are usually more prepared to share their initiative at one stage of the process than at another. Sherlock Holmes is a good example of someone who obviously took a lot of investigating and exploring initiative in seeking the murderer, but shared none of it with his friend Watson. Only when he formed his intention or conclusion did he take the initiative to share: "Elementary, my dear Watson." The following case describes an executive of even greater independent propensity: he shared little of what he gave attention to or of the intentions he formed or even of his actual "committing."

This man was chief executive of a small U.S. company, which found a British purchaser. The acquisition was seen as a growth prospect which would spearhead the British firm's drive into the U.S. When the company was acquired, its chief executive was a lone entrepreneur. He seemed hard-working and capable and became very friendly with the chairman of the British parent. Although warned of his protege's "loner" tendencies, the chairman confirmed him in his position and decided to build a team around him. Within 30 months, seven senior executives of undoubted calibre had been appointed and had resigned.

Typical complaints were that they were never given vital information, were not allowed authority, and had decisions pre-empted. Yet they all insisted that they had nothing against the chief executive as a person.

They liked him, thought he had guts, and knew him to be a man of compassion and generosity in his private life. When challenged by a consultant on 27 separate incidents where he could have shared his initiative, the chief executive had an answer for every one. For example, his failure to give vital information to his vice president for marketing before an important exhibition was, "Better that he finds out for himself."

The point of the story, again, is not the correctness or otherwise of the chief executive's independent initiative. It has its place, in context. But the strategy imposed by the chairman completely failed to take into account the individual action motivation of the person on whom it most depended for its implementation. The cost to the British group involved has been immense.

When behavior contradicts strategy, there are basically two alternatives: change the strategy or change the people. The former is worth considering seriously, on the principle that, if you have a good chef, you open a restaurant. In other words, you build a strategy which is consistent with the strengths of the top management team. Alternatively, you appoint or develop top managers likely to act consistently with the strategy.

Managers responsible for the implementation of strategy often have an ambivalent role in relation to others who want a say in its formation, such as non-executive directors, shareholders' representatives, community representatives, or political leaders. A so-called consensus may be reached on a strategic plan; but the executives who do the implementing have a lot of scope to distort it, without deliberate intent to do so.

The process of implementation can be monitored against the strategic plan. Whenever and wherever contradictions emerge, much can be achieved by discovering what are the prevailing initiatives among the top executives, and to what degree the initiatives run counter to the strategy which those concerned thought they were implementing. As strategy implementation is a continuous process, subject to updating according to circumstances (*i.e.*, the executives' reading of circumstances), there is a lot of scope to build in new initiatives which are both potentially within the individual's capacity to change and within the design boundaries of the strategy.

Had it realized the built-in contradiction, Hoover could either have abandoned the diversification strategy earlier (and shifted to the consequent new strategy) or recognized that disciplined procedures were necessary to bring about consistent implementation. Even that can fail, so strong is the power of individual action motivation; but sometimes it works. The British group which acquired the U.S. company should have recognized that it could never effectively build a team around such an independent entrepreneur; it might then have structured him in a lone position, with someone else as general manager.

Those who advocate that major change is needed, if people are to keep up with the fast-moving pace of present-day events, have promoted a range of "change agent" techniques. There is a movement to convert the practice known as "organization development" to "organization transformation," for example. But the leopard does not change his spots. Human beings can only modify and develop their behavior within the strict confines of the personality which they possess. What will not change more than marginally is the action motivation of the individuals who have the power to put strategies into practice. That being the case, there is surely a strong argument for making certain that strategy and motivation in the key individuals coincide, that there is no conflict.

Warren Lamb is head of Warren Lamb Partnership, management consultants.

31.
TOWARD A THEORY OF
CAREER MOTIVATION

Manuel London

Career motivation is viewed as a multidimensional construct. Components consist of individual characteristics and corresponding career decisions and behaviors.

The term motivation often is used to explain decisions and behaviors that cannot be explained by ability alone. Motivation is concerned with the direction, arousal, amplitude, and persistence of an individual's behavior (Campbell & Pritchard, 1976). Work motivation is a construct that generally refers to motivation to do one's current job. The term managerial motivation refers to the desire to engage in and meet managerial role requirements, *e.g.*, exerting leadership, conducting routine administrative activities (Miner, 1977). These constructs are limited in scope, however, in that they do not reflect the many individual characteristics and associated decisions and behaviors relevant to one's career.

The term career motivation encompasses the terms work motivation and managerial motivation and goes further to include motivation associated with a wide range of career decisions and behaviors. These include searching for and accepting a job, deciding to stay with an organization, revising one's career plans, seeking training and new job experiences, and setting and trying to accomplish career goals. Career motivation is defined as the set of individual characteristics and associated career decisions and behaviors that reflect the person's career identity, insight into factors affecting his or her career, and resilience in the face of unfavorable career conditions. Career motivation should be understood in terms of the relationship among individual characteristics, career decisions and behaviors, and situational conditions. Several authors have pointed to the need for theoretical models linking these variables over time (Brousseau, 1983; Dubin 1976; Raynor, 1978). Toward this end, this paper begins to develop a theory of career motivation by outlining an integrative, holistic framework for understanding psychological and organizational career-related variables and processes.

CAREER MOTIVATION COMPONENTS

Career motivation is conceptualized here as a multi-dimensional construct internal to the individual, influenced by the situation, and reflected in the individual's decisions and behaviors. The variables relevant to career motivation form a set of dimensions clustered a priori into domains. The dimensions are neither independent nor necessarily exhaustive of all possible important constructs. Each domain is not intended to be a sum of its dimensions. The dimensions support and extend the meaning of the domain and are likely to vary in importance to the domain. Each individual characteristic associated with career motivation corresponds to a situational characteristic and a career decision or behavior.

INDIVIDUAL CHARACTERISTICS

The individual characteristic dimensions are needs, interests, and personality variables potentially relevant to a person's career. These dimensions are clustered into three domains: career identity, career insight, and career resilience. The dimensions comprising these domains were derived from work on personality and individual assessments (Bray, 1982; Bray, Campbell, & Grant, 1974; Murray, 1938). Career identity reflects the direction of career motivation; career insight and resilience reflect the arousal, strength, and persistence of career motivation. Some of the dimensions (e.g., need advancement and commitment to managerial work) are most applicable to managers in hierarchical organizations.

Additional dimensions may have to be developed for studying career motivation in other contexts. Many of the dimensions, however, are very general (e.g., self-esteem, risk taking tendency, adaptability, self-objectivity) and are applicable to many types of occupations as well as to other areas of life. Each of the three domains and their dimensions are described below.

Career Identity. This is how central one's career is to one's identity. Career identity consists of two subdomains: work involvement and desire for upward mobility. Work involvement dimensions, which should be positively related to career identity, include job involvement, professional orientation, commitment to managerial work, and identification with the organization. Also, individuals who are high on career identity are likely to find career satisfaction to be more important than satisfaction from other areas of life (primacy of work).

The upward mobility subdomain includes the needs for advancement, recognition, dominance, and money. It also includes ability to delay gratification, which should be negatively related to desire for upward mobility.

Career Insight. This is the extent to which the person has realistic perceptions of him or herself and the organization and relates these perceptions to career goals. Goal flexibility and need change should be inversely related to career insight. Other relevant dimensions (goal clarity, path goal clarity, social perceptiveness, self-objectivity, realism of expectations, career decision making, and future time orientation) should be positively related to career insight.

Career Resilience. This is a person's resistance to career disruption in a less than optimal environment. To understand the meaning of career resilience more clearly, it should help to have a conception of its opposite: career vulnerability. This is the extent of psychological fragility (*e.g.*, becoming upset and finding it difficult to function) when confronted by less than optimal career conditions (*e.g.*, barriers to career goals, uncertainty, poor relationships with co-workers). Being high on career resilience (low on career vulnerability) does not mean that the person is insensitive to such environmental conditions, but rather that he or she will be able to cope more effectively with a negative work situation.

The dimensions under career resilience fall into three subdomains. One is self-efficacy, which includes the dimensions of self-esteem, need autonomy, adaptability, internal control, need achievement, initiative, need creativity, inner work standards, and development orientation. Another subdomain is risk taking, including risk taking tendency, fear of failure, need security, and tolerance of uncertainty and ambiguity. The third subdomain is dependency. This includes career dependency, need for superior approval, and need for peer approval. It also includes competitiveness, which should be negatively related to the other dependency dimensions.

Individuals will be more resilient the higher they are on the self-efficacy and risk taking dimensions and the lower they are on the dependency dimensions. Those low on career resilience are likely to be motivated to avoid risk, be dependent on others, seek structure, and avoid situations in which organizational outcomes depend on their behavior. Those high on career resilience are likely to do the reverse—take risks, be independent of others, create their own structure, and thrive on situations in which outcomes are contingent on their behavior.

Thus, career motivation is not a unidimensional construct but a set of variables, whose dimensions do not necessarily encompass all relevant individual characteristics; nor are the dimensions meant to be orthogonal. Furthermore, the grouping of dimensions into domains is theoretical at this point. Research will be necessary to refine and extend the dimensions, derive more coherent domains, and consider interactions among the dimensions. Table 1 lists and defines the individual characteristic dimensions and domains and should serve as a resource for identifying relevant variables for psychological research on careers and for suggesting how a given variable fits into a vector of related variables.

SITUATIONAL VARIABLES

Many elements of a person's work environment are likely to be important to career motivation. These include staffing policies and procedures, leadership style, job design, group cohesiveness, career development programs, and the compensation system, to name a few. (For the sake of parsimony, situational variables applying only to the work organization are presented. They could be extended to include nonwork variables.)

Table 1 links the individual characteristic dimensions of career motivation to situational characteristics. For example, career identity should be associated with the extent to which work attributes, such as the importance of one's job to the organization, contribute to one's self-image (career identity press). Career insight should be related to the amount of career information and guidance supplied by the organization (support for career development). Career resilience should be associated with variables reflecting the organization's strength and support. Conversely, career vulnerability should be associated with the degree of ambiguity, conflict, and uncertainty in the organization (organizational stress). Each of the situational characteristics should be viewed as a continuum that may vary from low to high at different times.

CAREER DECISIONS AND BEHAVIORS

Career decisions and behaviors include generating alternative courses of action, seeking information about them, evaluating the information, setting goals, making decisions to behave in various ways, and carrying out the decisions. The processes of setting career goals and making career decisions are cognitive but are manifest in observable actions.

Career decisions and behaviors may be linked to the individual and situational characteristics. This idea is captured in Table 1 in a set of behavioral dimensions. For instance, career identity should be related to giving up something of value for one's career (demonstrating career identification). Career insight should be related to seeking career information and setting career goals (career planning). Career vulnerability should be associated with increased absenteeism, task avoidance, and symptoms of stress (decreasing effectiveness).

Although each dimension outlined in Table 1 is conceptually distinct, overlap among dimensions is likely. For instance, career planning is relevant to several behavioral dimensions.

A CAREER MOTIVATION MODEL

One way to view career motivation is that it affects what will happen, or what a person hopes will happen, in the future. Career decisions and behaviors are guided by the outcomes that are desired and one's expectations for attaining them. This is known as prospective rationality (O'Reilly & Caldwell, 1981). Another view, compatible with the first, is that career decisions, behaviors, and situational conditions affect how one interprets the environment and one's psychological state. This is known as retrospective rationality (Salancik & Pfeffer, 1978). Although some individual characteristics may be quite stable, evolving during one's early life and supported by fairly consistent situational conditions, other dimensions are more sensitive to the environment. The level and importance of an individual characteristic to career decisions and behaviors will depend on the salience of different situational variables and their stability over time. The processes of prospective and retrospective rationality provide a basis for understanding the relationships among individual, situational, and behavioral variables associated with career motivation. These are general processes that may apply to other facets of life in addition to careers.

PROSPECTIVE RATIONALITY

This approach holds that choice processes are "based on a search for and use of information that allows the decision maker to form rational expectations about how good or bad the alternatives are likely to be" (O'Reilly & Caldwell, 1981, p. 598). Inferior information, misperceptions, or inaccurate interpretation of information may result in poor decisions and/or inappropriate or dysfunctional behaviors. Prospective rationality assumes that objective differences in organizations, jobs, and individuals account for variations in career decisions and behaviors.

Expectancy theory of work motivation provides an example of prospective rationality assumptions. The theory focuses on cognitions or expectancies of various outcomes and on the extent to which the outcomes are valued by the individual (Vroom, 1964). The assumption is that people cognitively combine information to determine maximally beneficial alternatives and then direct their behavior in a way most likely to achieve those alternatives (Staw, 1981). (See Naylor, Pritchard, & Ilgen, 1981, for a recent elaboration of this approach.)

Content theories of motivation focus on the needs, interests, and values people try to achieve (Campbell, Dunnette, Lawler, & Welck, 1970). These theories, exemplified by the work of Murray (1938), Maslow (1954), and Herzberg (1966), also assume prospective rationality in that they specify what an individual will try to achieve in the future.

RETROSPECTIVE RATIONALITY

This process begins with the idea that people spend much more time with the consequences of their actions and decisions than they spend contemplating

Table 1: Career Motivation Variables

Individual Characteristics	Situational Characteristics**	Career Decisions and Behavior***
DOMAIN I: Career Identity—how central one's career is to one's identity	Career Identity Press—work elements, such as importance of one's job, contribute to self-image	Career Identification—establishing career plans, giving up something of value for one's career, etc.
Work involvement subdomain: Job Involvement—interest in and satisfaction from one's current job	*Encouragement of involvement subdomain:* Job Challenge—the job's skill variety, autonomy, significance, etc.	*Work involvement subdomain:* Demonstrating Job Involvement—working long hours; recommending the work to others
Professional Orientation—identification with an area of specialization	Encouragement of Professionalism—support for involvement in professional activities, others in organization are professionally oriented, etc.	Professional Behavior—enhancing one's prestige in the profession, describing oneself as a professional rather than as an employee of the organization
Commitment to Managerial Work*—preference for managerial work compared to other types of work	Importance of Managing—emphasis on managerial roles (e.g., status and level of responsibility)	Managerial Striving—using and improving managerial skills; setting career goals aimed at managerial positions
Identification with the Organization—how central the organization is to one's identity	Press for Organizational Commitment—value of inducements (e.g., salary, pension) for individual contributions (e.g., good performance, staying with the organization)	Demonstrating Organizational Commitment—staying with the organization; investing in it; describing oneself as an employee of the organization

Primacy of Work*—satisfaction derived from one's career compared to other areas of life	Work Priority—intrinsic value of job and career compared to nonwork activities	Showing Devotion to Work—sacrificing non-work activities and responsibilities for work (e.g., relocating one's family, working overtime)
Desire for upward mobility domain: Need Advancement*—need to be promoted	Opportunities and rewards subdomain: Advancement Opportunities—the value of, and opportunities for, advancement	Desire for upward mobility subdomain: Striving for Advancement—furthering advancement possibilities (e.g., establishing a career path, requesting to be considered for promotion)
Need Recognition—need to be appreciatively acknowledged	Potential for Recognition—opportunities for recognition (e.g., through regular appraisal feedback, visible work)	Seeking Recognition—attracting attention (e.g., volunteering for important assignment, communicating work results to higher management)
Need Dominance—need to lead and direct	Leadership Opportunities—opportunities to assume leadership roles	Trying to Lead—requesting and assuming leadership roles
Financial Motivation—need to make money	Potential for Monetary Gain—value of, and opportunities for, financial rewards	Striving for Money—requesting a raise, changing jobs for a higher paying position, etc.
Ability to Delay Gratification*—willingness to wait for promotion and other career rewards (negatively related to desire for upward mobility)	Advancement Controls—time and experience requirements for promotion, salary increases, leadership opportunities, etc.	Accepting Slow Progress—not taking action to increase one's progress even when others are progressing faster

* Based on management assessment center dimensions (Bray, 1982; Bray et al., 1974).

** Relationships to the individual characteristic in the row are hypothesized to be positive.

Table 1: Career Motivation Variables (cont'd)

Individual Characteristics	*Situational Characteristics***	*Career Decisions and Behavior***
DOMAIN II: Career Insights—realistic perceptions of oneself and the organization and relating this to career goals	Support for Career Development—career information and guidance	Career Planning—seeking career information and performance feedback; seeking career goals
Goal Clarity—clarity of career goals	Structure for Goal Setting—existence of career alternatives, procedures, and assistance for setting career goals	Establishing Career Goals—identifying specific career goals and making them concrete (*e.g.*, putting them in writing)
Path Goal Clarity—clarity of means of achieving career goals	Path Goal Structure—existence of standard career paths; help in establishing a career path; extent career paths are realized	Establishing a Career Path—identifying how goals can be achieved and working toward them
Goal Flexibility*—willingness to modify or alter career goals (negatively related to career insights)	Organizational Flexibility—requirements and procedures for establishing and changing career goals; variety of alternatives	Changing Goals—changing goals in response to change in interests, circumstances, and influences
Need Changes—interest in new and different career experiences (negatively related to career insight)	Opportunity for Change—amount of change in the organization, opportunities for voluntary change, and assistance in adapting to change	Making Change—initiating change; expressing enthusiasm for new experiences and boredom with old experiences

Social Perceptiveness*—sensitivity to organizational and interpersonal factors affecting career progress	Visiblity of Organizational Process—organizational processes (e.g., appraisals, personnel decisions) are explicit, observable, and veridical	Responsiveness to Social Conditions—altering behavior to fit the situation; seeking information and personal contacts to take advantage of organizational process
Self-objectivity*—having an accurate view of one's strengths, weaknesses, and motives	Feedback Process—fairness and accuracy of performance and potential appraisal and review	Self-monitoring—keeping track of one's performance, trying to strengthen weaknesses that can be developed, and seeking assignments that use one's strengths
Realism of Expectations*—realism of expectations about career outcomes (e.g., advancement, salary)	Realistic Job Information—completeness and accuracy of information about career opportunities	Forming and Expressing Realistic Expectations—seeking information; comparing one's expectations to others'
Career Decision Making—tendency to be thorough and decisive in decision making	Favorability of Decision Context—existence of alternatives and information about them; time available for making decisions; revokability of decisions	Decision-making Behavior—seeking and evaluating alternatives and information; not wavering once alternatives are evaluated or regretting decisions after they are made
Future Time Orientation—tendency to anticipate the future and work toward future goals	Organization's Emphasis on Long-term—requirements for long-term planning; changes expected in the future; rewards for long-term accomplishments	Instrumental Behavior—working harder on projects that will affect one's career than on routine tasks; planning for the future and acting on those plans

* Based on management assessment center dimensions (Bray, 1982; Bray et al., 1974).

** Relationships to the individual characteristic in the row are hypothesized to be positive.

Table 1: Career Motivation Variables (cont'd)

Individual Characteristics	Situational Characteristics**	Career Decisions and Behavior**
DOMAIN III: Career Resilience—the person's resistance to career disruption in a less than optimal environment. The opposite is career vulnerability, extent of psychological fragility (e.g., becomes upset and finds it difficult to function) when confronted by less than optimal career conditions	Organizational Strength and Support—the clarity, harmony, and certainty of organizational processes and procedures. Other factors include openness of communication, integrity, stability, growth, and other indices of organizational effectiveness. The opposite is organizational stress—the degree of ambiguity, conflict, and uncertainty within the organization	Increasing Individual Effectiveness—demonstrating initiative, purposive action, and high performance. The opposite is decreasing individual effectiveness—demonstrating withdrawal, anxiety, and confusion (e.g., absenteeism, task avoidance, physical and/or psychological symptoms of stress, low performance)
Self-efficacy subdomain: Self-esteem—the extent to which the person has a positive self-image	*Encouragement of individual contribution and personal growth subdomain:* Positive Reinforcement—positive reinforcement and constructive feedback are given to employees	*Self-efficacy subdomain:* Showing Belief in Oneself—requesting difficult assignments; expressing one's ideas; constructively dealing with criticism
Need Autonomy—need to be independent (also relevant to dependency subdomain)	Encouragement of Autonomy—assignments are given to individuals not groups; individuals are encouraged to work alone; individual accomplishment is rewarded	Striving for Autonomy—choosing to work alone; taking independent action; not asking for assistance

Adaptability—acceptance of an adjustment to job and organizational changes	Organizational Change—frequency and extent of changes in task assignment, job structures, reporting relationships, work locations, policies, and regulations assistance given by organization in adapting to change	Demonstrating Adaptability—changing behaviors to meet changing demands; readily learning new procedures, rules, technology, etc.
Internal Control—belief that one can influence career outcomes (e.g., promotional opportunities, job assignments)	Amount of Individual Control—how much discretion the individual has in determining work methods and work outcomes	Taking Control—working hard to obtain valued outcomes; requesting assignments, promotions, and raises
Need Achievement—need to do difficult jobs well (apart from trying to advance)	Opportunity for Achievement—difficulty and importance of one's job; time span for goal accomplishment	Striving to Achieve—working hard on difficult tasks and seeking knowledge of the results; requesting projects that use one's skill and expertise
Initiative—need to take action to enhance one's career	Opportunity for Input—the extent to which employee's ideas are listened to and acted on; formal programs for input (e.g., MBO)	Taking Action for Self-benefit—letting career goals be known, requesting desired assignments, making the outcomes of one's work known to higher management
Need Creativity—need to create new methods, products, procedures, etc.	Support for Creativity—rewards are given for creative ideas and solutions; change is frequent and there are few standard procedures and routine tasks	Creative Behavior—searching for and offering innovative ideas and new procedures; applying a wide range of resources to one's job

---

* Based on management assessment center dimensions (Bray, 1982; Bray et al., 1974).
** Relationships to the individual characteristic in the row are hypothesized to be positive.

Table 1: Career Motivation Variables (cont'd)

Individual Characteristics	Situational Characteristics**	Career Decisions and Behavior**
Inner Work Standards* —desire to do a good job when something less will do	Demands for Quality—incentives for high quality work; explicitness of performance standards	Quality of Work—attending to details; taking time to do the best job possible
Development Orientation* —desire to expand one's skill or knowledge	Support for Development—tuition aid; in-house training programs; rewards for development	Seeking Development—taking courses, keeping up with developments in one's field, improving one's skills
Risk taking subdomain: Risk Taking Tendency—tendency to risk something of value (e.g., money, one's job, self-esteem) to gain something of value	*Risk taking potential subdomain:* Opportunity for and Value of Risk Taking—how positively risk is viewed (aside from the outcome); the opposite is emphasis placed on stability and not "rocking the boat"	*Risk taking subdomain:* Taking Risks—suggesting ideas contrary to those of others; taking a job with high rewards but little security; assuming responsibility for one's behavior
Fear of Failure—fear of not living up to one's expectations or those of others (negatively related to risk taking)	Consequences of Failure—visibility of failure; a failure can be the "kiss of death" for advancement, bad reputations spread quickly and die slowly	Response to Failure (or potential failure)— withdrawing from difficult situations; working in groups to avoid individual accountability
Need Security* —value of secure employment (negatively related to risk taking)	Job Security—the organization's reputation as a long-term employer; availability of jobs in the labor market	Seeking Security—keeping a secure job even though advancement possibilities and salary may be better elsewhere

Tolerance of Uncertainty and Ambiguity*—the degree to which one's work performance stands up under uncertain or unstructured situations	Organizational Uncertainty and Ambiguity—clarity, structure, and stability of work goals, methods, reporting relationships, policies, etc.; predictability of work outcomes	Seeking Structure—setting schedules; organizing work loads; acting without direction
Dependency subdomain (negatively related to career resilience): Competitiveness—need to compete with one's peers (negatively related to dependency)	*Interpersonal concern and cohesiveness subdomain:* Competitive Situations—employees are compared to each other for purposes of evaluation and reward	*Dependency subdomain:* Competing—taking jobs or assignments for which rewards are based on competition; trying to advance faster and further than one's peers
Career Dependency—expecting the organization or supervisors to guide one's career	Paternalism—supervisors act as mentors or sponsors to selected subordinates, make plans for and decisions about subordinates' careers, and are held responsible for subordinates' career development	Waiting for Career Direction—waiting for information about development; expressing the belief that the organization has a career plan for each individual
Need Supervisor Approval—emotional dependency on authority figures	Supervisor's Consideration and Control—supervisor develops friendships with selected subordinates and gives them more attention and latitude than others; sets goals and standards; monitors work	Deferent Behavior—trying to impress one's supervisor; being influenced by the supervisor (e.g., expressing the same opinions)
Need for Peer Approval*—emotional dependency on co-workers	Group Cohesiveness—co-workers develop friendly relationships and depend on each other for task accomplishment	Relying on Others—seeking task assistance from co-workers; being socially involved with them; being influenced by them

---

* Based on *management assessment center dimensions* (*Bray, 1982; Bray et al., 1974*).

** *Relationships to the individual characteristic in the row are hypothesized to be positive.*

future behaviors and beliefs (Salancik & Pfeffer, 1978). Individual characteristics, such as one's needs and one's self-concept, are cognitions that make sense out of past actions in a social environment (Pfeffer, 1980). The more ambiguous the environment, the more the worker will rely on social comparisons and past behavior to assess it. Individual characteristics are affected by the salience and relevance of information and by the general need to develop socially acceptable and legitimate rationalizations for actions.

Salancik and Pfeffer (1978) outlined three bases for retrospective rationality. One is social, another is environmental, and the third is behavioral. The social basis occurs when the job is so complex that the individual is uncertain how to react to it. Knowing how others evaluate the job suggests to the employee how he or she should react. Also, people are likely to agree with their co-workers so that they fit into the work environment. Moreover, people are influenced by what others say about them and by the advice given to them.

Individuals cognitively evaluate facets of the job environment. Objective characteristics of the organization affect the individual's perceptions of these characteristics. Judgments are a function of the positive and negative information a person has about the job.

Past behavior can be a determinant of individual needs states. It can serve as a source of information for constructing attitude statements (Bem, 1972). Also, it may influence future behavior in that individuals attempt to behave in ways that are consistent with the past, giving little thought to what might happen in the future (Staw, 1981). Retrospective rationality may be based partially on the need to justify one's behavior and the desire to appear competent in previous as opposed to future actions. There is considerable evidence that individuals try to maximize consistency between their behavior and their self-image (Baumeister, 1982). Moreover, they behave in ways that construct (create, maintain, and modify) their public self congruent to their ideal self and behave in ways that please the observer.

Retrospective rationality processes can serve as the basis for prospective rationality directed toward future actions. Cognitive social learning results in establishment of perceived self-competencies, expectancies, values, ways of encoding the environment, and self-regulatory mechanisms (Mischel, 1973). These, in turn, operate cognitively through different decision-making heuristics to affect future actions. Deci (1980) provides a similar formulation by arguing that individuals' perceptions, or cognitive evaluations, of the environment develop from their experiences. These perceptions and evaluations shape behavioral choices. Thus, both retrospective and prospective rationality processes may affect career decisions and behaviors (Staw, 1981).

AN INTERACTIVE MODEL

Figure 1 diagrams the proposed relationships among situational characteristics, individual characteristics, and career decisions and behaviors.

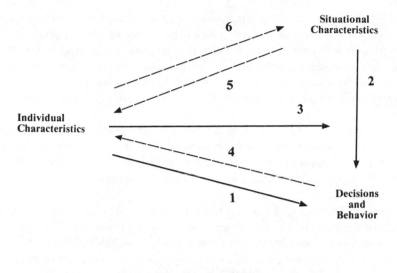

Figure 1
An Interactive Model of Career Motivation Components

The model emphasizes that career motivation is a multidimensional, dynamic process, not a unidimensional construct. The specific variables involved and their strengths vary over time and for different individuals in different situations. Individual characteristics are not necessarily stable traits in all environmental contexts. Some are stable for a long time, others are activated and become strong for a short period, and still others have little effect or never fully evolve. The nature of the interactions in the model also varies. Different types of interactions arise at different times depending on the variables involved and their strength. The numbers in the diagram referring to the linkages do not imply order of occurrence or importance. Rather, the model represents continuous processes of direct and indirect relationships.

Linkages 1, 2 and 3 describe prospective rationality processes. Linkage 1 refers to the direct effects of individual characteristics on decisions and behaviors, as when a person behaves in a certain way almost regardless of the situation. For example, risk taking tendency will lead to choosing career alternatives with higher values and lower probabilities of occurrence.

Proposition 1. Individual characteristics associated with career motivation will have a greater direct effect on career decisions and behaviors when the individual characteristics are stable and integrated into the individual's self-concept. This is evident when a decision or behavior fits into a pattern of decisions and behaviors typical of the individual.

Linkage 2 represents the direct impact of the situation on career decisions and behaviors. These are cases in which the situation restricts or in other ways determines individual actions. For instance, an organization may require that a new manager attend a set of training programs or enroll in a graduate degree program. As another example, the more cohesive the work group, the more likely social influence processes will affect career decisions and behaviors.

Proposition 2. Situational characteristics will have a greater effect on career decisions and behaviors the more the situational characteristics control or limit possible decisions and behaviors, define what decisions and behaviors are socially acceptable, and require justifying one's decisions and behaviors to others.

Linkage 3 represents the interactions that may occur between the individual and the situation as they affect career decisions and behaviors. The nature of the interactions that emerge will depend on the variables involved. Different theoretical approaches posit different independent and intervening variables. (For example, McClelland's 1971 need achievement theory holds that individuals with high need achievement will choose moderately difficult tasks, whereas those with low need achievement will choose very easy or very difficult tasks.) Each individual characteristic dimension associated with career motivation may interact with its corresponding situational characteristic to affect career decisions and behaviors (corresponding variables are those in each row of Table 1). In general, the strength of a main effect or interaction will depend on the strength of the independent variables (their stability, favorability, recency of occurrence, etc.). For instance, if the situation is such that the individual has discretion in determining work assignments, those high on the individual characteristics of internal control (the belief that one can influence career outcomes) are more likely to try to control their assignments than are those low on internal control. When there is little discretion in determining work assignments, internal control is not as likely to affect the individual's behavior.

The congruence or match between the individual and the situation is likely to affect what career decisions and behaviors will occur and their potential value to the individual and the organization. For example, consider an organizational environment low in encouragement of autonomy, discretion over career outcomes, opportunities for achievement, feedback on performance, and positive reinforcement for good performance. The resilient individual is likely to tolerate the situation for a while and, if it does not improve, look for better alternatives elsewhere. This may be negative for the organization if the individual is a valued employee. Alternatively, the individual may cease striving for autonomy, taking control, striving to achieve, and showing belief in himself or herself. This could lead to negative outcomes for the employee and the organization. As another example, consider the case of a vulnerable employee assigned to a supervisor who provides encouragement of autonomy, discretion over career outcomes, opportunities for achievement, performance feedback, and positive reinforcement. The subordinate is unlikely, at least initially, to be effective in this environment. Perhaps over time, he or she may become more resilient if the supervisor maintains this style of management.

Proposition 3. Career decisions and behaviors will be more effective (e.g., *have more positive outcomes for the individual and the organization) the greater the congruence between the individual and the situational characteristics.*

The motion of individual/situational congruence must be viewed broadly, taking into account sets of individual characteristics and sets of situational characteristics. For example, the individual's internal control will not moderate the relationship between the amount of individual control available and the extent to which the person takes control if the individual's need achievement and need autonomy are low. Also, the effectiveness of a particular career decision or behavior will depend on a number of factors, including the individual's ability and the conditions in the organization. A person with low ability who tries to take control over his or her career outcomes may not do so effectively. An individual who establishes specific career goals and puts them in writing may be wasting his or her time if the organization is in a state of flux.

Linkages 4, 5 and 6 describe retrospective rationality processes. Linkage 4 deals with how past decisions and behaviors affect individual characteristics. The tendency to maintain consistency between one's behavior and self-concept underlies this linkage. For example, establishing plans for one's career is likely to enhance career identity as long as the plans are likely to be put into effect. As another example, turning down a lucrative job offer is likely to enhance loyalty to one's present employer unless the decision can be changed easily or attributed to factors beyond the individual's control.

Proposition 4. Past career decisions and behaviors will have a greater effect on the individual characteristics associated with career motivation the more the decisions and behaviors have positive or negative consequences and the longer these consequences last.

Linkage 5 deals with how the current situation affects individual characteristics. For instance, receiving positive feedback for performance should lead to higher self-esteem and a greater sense of internal control, particularly when the task is such that the individual has control over the outcome. Increasing job challenge (e.g., by increasing the job's skill variety, task identity, feedback, autonomy, and significance) should positively affect job involvement unless such changes in task design are viewed as increased demands.

Proposition 5. Situational charactericics will have a greater effect on the individual characteristics associated with career motivation the more the situational characteristics are viewed as positive or negative, the more recently they occurred, and the more they control possible career decisions and behaviors.

Linkage 6 is the process of interpreting the situation. A high self-esteem individual would be likely to attribute a lower-than expected pay raise to external factors, such as the economy, if another justification is not provided by the supervisor. A low self-esteem individual would be likely to attribute a lower-than-expected raise to his or her own performance. To do otherwise in either case would be inconsistent with the individual's self-concept. However, if the pay raise is explained (e. g, everyone received the same percentage, or the individual's performance was lower than it should have been), then the causal attribution may not be affected by the individual's self-esteem.

Proposition 6. Individual characteristics associated with career motivation will affect how the situation is perceived the more the situation initially is ambiguous, uncertain, and/or cognitively inconsistent.

The propositions and associated linkages provide a framework for investigating and understanding career motivation and for generating more specific hypotheses about the effects of the components of the model. Changes in the variables and their effects may be observed over time. It should be recognized that the proposed relationships do not occur in isolation from one another or in a fixed sequence. Also, Figure 1 is a simplified version of the relationships because the individual, situational, and behavioral components of the model are vectors of interrelated dimensions.

The propositions express the primary linkages among the components of the model. Other relationships also may occur, although they may emerge more clearly in one of the above proposed relationships because of the sequence of events. Career decisions and behaviors may have a direct effect on the situation, as when an individual's requesting and assuming leadership roles is recognized and results in increased leadership opportunities. Also, career decisions and behaviors may moderate relationships between individual and situational characteristics. For example, individuals may not acquire a sense of internal control from new organizational policies allocating increased power and responsibilities unless they have behaved in a way that demonstrates power. However, this may appear from analyses over time as a sequence of the effects of the situation on behavior and the effects of behavior on the individual's psychological state. Another possibility is that the situation may moderate relationships between individual characteristics and career decisions and behaviors, as when effective leadership behavior does not result in the feeling of internal control and need dominance unless a formal statement detailing reporting relationships and responsibilities has been issued by the organization. However, this may appear as a strong relationship between the situation and the individual characteristics and a weak relationship between the behavior and the individual characteristics, particularly if the behavior has been ongoing and the situational characteristic justifying the behavior is of recent occurrence.

Recognizing the complexity of the model, a manageable approach to testing the propositions would be to investigate the linkage by studying sets of dimensions. The model cannot be tested in one study nor can it be tested by measuring a few variables. It requires an organismic, in-depth, longitudinal program of research. This should involve three types of assessment: one focusing on the individual characteristics, another on the situation, and a third on the career decisions and behaviors. An assessment center is one way to measure the individual characteristic dimensions. Techniques for assessing the situational characteristics and career decisions and behaviors include interviews, observations, ratings, diaries, and network analysis (see Lawler, Nadler, & Cammann for a review of such methods). The assessments should be repeated over time to test causal relationships among the components.

IMPLICATIONS OF THE MODEL

Traditional motivational strategies entail changing an element of the environment (e.g., the compensation system or the job design) to increase motivation and thereby enhance job performance. Another approach has been to hire people who have not only requisite skills and abilities but also a psychological profile that is believed (but unfortunately seldom empirically demonstrated) to be job related. The idea that some individual characteristics may change over time and be affected by situational conditions introduces possibilities for new motivational strategies. Once there is a better understanding of how the situation activates different individual characteristics, it will be possible to affect motivation by changing the salience of different situational variables. Attention may be focused on different elements of the environment by changing them or perhaps merely discussing them or communicating information about them. For example, a company may offer its employees a voluntary, self-administered career management program that consists of several workbooks. Because this requires considerable work with no immediate benefit to one's career, the program may be completed by relatively few employees. Just knowing that the program exists, however, may focus the attention of many more employees on their goals, factors that affect those goals, and their responsibility for their own careers. This could ultimately affect their career decisions and behaviors, although not necessarily in the way the program was intended.

How people interpret the environment has implications for motivational strategies. For instance, a given situational change may not affect motivation because it is not perceived as intended. Understanding which individual characteristics are relevant to interpreting different situations may suggest ways of controlling the process.

The multidimensional nature of career motivation suggests that motivational strategies will have to deal with broad sets of variables. For example, a new pay system may be designed and implemented along with a career development program, a supervisor-subordinate joint goal setting process, and new transfer and promotion policies as an integrated system. Such a system could be designed using knowledge about relationships among groups of situational characteristics, individual characteristics, and career decisions and behaviors. As another example, an employee communications program coupled with training to help subordinates set and carry out career goals may affect career insight variables. But these programs may have no effect if prior circumstances generated low career resilience. Consequently, programs to affect resilience dimensions (e.g., ways of providing constructive feedback while reducing the negative consequences of failure) also may be necessary.

SUMMARY

This paper outlines the components of career motivation and proposed relationships among them. The components consist of individual characteristics organized into three domains (career identity, career insights, and career resilience) with corresponding situational characteristics and career decisions and behaviors. The relationships among the components are based on prospective and retrospective rationality. Prospective rationality is the process by which individuals' career decisions and behaviors are affected by what they believe will happen in the future. The nature of the situation and the individual characteristic associated with career motivation affect career decisions and behaviors. Retrospective rationality holds that social learning and information processing influence individual characteristics. The importance of different individual characteristics will change with the salience of corresponding elements of the situation and one's decisions and behaviors. Testing the model requires an organismic, longitudinal assessment of each component. The results are likely to be valuable for designing new motivational strategies.

REFERENCES

Baumeister, R.R., "A Self-presentational View of Social Phenomena," *Psychological Bulletin*, (Vol. 91, 1981), pp. 3-25.

Bem, D.J., "Self-perception Theory," in L. Berkowitz, ed., *Advances in Experimental Social Psychology*, Vol.6 (New York: Academic Press, 1972), pp. 1-62.

Bray, D.W., "The Assessment Center and the Study of Lives" *American Psychologist,* (Vol. 37, 1982), pp. 180-189.

Bray, D.W., Campbell, R.J. and Grant, D.L., *Formative Years in Business: A Long-term AT&T Study of Managerial Lives* (New York: Wiley, 1974).

Brousseau, K.R., "Toward a Dynamic Model of Job-person Relationship: Findings, Research, Questions, and Implications for Work System Design," *Academy of Management Review* (Vol. 8, 1983), pp. 33-45.

Campbell, J.P. and Pritchard, R.D., "Motivation Theory in Industrial and Organizational Psychology," in M.D. Dunnette, ed., *Handbook of Industrial and Organizational Psychology* (Chicago: Rand McNally, 1976), pp. 63-130.

Campbell, J.P., Dunnette, M.D., Lawler, E.E., III and Weick, K.E., Jr., *Managerial Behavior, Performance and Effectiveness* (New York: McGraw-Hill, 1970).

Deci, E.L., *The Psychology of Self-Determination* (Lexington, Mass.: Lexington Books, 1980).

Dubin, R., "Theory Building in Applied Areas, in M.D. Dunnette, ed., *Handbook of Industrial and Organizational Psychology* (Chicago: Rand McNally, 1976), pp. 17-39.

Herzberg, F., *Work and the Nature of Man* (Cleveland, Ohio: World Publishing. 1966).

Lawler, E.E., III, Nadler, D.A. and Cammann, C., *Organizational Assessment: Perspectives on the Measurement of Organizational Behavior and the Quality of Work Life* (New York: Wiley, 1980).

Maslow, A.H., *Motivation and Personality* (New York: Harper & Row, 1954).

McClelland, D.C., *Motivational Trends in Society* (Morristown, N.J.: General Learning Press, 1971).

Miner, J.B., *Motivation to Manage: A Ten-year Update on the "Studies in Management Education" Research* (Atlanta, Ga.: Organizational Measurement Systems Press, 1977).

Mischel, W., "Toward a Cognitive Social Learning Reconceptualization of Personality" *Psychological Review* (Vol. 80, 1973), pp. 252-283.

Murray, H.A., *Explorations in Personality: A Clinical and Experimental Study of Fifty Men of College Age* (New York: Oxford University Press, 1938).

Naylor, J.C., Pritchard, R.D. and Ilgen, D.R., *A Theory of Behavior in Organizations* (New York: Academic Press, 1980).

O'Reilly, C.A., III and Caldwell, D.F., "The Commitment and Job Tenure of New Employees: Some Evidence of Post Decisional Justification," *Administrative Science Quarterly* (Vol. 26, 1981), pp. 597-616.

Pfeffer, J., "A Partial Test of the Social Information Processing Model of Job Attitudes," *Human Relations* (Vol. 33, 1980), pp. 457-476.

Raynor, J.O., "Motivation and Career Striving," in J.W. Atkinson and J.O. Raynor, eds., *Personality, Motivation, and Achievement* (New York: Wiley, 1978), pp. 199-219.

Salancik, G.R. and Pfeffer, J.A., "A Social Information Processing Approach to Job Attitudes and Task Design," *Administrative Science Quarterly* (Vol. 23, 1978), pp. 224-253.

Staw, B.M., "The Escalation of Commitment to a Course of Action," *Academy of Management Review* (Vol. 6, 1981), pp. 577-587.

Vroom, V.H., *Work and Motivation* (New York: Wiley, 1964).

Manuel London is a district manager of Basic Human Resources Research, American Telephone and Telegraph Company.

32.
LET'S PUT THE
WORK ETHIC TO WORK

Daniel Yankelovich
John Immerwahr

New jobs, new technology, and new values add up to a "high-discretion" workplace. But our management systems and incentives are geared to low-discretion workers, who are becoming less and less prevalent. We're losing an opportunity for worker commitment.

Despite the current recovery, the U.S. economy is at a crisis point. We are experiencing a *commitment gap* at precisely the moment when we have a tremendous need for dedication and commitment from our workforce.

The traditional American workplace was designed so that high productivity required only a limited commitment from the workforce. But this limited-commitment arrangement is no longer adequate in today's brutal and unforgiving world economic market. Many of our competitors, particularly Japan, have done so well precisely because they have been able to mobilize a workforce that is highly motivated and intensely committed to quality workmanship.

If America is to compete effectively, harnessing the nation's human resources must be an important part of our overall strategy. It is not that America has done poorly. Indeed, the limited-commitment model was phenomenally successful—so successful that we have been reluctant to reexamine it even when conditions have changed. Through most of this century the main thrust in American industry was to minimize the amount of discretion permitted frontline workers. Traditional "scientific management" sought to increase productivity by reducing work to a series of simple, routinized tasks, and by centralizing the managerial control of output and performance. The goal was to make productivity independent, as much as possible, of individual creativity and motivation.

But a number of changes, in both the workplace and the workforce, have dramatically altered these conditions. One of the most significant changes has been a marked increase in the amount of control or discretion that individual

171

jobholders have over their work. We use the term "discretionary effort" to describe the difference between the maximum amount of effort and care an individual *could* bring to his or her job, and the minimum amount of effort *required* to avoid being fired or penalized. It can vary widely from job to job and from person to person. A number of recent developments—new jobs, new technologies, and new values—have created a high-discretion workplace.

New jobs. The shift toward white-collar jobs has increased the amount of discretion in the workplace. White-collar jobholders are much more likely to have high-discretion jobs. The Public Agenda Foundation's survey of 845 working Americans found that almost half of all white-collar jobholders (49 percent) say they have a great deal of freedom in deciding how to do their jobs; in contrast, only one-third of blue-collar workers felt that way.

New technologies. We are at the beginning of a second industrial revolution, one that will increase the amount of discretion in the workplace—a course opposite that of the first industrial revolution, which made the individual worker less important. Close to half of American jobholders (44 percent) say that they have experienced significant technological changes in their jobs in the last five years. Just under three-quarters of this group say that the changes have made their work more interesting; and more than half say that technological changes have given them greater independence.

New values. In the past, many workers were willing to sacrifice a great deal of their autonomy in the workplace in exchange for a good income and an increasing standard of living for themselves and their families. Today, with higher education levels, dramatic changes in family responsibilities (because of the increase of dual-wage-earner and single-parent families), and the rise of new values stressing self-development over self-sacrifice, many jobholders are no longer willing to surrender their autonomy in exchange for material rewards.

The Public Agenda research shows, then, that American jobholders now have a great deal of discretion over the quantity and quality of effort they invest in their work. Only about 21 percent say that they have little or no control over how they do their jobs, and even fewer (only 10 percent) say they have little control over the quality of their work.

The vast majority say that they exert considerable control over their output, and discretion is even higher among those jobholders who are well-educated, who are in white-collar or service jobs, or whose jobs have been affected by technological changes. The faster rate of job growth in these categories, therefore, indicates that the movement to a high-discretion workplace will accelerate further.

But managerial skill and training have not kept pace with these changes; as a result, existing incentive and managerial systems are often out of sync with the changing realities and values of the American workplace. This is clearly reflected in problems with work behavior.

Rather than increasing their efforts, in response to the new competitive realities, American workers' work behavior is deteriorating. Fewer than one out of four (22 percent) say they are performing to their full capacities. Nearly half of the workforce (44 percent) say they do not put a great deal of effort into their jobs over and above what is required. A majority feel that, under the right conditions, they could significantly increase their performance. Moreover, there are indications that effectiveness is actually *decreasing*. Several surveys reveal, for example, a widespread impression that people aren't working as hard as they used to.

A HEALTHY WORK ETHIC

The commonly accepted explanation for the declining work effort is a weakening of the *work ethic*. Many leaders attribute this to the emergence of a new set of cultural values that stresses hedonism, leisure, narcissism, and self-satisfaction, and that is antithetical to the values of hard work and commitment to the job. This has, in turn, bred an uncharacteristic sense of defeatism among American leaders. Our findings and those of other organizations suggest, however, that the work ethic is in surprisingly good health in America and may even be growing stronger.

A Public Agenda study found that a majority (52 percent) aligned themselves with the strong form of the work ethic: "I have an inner need to do the very best job I can, regardless of pay." Three out of four workers believe they could be helpful in improving the quality and efficiency of their work. It is interesting to note, too, that nearly two-thirds say they prefer a boss who is very demanding in the name of high-quality workmanship.

The work ethic is more common among those who have high-discretion jobs. The natural home of the modern work ethic is an environment of high-discretion jobs, where work conveys a sense of purpose, challenge, and accomplishment. Generally speaking, better-educated jobholders are more inclined to feel that work has an intrinsic moral value. Those who value personal self-expression and the fulfillment of one's potential as an individual do bring new demands to the workplace, but expressiveness is not incompatible with hard and effective work.

Why hold back? If many Americans have an inner need to give their best to their jobs—and if, increasingly, they have a great deal of control over their level of effort—what is preventing them from giving more to their work?

The answer is that Americans receive messages from their jobs that run counter to their own work-ethic norms. The evidence indicates that a major reason for the decline in worker effort is that managerial practices do not take advantage of the work ethic—and sometimes thwart it.

First, almost half of the workforce believe that there is no relationship between how good a job they do and how much they are paid. Jobholders also see little connection between any increased productivity of their companies

Figure 1.
MOTIVATORS OR SATISFIERS?
(How jobholders rate job characteristics)
(percent of respondents)

FACTORS THAT ENHANCE PRODUCTIVENESS:	WOULD CAUSE ME TO WORK HARDER	MAKES JOB MORE AGREEABLE	BOTH
GOOD CHANCE FOR ADVANCEMENT	48%	22%	19%
GOOD PAY	45	27	22
PAY TIED TO PERFORMANCE	43	31	16
RECOGNITION FOR GOOD WORK	41	34	17
JOB ENABLING ME TO DEVELOP ABILITIES	40	27	20
CHALLENGING JOB	38	30	15
JOB ALLOWING ME TO THINK FOR MYSELF	37	33	17
A GREAT DEAL OF RESPONSIBILITY	36	28	14
INTERESTING WORK	36	35	18
JOB REQUIRING CREATIVITY	35	31	20

FACTORS THAT MAKE THE JOB MORE AGREEABLE:	MAKES JOB MORE AGREEABLE	WOULD CAUSE ME TO WORK HARDER	BOTH
NOT TOO MUCH RUSH AND STRESS	61%	15%	13%
CONVENIENT LOCATION	56	12	12
WORKPLACE FREE FROM DIRT/ NOISE/POLLUTION	56	12	12
WORKING WITH PEOPLE I LIKE	54	17	13
GETTING ALONG WELL WITH SUPERVISOR	52	19	12
BEING INFORMED ABOUT WHAT GOES ON	49	21	16
FLEXIBLE WORK PACE	49	20	12
FLEXIBLE WORKING HOURS	49	18	15
GOOD FRINGE BENEFITS	45	27	18
FAIR TREATMENT IN WORKLOAD	45	24	18

Source: Public Agenda Foundation survey

DOS AND DON'TS
FOR SUPPORTING THE WORK ETHIC

DO TIE remuneration directly to performance that enhances the efficiency and effectiveness of the enterprise.

DO GIVE public and tangible recognition to people whose effort and quality of results exceed the average satisfactory job performance.

DO ACCEPT wholeheartedly the principle that employees should share directly and significantly in overall productivity gains.

DO ENCOURAGE jobholders to participate with management in defining recognizable goals and standards against which individual performance can be judged.

DO GIVE special attention to the difficulties that middle managers face in supporting and enforcing programs to restructure the workplace.

DON'T PERMIT situations to develop where the interests of employees run counter to the well-being of the firm—e.g., by introducing new technology in a way that threatens employees' job security or overtime.

DON'T ATTEMPT to improve standards of quality unless you are prepared to accept the full costs—e.g., discarding substandard products, paying more for better components, or transferring or dismissing people who cannot do quality work.

DON'T PERMIT a significant gap to develop between management rhetoric and the actual reward system.

DON'T PRETEND that programs designed to increase productivity are really intended to enhance job satisfaction and the dignity of work.

DON'T SUPPORT special privileges for managers that serve to enhance the status of managers be widening the gap between them and those who actually do the work.

and their pay. More than seven out of 10 working Americans say they want more recognition for good work.

Second, while there have been frequent attempts to structure incentive systems to provide greater support for the work ethic, these have often failed to distinguish between *satisfaction* with the job and *effectiveness* in doing it. A focus on job satisfaction does not necessarily enhance work-ethic values; indeed, it may even undermine these values. If managers want to capitalize on the considerable human potential that already exists in the workforce, they must focus on motivators as well as satisfiers and not confuse one with the other (see Figure 1).

Third, nothing corrodes the work ethic more than the perception that employers and managers are indifferent to quality. Strict, even harsh, emphasis on the highest standards of quality reinforces the conviction that work has an intrinsic worth and meaning. Improving standards as a means of reinforcing the work ethic may involve the restructuring of jobs. In order to win worker commitment, it is important to place greater responsibility for quality on workers themselves, rather than on inspectors.

Fourth, a major deterrent to employee commitment has to do with status, authority, fairness, and prerogatives in the workplace. The traditional organization of the American workplace embodies a centralized control system with clearly specified job descriptions and lines of authority. Such an organization often distinguishes sharply between those who manage and those who actually do the work, a distinction reinforced by equally sharp status differences, large pay differentials between managers and hourly workers, less constraining rules of conduct for managers, and other prerogatives that reflect the fact the managers possess power and control.

These differences also reflect the assumption that individual jobholders are less central to the success of the enterprise than managers are. In a high-discretion workplace, symbols of status and privilege that are not distributed in accordance with performance are likely to undermine both the work ethic and high levels of performance. High commitment requires a sense of shared responsibilities, goals, and burdens; and this means that those lower in the hierarchy must be able to see themselves and their supervisors as sharing the same destiny.

There are, then, four major steps that managers can take to enhance and take advantage of the American work ethic:

1. Develop performance incentives that encourage rather than bypass the work ethic.
2. Set high quality standards that reinforce the idea that work has an intrinsic worth and meaning.
3. Distinguish between job improvements that enhance job satisfaction and those that actually enhance productiveness.
4. Flatten the hierarchy to eliminate artificial status barriers that undercut the work ethic.

Daniel Yankelovich is president and co-founder of the Public Agenda Foundation and chairman of Yankelovich, Skelly & White, Inc. John Immerwahr is professor of philosophy at Villanova University and a senior project consultant for the Public Agenda Foundation. This article is based on a major study, Putting the Work Ethic to Work, done by the Public Agenda Foundation.

33.
MOTIVATION: NEW DIRECTIONS FOR THEORY, RESEARCH, AND PRACTICE

Terence R. Mitchell

Emphasis is placed on the internal, unobservable aspects of motivation and the distinction between motivation and behavior and performance.

Over the last five years various professional commitments have led me to look at the field of motivation from both a theory-research perspective and a practical or applied perspective. The analysis of the theoretical and research literature has resulted in detailed and comprehensive review papers (Mitchell, 1979; Mitchell, in press). The attempts to deal with applications and implications were prompted by field research endeavors (Latham, Mitchell & Dossett, 1978) and the writing and revision of a textbook (Mitchell, 1978). Several ideas have emerged from these activities.

First, from the reviews of motivation theory and research (Campbell & Pritchard, 1976; Dorman, Greenhaus & Badin; 1977; Locke, 1975; Staw, 1977), it became clear that some shifts in the field were occurring. The overwhelming percentage of current papers are concerned with information processing or social-environmental explantions of motivation (Salancik & Pfeffer, 1977, 1978) rather than with need-based approaches or approaches that focus on individual differences. These latter approaches, represented by people like Maslow, have almost disappeared in the literature.

The information processing approaches are illustrated by the large amount of work on expectancy theory, goal setting, and equity theory. Theories focusing on the job environment, such as operant conditioning or job enrichment, and theories emphasizing social cues and social evaluations also have been important. These approaches have all been helpful in increasing the understanding of motivation.

A second trend, however, has not been so widely recognized. More specifically, when one reviews this research, it becomes readily apparent that most of the studies investigate only one theory in depth. Many studies set out to demonstrate that goal setting, operant conditioning, or expectancy theory, works. In other cases the research is concerned with fine-tuning the theory (*e.g.*: Is participative or assigned goal setting better? Should expectancies be added to or multiplied by valences? Is a variable or continuous schedule of reinforcement best?). These questions are important, but few studies have been designed to integrate theories, to test them competitively, or to analyze the settings in which different theories work best.

Several issues also emerged from the practical experiences and attempts to summarize applied principles. First, there are some preliminary questions that must be answered and requirements that need to be met before implementing any motivational system. These questions and requirements revolve around (1) how people are evaluated and (2) the demands of the task. In other words, to apply motivational principles, one must do some preliminary work involving other organizational factors.

Second, in attempting to apply motivational principles in an organization, one often runs into mitigating circumstances. There are situations and settings that make it exceptionally difficult for a motivational system to work. These circumstances may involve the kinds of jobs or people present, the technology, the presence of a union, and so on. The factors that hinder the application of motivational theory have not been articulated either frequently or systematically. The purpose of this paper is to review what is currently known about motivation, describe some theoretical areas in which ambiguity exists, and identify some situational constraints on the utilization of this knowledge.

The goal of this paper is not to provide a comprehensive source of references on the topic of motivation. Vast resources are already available for that purpose. There are whole books devoted to the topic (Korman, 1974; Lawler, 1973; Ryan, 1970; Vroom, 1964; Weiner, 1972), books of readings (McClelland & Steele, 1973; Steers & Porter, 1979; Tosi, House & Dunnette, 1972), and many review articles (Campbell & Pritchard, 1976; Korman et al., 1979; Locke, 1975; Mitchell, 1979; Staw, 1977). The material and principles discussed in this paper will be dealt with at a fairly global level. This is not to say that the ideas are not supportable or that a detailed level of analysis is not important. In most cases, at least one representative citation will be provided. However, the objective of the paper is to stimulate debate and interest in some issues about motivation that (1) have been discussed infrequently or (2) have recently emerged and need to be highlighted.

BACKGROUND

Many nonacademics would probably describe motivation as the degree to which an individual wants and tries hard to do well at a particular task or job. Dictionary definition describes motivation as the goad to action. The more technical definitions given by social scientists suggest that motivation is the group of psychological processes that causes the arousal, direction, and persistence of behavior (Atkinson, 1964; Campbell, Dunnette, Lawler, & Weick, 1970; Huse & Bowditch, 1977; Kast & Rosenzweig, 1979; Korman, 1974; Luthans, 1977). Many authors add a voluntary component or goal-directed emphasis to that definition (Hellriegel & Slocum, 1976; Lawler, 1973; Ryan, 1970; Vroom, 1964). Thus motivation becomes those psychological processes that cause the arousal, direction, and persistence of voluntary actions that are goal-directed.

Although there is some disagreement about the importance of different aspects of this definition (e.g., whether arousal or choice is more important), there is consensus about some underlying properties of this definition. First, motivation traditionally has been cast as an *individual* phenomenon. Each individual is unique and all of the major motivational theories allow in one way or another for this uniqueness to be demonstrated (e.g., different people have different needs, expectations, values, attitudes, reinforcement histories, and goals). Second, motivation usually is described as *intentional.* That is, motivation supposedly is under the employee's control. Most behaviors that are seen as influenced by motivation (e.g., effort on the job) typically are viewed as actions the individual has chosen to do.

A third point is that motivation is *multifaceted.* The two factors of greatest importance have been the arousal (activation, energizers) and direction (choice) of behavior. The question of persistence has been of minor importance, partly because the issue of maintenance of behavior (once it is started and directed) has received less attention and partly because some authors have defined persistence simply as the reaffirmation of the initial choice of action (March & Simon, 1958).

The arousal question has focused on what gets people activated. What are the circumstances that arouse people so they want to do well? The second question, that of choice, deals with the force on the individual to engage in desired behaviors. Given that the person is aroused, what gets him going in a particular direction? These distinctions are reflected in much of the writing on motivation.

The fourth point to make is that the purpose of motivational theories is to predict *behavior.* Motivation is concerned with action and the internal and external forces that influence one's choice of action. Motivation is not the behavior itself, and it is not performance. The behavior is the criterion, that which is chosen. And in some cases the chosen action will be a good reflection of performance. But the psychological processes, the actual behavior, and performance are all different things, and the confusion of the three frequently has caused problems in analysis, interpretation, and application.

So, given these elaborations, a definition of motivation becomes somewhat more detailed. Motivation becomes the degree to which an individual wants and chooses to engage in certain specified behaviors. Different theories propose different reasons, but almost all of them emphasize an individual, intentional choice of behavior analysis.

PRELIMINARY QUESTIONS

Given that one understands what motivation is, the next question concerns why it is important to management. Most organizations function under the principle of rationality (Scott & Hart, 1979). That is, the primary goal of management is to increase efficiency by getting the greatest output at the lowest cost. Therefore, any behaviors that contribute to greater efficiency will be actions that management will want to encourage. These actions might be coming to work, being punctual, or exerting a lot of effort. Because these behaviors often are assumed by management to be motivated—voluntary choices controlled by the individual —management often establishes what it calls a motivational system. This system is intended to influence the factors that cause the behavior in question.

The important point to make is that one must be clear in distinguishing between this motivation system and the definition of motivation as a cognitive, individual, intentional phenomenon. The motivational system is imposed from the outside. It is constructed according to the assumptions held by management about (1) what behaviors are important for effectiveness and (2) the factors that influence these behaviors. To make sure these assumptions are correct, some preliminary work should be done before any system is tried.

PERFORMANCE APPRAISAL

Although many organizational factors contribute to effectiveness, such as turnover, absenteeism, and technology, probably the factor that is described as most important and the one that management feels it can influence is job performance. Job performance typically is viewed as partially determined by the motivation to work hard, and, therefore, an increase in motivation should result in greater effort and higher performance. However, to have any idea about the effects of a motivational system, one must have a good performance appraisal instrument. Changes in performance must be detectable and demonstrable. There is not enough space to go into the merits of various appraisal procedures (Kane & Lawler, 1979; Kavanagh, 1981; Landy & Farr, 1980), but there are some generalizations that can be made about appraisal and its relationship to motivation.

First, it goes without question that both a reliable and valid system is needed, not only for issues of motivation but for issues of selection, promotion, counseling, and adherence to legal guidelines. In short, a sound appraisal device is necessary for many personnel functions.

But besides the methodological properties for the device, there are some substantive issues as well. The more closely a performance appraisal device fits with the definition of motivation, the easier it will be to assess the effects of motivational interventions or strategies. More specifically, if performance is defined in behavioral and individual terms and so is motivation, then the concepts and their measures show correspondence. They are less likely to be confounded by other factors.

This distinction is very important. Some appraisals use group or team goals as performance criteria as opposed to individual performance. Also, some appraisals emphasize outcomes (policies sold) as opposed to behavior (clients visited). The further away one gets from individual behavior, the more difficult it is to infer directly and unambiguously a change in motivation rather than a change in performance.

To some extent, however, the type of appraisal may be dictated by the technology or task with which people are engaged. In some cases group performance on outcomes may be the best one can do. This is a point that will be covered later, but at this juncture it is sufficient to mention that (1) a good performance appraisal device is necessary and (2) the closer this device is to measuring individual behavior, the easier it is to evaluate the effects of motivational systems or technologies introduced to management.

FACTORS INFLUENCING PERFORMANCE

Given that a good performance appraisal system is in place and that it measures individual behavior, the next question is: Does motivation make a difference for performance? Many years ago Vroom suggested the equation: performance = ability × motivation; and somewhat later the term "role perceptions" was added to the right side of that equation (Porter & Lawler, 1968). More recently, Campbell and Pritchard (1976) expanded that definition to performance (aptitude level × skill level × understanding of the task × choice to expend effort × choice of degree of effort × choice to persist × facilitating and inhibiting conditions not under the control of the individual). These authors recognized that performance is caused by at least four and maybe more factors. In order to do well one must (1) know what is required (role expectations), (2) have the ability to do what is required, (3) be motivated to do what is required, and (4) work in an environment in which intended actions can be translated into behavior.

The implication is that there probably are some jobs for which trying to influence motivation will be irrelevant for performance. These circumstances can occur in a variety of ways. There may be situations in which ability factors or role expectation factors are simply more important than motivation. For example, the best predictor of high school grades typically is intellectual endowment, not hours spent studying. In a paper entitled "Performance Equals Ability and What," Dunnette concluded that "ability differences still are empirically the most important determiners of differences in job performance" (1973, p. 22). Some of the problems referred to in this quote pertain to inadequate performance measures or poorly articulated theories of motivation, but part of the problem is that performance on some tasks simply is controlled more by ability than by motivation.

Another circumstance may occur in which performance is controlled by technological factors. For example, on an assembly line, given that minimally competent and attentive people are there to do the job, performance may not vary from individual to individual. Exerting effort may be irrelevant for performance.

One way to gain information about these issues is through a thorough job analysis. This type of analysis can help to determine what behaviors contribute to performance and the extent to which these behaviors are controlled voluntarily (motivated) or controlled by ability factors, social factors, or technology. Except for some recent work by Hackman (Hackman & Morris, 1975; Hackman & Oldham, 1980), this is infrequently discussed.

The implications of the points about job analysis, performance appraisal, the factors that contribute to performance appraisal, and the factors that contribute to performance boil down to one crucial point: *performance is not the same as motivation.* If one wants to assess changes in motivation or the influence of interventions on motivation, then one must measure motivation and its contributions to behavior. If performance is assessed globally or nonbehaviorally, then performance is not a good indicator of motivation. Even when performance is individually and behaviorally assessed, motivation may control substantially less than 100 percent of the variance in performance. That is, behaviors may be jointly determined by ability and motivation or some other combination of factors. When either of these two circumstances is true, the researcher or practitioner should seek to define and assess motivation separately. This point is frequently recognized (Lawler, 1973) and almost never practiced.

In summary, before any motivation system is installed, one must be sure (a) that there is a good performance appraisal system available, (b) that motivation is an important contributor to performance, and (c) that where motivation is clearly not the major contributor to performance, a separate measure of motivation or of behaviors clearly caused by motivation is developed. When these three conditions are not being met, there is little point in pursuing the topic further. If they do exist, then one has the opportunity to put into practice what has been learned from previous research on motivation.

RESEARCH REVIEW

As mentioned earlier, theories of motivation typically are concerned with the questions of arousal and behavioral choice. The purpose of a review of these topics is not to criticize the different motivational theories. All of them have revealed some aspects of motivation that have empirical support. But some of the *factors controlling behavior* that they emphasize are more or less applicable in various situations. It is hoped that an understanding of these mitigating circumstances can serve as an initial step in developing contingency models of motivation: models that describe when and where certain motivational systems will be most effective.

THEORIES OF AROUSAL

The most popular theories of arousal for many years have been those that emphasize needs. Theories that emphasize individual needs (*e.g.*, need achievement) or groups of needs (*e.g.*, need hierarchies) all postulate that the arousal process is due to need deficiencies. That is, people want certain things in their jobs and they will work to fulfill those needs.

The major implications of this research have been two-fold. First, these theories clearly recognize and make central the idea of individual differences (Alderfer, 1977). Different people are motivated by different things. The second widely accepted point is that organizations generally have overlooked upper level needs. The works of such people as Maslow, McGregor, Herzberg, and Alderfer all suggest that, in general, organizations spend much more time being concerned with the fulfillment of lower level needs (*e.g.*, through motivational systems emphasizing pay, hours of work, and the physical setting) than with the fulfillment of upper level needs (*e.g.*, through systems emphasizing autonomy, recognition, creativity, and variety).

In recent years there has been a shift away from these need-based theories of arousal (Salanick & Pfeffer, 1977, 1978; Weiner, 1972) to approaches that emphasize processes such as social facilitation or evaluation apprehension (Ferris, Beehr, & Gilmore, 1978). These theories suggest that people are aroused by the presence of others and the knowledge that other people are evaluating them. The social cues in the form of expectations given off by subordinates, co-workers, and supervisors become important causes of arousal.

Other current approaches emphasize some ideas of cognitive inconsistency—for example, Korman's (1976) work on self-esteem—or the match between task-related needs and the characteristics of the job. An example of this latter approach is Hackman and Oldham's (1980) theory of job enrichment suggesting that an enriched job is motivating only for those who have high needs for growth.

What almost all of these theories emphasize in one way or another is that arousal is seen as (1) current and (2) highly related to the social or task environment. Thus, instead of deep-seated needs developed a long time ago that reside solely within the individual, a much more external and present frame of reference is emerging. Central to almost all of the new approaches is the idea that the individual cognitively processes and evaluates a lot of information and that motivation is linked strongly to this information processing activity.

In summary, the arousal theories say (1) attend to individual differences, (2) try to attend to upper level (intrinsic) needs, (3) note that social expectations have powerful effects, and (4) note that current information is extremely important. In attempting to implement these ideas, however, difficulties often arise. Some of these obstructions are as follows.

First, there is a whole set of organizational factors that make it difficult to individualize rewards and emphasize upper level intrinsic needs. The larger the organization and the more heterogeneous the work force, the more difficult it becomes. Ideally one would like to let employees have some choices in their compensation—for example, cafeteria style plans (Lawler, 1976)—and let managers have greater flexibility in the administration of rewards. But in practice these strategies are hard to implement. Dealing with unions also tends to restrict this flexibility because their striving for equity often leads to solidifying reward systems rather than increasing the latitude of management.

The theories that focus on social cues and expectations require that people be observed and that management have some influence on social norms. One idea that strives to let evaluation apprehension operate at the appropriate level is to match the level of appraisal with those people who most frequently observe the work of the individual. So, for example, if supervisors do not directly observe the work of subordinates who do observe an individual, then have evaluations by the subordinate's peers be part of the appraisal process.

Influencing social norms is more problematical. Factors like organizational climate are known to be important, and processes such as team building may help to instill norms or expectations for hard work. However, very little theory or research exists that uses these norms as dependent variables. This is an area for further work.

In summary, some important things have been learned about arousal as an individual process, one that is frequently related to current social cues. However, practical limitations such as organization size, unions, or heterogeneity of personnel may limit attempts to implement the knowledge. Also, further work is needed on understanding how one can influence social norms and expectations.

THEORIES OF CHOICE

The major theories of behavioral choice are goal setting, expectancy theory, operant conditioning, and equity theory. The research on goal setting is quite clear. People work harder with goals than without goals. This is especially true if the goals are specific and difficult and if feedback exists (Locke, 1978; Steers & Porter, 1974; Yuki & Latham, 1978). The areas of ongoing research emphasize such issues as whether rewards directly influence motivation, or whether they influence motivation by changing the level of the goal.

Expectancy theory and operant conditioning are very different in underlying philosophy (cognitive versus noncognitive), but they generate similar principles of application. Both approaches argue that (1) rewards should be closely tied to behavior, (2) reward administration should be frequent and consistent, and (3) people are motivated by outcomes (expected or past).

Reviews of expectancy theory (Connolly, 1976; Mitchell, 1980; Schwab, Olian-Gottlieb & Heneman, 1979) and operant conditioning or social learning (Babb & Kopp, 1978; Davis & Luthans, 1980) are available. People doing research on both theories are concerned with issues that have to do with how to tie rewards to behavior, what sorts of schedules to use, how to measure various theoretical components, and so on. But, except for some minor disagreements (Mawhinney & Behling, 1973), the approaches are in agreement about principles of application.

Equity theory (Carrell & Dittrich, 1978; Goodman, 1977) suggests that people are motivated by a desire for fairness. When they believe they are being treated unfairly, they will behave in ways that they believe will restore their sense of equity. Although overreward (getting more than one should) and underreward (getting less than one should) are similar from a theoretical perspective, the research suggests otherwise. People are more comfortable (less likely to change their behavior) with overreward than underreward. If people feel that they are underrewarded and can do little about directly influencing their rewards, they are liable to be dissatisfied, work less, and be absent more frequently than when they feel that they are being treated equitably.

Without getting into detailed analysis, one can point out some important differences and similarities between these approaches. The most striking difference is the basic underlying motivational mechanisms postulated as the cause of behavior. These are (1) intentions to reach a goal, (2) expectations of maximum payoff, (3) past reinforcement histories, and (4) a desire for fairness. The similarities are that all four approaches define motivation as an individual, intentional process. Also, except for the operant approach, all of the others focus on relatively current information processing. In this respect, the arousal and choice models seem to be headed in a similar direction. Finally, three of the models define motivation as directly influenced by outcomes (expectancy, operant, and equity approaches); goal setting sees outcomes as indirectly influencing motivation through goal level and intentions.

In order to utilize the information generated from these approaches, one must be able to set specific individual goals, tie rewards to individual behavior, and treat people fairly and equitably. As usual, this is easier said than done. A number of circumstances or situations make it difficult to implement these ideas.

One major problem is that many jobs involve considerable interdependence (Lawler, 1973). People frequently must work with others in order for the job to be accomplished successfully. This interdependence often makes it difficult to specify or tease out individual contributions. To the extent to which there is failure to assess individual behavioral contributions accurately, there will be trouble with individual goal setting and reward administration. Either group goals or rewards may be used.

A second important factor is observability. Individual feedback and reward administration both depend on the extent to which one knows what employees are doing. In many cases, people work alone, or in relatively isolated situations (*e.g.*, within offices, on the road). To the extent that there is poor information about what people actually do, there will be difficulty with implementation.

A third problem has to do with change. In certain situations, jobs and people change fairly rapidly. The changes in jobs may be due to changes in technology, and the changes in people may be due to turnover. Note, again, that motivation emphasizes an individualized behavioral approach. Changes in jobs and people necessitate changes in the motivation system in the form of different behaviors to observe and different rewards to administer.

Finally, the heterogeneity of jobs causes difficulty as well. Each different type of job ideally should require a different job description, different behavior, and, therefore, a different reward system. These last two points focus on the compromise often required in implementing motivational principles. In many cases people or jobs must be lumped together. However, it should be recognized that, to the extent to which there is deviation from the individual behavior conceptualization of motivation, there probably will be a reduction in the effectiveness of the motivational programs and the ability to measure their impact.

DISCUSSION

An analysis of both the theory and practice described above results in some important statements about where research on the topic of motivation should go from here. In terms of theoretical development, it appears as if three things are needed.

First, more integration is needed. Except for a few papers—for example, Locke (1978) and Wofford (1979)—very little theoretical work has been done to suggest the additive or interactive effects of the various approaches. The empirical studies that do compare or combine approaches suggest that combining various factors can lead to an increase in motivation. For example, a paper by White, Mitchell, and Bell (1979) demonstrates that evaluation apprehension, goal setting, and social pressure all have significant effects on motivation and that these effects might be additive.

A second implication that follows the above line of reasoning is that contingency type models of motivation need to be developed and tested. More specifically, the question is no longer whether goal setting or operant approaches work, it is where and when they work best. The mitigating circumstances that were described make it more difficult for one theory to work than another. For example, social cues and evaluation apprehension may increase in importance with interdependence, and goal setting and expectant or operant approaches may become less feasible. With interdependence comes more social interaction and the chance to observe the behavior of others. Social cues and evaluation apprehension should be more salient. On the other hand, interdependence may make it more difficult to specify individual contributions and reward them. At this point there is nothing in the literature that suggests when and where different motivational strategies will be most appropriate.

The third issue complements the other two. Because many jobs are, in fact, interdependent, social, and subject to change, more theory and research needs to be generated on how group processes affect motivation. Strategies such as team building or other interventions designed to increase commitment and motivation need to be studied as motivational models. An understanding is needed of the effects of such interventions on motivated behaviors and how these behaviors contribute to performance. It is hoped that more attention to the above issues will result in a more comprehensive understanding of not only the causes of motivation but how and when and where different strategies should be used.

Exhibit 1
A Flow Diagram of Questions about Motivation

1. Can performance be defined in individual, behavioral terms? If not, develop a separate measure of motivation.
2. Is motivation important for performance, or are abilities and situational factors more important? If motivation is important, but not the same as performance, develop a separate measure of motivation. If one cannot meet the requirements of questions 1 and 2, it may not be worth it to proceed further. If, however, motivation is important for performance and performance is a good reflection of motivation or a good measure of motivation exists, then proceed with the analysis.
3. Is the reward system rigid and inflexible? In other words, are people and tasks grouped into large categories for reward purposes?
4. Is it difficult to observe what people are actually doing on the job?
5. Is an individual's behavior heavily dependent on the actions of others?
6. Are there lots of changes in people, jobs, or expected behavior?
7. Are social pressures the major determinants of what people are doing on the job?

If questions 3 through 7 are answered with a no, then some system combining a needs analysis with goal setting, operant, or expectancy and equity ideas should be effective.

Hand in hand with these changes in theory and research should come changes in practice. One of the first things that should be developed is a set of diagnostic questions that any manager should ask about the motivational process. A flow chart or decision tree could be developed such as the one presented in Exhibit 1. To some extent Exhibit 1 looks like the Vroom and Yetton (1973) model. Unfortunately, the Vroom and Yetton model is vastly superior in its level of detail, analysis, and support. For example, the weighting of factors 3 through 7 in Exhibit 1 is still unknown. There is little to guide one as to the order in which to ask the questions. But, more importantly, there is little guidance about what to do if the answers to 3 through 7 are yes. If what people do can be observed, if various rewards can be utilized, and if rewards can be tied to individual behavior without concern for social pressures or changes in the job, then systems are available that are ready to go. However, the situation is more ambiguous if the reverse of these conditions holds. The knowledge about how to influence motivation when correct behaviors are hard to define and observe, constantly changing, and under the control of interdependencies or social pressures, is severely limited.

The obvious implication for the practitioner is that the cost of implementing one of the more traditional motivation systems (e.g., MBO, behavior modification) might outweigh the benefit under these latter conditions. Until there are better answers to the question of how to influence motivation when these conditions exist, it will be difficult to develop any sort of comprehensive strategy for enhancing motivation. Thus, although the focus of current research is coming to recognize the importance of social processes, changes in jobs or people (Katz, 1980), and problems in flexibility and ability to give feedback (Ilgen, Fisher & Taylor, 1979; Nadler, 1979), few remedies for these problems have been developed. Until this is done, a substantial inadequacy will remain in the ability to understand and influence motivation on the job.

REFERENCES

Alderfer, C.P., "A Critique of Salancik and Pfeffer's Examination of Need Satisfaction Theories," *Administrative Science Quarterly* (Vol. 22, 1977), pp. 658-669.

Atkinson, J.W., *An Introduction to Motivation* (Princeton, N.J.: Van Nostrand, 1964).

Babb, H.W. and Kopp, D.G., "Applications of Behavior Modification in Organizations: A Review and Critique," *Academy of Management Review* (Vol. 3, 1978), pp. 281-290.

Campbell, J.P. and Pritchard, R.D., "Motivation Theory in Industrial and Organizational Psychology," in M.D. Dunnette, ed., *Handbook of Industrial and Organizational Psychology* (Chicago: Rand McNally, 1976), pp. 62-130.

Campbell, J.P., Dunnette, M.D., Lawler, E.E., III and Weick, K.E., Jr., *Managerial Behavior, Performance, and Effectiveness* (New York: McGraw-Hill, 1970).

Carrell, M.R. and Dittrich, J. E., "Equity Theory: The Recent Literature, Methodological Considerations, and New Directions," *Academy of Management Review* (Vol. 3, 1978), pp. 202-210.

Connolly, T., "Some Conceptual and Methodological Issues in Expectancy Models of Work Performance Motivation," *Academy of Management Review* (Vol. 1, No. 4, 1976), pp. 37-47.

Davis, T.R.V. and Luthans, F., "A Social Learning Approach to Organizational Behavior," *Academy of Management Review* (Vol. 5, 1980), pp. 281-290.

Dunnette, M.D., *Performance Equals Ability and What?* Technical Report No. 4009 (Minneapolis: Center for the Study of Organizational Performance and Human Effectiveness, University of Minnesota, 1973).

Ferris, G.R., Beehr, T. A. and Gilmore, D.C., "Social Facilitation: A Review and Alternative Conceptual Model," *Academy of Management Review* (Vol. 3, 1978), pp. 338-347.

Goodman, P.S., "Social Comparisons Process in Organizations," in B.M. Staw and G.R. Salancik, eds., *New Directions in Organizational Behavior*, Vol. 1 (Chicago: St. Clair Press, 1977), pp. 97-132.

Hachman, J.R. and Morris, G.G., "Group Tasks, Group Interaction Process, and Group Performance Effectiveness, in L. Berkowitz, ed., *Advance in Experimental Social Psychology*, Vol. 7 (New York: Academic Press, 1975).

Hellriegel, D. and Slocum, J.W., Jr., *Organizational Behavior: Contingency Views (St. Paul, Minn: West Publishing, 1976).*

Huse, E.F. and Bowditch, J.L., *Behavior in Organizations: A Systems Approach to Managing* (Reading, Mass: Addison-Wesley, 1977).

Ilgen, D.R., Fisher, C.D. and Taylor, M.S., "Consequences of Individual Feedback on Behavior in Organizations," *Journal of Applied Psychology* (Vol. 64, 1979), pp. 349-371.

Kane, J.S. and Lawler, E.E., "Performance Appraisal Effectiveness: Its Assessment and Determiants," in B. Staw, ed., *Research in Organizational Behavior*, Vol. 1 (Greenwich, Conn.: JAI Press, 1979), pp. 425-478.

Kast, F.E. and Rosenweig, J.E., *Organization and Management: A Systems Approach* (New York: McGraw-Hill, 1979).

Katz, R., "Time and Work: Toward an Integrative Perspective," in B.M. Staw and L.L. Cummings, eds., *Research in Organizational Behavior*, Vol. 2 (Greenwich, Conn.: JAI Press, 1960), pp. 81-128.

Kavanagh, M.J. "Performance Appraisal," in K. Rowland and G. Ferris, eds., *Personnel Management* (Boston: Allyn and Bacon, 1981).

Korman, A.D., *The Psychology of Motivation* (Englewood Cliffs, N.J.: Prentice-Hall, 1974).

Korman, A.K., "Hypothesis of Work Behavior Revisited and an Extension," *Academy of Management Review* (Vol. 1, No. 1, 1976), pp. 50-63.

Korman, A.K. Greenhaus, J.H. and Badin, I.J., "Personnel Attitudes and Motivation," *Annual Review of Psychology* (Vol. 28, 1977), pp. 175-196.

Landy, F.J. and Farr, J.L., "Performance Rating," *Psychological Bulletin*, (Vol. 87, 1980), pp. 72-107.

Latham, G.P., Mitchell, T.R. and Dossett, D.L., "The Importance of Participative Goal Setting and Anticipated Rewards on Goal Difficulty and Job Performance," *Journal of Applied Psychology* (Vol. 63, 1978), pp. 163-171.

Lawler, E.E., III, *Motivation in Work Organizations* (Monterey, Calif.: Brooks/Cole, 1973).

Lawler, E.E., III, "New Approaches to Pay Administration," *Personnel* (Vol. 53, 1976), pp. 11-23.

Locke, E.A., "Personnel Attitudes and Motivation," *Annual Review of Psychology* (Vol. 26, 1975), pp. 457-480.

Locke, E.A., "The Ubiquity of the Techniques of Goal Setting in Theories and Approaches to Employee Motivation," *Academy of Management Review* (Vol. 3, 1978), pp. 594-601.

Luthans, F., *Organizational Behavior* (New York: McGraw-Hill, 1977).

March, J.G. and Simon, H.A., *Organizations* (New York: Wiley, 1958).

Mawhinney, T.C. and Behling, O., "Differences in Predictions of Work Behavior from Expectancy and Operant Models of Individual Motivation," *Proceedings of the Academy of Management* (1973), pp. 383-388.

McClelland, D.C. and Steele, R.S. *Human Motivation: A Book of Readings* (Morristown, N.J.: General Learning Press, 1973).

Mitchell, T.R. "Organizational Behavior," *Annual Review of Psychology* (Vol. 30, 1979), pp. 243-281.

Mitchell, T.R., "Expectancy-value Models in Organizational Psychology," in N. Feather, ed., *Expectancy, Incentive and Action* (Hillsdale, N.J.; Erlbaum and Associates, 1980).

Mitchell, T.R., "Motivational Strategies," in K. Rowland and G. Ferris, eds., *Personnel Management* (Boston: Allyn and Bacon, in press).

Mitchell, T.R., *People in Organizations: Understanding Behavior* (New York: McGraw-Hill, 1978).

Nadler, D.A., "The Effects of Feedback on Task Group Behavior Review of the Experimental Research," *Organizational Behavior and Human Performance* (Vol. 23, 1979), pp. 309-338.

Porter, L.W. and Lawler, E.E., III, *Managerial Attitudes and Performance* (Homewood, Ill.: Dorsey, 1968).

Ryan, T.A., *Intentional Behavior: An Approach to Human Motivation* (New York: Ronald Press, 1970).

Slaancik, G.R. and Pfeffer, J., "An Examination of Need Satisfaction Models of Job Attitudes, *Administrative Science Quarterly* (Vol II, 1977), pp. 427-456.

Salancik, G.R. and Pfeffer. J., "A Social Information Processing Approach to Job Attitudes and Task Design," *Administrative Science Quarterly* (Vol. 23, 1978), pp. 224-253.

Schwab, D.P., Olian-Gottlieb, J.D. and Heneman, H.T., III, "Between Subjects Expectancy Theory Research: A Statistical Review of Studies Predicting Effort and Performance," *Psychological Bulletin* (Vol. 86, 1979), pp. 139-147.

Scott, W.G. and Hart, D.K. *Organizational America* (Boston: Houghton Mifflin, 1979).

Staw, B.M., "Motivation in Organizations: Toward Synthesis and Redirection," in B.M. Staw and G.R. Slanick, eds., *New Directions in Organizational Behavior*, Vol. 1 (Chicago: St. Clair Press, 1977), pp. 54-95.

Steers, R.M. and Porter, L.W., "The Role of Task-goal Attributes in Employee Performance," *Psychological Bulletin* (Vol. 81, 1974), pp. 434-452.

Steers, R.M. and Porter, L.W., *Motivation and Work Behavior* (New York: McGraw-Hill, 1979).

Tosi, H.L., House, R.J. and Dunnette, M.D., *Management Motivation and Compensation: A Selection of Readings* (East Lansing, Mich.: MSU Business Studics, 1972).

Vroom, V.H., *Work and Motivation* (New York: Wiley, 1964).

Vroom, V.H. Yetton, P.W., *Leadership and Decision Making* (Pittsburgh: University of Pittsburgh Press, 1973).

Weiner, B., *Theories of Motivation: From Mechanism to Cogation* (Chicago: Rand McNally, 1972).

White, S., Mitchell, T.R. and Bell, C.H., "Goal Setting, Evaluation Apprehension and Social Cues as Determinants of Job Performance and Job Satisfaction in a Simulated Organization," *Journal of Applied Psychology* (Vol. 62, 1977), pp. 665-673.

Wofford, J.C., "A Goal Energy Effort Requirement Model (GEER) of Work Motivation," *Academy of Management Review* (Vol. 4, 1979), pp. 193-201.

Yukl, G. A. and Latham, G.P., "Interrelationships among Employee Participation, Individual Differences, Goal Difficulty, Goal Acceptance, Instrumentality and Performance," *Personal Psychology* (Vol. 31, 1978), pp. 305-324.

Terence Mitchell is professor of management and organization and of psychology at the University of Seattle.

34.
FIVE STEPS TO IMPROVING
EMPLOYEE PERFORMANCE

Michael Smith
Jan Wing

> This model formalizes the steps that successful managers have been using for years to help their subordinates.

As a supervisor, it is your responsibility to take corrective action for inadequate performance. But if you're like most supervisors, you've probably wondered if the time and effort you have devoted to trying to improve subordinate performance haven't been wasted, given the return. Most managers find that their efforts don't lead to improved performance. Below is a five-step model that can help you deal more effectively with performance problems. It isn't the only approach to upgrading performance, but it has been shown to be 75 percent effective. It involves:

1. Looking at a subordinate's total performance and focusing on significant behavior requiring improvement
2. Agreeing on a description of current performance
3. Finding out why expectations are not being met
4. Developing a performance improvement plan
5. Making sure improvement provides a payoff

At first glance, this model may seem an overly complicated way to help someone improve. But all this model does is formalize the steps that successful managers have been using for years to help their subordinates.

STEP 1: LOOK AT TOTAL PERFORMANCE
AND FOCUS ON PROBLEMS

In discussing job performance with an employee, it's important not to concentrate exclusively on poor performance. Discussions with subordinates about performance should include a review of the results that were on target as well as those that weren't.

When the most important aspects of an employee's job were done as expected or better, the discussion should focus on maintaining performance at that level. But when significant parts of the job were not performed as expected, then the focus should be on improvement. Your objectives are to improve performance in those areas that are most important to the organization and to your subordinates, eliminate any negative behavior that severely interferes with others' performance, and see that positive changes in employee behavior and performance are maintained. You shouldn't try to accomplish too much at one time. Select one or two areas that, if improved, would change your evaluation of the subordinate. Trying to do more than this will increase the likelihood of failure, frustration, and more poor performance.

STEP 2: AGREE ON A DESCRIPTION OF CURRENT PERFORMANCE

Little will be accomplished if you and the subordinate are talking at cross purposes. This can happen if the discussion isn't specific with regard to your expectations and to how far off the employee's current performance is from those expectations.

Zeroing in on specific areas for improvement isn't easy. Many times a manager will talk with a subordinate about poor performance but when the conversation is completed, the employee is still uncertain about what needs to be done to satisfy the supervisor. To understand why confusion occurs, look at the samples of managerial comments that follow. The comments on the left are not specific enough. The comments on the right are clear enough for the subordinate to know what the manager is talking about.

Sample Performance Descriptions

Manager did say: "You don't plan well."	Manager should have said: "By waiting until one week before deadline and not in some way doing the work a little at a time in the eight weeks you had, you made on-time delivery impossible."
"You have no sense of urgency."	"I asked you to prepare a status report for the division manager. I didn't expect to wait three days while you finished your regular quarterly reports."

"You don't listen to people."   "When your subordinates talk to
                                       you, you shuffle paper, look for
                                       misplaced memos, and move
                                       around your office."

In your meeting with a problem employee, you may wish to indicate in a general way that there is a problem and ask the subordinate for his or her perception of the situation. Or you may prefer to state your position first. However, it is always worthwhile to ask for the subordinate's viewpoint. It enables you to determine if the subordinate understands what is being said as well as how he is reacting to your comments.

It's your responsibility to do whatever you can to make sure your message is getting through. Mention dates, times, people involved, quality and quantity standards to be met, and how far off performance was from the standards.

STEP 3: FIND OUT WHY EXPECTATIONS ARE NOT BEING MET

It's always easier to solve a problem when you know the cause. With performance problems, though, that's not always a simple matter. Raising performance questions brings out defensiveness in employees. The number of excuses given will be directly proportional to the way you question the employee or the way people who make mistakes are treated in your organization. If you ask, "Why did you make that mistake?" don't expect a straight answer. If you normally "hang" people who make mistakes, don't expect them to admit readily to any kind of error or substandard performance.

The likelihood of hearing excuses is no reason to avoid asking for subordinate input. There may have been valid reasons for the poor performance. You, as well as the employee, will benefit from an objective discussion of what happened. Avoid making assumptions about the subordinate and his or her actions. It's very easy to ascribe poor performance to carelessness, incompetence, or some other mortal sin, when the real reason is much more mundane. We have found that poor performance most often stems from one of seven reasons: unclear expectations, lack of feedback, interference, the right thing is too hard to do, the wrong thing is too easy to do, lack of practice, and lack of knowledge or skill. Once causes like these are identified, it is much easier to work with the subordinate in improving performance. Possible solutions to the seven problems are shown in the following table.

Seven Causes of Poor Performance

Causes of problem   *Possible solutions*
1. Subordinate doesn't know   Establish standards,
what is expected.   expectations, and/or objectives.

2. Subordinate doesn't get feedback about the level and the quality of actual performance	Establish some means of giving timely feedback. This could be periodic discussions with you or a self-monitoring system, such as a simple PERT chart.
3. Expected performance is difficult, "punishing," or in some way less desirable for the subordinate.	Remove or reduce the inhibiting factors to correct performance. Try to make performance matter.
4. Subordinate knows how to do what is expected but is "out of practice."	Provide practice.
5. Subordinate doesn't know how to do what is expected.	Arrange for training. Look into the availability of reference materials and other aids.
6. Something in the work environment interferes with performance.	Look at priorities, time expectations, mix of duties, physical environment, availability of resources to determine the source of interference.
7. Performing below expectations is easier, "rewarding," or is some way more desirable for the subordinate.	Be sure expectations are known and the consequences for not performing up to expectations are also known (effect on future performance appraisals, your displeasure, interference with others' work). See if performing as expected can be made less difficult or more rewarding.

In applying a solution, remember that it will work only if the proper motivation exists. Almost everything one does has a payoff; otherwise, one wouldn't bother doing it. This is particularly true about job performance. An improvement will not occur if there is no payoff or an unwanted payoff for the subordinate.

Some managers believe that improved performance will come about only through the internal motivation of the individual employee, perhaps assisted by the boss arranging for a more positive or a more explicit payoff. This is generally true. But there is another side to the motivation equation. A subordinate will also work to expected levels because not doing so will result in an unwanted payoff like constant supervisory attention, no raise in pay, or termination. Making clear to an employee the consequences of continued poor performance is a valid course of action, although it should only be used as a last resort. Like aspirin, threats mask the symptoms but they don't fix the underlying problem.

STEP 4: DEVELOP AN IMPROVEMENT PLAN

Telling an employee that his or her performance must improve isn't enough to bring about change. An improvement plan must be developed. Ideally the subordinate should be a willing partner in the plan's development. Depending on the subordinate's willingness to take responsibility for his or her own actions, you as a manager will be more or less involved in setting up the plan. Whatever the extent of your involvement, however, be sure:

The plan includes a set of objectives. These objectives should help close the gap between expected and actual performance. They should include a description of the expected quality and quantity of work, the date by which change will be apparent, and anything else that is appropriate. If the gap between expected and actual performance is too big to correct immediately, improvement can occur gradually, in increments. It's better to have three small progressive successes and retain an employee than one big failure.

Objectives should be jointly developed unless the subordinate won't cooperate. In that case, you should set the objectives.

The plan is specific enough. It should include who does what, by when, and with what resources. Ideally, these issues should jointly be determined with the subordinate doing most of the work. This way the employee feels ownership of the plan and will be more committed to its achievement. But, again, with an extremely poor performance or an unmotivated one, the manager may have to do most of the work.

The plan includes some method of measuring progress. Specific feedback must be given frequently. The most effective feedback method is one that allows the employee to monitor his or her own performance. You might also consider providing ongoing feedback or periodically meeting with the subordinate to provide feedback on his or her progress. Whatever the system used, the feedback must be intensive until performance improves and stabilizes at the expected level.

What we're describing is nothing more than a very specific objective-setting process. But because of its importance to improved performance, if the employee won't actively participate, you will have to do the lion's share of the work.

You might resist having to do much of the work. "If he (or she) won't change, that's Jim's (or Jane's) problem," you might say. That's true to a degree. But the employee was productive once or was well enough thought of to be hired in the first place. It is a manager's responsibility to manage performance, and that includes taking the time and effort to evaluate the employee's total performance, establish a description of current performance, show how expectations are not being met, and initiate or develop an improvement plan.

There is no easy formula for the amount of time you allow for improvement to take place. This decision will be based on the subordinate's length of service (more for a long-time employee, less for a newer one), the complexity of the tasks involved (the more complex, the more time), the importance of the performance to the organization, and so on.

STEP 5: MAKE SURE IMPROVEMENT PROVIDES A PAYOFF

The last step in the model—making sure there's a payoff for improved performance—is essential to the model's success, since as we've mentioned people only change when they see some valued payoff in changing. The payoff may be gaining or maintaining something they want or it may be avoiding something that they don't want. Whatever the payoff, it must be linked to the performance. Whatever you have promised, make sure you deliver. No matter what it is—a better appraisal, continued employment, praise, more responsibility, a salary increase, a transfer, or special assignment—the expected payoff must be given. This way you ensure your credibility as a manager and make it easier on yourself to work with this subordinate and others in the future.

One final word of advice about overseeing the work of employees: In devoting time and attention to marginal performers, don't neglect your good performers. They require feedback and attention just as much or more than their less efficient colleagues.

Michael Smith is manager, Human Resources Development, Research-Cottrell. Jan Wing is a senior training specialist, Research-Cottrell.

Part V
MOTIVATION—SYSTEMATIC APPROACHES

35.
A COORDINATED APPROACH TO MOTIVATION CAN INCREASE PRODUCTIVITY

James M. McFillen
Philip M. Podsakoff

Too often, effective management strategy has been sacrificed for convenience.

For at least 40 years, the attention of academicians and managers in the United States has shifted steadily from employee performance to employee satisfaction. Organizations have developed programs in the areas of compensation, job design and supervisory leadership—all aimed at making employees feel better about their jobs and their employers. And evidence suggests that industry's efforts in behalf of employee satisfaction have been successful.

Although U.S. workers overwhelmingly express satisfaction with their jobs, their productivity improvement has slowed appreciably. Recent reports paint a picture of a steady decline of U.S. industrial productivity relative to other industrialized nations.

But hourly compensation in the United Sates has been rising over the same period that productivity has been slipping. The cumulative effect has been a rise in labor cost of over 220 percent during the 20 years from 1957 to 1977. Coupled with the increased costs of energy, government regulation, taxes, etc., this damaged America's economic position at home and abroad.

When the wages for a given year are adjusted by the inflation rate for that year, the results indicate a leveling off of real compensation. The effect of inflation exceeding productivity improvement is that the real economic gains of employees have ceased. All of industry's efforts to improve productivity have gone into offsetting the rapidly rising cost of labor, such that the real unit labor cost has remained relatively stable. Organizations have had to run faster to stay even.

Numerous reasons have been cited for America's poor performance. The finger has been pointed at problems of capital formation due to taxation, savings patterns, and a general redistribution of wealth. A second target has been the effects of government regulation and legislation in the areas of safety, pollution, employment, and energy. Changes in work force composition and competence have been offered as a third cause.

The examples used to support this conclusion are the lower skills, training, and experience brought to the workplace by teenagers, minorities, and women, who increased their labor participation rates in the '70s.

The final cause is changes in the motivation and work ethic of the American worker. This is best exemplified by the declining role of work in a person's life, coupled with the rising demand for more leisure. For whatever reason, it has become apparent that American industry is getting less work per dollar of wages than it did just a few years ago.

PLACING BLAME

Most of the causes of lowered productivity appear to be beyond the control of an individual manager, and many seem beyond the influence of an organization's management team. However, productivity is not strictly a function of variables external to the firm, over which management has no control.

A closer examination of the motivational causes of lowered productivity shows that many management policies and practices are at least partially to blame for the change in employee attitudes toward work. Many potentially powerful tools lie within management's control if only management chooses to develop an overall strategy for performance improvement. This strategy must utilize the various elements of human resource management in a unified program consistent with enhancing employee motivation to work. Too often, effective management strategy has been sacrificed for ease of administration, standardization, and a preference for equality of treatment over equity.

Management has frequently dismissed or diluted some of the most influential practices, while at the same time opting for isolated programs in which performance on the job is to be encouraged by allowing good workers to escape from the workplace through flextime, modified work weeks, and other opportunities for increased leisure time. Such programs usually provide a job change designed to improve the quality of work life with the hope that employees will reciprocate with increased performance or reduced personnel-related costs. The results frequently are a set of conflicting incentives and policies. Motivation should be a positive, active concern of management, rather than a negative, passive issue to which managment responds only when something goes wrong.

To develop a consistent, unified strategy for increasing employee productivity through motivation, management must develop a framework for motivation that allows the policies and programs in human resources management to be coordinated. Without some underlying framework, the interdependence of the wide variety of policies and programs involved will be difficult to identify and their administration will be confusing and conflicting. Motivation is complex, but its importance and potential contribution are so great that management must attempt to fashion some overall direction for their motivation efforts. Motivation must not be left to chance with the hope that some combination of elements will prove motivating.

MANAGEMENT MISTAKES

To understand the importance of management philosophy and practice in the productivity problem, the context of the human resources side of the issue must be considered. Management has played a major role in developing the conditions of motivation found in business today, and therefore must accept responsibility for the demotivating effects of current management practice. A fundamental problem has been the adoption of a philosophy suggested by the human relations movement that employee satisfaction causes employee performance. Adherence to this philosophy has led to a major change in the way organizations try to motivate their members.

Under this philosophy, providing employees with things they desire is expected to make employees more satisfied with the firm, or more indebted to it, with the hope that they will be more productive. The result of this practice, as most managers can attest, is not improved productivity, but rather increased costs. If providing boosts in wages or other employment benefits prior to increased performance were the key to improving motivation and productivity, then establishing and raising the minimum wage should have been a major boon to worker productivity.

The fact is that negotiated, legislated, or management-mandated increases in the general wage do not result in improved worker output. Management has, instead, reduced employment and substituted machines and automation to improve productivity as a way to offset increased labor costs.

A related management practice has been a general movement away from performance-related rewards. This is true with regard to financial and non-financial rewards. Some firms have felt compelled to abandon the use of financial incentives in favor of hourly or salary-based compensation, due to management philosophy, policy ease, or external pressures. Regardless of the reason, the long-term effects have been the same: The relationship between employee compensation and daily performance has been seriously diminished.

Annual merit increases or across-the-board wage adjustments are not satisfactory substitutes for performance-related compensation. Coupled with the effect of inflation upon the financial resources available for pay raises and the neglect and misuse of performance appraisals by management, the transition to salary and hourly pay has all but eliminated the tie between performance and earnings, and has eroded employee belief that their economic gains are somehow tied to the gains of the firm. If managers wish to test their firm's effectiveness on this issue, they need only ask what advantages or benefits accrue to high-performers that do no accrue to low-performers. If the list is short and of little value, then the organization has seriously reduced the effectiveness of its reward system.

DEMOTIVATING MESSAGE

More and more managers are finding that although their organizations give "lip service" to providing merit raises or other financial incentives, the allocation of such rewards often is quite arbitrary due to the use of poor appraisal practices or to a dependence upon seniority and cost-of-living as the principal criteria for raises. The results are the same.

The only consistent message to employees is that performance does not determine compensation. What does influence compensation is the action taken by unions, government, and management independent of any employee efforts toward increased productivity. Increased pressure on management, not increased performance, is the key to earning more. The motivation implications should be obvious, and the focus of employee efforts readily apparent. Management must consider the long-term costs as well as the short-run benefits of such practices.

Non-financial rewards have grown increasingly important with the growth in non-contingent compensation. Hourly pay, salary, and fringe benefits basically encourage employees to do only what is necessary to maintain employment. If management expects employees to go beyond this minimum level of acceptable performance, the burden falls upon non-financial means of motivation. Management either must hire only those individuals whose dominant characteristic is intensive self-motivation, or use its own managerial skills to arouse employee motivation. The problem in depending upon either of these two solutions is that neither is very likely. Self-motivation relies essentially upon self-interest and only rarely do jobs and self-interest significantly overlap. As for managerial skills, individuals in management positions frequently lack either the time, inclination or skill to motivate others.

For various reasons, managers are unable or unwilling to invest the degree of involvement and effort required to really encourage subordinates to perform. When advised on using feedback, recognition, and participation as motivation tools, managers commonly respond by claiming they do not have the time to become so involved in the interpersonal side of motivation. The organization and its managers, however, find the time and resources to deal after-the-fact with the results of low employee motivation and commitment to performance. Managers are forced to find the time to fight the fires that erupt; it's just the prevention that suffers from such low priority.

Organizations frequently turn to complex programs, such as job enrichment and MBO, as solutions to motivation problems. Management employs a promising new program only to find that the benefical effects are short-lived or that the few benefits are buried by an avalanche of forms, meetings and procedures. The disruption and disillusionment that frequently follow dampen enthusiasm and produce a disdain for future efforts to enhance motivation. At the heart of the failure is a fundamental problem: Management has failed to utilize a framework for motivation that facilitates the development and integration of human resource programs and policies.

New programs are planned, but they are not integrated with existing systems. A framework is needed that allows motivation problems to be analyzed logically and systematically, and that permits management to assess in what manner a given program might contribute to or detract from motivation.

DEFINING MOTIVATION

Before a framework can be developed, some common idea of what is meant by motivation must be established. When a manager says an employee is unmotivated, what the manager really means is that the employee is not motivated to do what the manager wishes to be done, but instead is motivated to do something the employee, or the work group, or someone else wants done. This, then, is a matter of direction of motivation and not a matter of being motivated or unmotivated.

All employees exhibit motivated, purposeful behavior. The problem is that the employees' purposes are not always the same as those of management. The question for management then is how to create situations that motivate employees in the desired direction.

A manager's concept of motivation appears to have two components. The first involves the effort or attempt to perform: Does the employee try to do what is asked? The second involves the actual performance or results accruing from the employees' efforts: Does the employee actually accomplish what is asked? Although one component might seem to imply the other automatically, the fact is the components may be considered as separate elements.

For example, it is easy to see how an employee's efforts might be blocked or misdirected and therefore fail to result in satisfactory performance. The employee might be willing, but lack the proper skills or have the wrong idea as to what is expected. What is sometimes harder to see is that performance attributed to one employee may have resulted from the efforts of others or from the wrong kind of effort. Like Tom Sawyer's fence painting, an employee's performance could be due to misplaced efforts, as in taking short-cuts or getting others to do the employee's work. Performance might also emerge from the natural interdependence of the work as when performance is a function of group rather than individual effort.

Similarly, a lack of effort may be due to a lack of incentives, or to competing incentives, or to past failure. Employees engage in their personal cost-benefit analysis and opt for those bargains they perceive as profitable for themselves. Managers must examine the work situation from the employee's perspective. A recent example of this problem was a supervisor for a large appliance manufacturer who could not understand why a college-educated hourly worker would not transfer from a $7.50 per hour, late-shift janitorial job to the assembly line, where the employee could earn 10 percent more per hour.

As the situation was examined, it became apparent that not only would the job change mean a decline in autonomy—which was important to the college graduate—but it would also mean a sizeable increase in the amount of effort required. Management was expecting the employee to voluntarily switch from a job requiring an honest five hours of work per eight-hour shift to one requiring seven-and-one-half hours on the line. For this 50 percent increase in work, the employee was offered a 10 percent increase in pay. All motivation-related issues must be viewed from the perspective of the one being motivated, not of the one trying to do the motivating.

EFFECTIVE FRAMEWORK

Creating a framework for motivation requires a consideration of what encourages effort and what channels that effort toward satisfactory job-related performance. Such a framework must include the specification and description of what is to be done and the elements that contribute to a willingness to perform. This willingness results from an interaction between the incentives for performance and the employee's knowledge and confidence regarding performance. A simplified version of a model of motivation developed by Vroom and extended and elaborated by Campbell, Dunnette, Lawler and Wcick, can serve as the origin for a framework of motivation (see the table).

BARRIERS TO PERFORMANCE

The limits to the effort-performance relationship are quite different from those affecting the performance-outcome relationship, but all of the limits share the requirement for viewing motivation from the perspective of the employee. The common effort-performance limits fall into four categories:

- Doubts about ability, skill or knowledge
- Physical or practical possibility of the job
- Interdependence of job with other people or activities
- Ambiguity surrounding the job requirements

Employees may be reluctant to try to perform, because they doubt their capacity to do the job, or doubt whether the job can be performed as described.

Table
A Motivation Framework

Effort ◆ ◆ ◆ Performance ◆ ◆ ◆ Outcome

Barriers to performance   Limits on incentive

1. Doubts about ability,   1. Linkage between performance
   skill, or knowledge   and outcome
2. Physical or practical   2. Knowledge of outcome
   possibility of job   3. Incremental nature of
3. Interdependence of job   outcomes
   outcomes with other   4. Indivisibility of outcomes
   people or activities   5. Time span between performance
4. Ambiguity surrounding   and outcome
   job requirements

If employees doubt whether they can be successful at their jobs, their expectation of receiving rewards also will be reduced. Assuming no change in the level of promised outcomes, motivation declines as the odds against success becomes higher. Employees discount the value of trying as the probability of successful performance diminishes. Past failure in the same or similar work can contribute to doubts about whether successful performance will follow effort.

The barriers due to interdependencies arise when the employee's desired activity is entangled with the activities required of others or with other activities in which the employee is engaged. If an employee's work is dependent upon work by others prior to or simultaneously with his own work, the employee is less likely to feel that he is able to control the level of performance. The necessity to coordinate with others dampens one's expectation of successful performance unless similar situations in the past have proven satisfactory.

All managers have experienced that initial sense of anguish when a new committee is formed to handle some complicated problem. Similarly, when an employee is faced with several highly interdependent tasks, the problem of coordinating and prioritizing those tasks appears. When some of those tasks are in direct conflict due to time or resource limitations or to conflicting goals, the effect is to lower the employee's expectation of successfully completing all or part of the tasks. Therefore, interdependencies that are not carefully coordinated and controlled by management will result in lowered employee motivation.

The final category of barriers to the effort-performance relationship is ambiguity. Ambiguity can take many forms. It may appear as poor communication regarding what is to be done, or confusion over methods or authority. Employees who are unsure what is expected of them may be hesitant to act or, worse, may embark on their own interpretation of what is to be done. In essence, management leaves performance to chance when it allows ambiguity to develop around the task. If the intent is to test an employee's initiative, ambiguity might serve a useful purpose. In daily management practice, however, unnecessary ambiguity about the task is likely to reduce an employee's confidence in a successful performance and therefore reduce motivation to perform. Highly ambiguous work coupled with highly important outcome can also be damaging by inducing high levels of employee stress.

LIMITS ON INCENTIVE

In examining motivation, managers must ask themselves why an employee should desire to do what is asked. The answer lies in whether accomplishing the desired performance will result in outcomes accruing to the employee that otherwise would not have been available. Does performance result in outcomes that non-performance does not? There are five limits that affect the employee's perception of the performance-outcome relationship:

- Linkage between performance and outcome
- Knowledge of outcome
- Incremental nature of outcomes
- Indivisibility of outcomes
- Time span between performance and outcome

Much of what management, organized labor, and government have done in the area of employment has driven a wedge between performance and outcome. Salary, fringe benefits, seniority-based raises, and ineffective performance appraisals all contribute to reducing the linkage between pay and performance. The result is that one's earnings are not influenced by what one does on behalf of the organization, but rather by the power or influence employees collectively have over the organization—or by the benevolent actions of management. The former defeats management's ability to manage and the latter creates a childlike dependence for the employees. Similarly, managers fail to use feedback, praise, and recognition in a manner consistent with encouragement performance.

The performance-outcome linkage also is weakened when the receipt of outcomes is clouded by ambiguity. The confusion may be due to a lack of knowledge of outcomes, to a discounting of the value of outcomes because of their incremental nature, or to an inability to limit the benefits of some outcomes (such as department bonuses only to those employees who deserve them). All three cause employees to doubt that they receive anything significant for their role as a high-performer. Employees may be unaware of benefits that accrue to those who perform well or may perceive each benefit in such a piecemeal fashion that the total value of the benefit goes unappreciated. Employees subject to group-based incentives often feel short-changed because unequal performances are rewarded equally. Since individual motivation is weakened, the best performers tend to drift downward to the level of the mediocre performers.

The final limit to the performance-outcome relationship relates to the problem of the timing of reward allocation once desired performance has occurred. The annual bonus or annual salary increase is an example of the timing problem.

An employee receiving a merit raise in July for performance during the prior year associates that raise less with daily performance than if merit increases were allocated more frequently but covered shorter periods of time. When incentive pay lags two, three, or four weeks behind the date of performance due to the complications of administration, employees tend to lose the immediate association between pay and performance, which in turn weakens the performance-outcome linkage engineered into the compensation system. The key element in this problem is the immediacy of the outcome accomplished by actually allocating the rewards or by providing employees with tangible evidence of their current performance and upcoming rewards.

INTERDEPENDENCE

The effort-performance barriers are damaging to the level of employee motivation. Since they affect motivation through a different route than the performance-outcome limits, they require different resolution strategies. Although different solutions are required, the effects of the two sources of limits are not totally independent. Management can attempt to heighten an employee's motivation on a difficult task by increasing the value of a performance-contingent reward or by strengthening the contingency between task performance and rewards. This balancing act has its limitations. Attempting to offset very low performance probabilities by making the performance-related outcomes more important can induce high levels of stress and frustration in employees. A manager may not achieve positive results by telling an employee, "I know you don't think you can handle the job, but if you don't try you're fired." Here the payoff for performance is high (keeping one's job), but it does not overcome the limits perceived by the employee. The motivation to try may be higher, but so may be the anxiety.

APPLICATION OF THE FRAMEWORK

The framework of motivation developed here suggests three key areas of management responsibility:

- Performance definition
- Performance facilitation
- Performance encouragement

Attention to these areas will reduce the limits to motivation and will serve as a guide to the coordination and integration of human resource policy.

Performance definition involves the initial disclosure of what is expected from employees and a continuous process of orienting employees toward job performance. It involves three elements: goal, measures and assessment. Establishing goals is critical to motivation. Employees might be instructed as to what the work goals are or be permitted to participate in the actual goal-setting process. Participation in goal setting tends to increase employee acceptance of the goals. In either case, the goals need to be precise, reasonable, and specific as to the what, how, and when of performance. Goal setting improves the direction of effort as well as enhancing accountability.

Goals also help employees to understand their relative contributions to the firm. For example, an electronics manufacturer had trouble with performance quality along an assembly line. Management discussed the quality standards and the reasons behind each standard with the employees. The discussion included a display along one wall of the work area that demonstrated the effects of one operator's error upon subsequent work stages and the final product. The display made it quite evident that the performance goals were not arbitrary.

The presence of goals, however, is not sufficient. Management also must find a means for operationalizing and therefore measuring the goals. Goals such as making the company successful not only lack specificity as to what level of success is desired, but also fall prey to many potentially competing measures of success. A goal that has no direct or surrogate measure is of little use to management beyond window dressing.

The third aspect of performance definition is assessment. Management can identify measurable goals, but if there is no intent to assess individual or organization performance on those goals, the goals will serve no purpose motivationally. In fact, goals that are started but that go unassessed over time send important messages to employees about management commitment to those goals and raise questions about management commitment in other areas. Sloppy, unprofessional assessment of performance not only tarnishes management's image, but potentially leads to misinformation about the performance of individuals as well as of the organization. Misinformation makes the accurate rewarding of performance impossible and therefore reduces the motivating potential of the reward system. Assessment also encourages a continuing orientation toward job performance.

Performance definition aids establishment of effort-performance and performance-outcome relationships. It helps determine the ability and knowledge required for the job, clarifies interdependencies and conflicts, and improves directionality of effort through reduced ambiguity. Performance definition also makes possible the creation of a performance-outcome linkage. The pivotal connection of performance definition to motivation should be readily apparent.

The second key area, performance facilitation, involves elimination of

roadblocks to performance. Its major contribution to motivation is that it increases the effort-performance relationship. To facilitate employee
performance, management must be active in:

- Removing performance obstacles
- Providing means and resources for performance
- Selecting proper personnel

When designing jobs, management must create highly supportive task
environments. Jobs should be free of unnecessary obstacles to performance.
These obstacles frequently take the form of poorly maintained equipment,
cumbersome management practices, and poorly designed work methods. The
effect of these is to make it more difficult and frustrating to do the assigned
work. Motivation declines as employees develop the opinion that management
is apparently unconcerned about getting the job done.

A similar problem develops when management fails to commit the resources
necessary for performance. This is typified by organizations that try to do
everything on a "shoestring" budget. Assigning minimal financial, human, or
material resources can be self-defeating and extremely costly in terms of
performing the task at hand, as well as in terms of future employee motivation
to perform. Such practices cause employees to doubt whether the assigned task
can be done well, and signal the relative importance management assigns to
the task.

The final element of performance facilitation is the proper selection of
personnel. Although selection has been made more complicated by equal
employment legislation, management cannot afford to back away from proper
selection policy. Selection, training, and placement are essential to employee
motivation to perform. Poor staffing procedures guarantee reduced motivation
by placing employees in jobs that either demand too little from them or require
more than their skills and abilities can supply. The result is higher turnover and
absenteeism as well as reduced performance. An additional effect is the hiring
of more employees than are actually required. This means generally higher
fringe benefit costs as well as higher wage costs. Productivity is reduced and
costs increased simultaneously.

THE FINAL KEY

Performance encouragement is the final, key area. In order to encourage
employee performance through the performance-outcome linkage,
management must be concerned with five issues:

- Value of reward
- Magnitude of reward

- Timing of reward
- Likelihood of reward
- Equity of reward

Value and magnitude of reward relate to the choice of rewards to be used in an organization. Much has been said in the popular literature about the changing values of American workers. Management must offer outcomes to employees that are attractive in both value and magnitude. Job redesign, cafeteria pay systems, and altered work weeks all have been attempts to offer employees outcomes they value.

Sometimes, however, the problem is not one of value, but rather of amount. For example, an organization may offer insufficient inducement to exert more effort. A manager in a government agency complained that the new breed of employees was not as motivated as it should be. Even though the employees were eligible for merit increases, the manager felt that they just did not seem to put much effort into their jobs.

When asked how much of a raise he gave his top performer, the manager proudly stated, "Why, I gave him eight percent." When asked what his worst performer received for a raise, the manager responded, "Seven percent, but the difference really was based on merit." One may argue whether seven percent is of sufficient magnitude given 10 percent inflation, but the belief that a one percent differential is sufficient to reward high performance is purely wishful thinking.

The issues of timing and likelihood of reward apply to the linkage between performance and outcome. As discussed under the framework for motivation, management practices that serve to seriously dilute the relationship between performance and subsequent reward destroy the reason for employee performance. Whether the reward is in the form of raises, incentive pay, promotions, or recognition for a job well done, timing and likelihood are fundamental to an effective reward system. Outcomes that are delayed in coming lose their potential for motivation just as do outcomes that accrue independent of performance.

Many production incentive systems require lengthy delay in the allocation of rewards. In the tubing department of a major steel producer, the production bonus was computed daily as a function of the employee's job and production level for the day. The incentive was included on payroll checks distributed two weeks later. Since employees commonly worked on three or more different machines in a given week and their levels of performance varied as a function of both the product and the quality standards involved, employees found it nearly impossible to account for the fluctuations in incentive pay that occurred on their checks each week. Employees either doubted whether performance was related to pay or believed the formula was too complicated for them to understand. The result was a feeling that the production bonus was like dropping coins in a slow machine; the payoff was by chance.

The final issue, equity, affects the magnitude and likelihood variables. Equity is simply a judgment about whether one gets what one deserves, and is made in reference to employees who believe they work harder than other people in similar jobs and who believe they should receive more in return from the organization.

This means they expect a greater magnitude of rewards. If they fail to receive those increased rewards they may reduce the quantity or quality of their performances and come to believe that reward is unrelated to performance. Experience has shown that people have a much greater tolerance for being inequitably overpaid than for inequitably underpaid. Treating all employees equally invariably results in inequitable treatment, because people rarely perform equally. The high-performers are underpaid and hence reduce their level of performance. Low-performers are overpaid but find numerous ways to justify it rather than increase their performance. Equal treatment, therefore, reuslts in equally low performance for all employees over time or results in the good employees quitting to take jobs with firms that will appreciate their contribution.

Inequity often occurs in well designed but poorly administered reward systems. Employees read management's intentions not from what management professes to do but from what, in fact, occurs. Inattention to the details of the reward system's administration—for example, performance appraisal—guarantees feelings of inequitable treatment.

IMPLICATIONS FOR MANAGEMENT

Many causes of lowered or static levels of employee productivity exist. Employee motivation is only one of the contributors. In fact it is hard to say what percentage of the productivity problem is attributable to changed attitudes toward work. Some experts go so far as to say that productivity cannot be improved by employees working harder, but rather that employees must work smarter. However, if recent estimates are accurate and the average employee works only four hours out of every eight-hour shift, there appears to be room for employee-based improvements in productivity. The fundamental point to remember is not whether working smarter or harder is the answer, but that prevailing management practice often fails to reward employees for either working harder or smarter. Management has been racing to get increasing productivity from a declining employee commitment to performance.

The call for performance-contingent rewards is not a request for a return to the sweatshop. However, future personnel practice must renew the relationship between employee performance and employee outcome. The complexities of human motivation make a coordinated human resource policy essential in modern organizations. Failure to apply a logic or framework to management practice produces confusion and conflict in personnel administration. In formulating future human resource policies, management must:

- Quit relying on employee indebtedness to encourage performance and instead consider what the organization owes to good performers.
- Be aware of the context of performance and productivity problems in the organization.
- Examine the motivational properties of the personnel policies and practices in the organization within the context of a motivation framework.

Improved productivity deserves the attention of management and labor. It is worth management's time to design and administer programs that encourage improved employee productivity. Management would do well to add this new slogan to guide future personnel practices: productivity is no waste of effort.

James M. McFillen, is an assistant professor of management sciences at Ohio State University. He received his D.B.A. in organizational behavior from Indiana University. Philip M. Podsakoff is also an assistant professor of management science at Ohio State. He received his D.B.A. in organization behavior from Indiana University.

36.
TRACKING MOTIVATION

Kenneth A. Kovach

Surveys help gauge employee needs.

Traditionally, the area of employee motivation has caused administrative managers as many problems as has any other single functional area. The problem of motivating employees seems to have, at best, nebulous and temporary solutions. These solutions are a function of the job and educational level of the employees to be motivated, the management style being practiced, and the "organizational climate" as indicated by company policies.

All of these factors, of course, are subject to change. Even if a manager was able to take them all into account, assess their impact, and arrive at the most appropriate technique to motivate employees, such a solution could only be applied until one of the factors began to alter.

Thus, while problems in other functional areas—financial reporting procedures, personnel hiring policies, accounting techniques for depreciation—can be addressed in a more quantitative, factual way, with solutions put in place for extended time periods, the area of employee motivation lends itself more to subjective, situational solutions.

Unfortunately, the formal motivation theories of the last 75 years have often been offered up by their advocates not as temporary, situational solutions, but as *the* solution or, at best, a solution. Unfortunately, few things in life are that simple. What motivates one particular employee may not motivate another in an identical situation.

Maslow notwithstanding, we do not all have the same need hierarchy. Suppose, after fulfilling our basic needs for food and shelter, we prioritize our remaining needs differently. The organization may offer us what Maslow contends are second-level needs. But what if this is the next level of needs for one employee, but not for another? All of a sudden, the need hierarchy theory of motivation is in trouble.

The point is that even with one of the most widely known, respected, and practiced theories on motivation, there is a problem that is symptomatic of all such theories. That is, the effectiveness of the motivation technique employed is dependent on the individual value system of the employee. No one person or one theory has the answer. Yet, these theories attach a universality to themselves which can cause serious problems when applied in individual situations. This is the "situational" problem of present motivation theories.

The other reason present-day motivation theories run into trouble is the "temporal" or time problem. What motivates an employee or group of employees now may not necessarily motivate them in the future. Money may motivate our group now, but if, due to a profit-sharing plan, some of us accumulate a nice nest egg in the next five years, money may not have the influence in directing our behavior that it once did.

As conditions such as financial position, job security, peer status, etc., change over time, so do motivators. While this may appear to be obvious, it is a point that is almost universally overlooked when deciding upon and applying motivation theories.

THE FIRST STEP

What then is the solution? If a manager could periodically assess what it is that will motivate particular employees at the present time, he or she will have taken the first important step toward a sound theory of motivation.

The mistake managers make today is that once they decide to make such an assessment, they then use a self-reference criterion. Stated simply, they assume that what motivates them will motivate their employees. This is a crucial mistake.

That you are in a managerial position, and hence concerned with the motivation of others, means that your financial, social, and employment aspirations are different from those of your employees. Different things will motivate you, and the use of a self-reference criterion will doom your efforts to failure.

The most direct, efficient, and inexpensive solution to the problem of motivators is attitude surveys. Once set up, they are remarkably inexpensive to administer and, if properly structured, easy to evaluate. They avoid the self-reference problem, provide insight for management into employee attitudes, which can be a key to motivation, and, if given frequently enough, can be used to overcome the situational and time problems discussed earlier.

In a group of 50 to 100 employees, it is reasonable to administer an attitude survey twice a year. The survey should be structured so that the results can be easily tabulated. The last thing a supervisor needs is 1,000 essays crossing his or her desk every six months. For that reason, a survey that uses a Likert Scale is desirable in all but the smallest companies. There are many variations of the Likert Scale, but the two depicted in this article are the most common.

COMMON LIKERT SCALES

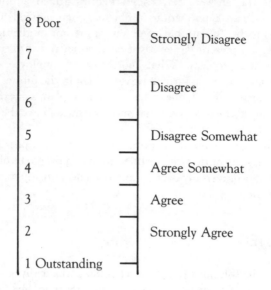

8 Poor

           Strongly Disagree

7

           Disagree

6

5   Disagree Somewhat

4   Agree Somewhat

3   Agree

2   Strongly Agree

1 Outstanding

HOW IT WORKS

The survey can assess attitudes such as how an employee feels about a supervisor, pay, new company work rules, particular fringe benefits, the variety or difficulty of a job, etc. Employees should either be asked directly about these matters (in which case the one-to-eight scale can be used) or be presented with a favorable or unfavorable statement about the particular matter (in which case the second scale can be used).

A survey can address 10 to 15 areas, each area having its own scale. If more than 15 areas are addressed, employees become less conscientious in their responses. Care should be taken to convince the subjects that their responses will be kept anonymous. While this will occasion a few "crank" responses, overall it will provide more meaningful information in such sensitive areas as attitudes toward immediate supervisors.

The scale should be constructed with an even number of choices, so as to avoid a "middle" choice. Adjectives should be chosen to avoid middle-of-the-road responses. This is a very important and often violated rule of Likert Scales. By removing the "average" choice, the respondent is forced to choose one or the other side of each issue.

Surprisingly enough, such a system causes a better, wider dispersion in responses. Those who would have chosen the middle box in the odd scale do not choose one of the middle two in the even scale. Their responses now become more distributed across the entire scale.

The scale responses can then be assigned numerical values for tabulation. For example, on a six-point scale ranging from outstanding to poor, outstanding may be assigned a value of five and poor a value of zero. This makes tabulation, comparing, and trend analysis simple. It will not, however, answer the question of *why*.

Suppose, for example, that we discover from a Likert Scale attitude survey that a particular company policy or a particular supervisor scored lowest as far as employee attitudes. To find out why, it is necessary to leave one or two blank lines after each scale for comments.

Should an employee choose a response at either end of the scale, they can then be asked to comment about the response. The responses can be scanned for a pattern.

ASSESSING ATTITUDES

Periodic attitude surveys are one of the most direct, efficient, and inexpensive ways to help discover what motivates employees.

General attitude surveys, such as the example below, can serve as the first step in discovering trends of satisfaction or dissatisfaction in particular work areas. Responses can point to specific areas where a second survey may be helpful, where queries can be slanted for a company's unique environment and situation.

Attitude surveys that use a Likert Scale, as depicted in the table, are easy to tabulate. A well-constructed Likert Scale avoids middle-of-the-road responses.

Each question would have below it a Likert Scale. Employees would check the appropriate area on the scale to indicate how satisfied they are with various aspects of their jobs.

GENERAL ATTITUDE SURVEY

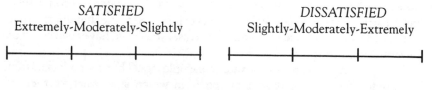

SATISFIED
Extremely-Moderately-Slightly

DISSATISFIED
Slightly-Moderately-Extremely

Economic Issues
1. Indicate your satisfaction with your pay.
2. Indicate your satisfaction with your fringe benefits.
3. Indicate your satisfaction with your promotional opportunities.

Social Issues
1. Indicate your satisfaction with your supervisor.
2. Indicate your satisfaction with your co-workers.
3. Indicate your satisfaction with your subordinates.

Task Issues
1. Indicate your satisfaction with your normal work assignments.
2. Indicate your satisfaction with the variety in your job.
3. Indicate your satisfaction with the amount of work required in a typical day.
4. Indicate your satisfaction with the hours of work required of you in a typical day.

Overall
1. Indicate your overall satisfaction, considering all aspects of your employment.

Responses can be categorized by job, level, department, occupation, division, or whatever is appropriate. It may come to light that while overall the employees are very satisfied with a particular feature of work, those in one department are very dissatisfied with that feature. This is the type of valuable information that can serve as the basis for decisions affecting motivation.

TELLING IT ALL

Finally, once the analysis is complete, the results of the survey should be made available to the participating employees, no matter what the results show. If employees are generally happy with a particular area, telling them the results makes you or the company look good. If employees are unhappy with an area, but you or the company can do something to correct the situation, again, reporting the results enhances your, and the company's, position. If employees are unhappy with an area and nothing can be done about it—the worst possible case—feedback is still essential.

Explain why nothing can be done: economics, legal requirements, company policy, etc. If you cause one employee out of 10 to see why nothing can be done, you have made an important step forward. If you don't report results, many participants will believe that you never intended to use that information, but were only trying to pacify them. In this case, you would have been better off never having run the survey.

You as a manager, cannot motivate your employees. That door is locked from the inside. You can create an atmosphere in which it is easier for them to motivate themselves. And a properly administered attitude survey can be the key.

Kenneth A. Kovach is associate professor of personnel and industrial relations at the School of Business Administration at George Mason University, Fairfax, Virginia.

37.
PERFORMANCE COACHING: HITTING THE BULL'S-EYE

Ellen J. Wallach

In supervising employees, a manager should be realistic in his or her expectations. People usually don't change overnight.

Here is the challenge. You are an archer standing in a field. It is a foggy day. In the distance, there are targets of various sizes. Some sway in the breeze, some have fallen over, some seem to lack a bull's-eye, and none are marked with point values. It is impossible to see all the targets at once, and every so often someone adds, moves, or removes a target. You have been given a bow and an unlimited number of arrows. You will have six minutes to accumulate as many points as possible. What are your chances of success? Not too good? Would you like some help?

So would your employees. The performance challenge facing them is quite similar. Your employees are motivated to do their best (they would be thrown out of the game otherwise), and they have the necessary education and experience for the job (they were hired for it). But in order to give their best performance, they need your help. They cannot aim their arrows for maximum points unless they can see the target clearly, know how they will be scored, and receive coaching on their shooting.

THE TARGET/JOB DESCRIPTION

To be successful, employees need clear, relatively stable targets that are within range. Performance standards that are a part of their job descriptions should provide these targets. But most job descriptions are written for recruitment purposes. Often, also, descriptions are too dated to provide the guidance employees need. No wonder, then, that employees' perceptions of their jobs—based solely on their reading of job descriptions—are so often wrong.

When was the last time you and your employees compared understandings of their jobs? Do you have a current, shared agreement on their major tasks, roles, and responsibilities with each member of your team? To find out how your understanding of an employee's job compares with that of the employee, ask him or her to write a description of the work. Independently, you do the same. You may be surprised by the differences.

An up-to-date job description can eliminate much of the misunderstanding. Such a description should include the major tasks, roles, and responsibilities of the job, current comparative importance of the different tasks, and the amount of time that should be spent on each. The last is often neglected in job descriptions, although time is money and without direction employees may spend valuable time on tasks that are often not worth the expenditure.

Of course, priorities constantly change. These changes should be communicated to employees on an on-going basis. Too often an employee leaves his or her boss's office mystified and frustrated, after being told, "Why were you wasting your time on x? My boss is waiting for y!" "Why," says the employee (too often to himself or herself), "didn't someone tell me?"

The more specific your communication with your employees, the better their chances of hitting the target. You can't hit something if you don't know what it is.

SCORING POINTS/PERFORMANCE CRITERIA

Archers need to know not only which targets to aim at but how their arrows will be scored. Likewise, employees need to know what it takes to get an "outstanding" rating and whether performance will be judged based on results in a limited number of key job areas, by general results, by how well behavior appears calculated to produce results, or by fulfillment of certain unwritten objectives.

If how a person does a job is as important as what he or she does, then that person should know it. Meeting objectives while alienating co-workers, for instance, may not merit an outstanding rating. If an employee knows this, he can adjust his work behavior accordingly. The more clearly you communicate the way things should be done, the more successful your employees will be in meeting the expectations of the corporate environment.

COACHING/PERFORMANCE FEEDBACK

In our analogy, no one was telling you where your arrows were hitting, or if they were hitting. Clearly, effective coaching would have improved your score. Likewise, coaching and performance feedback can improve one's score on performance rating sheets.

Effective feedback does not mean once- or twice-a-year performance appraisals; it means on-going coaching and review of progress.

Understanding and achieving standards of performance is easier for your employees if you provide them with the following six types of feedback.

Honest. If an archer's arrows are barely hitting the target yet you keep saying, "wonderful," you not only haven't helped the archer improve, you've confused him or her as well. The archer won't even know that improvement is needed.

Too often, managers aren't totally honest when they give feedback. For one thing, they don't differentiate among staff, often rating a substandard worker the same as a top performer. Likewise, they don't differentiate for each individual, that is, they don't break down job performance in terms of specific tasks.

Specific. Telling you your arrow was too far from the bull's-eye isn't as helpful as saying it was six inches too far to the left. Likewise, an employee should be told as clearly as possible why his or her performance was below par. If feedback is too general, subordinates will not understand how to correct their behavior.

Behavior-oriented. It is easier for an employee to accept feedback when it describes specific behavior than when it makes judgments about the employee as a person. Labeling another's behavior does not encourage constructive communication. Telling a worker that he is "too aggressive," for instance, will only make him more so. Instead, the employee should be told when he was aggressive and why such behavior is considered aggressive. One person's aggression is another's assertiveness. To be effective, feedback must describe specific behavior and its consequences.

Constructive. Managers need to identify not only what is wrong but how it can be corrected. It is not enough to tell someone how well they are doing. A supervisor should also suggest ways for the person to improve. If I told you that your arrows were not reaching the target, you would know that improvement was needed, but you still wouldn't know where. However, if I suggested that you change your stance and pull harder on the bow string, then you would know how to improve.

Balanced. If your subordinates kept a record of the feedback that you gave them in a typical week, what would they find? Mostly positive comments, mostly negative ones, or none at all?

The experience of hundreds of companies shows that "none at all" would be the most likely response, followed by a distant "mostly negative."

Too often managers have a "straw that broke the camel's back" approach to giving feedback. They avoid giving negative feedback because it's not worth the effort, they don't have the time, or the performance problem is "no big deal." Meanwhile, dissatisfaction with the employee mounts. Finally, an incident, often relatively insignificant, triggers an angry outburst and a barrage of complaints. The employee finds himself or herself hit with weeks of stored negative feedback at once. This is too much for the individual to absorb, much less use.

Regular feedback of a positive nature is most effective in reinforcing what the employee does well. It is also far easier for an employee to receive suggestions for improvement without being defensive if he or she has been recognized as well for good performance. It is easier for employees to hit the bull's-eye if they know their strengths as well as their areas needing improvement.

Timely. It will take longer to improve your archery score if feedback is given after every six arrows than after each arrow. The closer to the event that feedback is given, the more effective. Also, the more frequently it is given, the more effective the feedback.

In supervising employees, a manager should be realistic in his or her expectations. Usually people don't change overnight. An employee who is learning and growing will sometimes falter. When that happens, his or her supervisor should provide encouragement and support. The challenge of supervision is in helping employees hit the bull's-eye.

Ellen J. Wallach is a career development consultant in Lexington, Massachusetts.

38.

A FIVE-ROLE SYSTEM FOR MOTIVATING IMPROVED PERFORMANCE

Robert E. McCreight

The manager or supervisor is called upon to play several roles in today's organization, but the most demanding of these roles is that of human resources manager.

In the role of human resources manager, the principal objective is to manage and motivate improved employee performance. Actually, the role can be divided into five smaller roles: the goal setter, the trainer, the mentor, the evaluator, and the decision maker. Each of these smaller roles, when successfully integrated with the others, enables managers and supervisors to motivate improved employee performance.

In carrying out these five distinct roles, the manager or supervisor should deliberately build skills for taking the actions that support each role. This does not necessarily mean that any new behavior must be learned. It does mean that certain types of behavior that set the manager or supervisor apart from employees must be emphasized and developed.

THE GOAL SETTER

The goal setter makes all basic determinations about what, how, when, and how well the work of each employee must be performed. The supervisor who fills this role has the opportunity to reconcile organizational goals with performance goals established for each employee.

Individual employee performance goals include the accomplishment of all tasks described in the job description, and the attainment of any project goals that the supervisor assigns to an employee during the fixed period of time. The supervisor or manager must define the principal tasks and project goals expected of each employee. In developing these goals, standards for quality and quantity can be specific for each task or project.

The goal-setting event is based partly on the supervisor's assessment of the employee's capabilities and partly upon the particular goals to be achieved. The importance of the goal-setting event stems from the opportunity it gives employees to clarify their principal performance responsibilities and discuss with their supervisor how they will be evaluated during the course of the coming year. Once it is clearly established that certain well-defined accountability requirements will be used to objectively assess employee performance, both supervisors and employees can focus on the job to be done.

There is also room for caution in the implementation of this role. While supervisors may establish performance goals and standards, consideration should be given to making this process one in which the employee is an active participant. Standards which are both realistic and challenging can play a major part in stimulating the motivational energy needed to sustain the desired level of employee performance. Overall, the function of the goal-setter role is to identify performance requirements for each employee, and to secure agreement with each employee on both the requirements identified and the means of evaluating performance against those requirements. In the goal-setter role, the supervisor or manager leads employees to the attainment of individual and organization goals.

THE TRAINER

Closely related to the goal-setter role is the role of trainer. Here the required behavior ranges from explicit how-to-do-it instructions to more subtle guidance on the performance of assigned tasks or projects.

The trainer role rests on the assumption that each employee has weaknesses that the supervisor must recognize. This role also assumes that unless the tasks assigned to employees are clearly communicated, demonstrated, or discussed, each employee may approach the job differently, or incorrectly. What job priorities are set and how job procedures are monitored will depend upon the employee and work to be done. There is no doubt, however, that misunderstandings about priorities, procedures, and the use of independent judgment can occur if these matters are never discussed or clarified.

The supervisor or manager can model the desired performance, demonstrate a particular procedure, or suggest an approach in handling a task problem. By carefully focusing discussion upon the skills and behavior needed to get the task done, the supervisor establishes a positive, educational, and objective climate. Moreover, the "do this, do that" style of supervision is avoided; and employees will have the opportunity to offer suggestions that could have a beneficial effect on productivity. In the role of trainer, the supervisor aims at building a collaborative environment for problem solving and performance improvement.

THE MENTOR

A mentor provides performance feedback to employees not only about job goals and projects already established but also about unforeseen problems and new priorities. Feedback and coaching are essential at random and specified times during an employee's evaluation period. Feedback tells employees how well they have been performing all assigned tasks and projects. Coaching tells employees what kind of performance should be continued and what kind of performance should be changed.

As a mentor, the supervisor or manager should do more than guide the employee to more competent performance. The key is to encourage employees to devise their own plans for performance improvement and self-development. The employee's readiness to assume more difficult responsibilities or willingness to take on new tasks should be monitored by the mentor.

The ways in which the mentor role can be applied by supervisors or managers permit flexibility of emphasis. This role allows an early warning to be communicated to marginal performers, yet it also creates the climate for motivating above-average performers to keep doing their best. The principal objective of mentoring is to review and reinforce the employee performance when it will have the most motivational impact.

THE EVALUATOR

The fourth role that supervisors and managers can play is that of evaluator. The challenging tasks of the evaluator include the comparison of employee performance to established goals and the diagnosis of factors that may influence marginal or substandard performance.

Since the manager or supervisor cannot afford to rely on intuition or memory, he or she must properly and accurately document employee performance events during the evaluation period. Such documentation helps the supervisor or manager remain objective and apply good judgment. If the employee is to be held accountable for the quality of performance demonstrated, it is equally reasonable to hold the supervisor accountable for evaluating that performance.

Besides evaluating actual performance against established standards, the supervisor should examine the extent to which the work environment, the employee's skills, or the nature of the task itself, influenced employees to demonstrate marginal or substandard performance. If the employee's skills need sharpening, then training may stimulate the level of performance desired. However, if it appears that the nature of the task itself is so complex or difficult that marginal performance is likely, then employee training may not be the appropriate solution.

The performance analysis or diagnostic dimension of the evaluator's role will require additional skills that differ in significant ways from the skills employed in the mentor or trainer roles already discussed. Skill in determining the basis for substandard or marginal performance, as well as in developing approaches to deal with marginal performance situations, is a typical example. The major objective of the evaluator is to determine whether employee performance goals have been met, and what actions might be appropriate in dealing with marginal or substandard performance.

THE DECISION MAKER

The fifth and final role in the managerial system for motivating improved employee performance is the role of decision maker. Closely linked with all the other roles already discussed, the decision maker role requires that the supervisor or manager take some specific action based upon the employee's performance during the entire evaluation period.

Specific actions may include promotions, cash awards, special salary increases permanently added to base pay, reassignments, reductions in grade, and removal from service. Whatever action is eventually taken by management will also serve to stimulate improved performance. Outstanding performance is judged upon the objective criteria formulated during the evaluation period. Marginal or substandard performance that results in reassignment or removal must also be based on the same criteria.

Both outcomes can motivate improved performance by demonstrating that performance really counts and that certain kinds of performance result in different, but reasonable, actions. Failure to recognize and reward outstanding performers will cause as much discord among employees as failure to deal effectively with marginal performers. The responsiblity of supervisors and managers is to take appropriate action in both situations. Deciding upon the appropriate action to take and following through with that action are the most important functions of the decision-maker role.

The actions taken during each phase of this five-role managerial system will set the stage for the next evaluation period. Employee performance during the preceding evaluation period will determine the goals of the next period. It is then up to the manager or supervisor to motivate employees to reach those goals.

Robert E. McCreight, is associate director, Labor Relations Training Center, U.S. Office of Personnel Management, Washington, D.C.. He holds an M.A. in public administration from George Washington University. He has more than 10 years' experience in personnel and labor relations at the federal, state, and city levels of government.

39.

ACTIVATION THEORY AND JOB DESIGN: A USABLE MOTIVATIONAL TOOL FOR SMALL BUSINESS MANAGERS

Gene Milbourn, Jr.

Activation theory explains how and why workers respond to routine work in ways that they do.

Small business managers are held responsible for the functions of planning, organizing, controlling, leading, and motivating employees toward organizational objectives. The manner in which a manager pursues corporate objectives is largely dependent upon certain assumptions that the manager makes about the nature of people. The autocratic and dictatorial "Theory X" manager subscribes to the rational, economic, predictable, and self-actualizing model: Management's point of view toward workers defines and sets boundaries within which workers will carry out their functions. "Theory X" managers will allow less employee freedom than will "Theory Y" managers. The areas in which more freedom can be allowed by "Theory Y" managers include such activities as work design, work planning, control over work methods, procedures and work pace, self-evaluation of performance, and participation in goal setting.

MOTIVATION DEFINED

Before we consider how managers can motivate workers toward higher task performance, it is important to examine why people choose to work in the first place. The jobs people do have the following motivational implications:[7]

1. They provide *wages* to the role occupant in return for his services.
2. They require from the role occupant the *expenditure of mental or physical energy*.

3. They permit the role occupant to contribute to the *production* of goods and services.
4. They permit or require of the role occupant social *interaction* with other persons.
5. They define, at least in part, the *social status* of the role occupant.

Motivation has only recently become studied as a unique or distinct psychological process. It has been difficult to separate behavior referred to as motivated from that associated with the emotional, perceptual, learning, and thinking processes. However, English and American psychologists in the 1880s began to write about voluntary action and propensity to act. One expert maintains that motivation is concerned with "how behavior gets started, is energized, is sustained, is directed, is stopped, and what kind of subjective reaction is present in the organism while all this is going on."[5] Another defines motivation as "a process governing choices, made by persons or lower organisms, among alternative forms of voluntary activity."[7] One other suggests "that an individual's motivation has to do with the direction of his behavior, or what he chooses to do when presented with a number of possible alternatives; the amplitude, or strength, of the response (*i.e.*, effort) once the choice is made; and the persistence of the behavior, or how long he sticks with it."[1]

Business managers are normally conversant with Maslow's hierarchy of needs and with Herzberg's two-factor theory, although both have serious limitations. The theories fail to address the fundamental questions and issues in motivational theory regarding the direction of behavior, the amplitude of responses, and the persistence of the behavior. Nor do they develop any theoretical concepts to explain why the job should affect performance.

There are several underlying principles from other investigations that have a great deal of support. Generally, we can say that high performance results when:

1. Managers manipulate (change) incentives to induce employees to increase task effort rather than manipulate workers directly.
2. Employees are able to use their valued abilities and skills in becoming task competent.
3. Employees perceive valued and equitable rewards to be linked to task performance.
4. Employees acknowledge a differential reward system based upon performance within the organization.[4]

THE CONCEPT OF COMPETENCE

A critical responsibility of any manager or supervisor is to ensure that the jobs people do have been properly planned and organized so that workers can become competent in their responsibilities. A feeling of competence gives workers a sense of efficacy or a feeling of being "fit to live." This mastery of job responsibility has been discovered as being an important factor affecting the level of both work and life satisfaction.

Robert White has offered a convincing argument that the striving to be competent or effective in dealing with the environment is to be considered a significant and innate motivating force. Individuals will strive to become effective in interacting with the environment for no obvious reason other than to master or control it. As White stated.[8]

> The instinct to master has an aim—and it follows hedonic principles by yielding "primary pleasure" when efficient action enables the individual to control and alter his environment.

The motivations implication for small business managers is to plan, organize, and control work in such a way that workers can apply all their resources to their jobs. In other words, a manager must structure a work situation so that workers can use their valued abilities and skills in becoming competent in the job they were hired to do without having to dilute their resources with time-consuming, non-task activities.

ACTIVATION THEORY, COMPETENCE, AND JOB DESIGN

Why do we frequently observe employees at all organizational levels engaging in the following activities or behaviors?

1. Restlessness
2. Changing posture
3. Taking unauthorized breaks
4. Stretching
5. Daydreaming
6. Engaging in horseplay
7. Feeling irritable
8. Performing poorly and having poor work attitudes

The job is the strongest motivating factor in the work environment. Unfortunately, over a period of time the job may fail to stimulate the worker sufficiently for him to maintain a comfortable level of arousal and alertness.[2] The job stimulation level may become so low that an employee not only experiences boredom but also lack of alertness, muscular uncoordination, and decreases in sensory sensitivities. The consequences of tedious work may contribute to poor task performance and poor work attitudes as depicted in Figure 1. The opposite situation may occur when a worker is in the very early stages of

Figure 1
Expected Consequences of Low and High Job Activation Levels

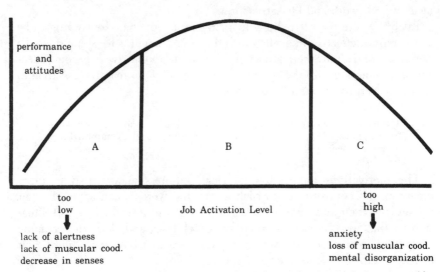

Area A, job stimulation too low, job enrichment needed; area B, job stimulation compatible with worker; area C, job too high in stimulation, job redesign needed.

learning. Here the job stimulation level may be too high, causing the worker to experience anxiety, loss of muscular coordination, and mental disorganization.

Activation theory is a neuropsychological approach to understanding worker behavior toward routine work. Activation theory:

> . . . anticipates any number of behavioral outcomes in tasks which require the constant repetition of a limited number of responses to stimulation which is configuratively simple and temporarily unvarying. . . . As the individual becomes familiar with surroundings and learns the responses required in the repetitive task, a decline in activation level is expected.[6]

It is important to realize that all work tends to become routine or repetitive after the job has been learned and practiced over a period of time. Some jobs become routine sooner than others due to the limited variety and the absence of difficulty in the tasks performed. Repetitive jobs are not inherently boring and monotonous. The same job may be stimulating to one person while boring to another.

Each person desires a particular level of stimulation where he can function best; this level is called the *characteristic activation norm.* Some workers function best under complex and stressful situations while others function optimally under more structured and less stressful situations. When a job fails to provide adequate brain stimulation, a worker seeks ways to increase stimulation to the level of the characteristic norm. A wide range of dysfunctional, non-task activities are pursued to offset a decline in the job stimulation level:[6]

> Additional cortical stimulation resulting from thoughts of an anticipated hunting trip or the recall of a recent encounter with a sexual partner may offset a decline in activation level. The individual may increase . . . stimulation and thus sustain activation level by stretching, alternating position, or otherwise varying their position at the task site. Leaving to visit the water fountain, another department, or the restroom not only increases . . . stimulation but results in greater stimulus variation.

Other dysfunctional behaviors such as social conversations, complex group relationships, gambling, and horseplay also introduce variations which serve to reduce the degree of monotony at the work site.

If patterns of dysfunctional activity are observed, managers can consider enriching jobs through job redesign. To motivate workers through the work itself, a job must:

1. Allow workers to feel personally responsible for an identifiable and meaningful portion of the work
2. Provide work outcomes which are intrinsically meaningful or otherwise experienced as worthwhile
3. Provide feedback about performance effectiveness.[3]

The job characteristics of jobs that can be changed to provide intrinsic motivation through the work itself are:

1. Variety: the degree to which a job requires employees to perform a wide range of operations in their work and/or the degree to which employees must use a variety of equipment and procedures in the work.
2. Autonomy: the extent to which employees have a major say in scheduling their work, selecting the equipment they will use and deciding on procedures to be followed.
3. Task Identity: the extent to which employees do an entire or whole piece of work and can clearly identify the results of their efforts.
4. Feedback: the degree to which employees receive information as they are working which reveals how well they are performing.[3]

The motivational value from enriched jobs is derived from the rewards associated with *performing well*. The worker will only receive intrinsic rewards such as feelings of accomplishment, achievement, and competence through effective performance. In other words, the worker rewards himself. Ineffective performance cannot be rewarded. Additionally, jobs can be designed only to reinforce successful job performance. Since intrinsic rewards are distributed on a variable ration schedule (behavior reinforced infrequently), feelings of achievement, accomplishment, and competence are immediately distributed or received by the worker. Therefore, workers can see a clear relationship between how hard they are trying and how well they are being rewarded.

Several considerations should be noted regarding the use of job enrichment programs. Available evidence suggests that job enrichment programs are more likely to improve work quality than work quantity. Indiscriminate application of job enrichment principles may have either no positive effects or negative effects on certain groups of workers. It has been found that urban blue-collar workers respond unfavorably to enriched jobs while rural blue-collar workers react with increased job performance and satisfaction. Some researchers believe that the urban workers are alienated from middle-class norms which value work as a creative, stimulating, and central focus in one's life. Making jobs more complex, challenging, interesting, meaningful, uncertain, autonomous, etc., through job enrichment programs has the effect of making jobs more difficult, *i.e.*, less desirable for the urban blue-collar worker.

SUMMARY

Motivation was defined as "a process governing choices, made by persons or lower organisms, among alternative forms of voluntary activity." Motivation is concerned with: (1) the direction of behavior, or what a person chooses to do when presented with a number of possible alternatives, (2) the amplitude, or strength, of the effort once a choice is made, and (3) the persistence of the behavior, or how long he sticks with it. The paper suggests that small business managers structure or design a work situation where workers can use their valued abilities and skills in becoming task competent. Competency was viewed as a strong and innate motivational force.

Over a period of time after the job has been well-learned and practiced, it may fail to stimulate the worker sufficiently for him to maintain a comfortable level of arousal and alertness. The job stimulation level may become so low that an employee not only experiences boredom but also lacks muscular coordination and experiences a decrease in sensory sensitivity. Dysfunctional worker reactions may take many forms, from taking unauthorized breaks to engaging in horseplay.

Job enlargement is viewed as a technique for increasing the job stimulation level to a point where the worker can feel comfortable and alert. Job enlargement can motivate workers through: (1) allowing the workers to feel responsible for a meaningful portion of work, (2) providing rewards which are experienced as worthwhile, and (3) providing meaningful feedback about performance. Indiscriminate use of job enlargement programs should be avoided.

REFERENCES

1.   Campbell, J.P., Dunnette, M.D., Lawler, E.E. and Weick, K.E., *Managerial Behavior, Performance, and Effectiveness* (New York: McGraw-Hill, 1970).

2.   Francis, G.J. and Milbourn, G., *Human Behavior in the Work Environment* (Santa Monica, Calif.: Goodyear, 1981), Chapter three.

3.   Hackman, J.R. and Oldham, G.R., *Work Redesign* (Reading, Pa.: Addison-Wesley, 1980), pp. 71-95.

4.   Hampton, D.R., Summer, C.E. and Webber, R.A., *Organizational Behavior and Human Performance* (Chicago: Scott, Foresman and Co., 1983), Chapters one and six.

5.   Jones, M.P., *Nebraska Symposium on Motivation* (Lincoln, Neb.: University of Nebraska Press, 1955), p. viii.

6.   Scott, W.E., "Activation Theory and Job Design," *Organizational Behavior and Human Performance* (Vol. 1, 1966), pp. 14-20.

7.   Vroom, V., *Work and Motivation* (New York: John Wiley, 1964).

8.   White, R.W. "Motivation Reconsidered: The Concept of Competence," *Psychological Bulletin*, (Vol. 66, 1959), pp. 291-302.

40.
IT'S SMART TO GET YOUR PEOPLE TO WORK SMART

Ian Rolland

It's impossible to overstate the importance of job satisfaction. No motivation program can be effective if employees see the work itself as boring or meaningless.

It has become gospel that this country must improve its productivity if it is to remain competitive here and abroad. It should also be obvious that to do this, management must fully utilize all available resources, human as well as technological.

Productivity requires people who work hard, supported by available technology. But maximum productivity requires one thing more: people who work *smart*.

In organizations where large numbers of employees work smart, productivity improvements stem from the workforce itself. Those who spend days routinely punching data into a computer may find additional uses for that technology which management—removed from details of the daily operation—had not considered.

Given encouragement, individuals within a work area may develop a more efficient division of labor.

I can tell you that in my organization many such ideas surfaced once we had made a conscious effort to tap the reservoir of employee creativity. The result has been productivity increases we in top management could not have otherwise reasonably expected.

Despite all the humanistic management theories of the last two decades, American business often fails to encourage employees to work smart, and therefore fails to maximize productivity. Management hires individuals to perform a single task or a repetitive series of tasks, but leaves their people ignorant of the larger effort to which they contribute. Management too often fails to encourage employee suggestions, and sometimes actually scorns such initiatives.

In such organizations, stimulating the upward flow of ideas will require nothing less than a fundamental change in the corporate environment. Employees must learn to sacrifice some of the security that comes with routine—for their betterment and for that of the organization. Equally important, managements of companies large and small must become more entrepreneurial in their approach to both work and people. We must be receptive to and act on good ideas, regardless of their origins.

How does an organization effect so basic a change?

A good place to start is some adaptation of the "quality circle" concept. We need to bring together employees at all levels who do the same job or are located in the same unit to regularly discuss their jobs and how to do them better. The flow of good ideas that results, once employees know management is listening, can be gratifying beyond expectations.

Of course, there is another side to the coin. Some employees will literally think their co-workers and themselves out of jobs. Because workforce-generated productivity depends on such initiatives, we cannot afford to reward such ideas with a place in the unemployment line. Staff reductions made possible by workforce-generated productivity improvements should be accomplished through attrition. Employees who think themselves out of jobs should receive training that prepares them for positions with more importance to the organization and more personal satisfaction to themselves.

It's impossible to overstate the importance of job satisfaction. No motivation program can be effective if employees see the work itself as boring or meaningless. We need to structure all positions around principles that make jobs meaningful to both workers and the organization. In practical terms, this means allowing more employee discretion and independence in planning the work. This might be accomplished by combining tasks done within a work area and forming natural units of work. When possible, employees should be allowed to do the whole job. We also can form client relationships and add functions to broaden a job's level of responsibility.

The performance appraisal itself can and ought to be a developmental tool rather than a mere rating mechanism. Properly administered, the appraisal can identify strengths upon which the employee can build and indicate weaknesses that might be addressed by training.

Instituting a program so fundamental and sweeping will not be easy. Some supervisors will be uncomfortable with anything less than a traditional, authoritarian approach to work and people, and some employees will not be up to the new dimensions of their jobs.

But my experience indicates that such instances will be few and they will be more than offset by improvements in both job satisfaction and productivity.

Ian Rolland is president and chief executive officer, Lincoln National Corp., an insurance holding company.

41.
MOTIVATE!

Don Caruth
Robert M. Noe III

Six dynamic solutions to an age-old challenge

What do we really know about motivation? In some instances, research findings have been grossly misinterpreted. In others, experience simply has not borne out what we have been taught. Despite the many volumes written about motivation in the past two decades, the concept of motivation is not generally understood. Consequently, a number of misconceptions have been perpetuated about motivation. Following are six motivation myths.

MYTH NUMBER ONE: MANAGERS CAN MOTIVATE

Managers can't motivate; neither can mothers, fathers, ministers, or coaches. Motivation is strictly internal. People can't be motivated until they decide to motivate themselves, and until they are willing to exert effort. An employee can't be motivated until a need is activated—not the manager's need but the employee's need.

This need causes certain employee behavior. From this you might be tempted to conclude, "What's the use? Managers have no role in motivation." Nothing could be further from the truth. While much of a firm's psychological climate is beyond the control of middle managers, each manager can do things to cause employees to motivate themselves.

For example, jobs often can be restructured to make them more challenging and meaningful. Enriched jobs encourage certain people to become motivated to produce more.

The key is for managers to know their employees and their needs. Then they should create a climate which will permit their people to satisfy these needs. Managers are not motivators, but they can inspire and encourage subordinates to motivate themselves.

MYTH NUMBER TWO: MONEY CAN'T MOTIVATE

While money often may not be the most important consideration for employees, it quickly becomes so if not adequately supplied. However, for money to motivate, it must be related to job performance. In sales jobs this is relatively easy to do. Moreover, various incentive compensation plans have stood the test of time. In jobs where work can't be precisely measured, management must have a valid performance appraisal system in place. This is an arduous and ongoing task.

Remember that money is a symbol. It can represent anything from security to prestige to achievement. Consequently, its motivational powers are quite diverse. However, it is clear that money can and does motivate many people.

MYTH NUMBER THREE: A HAPPY WORKER IS A PRODUCTIVE WORKER

The only certainty about happy workers is that they are not unhappy. True, some very productive workers are happy. But, at the same time, some happy employees are unproductive.

By maintaining high morale and job satisfaction, an organization may achieve important purposes. For example, workers may enjoy less stressful environments. However, many years of research have continued to support the notion that morale and improved productivity are essentially unrelated.

MYTH NUMBER FOUR: MOTIVATORS ARE UNIVERSAL

This is not true. However, if you were to examine many existing compensation plans, you would reasonably deduce that all people are motivated by the same factors. The rewards system is essentially identical for large groups of employees. Pay increases are provided on the same basis as are vacation, life insurance coverage, hospitalization, and other benefits. Apparently, it is assumed that all employees will respond to the same types of rewards.

Recent interest in cafeteria compensation plans, which offer an array of benefits which employees can choose from, suggests that conventional thinking may be awry. Firms that have implemented cafeteria plans have found that individuals desire different forms of compensation. Older workers may want to emphasize security and richer retirement plans. Younger employees may prefer cash and want to forgo some other benefits. Single employees may simply want more time off. Although there are numerous administrative problems inherent in cafeteria plans, having all employees subject to a simple, generalized compensation plan is rather weak. People have individual needs. Consequently, managers should address those specific needs.

MYTH NUMBER FIVE: MOTIVATION IS A SCIENCE

If motivation were a science, we would know by now how to get each employee to motivate him or herself. Although there are some general concepts and theoretical guidelines, we are still far from reducing motivation to a formula.

Motivation is essentially an art. A manager must understand each of his or her employees, comprehend his or her level of need and its intensity, and try to establish the conditions and circumstances that result in motivated workers.

MYTH NUMBER SIX: MANAGEMENT ALWAYS KNOWS WHAT MOTIVATES

Perhaps some managers really do. But in general this concept is also mythical. There are distinct differences in the perceptions of what supervisors believe their employees want and what employees actually prefer. In one series of surveys, originated in 1946 and replicated several times since, supervisors have consistently put "good wages" at the top of the list of job factors most important to employees. Employees have just as regularly ranked "good wages" as fifth in importance. "Appreciation of work" and a "feeling of participation" have been ranked at the top of the list by employees but near the bottom by supervisors.

Supervisors have tended to rate higher lower-order needs (psychological and safety needs). However, employees have given higher ratings to upper-level needs (ego and self-actualization needs). Managers should pay attention to what employees think is important.

Managers do not always understand what motivates their employees. However, by dispelling the myths about motivation, by seeking to discover what employees want, and by helping them satisfy their needs, you will be far ahead of less astute managers.

Don Caruth, Ph.D., is associate professor of management, and Robert M. Noe, III, Ed.D., is professor of management. Both are in the department of marketing and management at East Texas State University.

42.
MANAGEMENT GUIDELINES: UNDERSTANDING NEEDS

George Miller

A manager's ability to lead and motivate others can be increased significantly through self-insight and understanding of needs of others.

Some managers may think that being able to motivate others is a natural talent. Certainly some individuals seem to have started in life with a high degree of empathy and the ability to move people. But whatever one's ability to lead and motivate others, it can be increased significantly through self-insight and an understanding of the needs of those reporting to one.

It is unrealistic to hope for a full understanding of why we behave as we do. However, behavioral scientists have scratched the surface of understanding human behavior, and their findings are discussed in the following 12 guidelines.

Guideline 1: Insight into one's own motivations, attitudes, and feelings increases sensitivity to the needs of others, leading to greater managerial effectiveness.

If we don't understand ourselves, we are handicapped in understanding and working with others. Managers are often only dimly aware of their own motivations and feelings. Without realizing it, they sometimes project onto employees their own fears, hostilities, frustrations, likes, and dislikes. As they begin to understand themselves better, they can be more aware of the effect of their behavior and attitudes.

It also helps if a manager visualizes things from the other person's perspective. Of course, a supervisor can never do this completely. But the closer he or she comes to being able to do so, the more effective the individual will be in predicting behavior, selecting people for complex assignments, and motivating them to do their best.

Some managers study motivation and leadership to manipulate people. Very often these efforts boomerang. An understanding of their own needs and those of their employees can go a long way toward explaining why manipulation won't work.

Application. There is no quick method for developing self-insight and empathy. Some people may start off with greater sensitivity than others, but each person can increase sensitivity within his or her potential range. In developing this sense, a manager must remember that self-understanding and sensitivity to the reaction of others is a journey, not a destination; that is, we can constantly learn more about human behavior and our interactions with others. The process begins, however, with acceptance of the need and its value.

There are essentially three methods we can use to increase self-knowledge and sensitivity. The first is to do the job mainly by ourselves through study, introspection, and the help of a friend whom we trust to hold a mirror up to us. The second is to seek the help of a professional. The third method is through interaction with groups known as T-groups or sensitivity training. The accompanying list of questions can help a manager with the first approach. A manager who asks himself or herself these questions and tries to answer them in depth is well on the way to improvement. His or her defensive attitudes will begin to change, and he or she will be easier and more relaxed in interactions with associates and employees.

Developing Self-Insight

The following questions are not easy to answer. If they were, the person answering them would already possess great self-insight. It is suggested that these questions be answered with the help of a close friend or spouse. This does not mean that the advice will necessarily be right, but it will give an additional perspective.

1. Do I resent constructive criticism?
2. Do I fear looking within myself to examine my motives?
3. How do I really see myself? Is my self-image based on my real capabilities and values? Do I limit my potential by a self-concept not based on facts? Conversely, do I limit my achievements by choosing goals that are beyond my capabilities?
4. Are my actions and my behavior in conflict with my assertions? For example, am I really authoritarian in belief and practice while giving lip service to participation?
5. How do others see me? Do they see me as a Theory X manager or a Theory Y manager?
6. Am I aware of the source of my values and interests? Have I thought them through? Do they represent a set of values I have unconsciously defended without examination?

7. Am I really interested in helping my subordinates or do I use discussions to show them how clever and superior I am? Do I engage in a game of "oneupmanship" with them, disguised as coaching and development?
8. What kinds of situations and people irritate me, and why? What frustrations in my past trigger these reactions?
9. What kinds of people and situations do I like? Why?
10. Do I judge others by my own standards without examining the worth of their standards?
11. Do I expect others to like and dislike the same things I do? Do I acknowledge the uniqueness of each human being but then expect each one to be a carbon copy of myself?
12. Am I a good subordinate but a poor boss, or vice versa? Do I assume a paternal role with my subordinates and a dependent role with my superior?
13. How is my sense of humor? What kind of humor do I typically engage in and respond to? Why do I find certain things funny?
14. Do I use activity as an escape or as a basis of self-actualization? Can I stand being alone for periods of time?

Guideline 2: Awareness of the two polarities that motivate one—a side that isolates and a side that causes one to affiliate—promotes understanding in dealing with behavior that is often paradoxical.

Mankind seems to want to eat its cake and have it at the same time. In essence, we want to belong and be part of the group, but we also want to stand out in that group. These conflicting needs permeate all of life and are manifest in politics and business as well as in social situations. Much of a manager's time is spent in a game of oneupmanship, often with the very same people the person wants to have like and accept him or her.

Application. Managers should recognize these two sets of needs within themselves and in others and plan for them. There is a place for both group and individual recognition.

Guideline 3: People are motivated either by a desire to obtain something they value but do not have or by concern that they may be deprived of something they value and do have.

People are motivated positively by an opportunity to increase their satisfactions and negatively by concern or fear that their satisfactions will be decreased. For example, a person who values security highly will be motivated to get a job that promises stable employment. Once the individual gets the job, he or she will be motivated negatively by the threat that the job may be lost. A person who values prestige highly will be motivated positively by a chance to increase personal status and negatively by fear or concern that he or she may lose status.

It is important to remember that a need, when gratified, ceases to be a motivator in a positive sense. A person whose stomach is full is generally not motivated by an offer of more food. By the same token, a gratified employee is not necessarily a more productive one. Improved working conditions are important for morale but are not effective incentives for increasing production once they have been obtained. This is where negative incentives come in. They are very real and powerful motivators. They are particularly effective on a short-term basis. Over the long pull, however, they have a corrosive effect, blocking powers of concentration and creativity. That's why negative motivators should be used sparingly. Another reason for using negative motivators selectively is that great effort must be put forth for minimal results. When individuals are positively motivated to do things, they do them willingly, and the manager does not have to stand over them or play police officer.

Application. We can gain the cooperation of others through both negative and positive incentives. While maximum effort should be directed toward using positive incentives, there are occasions when negative incentives should be used. Unfortunately, by nature and background, some people respect only fear and force. Therefore, penalties for violating company policies and rules still have to be a part of a manager's arsenal. One can talk about the satisfaction of doing stimulating work but for many people work is still drudgery. These people have to be prodded to work as they are able and trained to do.

If a manager relies solely on negative incentives, however, something is very wrong. Either the problem lies within the manager or the selection system. If it is the former, then the supervisor is not leading but rather driving his or her employees.

Guideline 4: Realizing that human behavior is motivated by a hierarchy of needs, with higher needs generally inactive until lower ones are gratified, enables a manager to develop a system of incentives for optimum performance.

According to Maslow's hierarchy of needs, when lower or basic needs such as security or affection cannot be satisfied, it is difficult for a person to move into a position where he or she can satisfy higher needs such as self-respect and self-realization. So far as this motivational theory is concerned, healthy people are those who have sufficiently gratified their basic needs and are functioning at the self-realization level. That is, they are fulfilling the need to use their talents and abilities for the sheer satisfaction of actualizing their potentialities. This need is present in everyone. The problem is that people get hung up or blocked in satisfying their basic needs and consequently are unaware of these higher needs. Gratification of one need opens the consciousness to domination of another, higher need.

Although there is a normal priority of needs, the order is not necessarily the same for everyone. The basic nature and background of an individual influence his or her need structure. For example, some people seem to be loners; the social need does not seem to be very strong in them. In a communal society, security would not generally be as important as in a competitive culture. Acceptance by the group would take priority.

The hierarchy concept is not a static one. One need or a combination of needs may be dominant at one time while another set of needs may be more important at another.

Application. Understanding people's needs is important in establishing a system of incentives. Originally, security and individual competitiveness were the only two needs that industry directed its efforts toward. Today, much effort is being directed toward tapping needs for self-realization and self-actualization.

Guideline 5. Awareness that an employee is predominantly motivated by a need for security enables management to provide conditions that reduce feelings of insecurity and optimize performance.

It is doubtful that there is such a thing as a completely secure person. Indeed, it is questionable whether such a state of existence would be desirable. Some people, however, are dominated by the need for safety. These individuals live with feelings of apprehension and insecurity that affect their behavior. Every manager has one or two such individuals under his or her supervision. Anxiety and insecurity are a matter of degree. When they get out of hand, then professional assistance is required. Under normal circumstances, however, persons dominated by feelings of insecurity are able to make their way in the world if not subjected to too much stress. It is only when they are subjected to critical, unfeeling supervision that their performance and health suffer.

People dominated by feelings of insecurity try to conceal their fears. Therefore, keen sensitivity and observation are frequently needed to disclose the condition.

Application. Managers should look for the following clues to domination by the safety need:

- Avoidance of competitive situations
- Strong need for structure, rules, and regulations—a desire for prescriptive supervision
- Strong need for the familiar
- Dependency on others
- Extreme punctuality
- Over concern for health and welfare

When a manager identifies a subordinate with a strong security need, he or she should assign the individual to those activities where the person would be most effective. Jobs that involve pressure and challenge are not for this employee. The manager would best consider making the employee a part of a group effort. It is in this kind of situation where the safety-motivated person usually puts forth his or her best effort. For someone stuck at the safety need level, the most effective incentive might be a group bonus plan. Stable job assignments and written procedures and operating rules are also important to this employee.

Guideline 6: Where the need to belong and receive social acceptance and approval dominates, a manager should develop a separate system of incentives and provide work conditions that satisfy this need.

When someone has been deprived of affection in his or her early years, he or she is often dominated by the social need in adulthood. Such an individual has an especially strong need to be accepted and made a part of a group.

As in the case of those stuck on the safety need level, there are clues to help managers in identifying employees with strong social needs. A manager should look for strong friendship and cliques within the formal organization and in-dividuals who adopt the customs or characteristics of a superior or group in order to fit in. Irresponsible behavior may also be a clue since it can signal an individual's inability to identify with a group; it is a manifestation of the person's feelings of frustration.

As an outlet for such an individual's needs, a manager might consider appointing the person to serve on an employee committee. The supervisor should promote cohesion within the work group by developing common goals among its members and by reducing any friction that might exist between in-dividuals within the group. The manager should also consider the worth of group competition and group bonus plans.

In the past, unions have been more effective in appealing to employees' social needs than management. Management often believes it is necessary only to appeal to the security need. This is why some strikes don't seem to make sense. But workers don't only strike for more money or perks. They often strike for satisfaction of social needs that they feel are being frustrated in their work situation.

Guideline 7: There are employees who are driven by the urge to dominate others. Awareness of this enables management to provide the kind of supervi-sion that keeps performance within limits.

The ego need is manifested in people in a drive for power over others. This need is usually a reaction against basic feelings of insecurity and inferiority.

A person with the need to dominate others rarely makes a good manager even though he or she may be benevolent or paternalistic. Such persons may be competent enough to run a business, but they usually leave no legacy of talent. Only dependent people are permitted on their teams.

Application. A person driven by the need to dominate others should not be assigned to a supervisory position. Such an individual tends to stifle creativity and initiative. A power-hungry person in a staff capacity should be carefully supervised to see that he or she only gives advice, counsel, and service.

Guideline 8: Awareness that someone is motivated by the need for prestige and status enables management to provide work conditions and incentives that optimize that individual's performance.

Status anxiety is a term now used in industry to describe the condition of someone unable to do his or her work because of concern over status and inability to effect a change. Usually extreme concern for status is a reaction to early feelings of inferiority, manifested in a different way than the need to dominate.

Application. People reveal their motivations by their interests and personal objectives. No one clue should be regarded as especially significant by itself. It is when a number of clues begin to form a motivational pattern that runs counter to the person's vocation and financial and social position that the predominating inner need for status is revealed. For example, the kind of car a person drives, the clubs he or she belongs to, where the individual lives and his or her acquaintances, name-dropping tendencies, and preoccupation with such status symbols as a parking space with one's name on it and the quality of one's office carpet, are all clues to the intensity of the status need.

Someone with a strong need for status should be given opportunities for recognition. As incentives, he or she should receive letters of commendation for accomplishments, special privileges such as a seat in the executive dining room, and protection from loss of face when he or she errs. Titles are very important.

Guideline 9: Employees with the need to give should be given opportunities to serve.

This need ranges from the need to give material things to the need to give of oneself. It is found in teachers, social workers, and the clergy, but it is also found in ordinary workers who enjoy helping others. They often are people of great warmth and friendliness.

Application. People dominated by this need make excellent teachers and are of great service in training and developing people. The manager with such people as subordinates can make excellent use of their abilities internally in training and development and externally in customer service.

Guideline 10: Someone motivated predominantly by a need for achievement should be given work assignments that provide opportunities to excel and get things done.

People with the need for achievement also seek power but it is not simply for the sake of power or to dominate; they seek power to accomplish their goals. This is the urge that drives many managers. They are more in competition with themselves and the environment than they are with other people.

People motivated by a need for achievement find challenge and satisfaction in being managers because of the opportunities the position provides for accomplishment. Since accomplishment is the key factor in their motivation, they can take orders as well as give them. They usually receive authority because of their competence and hard work. With the need for achievement are an associated urge for action and a desire to excel. Individuals motivated by a need to achieve are usually bored with inactivity. They seek and accept external rewards more as evidence of achievement than because of prestige needs.

Application. Assignments that are challenging and require a self-starter should be given to managers and employees motivated by this need. If the individual is competent in the task to be performed, all he or she will need is clarification of the goals and some broad control limits. However, because of the person's strong need for action, he or she may find it hard to look beyond the immediate needs of the task. To avoid the problems that can arise from short-range thinking, the overall, long-term needs of the organization should be brought to the person's attention and made part of his or her responsibility.

Guideline 11: Opportunities to optimize performance should be provided those individuals predominantly motivated by the need to actualize their abilities.

Each of us has an essential nature that is our true identity. This represents our potentialities, not final actualizations. It is either shaped or stifled by culture and environment. Although in most cases the inner nature is weak and stifled by enculturation, it rarely disappears or dies completely. It persists underground, unconsciously. It is the cause of the dissatisfaction in successful people who have been busy satisfying deficiency needs for security, affection, and the like.

Application. A supervisor who is fortunate enough to supervise a self-actualized person would best give the individual as much opportunity as possible within very broad control limits. Such an individual does not have to be motivated; he or she is self-motivated. The person's incentive is the opportunity to perform and exercise his or her abilities.

Guideline 12: Awareness of how a manager really views his or her subordinates yields insights into the dynamics that take place in interactions with them.

Managers' actual attitudes and assumptions regarding the people reporting to them may vary widely from those they sincerely believe they hold. Managers tend to be people-oriented or task-oriented without realizing it. This tendency is most clearly manifested in superior/subordinate relationships.

People-centered supervisors see their jobs as essentially accomplishing results through people. Job-centered supervisors think primarily of the work itself and only secondarily of the people involved. Managers who are thing-oriented regard people in the same impersonal way that they regard inanimate objects. If a machine wears out, it is replaced; if an employee ceases to be productive, he or she is terminated. People who are task-oriented are not deliberately cruel; they simply lack the capacity to put themselves in another person's place and understand how he or she feels in the situation. Managers who are people-oriented don't pamper employees but they are capable of seeing things from another person's perspective and taking this into consideration in getting results.

Application. There are various degrees of people- and thing-orientation. The following questions have proved helpful in analyzing managerial orientation.

1. Do you view employees as identical units of labor? Are they merely extensions of machines and the activities they undertake?
2. Do you view employees as individual units of labor? That is, are you aware of their individual differences but only to the extent that the differences affect their work assignments?
3. Do you view employees as individual human beings with different needs and values but only in relationship to yourself and the job? That is, do you fail to take into consideration the relationships that exist between each worker and his or her peer group that occasionally may be more powerful than the relationship with you?
4. Do you work with your employees with full awareness of the informal relationships that influence their behavior, in addition to their relationship with you?

43.
COACHING . . .
A MANAGEMENT TOOL
FOR A MORE
EFFECTIVE WORK PERFORMANCE

G. Eric Allenbaugh

Coaching is far broader and more effective than performance evaluation: It is a collaborative process that contributes to a winning situation for the individual, manager, and organization.

"Getting things done through others," the most commonly accepted definition of management, strongly conveys the indication that managers need employees more than employees need managers. Managers receive their rewards and punishments for what employees do or do not do; their role, therefore, must be focused on helping employees succeed, for managers themselves can only succeed in direct proportion to the success of their employees.

The most significant contribution a manager can make to his organization is to develop himself and others—whether subordinates, colleagues, or superiors—to perform at optimum levels. The effective manager must ask of others: "What can I do that will enable you to function even more effectively on the job?" Imagine the organization-wide impact when managers at all levels openly explore this question with others, listen to what others have to say, and then embark on a course of positive action.

The effective manager, then, focuses on making strengths productive. To achieve the best results he has to effectively use all the available strengths—those of the subordinates, the boss, and himself. He starts with what a person should be able to do well and then demands that the person really do it. What can you do uncommonly well? What can each of your subordinates do uncommonly well? And your boss? Are you using those strengths effectively and getting appropriate results?

WHAT MOTIVATES PEOPLE?

For managers and employees who are really prospering in their jobs, work is likely to be a lot like play. Behavioral scientists have found that three psychological states are essential in determining a person's motivation and satisfaction on the job. These three core job dimensions are:

Experienced meaningfulness. The person must perceive his work as worthwhile and important by his own personal values and standards.

Experienced responsibility. The employee must believe that he is personally accountable for the outcomes or results of his efforts.

Knowledge of results. He or she must be able to determine, on some fairly consistent basis, what was done well, what opportunities there are for improvement, and exactly what is on target.

In study after study, employees and managers ranked these three factors higher than both pay and benefits as job satisfiers. Finding out what the employee values and integrating this into the job design, then, can lead to increased self-motivation, better work performance, greater work satisfaction, increased productivity, and lower absenteeism and turnover.

Unfortunately, not everybody is able to become internally motivated, even when the motivating potential of a job is high. Those with limited job growth needs may respond less eagerly or even balk at being pushed or stretched too far. Those individuals who have been coached and counseled to perform at a higher level, but who still do not meet standards, should be removed from their positions. But most employees with high growth needs will respond eagerly when they have jobs that contain the three job dimensions.

The majority of cases of nonperformance or ineffective performance can be attributed to managerial failure. Most ineffective performance can be traced to:

Lack of direction. Managers need to orient and train employees initially and then clarify the employees' functions, authority, responsibilities, and expectations (FAREs) on an ongoing basis. If orientation, training, and coaching are not performed well and on a timely basis by managers, subordinates will often gain only limited understanding of their jobs. In effect, employees frequently do not know what they are supposed to do, how to do it, or why they are supposed to do it.

Lack of feedback. Feedback and knowledge of results are important elements in motivating the employee. For satisfaction, growth, and development, employees need to get feedback on what they have done particularly well, what opportunities they have for improvement, and what they are doing just right.

THE VANISHING APPRAISAL

Most businesses and organizations have a policy that the performance of each individual shall be reviewed at least annually. However, this policy is often ignored. Performance appraisal systems are often "in the process of revision." Additionally, top executives require managers to conduct annual performance appraisals for their subordinates, yet seldom participate themselves.

A number of studies reveal that performance appraisals are done poorly and neither the individual nor the organization tend to be satisfied with the process for a variety of reasons.

1.   The focus of most appraisal systems tends to be on individual weaknesses. For a boss to concentrate on faults and weaknesses not only is distasteful but also erodes the relationship with his subordinates.

2.   Performance appraisal systems are often used to accomplish two conflicting objectives: determining the rewards an individual will receive and providing counseling and feedback for improvement and development. These goals call for different discussion emphases and can have different effects on the employee. When the performance evaluation is used in determining the rewards an individual will receive, employees have a reason for defending their performance and presenting themselves in the best possible light. Under such circumstances, they are likely to give invalid data about themselves in order to look good. As such, the performance appraisal serves neither purpose well.

3.   Subordinates tend not to hear criticism and often respond negatively to such feedback. This condition is accentuated when trust levels are relatively low and when interpersonal communication skills are not well developed. Management studies have concluded that rather than serving as a stimulant to more effective behavior, such negative feedback can lead to a deterioration of performance—just the opposite of what the performance appraisal system was intended to do.

Because of the stress and discomfort in the appraisal process, lack of valid data, conflict of interest, and focus on negatives, there is little incentive for either the boss or the employee to participate. With so few positive outcomes, it is no wonder that performance appraisals tend to vanish from the organization.

THE COACHING ALTERNATIVE

Coaching is a positive process of enabling strengths to be used productively. While far broader in concept and application than performance appraisals, coaching includes evaluation as part of the process. Coaching is defined as an ongoing, face-to-face, behavior-influencing process by which the manager and employee collaborate to assist in achieving: increased job knowledge; improved skills in carrying out job responsibilities; higher levels of job satisfaction; stronger, more positive working relationships; and opportunities for personal and professional growth. As a process for influencing human behavior, coaching can be contrasted with teaching, training, and counseling. Teaching and training emphasize the development of knowledge and skills. Counseling focuses on personality and psychological factors of performance. The coaching process lies between these two poles and has some characteristics of each.

As a collaborative process that emphasizes the employee's strengths, coaching tends to overcome most of the objections of the performance appraisal process. Because of ongoing feedback, employees know where they stand with their supervisor and are generally more receptive to interactions of a developmental nature. Furthermore, as coaching is not necessarily linked with rewards, employees tend to be more open and honest in self appraisal and managers tend to be more comfortable in exploring performance factors.

The success of the coaching process depends completely or partially on the attitude, knowledge, skill, and understanding of the manager. If the process is explored with the genuine spirit of enabling strengths to be used most productively and to contribute to the quality of working life, both the manager and the employee will participate with enthusiasm.

The central principles of coaching are:

1. Coaching emphasizes the job, not the person. It stresses development of knowledge and skills, not the success or failure of the employee as a person. While managerial awareness of employee personality characteristics and values is helpful, the emphasis is on improving job performance, not on changing the employee's personality.

2. Coaching implies respect for the dignity and worth of the individual, for the right to be an individual, and for the right to personal privacy.

3. Coaching starts with the employee's current level of performance as a baseline.

4. Coaching identifies realistic incentives that have personal meaning for the employee and identifies outcomes valued by the employee. Linking these outcomes with staffing and work assignments results in powerful individual motivators to perform at an optimum level.

5. Effective coaching leaves both the manager and employee with greater knowledge and more understanding of the employee's job - in addition to improving the manager-employee relationship.

6. As an ongoing participative process, coaching assures that the manager and the employee agree on performance goals, on how performance is to be measured, and on appraising performance against those goals. Thus coaching focuses on collaborative measures to attain objectives and results.

7. Coaching necessarily starts at the top of the organization with the president or chief executive officer. Not only does this enable top executives to function effectively, but their commitment to the process communicates an important message to the workforce.

Virtually every contact with the employee provides an opportunity for coaching. The foundation of coaching, however, is clarification of the FAREs, both when the employee is new to the position and as the employee develops or the job changes. The widest range of coaching opportunities is available in clarifying job responsibilities, defining levels of authority, and reviewing progress with the employee.

In addition to the many one-to-one contacts between manager and employee, group sessions provide excellent time-saving coaching occasions. The group experiences and perspectives can also provide valuable dimensions to the process. Group coaching examples include:

- Philosophical exploration of a subject
- Affirming standards and expectations
- Defining goals and objectives
- Periodic progress reports on goals and assignments
- Discussing successful and unsuccessful projects
- Strategizing, simulating, and role-playing important events or activities in preparation for the actual situation

COACHING TECHNIQUES

To coach effectively, the manager must be skilled in a number of techniques, such as:

Observation. Since most communication is transmitted by tone of voice, inflection, body language, and other non-verbal methods, observation of these methods is a powerful source of information to increase your understanding. Observation of the employee's interactions with co-workers and job performance factors is also an important information source.

Analysis. Analysis in coaching is the process of determining what responsibilities a particular job requires and what degree of authority must go with the job if it is to be done well. In the coaching process, the analysis is done in collaboration with the employee. An important part of this process is to explore the employee's values, wants, and needs. Integrating these elements into the job and work assignments when possible powerfully motivates performance.

Working through. "Working through" is that portion of the coaching interview where the manager and employee wrestle with a problem they have uncovered. By focusing on the problem as an opportunity for improvement, by maintaining a climate of acceptance and dignity, and by identifying the issue as a mutual one, the probability of a positive outcome is enhanced.

Channeling. Channeling is a means of guiding the coaching interview to assure that it focuses on a positive, supportive atmosphere, on an open exchange of ideas and mutual decision making, and on development of action plans that will contribute to individual and organizational development. Active listening skills, such as paraphrasing, summarizing, perception checking, and asking purposeful questions are instrumental. Also essential are assertive "sending" skills such as saying what you want, telling, communicating ideas and intentions, describing behavior, and describing feelings. In an atmosphere of trust and respect, significant progress can be made in developing an individual through an open exchange of thoughts and feeling.

Delegating. A fundamental aspect of every manager's job is the ability to delegate. Delegation encourages initiative, satisfaction, and personal and professional growth and enables managers to focus on high-priority issues. As such, this tool is an important part of the coaching process. Effective delegation requires that the manager:

1. Explain what has to be done and why the job is important.
2. Delegate in terms of results. Let the subordinate determine the means for achieving results where possible.
3. Give the employee the entire problem, not just a series of tasks.
4. Encourage the employee to think through the entire problem or issue.
5. Assign appropriate authority level: act on own, act and report, consult then act, or wait to be told.
6. Agree on a deadline.
7. Ask for feedback and check out understanding.
8. Provide for follow-up and controls.
9. Resist the temptation to get involved in the delegated assignment—let go!

Giving feedback. One factor that both motivates employees and contributes to their work satisfaction is knowledge of results—feedback. For psychological and developmental reasons, employees need to know where they stand, what they are doing well, and what opportunities they have for improvement.

ROLE CLARIFICATION STEPS

A critical part of the coaching process is to first clarify the FAREs. While several methods may be used, a relatively simple three-phase approach places primary responsibility on the employee to clarify the FAREs.

Phase I: employee self-evaluation. The employee acts on his or her own to:

1. Identify major job functions and record each on eight- by five-inch cards.

2. Identify related responsibilities on the back of each function card.

3. Assign one of the following authority codes to each of the responsibilities: act on own, act and report, consult then act, or wait to be told.

4. Prioritize major function cards, characterizing them as high, medium, or low priority.

Phase II: meeting with supervisor. The employee arranges a meeting with his or her respective supervisor for the purpose of coming to agreement about the FAREs. At this meeting, manager and employee:

1. Seek agreement of FAREs. Arrange the eight- by five-inch cards on a table for easy view by both the employee and manager. The manager provides feedback about the functions, authority, and responsibilities as perceived by the employee. Functions can be added or deleted and authority codes altered in the clarification and negotiation process with the employee.

2. Seek agreement on priorities. Once functions, authority, and responsibilities have been clarified, the employee can arrange cards in priority groups: high, medium, and low. The manager then provides feedback to either confirm the employee's perceptions or modify priorities.

3. Establish performance goals. Having clarified the job, manager and employee now collaboratively identify specific performance goals related to continued growth and development.

4. Record results of clarification process. Following the clarification interview, the results can easily be recorded by preparing a typed copy of the information from the prioritized function cards (including the newly established performance goals) and distributing copies to both the manager and employee.

Phase III: implementation. Here the data generated from the employee/manager session are put into practice as follows:

1. Trial adoption. Once the job and expectations have been clarified, a mutually agreeable trial period should be implemented.

2. Feedback. During the trial period, formal and informal feedback should be provided to indicate both the "well dones" and "opportunities for improvement."

3. Formal adoption. Once both the employee and manager are satisfied with the clarified FAREs, the job description should be formally adopted.

4. Revise FAREs as appropriate through coaching. Through ongoing coaching, the FAREs will require modification to encourage greater responsibility and authority levels for the employee, higher standards of performance, and adoption of changing individual and organizational needs.

FEEDBACK

After the FAREs have been clarified, virtually every contact with the employee presents an opportunity for coaching.

Informal feedback regarding both the "well dones" and "opportunities for improvement" is an invaluable source of information for the employee's development. Knowledge of results is both an important element of job satisfaction and an essential element for improving performance. The success of an employee is a high-priority managerial function.

Feedback is also important during FARE clarification and coaching sessions. Feedback should be transmitted in both directions.

Feedback to employee. In the coaching process, the employee is encouraged to think through his or her own performance and develop suggested action plans for managerial consideration. Prior to the formal coaching meeting, the employee completes a self-evaluation and then presents it to the manager for review and feedback. This process reduces or eliminates many of the problems associated with traditional performance evaluations completed by the manager for the employee and encourages a more open discussion for growth and development purposes. While this process is usually applied to general performance factors, it can certainly be more focused on individual projects as well.

A suggested format for the employee self-evaluation is as follows:

Self evaluation. The employee completes the following sentences: "To be even more effective, I will do more of or start doing _____ .... do less of or stop doing _____ .... continue doing _____ ."

Proposed action plans. For each of the "do more of's" or "do less of's," a specific action plan should be proposed answering the question: "Who is going to do what by when?"

A Manager's Feedback. After the employee has given a best shot at self evaluation, the manager has the opportunity to provide feedback regarding both the points of the evaluation and the action plans. After appropriate modifications are suggested, the manager and employee work through differences and come to an agreement. The final product can then be placed in the employee's file and reviewed at the next formal coaching session.

Feedback to manager. Recognizing that a primary function of management is to enable employees to be as successful as possible, it is critical that managers be open to feedback from employees regarding the working relationship, development process, and the job itself. Peter Drucker encourages managers to ask: "What can I do to enable you to be more effective on the job?" Taking this a step further, the following format is suggested: "To enable you (the employee) to be even more effective on the job, what can I (your supervisor) do more of or start doing? Do less of or stop doing? Continue doing?"

Encouraging such feedback from the employee will provide ideas to improve managerial performance, create a climate for more effective performance, enhance interpersonal trust, and contribute to the quality of working life. The risks are minimal. Some managers may fear getting negative feedback, but it is far better in the long run to work through these issues than to permit such feelings to go underground. In an open, caring environment of mutual exchange, both the employee and the manager win.

G. Eric Allenbaugh heads his own consulting firm, Organization Effectiveness Consultants, based in Eugene, Oregon.

44.
MOTIVATING EMPLOYEES IN AN AUTOMATED OFFICE

Edward D. Garten
Frances J. Garten

> As departments convert from manual to automated systems and even become computer-dependent, employees may become anxiety-ridden about how they will fit in.

The 1980s portend a substantial increase in the use of electronic-based equipment in office and plant operations. For many employees, this will mean a significant change in the work environment. As they find themselves surrounded by terminals and other evidence of the new technology, these workers may begin to question their worth to the organization and to seek confirmation of their value. But this is only one of a number of employee needs that may increase and require supervisory attention.

SUPERVISORY CONCERNS

Variety. If the automation-assisted assignments are dull and repetitive, employees may grow bored with the work and their motivation and productivity may decline. The need for variety is almost always present among employees but is particularly important to employees who see themselves as present-day versions of Chaplin's hero in "Modern Times." In most automated workplaces, there should be sufficient tasks to satisfy employees' psychological need for variety, and supervisors should be alert to opportunities for fulfilling this need by incorporating varied tasks into individual jobs.

Task Certainty. New and even experienced employees will approach change in the form of automation with some trepidation. Although the concerns are not always put into words, they include employee fears that they may not be capable of learning the new tasks or that they won't be able to develop the competence that management may demand over the short term. Workers want and require some measure of task certainty or at least need to believe that within a short time they will be comfortable with the tasks that they are expected to perform. Sensitive supervisors can go a long way toward instilling the self-confidence that these workers need.

Interaction. Workers in equipment-laden work environments have a strong need for human companionship. They need to interact with each other. This interaction should be encouraged by their supervisors and should take two forms. First and foremost is social interaction, the development of friendships among co-workers. The second involves interchanges between employees in which job-related information is shared, thus leading to the resolution of on-the-job problems. Supervisors have to be sensitive to both levels of need and to find ways of satisfying both.

IDENTIFICATION WITH THE ORGANIZATION

Almost all of today's workers desire a sense of growth and challenge on the job and a clear, if only general, understanding of how their work fits in with the rest of the operation. But employees working in a highly automated unit of an organization have a particularly strong need to identify with the whole operation, not to feel themselves merely a cog in the machine. The heads of such units have the responsibility of providing their subordinates with a sense of their significance in the grand scheme of things and in the achievement of the end product.

Autonomy. Employees who work alongside of the latest technological marvels need to feel in control, not subordinate to the equipment. They want to feel that they—not the equipment—are responsible for the achievement of results. Supervisors should manage in a manner that offers these employees as much opportunity for autonomy as possible without jeopardizing departmental goals.

A CLEAR BASIS FOR MOTIVATION

As departments convert from manual to automated systems and even become computer-dependent, employees may become anxiety-ridden about how they will fit in. They may worry about job security and their place in the new order and also may experiecnce need for a feeling of self-worth. Failure to provide reassurance can lead to a decline in motivation and productivity that can erode any economic benefits from automation.

Edward D. Garten, Ph.D., and Frances J. Garten, M.S., operate their own consulting firm, Garten & Garten Management Consultants, in Cookeville, Tennessee.

Part VI
THE THEORY
OF MOTIVATION

45.
WHY EMPLOYEE MOTIVATION HAS DECLINED IN AMERICA

Philip C. Grant

It might take years to reverse this downward trend.

Years of consulting in the field of human resources management have convinced me that employee motivation is on the decline in America, and has been for some time. Managers regularly assert that employees today just will not work like they used to. Further, my own observations suggest that more employees than in years past exert just enough effort at work to get by—no more.

In my opinion, employee motivation has been declining for a long time. This trend, however, has been camouflaged by rapid technological advance. Through the '50s, '60s, and early '70s, innovations in technology which led to productivity increases, occurred with such frequency that the decreasing contribution of employees was largely unapparent—or ignored. Few cared whether employees were motivated because it was believed that improvements in technology would overcome any human frailties.

But a new era is upon us. Technological growth in numerous sectors is slowing and the impact of declining motivation is becoming evident. In the last two years, the productivity of our economy has actually decreased.

To remain competitive in world markets, America can no longer neglect its human resources. Further decline in employee motivation cannot be tolerated. Human potential must be more fully utilized. The questions are: "Where do we start? How do we reverse the downtrend?" Reversal must begin with identifying the forces causing the decline. Only after this, can progress be made toward increasing motivation.

GREATER INSTABILITY AND DIVERSITY OF VALUES

Since the early '60s, the values of Americans have become increasingly unstable. Rapid change in what people believe has become the norm. People of all ages now find it difficult to decide just what is really worthwhile in life. Individuals frequently redirect their interests and life pursuits. Career aspirations, social relations, hobbies, jobs, and on-the-job goals are being changed at a rapid pace. Numerous individuals are choosing not to spend extended periods of time with any one interest or goal.

In addition, people have come to desire a fuller sampling of life and now distribute their waking hours among numerous at-work and away-from-work pursuits. For example, employees participate in more at-work socialization and recreation activities, and more away-from-work hobbies, clubs, community affairs, and self-development activities than ever before.

The reasons for this growing instability and diversification of values, interests, and goals are many. Greater affluence, more leisure time, higher education, less physically demanding work, and growth of the media have all contributed.

But such instability and diversification interfere with employee job motivation. Job motivation cannot develop when goals are unstable, since high effort in a given direction takes time. Employees who constantly switch jobs or on-the-job goals are not allowing themselves sufficient opportunity to exert high effort in a single direction. Diversification of goals stymies job motivation by causing one's efforts to be drawn away from the job.

Off-the-job goals compete with on-the-job goals and siphon away a portion of one's effort capacity. A greater diversity of off-the-job goals can well mean a decrease in the amount of effort available for application on the job.

MORE GUARANTEED REWARDS

Today, more companies are offering more guaranteed rewards than ever before. Incentive- or performance-based reward systems are being abandoned. Unions have fought for and won fixed wages and ever larger performance-independent fringe packages. Companies have found that to attract new employees, they must frequently guarantee salaries and wages.

Some companies have adopted guaranteed wages because they are less costly and legally risky to administer. The government has entered the act by passing a minimum wage law and establishing unemployment compensation, both of which represent rewards granted independent of employee performance.

Guaranteed rewards, however, destroy employee motivation. For one to exert high effort, one must realize greater satisfaction at high effort levels than at low effort levels. For this to be possible, the rewards for high effort must be greater than the rewards for low effort, because the costs of high effort—fatigue, boredom, stress, etc.—are greater than for low effort. Rewards received independent of effort level and performance mean higher satisfaction with low effort, because with low effort the costs are less.

INSTABILITY OF REWARDS TO SATISFY EMERGING NEEDS

Over the years, the socioeconomic climate in America has changed dramatically. Thanks to technology, there has been a marked increase in the standard of living for most Americans. Today, the majority of U.S. citizens have enough money to buy what they want and to live where and how they want. They have the time and financial resources to enjoy extended leisure time with family and friends. Most feel they are quite well-to-do both economically and socially.

In addition, improvements in medicine and the increased availability of health services have given Americans a heightened sense of security in life. Industry's adoption of less hazardous work environments has further enhanced the worker's sense of security and well-being. As Abraham Maslow contends, the lower-level needs (economic, security, and social) of the employee have been largely fulfilled. As the lower-level needs have become satisfied, the higher-order needs of self-esteem and self-actualization have emerged as the most predominant and least satisfied.

For employees to be motivated, they must receive valued rewards. Rewards matched to one's most intense or predominant needs will be perceived as valuable. Rewards suited for satisfying needs already well satisfied will not be perceived as valuable. Since most organizations have not adjusted their rewards from those appropriate only for satisfying lower-level needs to those incorporating mechanisms for satisfying the emerging, predominant higher-order needs, rewards are now perceived as less valuable than in the past.

A DISAPPEARING WORK ETHIC

In recent years, the Protestant work ethic has foundered and stumbled. Fewer individuals today believe that hard work is the mark of a righteous person. Fewer believe that all good automatically comes to those who work hard. Taking great pride in one's work is fast becoming obsolete. Hard work and quality individual output are no longer widely viewed as synonomous with personal success.

Many reasons for this disappearing ethic can be cited. The growing affluence of our society, the growing role of technology in production, increasing specialization, and the erosion of small business are some contributing factors.

For employees to be motivated, they must receive valuable outcomes for high effort. For those with a strong work ethic, high effort in-and-of-itself generates satisfaction with employment. But among American workers, the perceived values associated with hard work and work well done are diminishing.

REDUCED COSTS OF FAILURE

In our society, mechanisms for reducing the frustrations, anxieties, dis-appointments, and losses of personal pride and property resulting from failure are on the increase. Today, social counselors and psychiatrists ease the pain of clients experiencing emotional lows as a result of failure. Liberal divorce laws make it simple to walk away from the failings of marriage. Bankruptcy law allows individuals and companies to avoid high financial burdens incurred from failure. Alternative schooling exists for those who cannot make it in the traditional educational system.

Government-sponsored welfare supports those who fail to find work. Alternative jobs exist in relative abundance, making it possible for those who fail at one job to be retrained for another, or find employment in another company. Legislation now makes it difficult to release employees for failure to perform. Psychologists have convinced managers not to use various discipli-nary procedures and penalties for poor performance. Finally, unions have negotiated freedom from penalty for numerous types of nonperformance. The evidence is clear: penalties for lack of success are fast becoming extinct.

These developments are contrary to requirements for high on-the-job motivation. When people learn to expect no penalty for low effort and poor performance, such effort and performance can be attractive. In fact, some will actually experience high on-the-job satisfaction when exhibiting low effort and performance, if rewards are independent of performance and no costs (in the form of penalties) are incurred as a result of the low effort and performance. Imposing penalties for low effort is often the only way to stimulate motivation.

RISING INCOME AND PROGRESSIVE TAXATION

Throughout most of the history of the United States, the general level of wages and salaries has been on the increase. Part of this increase has occurred because of inflation, but a substantial portion of the increase has been real. The standard of living of most Americans has continually advanced.

Coupled with this income increase have been progressively larger income tax deductions. Our system of progressive taxation causes larger percentages of high income than of low income to be deducted for taxes. Because today's incomes are much higher than in past years, people now pay a significantly greater share of their incomes in the form of taxes.

To stimulate motivation, rewards must have high value. But as one's income level rises, additional increments are perceived as less and less valuable. This law of diminishing returns is encountered with all types of rewards. Progressive taxation compounds the effect as ever-increasing percentages of rising income are subtracted for taxes.

Those in high income tax brackets, therefore, tend to be unwilling to exert extra effort in pursuit of opportunities to earn added income. Because of diminishing returns and progressive taxation, any additional income is perceived as lacking sufficient value to cover the additional costs (fatigue, stress, and boredom) of increased effort.

MORE GROUP PRODUCTION AND PROBLEM SOLVING

In the past, discoveries were frequently made by individuals working alone in the laboratory. Innovations were often the product of individual effort, and production and problem solving were the responsibilities of individuals. With the growing complexity of business and technology, however, a need for team effort has emerged. Rugged individualism is no longer in demand. Now, groups instead of individuals are assigned responsibilities and held accountable for performance. Problems and projects are often too large for one man working in isolation.

When groups serve as the basic unit for production, individual employee motivation can be hurt in at least two ways. First, individuals in a group are not likely to perceive strong links between individual effort and group performance. The effects of both positive and negative individual contributions are less apparent and have less impact on total performance when the contributions of many others are added in. Employees may not see how their individual efforts really make a difference.

Second, individuals in a group are not likely to perceive a strong link between group performance and individual rewards. When performing as team members, rewards (and penalties) are shared. Sharing can cause individual members to perceive the value of rewards as diluted. Also, an individual's sense of accomplishment is often lower in a group because real accomplishment is not a product of the individual but of the entire team. Similarly, criticism for nonperformance often does not carry high negative value for the individual because such criticism is dispersed over many team members.

DECREASED EMPLOYEE LOYALTY

The rise of unions, the birth of new professions, increased organizational size, increased specialization, and the increased physical mobility of employees have resulted in decreased worker identification with the company. Employees have shifted their allegiances from their employing organizations to unions, professional associations, and various away-from-work groups and institutions. Employees no longer live and breathe only for the company. Psychological detachment and resultant low employee loyalty are now commonplace.

Decreased loyalty, however, causes reduced motivation. It means absence of a sense of obligation to the company. Employees lacking loyalty do not internally accept company goals. Employees with high loyalty, on the other hand, feel commitment to these goals. They feel they owe a fair day's work for a fair day's wage. They believe the organization deserves their best effort. They feel good when exerting high effort because it is seen as in the best interest of the company, and what is best for the company is best for them.

LESS SUPERVISORY POWER

Over the years, the supervisor's authority has eroded. At present, formal authority does not demand the respect it once did. Today, the control of rewards and penalties often resides with the union or with the personnel department instead of with the supervisor. Equal employment opportunity laws prevent the supervisor from exercising a free hand in hiring, firing, and other employment practices.

Supervisors today also have less expertise in many of the specialized fields which they must manage. Further, supervisors are no longer people in the know. Growing company size and specialization have reduced the supervisor's role as an information source. In short, the bases of supervisory power are vanishing.

But to influence employees, supervisors must have social power. To motivate, supervisors must not only control the application of rewards and penalties, but also control employee access to information and other resources that employees value. If supervisors lack such control, they can not entice employees to exert high effort.

SHORTER TIME PERSPECTIVES

In recent years, Americans have markedly transformed their horizons. Young and middle-aged citizens in the late '40s and '50s were future oriented. They planned for the future. They saved for the future. They were willing to sacrifice in the present for the promise of better times ahead.

But the world political and economic climate has changed, and with it people's time horizons. Individuals now see rapid change and uncertainty as the norm. People are sensitive to growing resource shortages, exploding populations, an increasingly risky world military posture, and a host of other seemingly unsolvable problems. Because of this, human beings want instant gratification. Spend now; don't wait for the future. Enjoy now; there may not be opportunity later. Investment is out of the question.

But if employees are not interested in long-run payoffs, they will not be willing to exert the extra effort required to generate such payoffs. If such rewards as future higher income, promotions, and recognition are not valued, the high effort necessary to realize these rewards will not be exerted.

CONCLUSION

These, then, constitute ten possible reasons for declining motivation. The list is not exhaustive. What is interesting and at the same time disturbing is that the forces causing the decline seem to be of great variety. No one or two factors can be singled out. Just to reverse the downtrend will, therefore, be a formidable task. To recover lost ground will take years, if not decades—and that is being optimistic. It may well be, considering the variety and strength of these forces, that a broad-based, concentrated attempt to restore employee job motivation can never be launched. Must we then accept lower motivation as inevitable?

REFERENCES

Bernstein, P.L., "Is Work Necessary?" *American Child* (Jan. 1964), pp. 15-19.

Grant, Philip C., "A Model for Employee Motivation and Satisfaction," *Personnel* (Sept.-Oct. 1979), pp. 51-57.

Grant, Philip C., "Explaining Motivation Phenomena with the Effort-Net Return Model," *Nevada Review of Business Economics* (Spring 1982), pp. 29-32.

Kovach, K., "Improving Employee Motivation in Today's Business Environment," *MSU Business Topics* (Autumn 1976), pp. 5-12.

Maslow, Abraham, *Motivation and Personality* (New York: Harper and Row, 1954).

Megginson, Leon C., *Personnel: A Behavioral Approach to Administration* (Homewood, Ill.: Richard D. Irwin, Inc., 1967).

"New Tool: Reinforcement for Good Work," *Psychology Today* (April 1972), pp. 68-69.

Northrup, B., "Working Happier," *The Wall Street Journal* (Oct. 25, 1974), p. 1.

Schrank R., "How to Relieve Worker Boredom," *Psychology Today* (July 1978), pp. 79-80.

Skinner, B.F., *Contingencies of Reinforcement* (New York: Appleton-Century-Crofts, 1969).

Solcum, J.W., Jr., "Motivation in Managerial Levels: Relationship of Need Satisfaction to Job Performance," *Journal of Applied Psychology* (Vol. 55, 1971), pp. 312-316.

Steers, Richard M. and Lyman W. Porter, *Motivation and Work Behavior* (New York: McGraw-Hill, 1979).

Vroom, Victor, *Work and Motivation* (New York: John Wiley and Sons, 1964).

"What Happened to the Will to Work?" *Nation's Business* (May 1965), pp. 56-60.

Will, George, "How to Cut Taxes and Prosper," *Newsweek* (May 26, 1980), p. 100.

Philip C. Grant holds an M.B.A. from the University of Maine and a Ph.D. in management from Walden University.

46.
MASLOW, MOTIVATION AND THE MANAGER

J.B. Gayle
F.R. Searle

Knowing what factors motivate you can go a long way toward ensuring successful management/employee relations.

In the late 1950s, Frederick Herzberg and his associates at the Psychological Service of Pittsburgh conducted a study in which they asked some 200 engineers and accountants from 11 different firms to recall incidents in their recent experience which made them feel either particularly good or particularly bad about their jobs. The results of this study gave rise to Herzberg's two-factor theory which is considered by many to be one of the significant mileposts in the development of an understanding of motivation.

In essence, this theory suggests that the factors involved in producing job satisfaction are separate and distinct from the factors that lead to job dissatisfaction. Since separate factors are involved, it follows that these two feelings are *not* opposite of each other. Thus, the opposite of job satisfaction is not job *dissatisfaction,* but rather *no* job satisfaction. Similarly the opposite of job dissatisfaction is not job *satisfaction* but *no* job dissatisfaction.

Following this approach, Herzberg identified a group of "hygiene" factors such as company policy and administration, supervision, interpersonal relationships, personal life, working conditions, salary, and security. These factors are considered basic, and deficiencies in them can create job dissatisfaction but are not capable of motivating an employee to work harder than would be expected under normal circumstances. A group of "motivator" factors was also identified and included achievement, recognition for achievement, the work itself, responsibility, and growth or advancement. These factors are said to be capable of creating job satisfaction, but only if there is an acceptable level of hygiene factors.

Despite criticism that Herzberg's findings were "methodology bound" and that different conclusions could have been drawn from the same results, the theory has been supported by a large number of studies and, in addition, is intuitively appealing. For instance, as a basic example of a hygiene factor, one might consider the availability of bathrooms to the employee. While the failure to provide adequate toilet facilities would undoubtedly lead to a great deal of job dissatisfaction, no amount of such facilities would be expected to motivate the employee to a greater than normal level of productivity.

A significant limitation of the two-factor theory is that Herzberg, like many investigators, views employee/management interface as a one-way channel through which management satisfies certain perceived employee needs in the form of hygiene and motivator factors, thereby motivating the employee to achieve some corresponding level of productivity.

A more useful view would be that hygiene and motivator type factors exist in both management and employees in a kind of *mirror image* relationship. In other words, there are factors which could cause a manager to be dissatisfied with an employee, but which would not lead to rewards for the manager in the form of merit raises or a position of greater responsibility. Likewise, there are also factors similar to Herzberg's motivators which could lead to a manager receiving rewards, but only provided that the hygiene factors are at acceptable levels.

For example, consider the employee and management hygiene and motivating factors in Figure 1. Without attempting to justify this exact listing, it appears that the hygiene factors on both sides of the interface result at least in part from a need for order and security. Thus, the employee needs to be able to count on continuity of employment under reasonable working conditions at an acceptable level of pay. Management needs to be able to count on the availability of an employee who will accept direction and carry out assignments in accordance with established policies.

As is often pointed out, the essentially negative nature of employee hygiene factors is consistent with Maslow's hierarchy of needs, which represents another well-known milepost in the development of an understanding of motivation. Thus, since most employers provide a high level of hygiene factors, such levels have come to be expected and are only of concern when not realized. Similarly, a managerial hierarchy of needs could be defined which would serve to explain the negative nature of managerial hygiene factors. Thus, since most employees conform to established policies, such conformance is only of concern to management when it is absent. Motivator factors, on the other hand, involve aspirations not so readily attained and thus represent higher levels in the hierarchy of needs for both the employee and the manager.

The benefits of recognizing that a "mirror image" of Herzberg's employee theory exists in the form of a management "two-factor theory" can be significant. Such recognition should begin with the interview-hiring process of prospective professional and management employees. The employment deliberations rarely go further than simple employee personality and skills vis-

Figure 1.
EMPLOYEE/MANAGEMENT FACTORS

EMPLOYEE FACTORS		MANAGEMENT FACTORS	
Hygiene	Motivator	Hygiene	Motivator
1. Supervision	Recognition	Attendance	Level of supervision required
2. Working conditions	Responsibility; Challenge	Acceptance of work assignments	Responsibility
3. Job security	Growth potential	Acceptance of management; Working relations with other employees	Creativity Attitude

a-vis the compensation package. Deliberate consideration of the two factors (hygiene and motivator) by *both* parties to the employment contract could help reduce future conflicts following hiring. Both parties should attempt to establish that the hygiene and motivator factors on both sides are compatible.

Although the prospective employee generally considers such factors as pay level, fringe benefits, type of work, etc., he or she may neglect a myriad of management policies affecting promotional opportunities, established work schedules, overtime pay, retention rights in layoffs, etc. Similarly, although management attempts to ensure the prospective employee's ability to accomplish the required duties, there is usually no attempt to determine his or her attitude toward sick leave, personal and/or family matters, support for controversial political movements, and other factors which could cause dissatisfaction on the part of the manager.

As one might expect, conflicts often arise after a period of time due to failure to negotiate an explicit contract or agreement which is acceptable to both the employee and the organization. Personnel actions which sometimes result from these conflicts can affect the employee's future employment and can cause loss of morale within the organization.

Such conflicts frequently result from a mismatch of individual and managerial hygiene factors. For example, it is not uncommon for a highly productive employee to object to reporting to work on a regular schedule, arguing that he or she frequently works overtime to finish urgent assignments. Management may well agree with the basic premise of the argument, but still insist that the employee report as scheduled to avoid complaints of inequity by other employees whose productivity levels may be somewhat lower.

In such an instance, the employee may become dissatisfied, resulting in a decrease in level of performance. This, in turn, may cause management dissatisfaction, resulting in increased job pressure on the employee. This increased job pressure is likely to result in further employee dissatisfaction and so the cycle continues, ultimately leading to secession or termination of employment. Or one party will elect to accept some level of dissatisfaction as preferable to the consequences of further escalating the conflict.

Since the costs of conflicts are likely to be significant for both parties, management actions to minimize their frequency would clearly be beneficial. A two-part approach could start with managers carefully reviewing existing and proposed personal policies and regulations from a standpoint of their needs. Certainly management has many legitimate needs and these should be documented in clear and explicit fashion. Unfortunately, many times management *policies* tend to far outnumber expressed management *needs*. Clearly one of the more important steps management can take is to limit personnel policies and regulations to areas of real needs and to ensure that they are compatible with constraints imposed by work requirements and organizational policies.

The other half of the approach should be an attempt to ensure a full understanding of management policies by potential employees prior to any offer of employment. All too often, the first knowledge of such policies comes from a briefing or handbook the employee receives on his or her first day of work.

Management's failure to ensure understanding of managerial policies by potential employees usually does not stem from an attempt to deceive. At first, managers are interested only in identifying the most desirable candidate for the position. However, once that identification has been made, the interest shifts to presenting the organization in the most favorable light, and this is not well served by pointing out that opportunities for future advancement may depend on equal opportunity considerations rather than productivity, or that management takes a dim view of any employee who is frequently absent, regardless of the reason. Although discussions of such matters may not constitute the most effective recruiting technique, they should reduce the likelihood of future conflicts due to the existence of incompatible managerial and employee hygiene factors.

Many studies and articles have been completed on the factors which act to create employee job satisfaction and to motivate employees to higher productivity, but few have considered the impact of the factors that cause *management* to be satisfied with the employee as well as those that motivate management to provide more than normal rewards to the employee. Employer/employee relations can be improved if the hygiene and motivator factors of *both* parties are carefully considered—not just those of the employee.

REFERENCES

Dunnette, M.D., Campbell, J.P., and Hahel, M.D., "Factors Contributing to Job Satisfaction and Job Dissatisfaction in Six Occupational Groups," *Organizational Behavior and Human Performance* (Vol. 2, 1967), pp. 169-174.

Herzberg, F., Mausner, B., Peterson, R.O., and Capwell, O.F., *Job Attitudes: Review of Research and Opinion* (Pittsburgh: Psychological Services of Pittsburgh, 1957).

Herzberg, F., Mausner, B., and Snyderman, B.B., *The Motivation to Work* (New York: John Wiley and Sons, 1959).

Hunt, J.G. and Hill, J.W., "The New Look in Motivational Theory for Organizational Research," in Tosi, H.L. and Hammer, W. Clay, eds., *Organizational Behavior and Management—A Contingency Approach* (St. Clair Press, 1974).

J.B. Gayle, Ph.D., is associate professor of management science at Florida Institute of Technology, Melbourne, Florida. He has held management positions with the U.S. Bureau of Mines and the National Aeronautics and Space Administration (NASA). F.R. Searle, D.B.A., is associate professor and chairman of graduate programs in the management science department of the Florida Institute of Technology, Melbourne, Florida. He has had extensive experience as an aeronautics engineer.

47.
IN SEARCH OF MOTIVATION

Michael E. Cavanagh

It's what's inside that counts.

The question most asked of business consultants is "How can we motivate our employees?" The answer most given by consultants is "You can't." The reason for this answer is that the question typically implies that somewhere there are strategies, techniques, or gimmicks that, once discovered and implemented, will double or triple employee motivation and productivity. Consultants realize that genuine and lasting employee motivation is not something management does, but rather a process that management fosters and allows to happen.

In attempting to understand motivation, it is important to distinguish between the two types: external and internal. External motivation consists of a system of promised rewards and threatened punishments. Rewards are salary raises, promotions, and psychological stroking. Punishments include no salary raises, no promotions, being "called on the carpet," being transferred to a less desirable job or location, or being fired.

The problem with motivation by reward is that, sooner or later, a ceiling will be reached on raises, promotions, and psychological stroking. As rewards gradually decrease, employee motivation typically drops to negligible levels, even though the employee may be receiving a good salary and have decent status considering his or her abilities.

THREATS BREED RESENTMENT

The problem with motivating by threat of punishment is that it breeds employee fear and resentment that are likely to be expressed, consciously or unconsciously, in psychological sabotage. Sabotage consists of any behavior that interferes with the successful achievement of company goals. Common types of sabotage are complaining, criticizing, spreading gossip, absenteeism, tardiness, wasting time, forgetting important details, communicating false information to superiors, failure to report problems, carelessness, laziness, rudeness to customers and clients, and taking the path of least resistance. Motivation by threat creates a vicious circle: threat, resentment, sabotage, more threat, more resentment, more sabotage, and even more threat.

Internal motivation is a far more complex phenomenon than the carrot and stick approach to reward and the "You'd better produce or else" strategy of punishment. Internal motivation develops from an atmosphere that includes four dimensions: the personal qualities of the employee, the nature of the job, the qualities of the supervisor, and the company philosophy.

FIVE PERSONAL QUALITIES

At least five personal qualities pertain to job motivation: ability, needs, frustration tolerance, self-esteem, and outside supports.

When a person's abilities (intelligence, creativity, energy, maturity) are reasonably consonant with the requirements of the job, this will act as a motivating force. When the employee's abilities are significantly higher or lower than those demanded by the job, this typically constitutes a contra-motivational factor. This principle should be kept in mind, especially when an employee is being considered for a job transfer or promotion. Motivation may be good until an employee is shifted to a job that is significantly above or below his or her abilities. When this occurs, a good employee turns into a problem employee.

When an employee's needs (the need to be, not just feel, secure, liked, appreciated, effective, comfortable, important, subordinate, autonomous, trusted, social) are reasonably met on the job, internal motivation will incubate and grow. When needs are continually thwarted, motivation may never become ignited and work becomes a place to make the most money for the least effort.

Employees with good frustration tolerance are able to be reasonably patient in the face of obstacles, are willing to forgo immediate satisfaction for long range goals, and are capable of assimilating periodic disappointment and failure without becoming more than temporarily demoralized. Employees with poor frustration tolerance who have jobs that require at least average tolerance are likely to become irritable and cynical, qualities that preclude good motivation.

SELF-ESTEEM HELPS

Employees who have an inherent sense of self-esteem possess a healthy pride in themselves that moves them to do good work, whether or not there is anyone else present to notice or affirm their efforts. They appreciate acknowledgment of their good work, but don't need it in order to function. Employees with poor self-esteem lack a basic pride in themselves and, therefore, function adequately only when they are continually refueled by the guidance and support of supervisors. This gradually wears down the supervisor and eventually creates mutual frustration and resentment.

Employees who have a satisfying personal life (family, friends, hobbies, interests, a sense of purpose in life) are able to bring energy to their work because they are continually replenished by their home and social life. In addition, they are able to place work in a healthy perspective: a bad day at work can always be rehabilitated by a good night at home. On the other hand, employees whose whole life is their work overreact to frustration, failure, or injustice at work because work is their life, not just one-third of it.

THE PERFECT MATCH

It is important that companies match the requirements of the job with the qualities of the employee. In the real world, this can seldom be done perfectly, but the closer the match, the better the chances are that internal motivation will develop. For this reason, serious attempts to find the right person for the right job are well worth the effort.

A good match can be accomplished by constructing questionnaires for applicants to complete, by carefully phrasing letters to former employers or teachers that will measure the qualities described above, and by skilled interviewing, especially in a setting where the applicants can be interviewed as a group. In this situation the interviewer (or, better yet, the interviewers) can healthily challenge the applicants and encourage them to interact, challenge, and compete with each other. This will afford the opportunity to see each applicant in action—to see his or her strengths or weaknesses in technicolor rather than in the black and white shots that the traditional job interview renders.

Simply asking applicants questions such as "Jim, how well do you handle stress in your life?" is naive and a waste of time. It is unlikely that Jim will respond, "Well, frankly, I cave in under stress," or "I punch the person closest to me," or "I get drunk."

GOOD OR BAD?

Too often the nature of the job is ignored when considering job motivation. There is no such thing as a good job or a bad job. What is a good job for one person may be a terrible one for another.

For example, collecting garbage may be a good job for one person because it pays well, offers outdoor work and good exercise, provides a sense of camaraderie among workers, and is not intellectually threatening. For another person, collecting garbage may be the worst job in the world because the person hates garbage, finds the hours terrible, thinks his fellow workers are morons, and sees no intellectual stimulation or existential meaning to the work. For the first person, the job itself is a significant motivator. For the second person, it is a significant demotivator.

There are four basic types of jobs:

- a job that meets the needs of the person and is likely to lead to an even better job
- a job that meets the needs of the person but is not likely to lead to advancement
- a job that does not meet the needs of the person but is likely to lead to a better job
- a job that does not meet the needs of the person and is not likely to lead to a better job

Each of these types of jobs will motivate or demotivate employees in different ways. Attempts to externally motivate people in demotivating types of jobs will soon crumble under the weight of the job itself. Until the needs of the person change or the elements of the job change (or both), there will be a continuing motivation problem.

THE IDEAL SUPERVISOR

Certain qualities that supervisors can possess, or work toward possessing, will enable them to be inherently and naturally motivating supervisors. When supervisors possess these qualities, at least to a greater rather than a lesser extent, they no longer need to use external motivation—just as a track star doesn't need a cane. Such qualities include honesty, supportiveness, empathy, accessibility, fairness, openness, insight, and interest.

Good supervisors level with their employees in all areas, even when it means casting themselves, the company, or the employee in a less than positive light. They recognize that 95 percent honesty means five percent dishonesty, a fact that can create a distrust that makes the 95 percent honesty suspect and irrelevant.

Supportive supervisors communicate the message: "We're on the same team, so when you do something well, I'll be the first to let you know, and when problems arise, we'll work on them together." This is in contrast to the supervisor who communicates, "You get paid for doing things correctly, so don't look to me for a pat on the back, and if you get yourself in a jam, you get yourself out of it."

HEALTHY COMPASSION

Supervisors should possess a healthy and appropriate compassion for their employees, which is communicated by a demeanor that says: "I know how you feel. You're in an objectively difficult situation." In some situations, all that a supervisor can give a person is empathy; often that is enough to get the employee over a hurdle. Instead of empathy, low-motivating supervisors offer war stories ("You should have seen what I had to put up with when I had your job.") or off-the-rack nostrums ("Don't worry about it—just do the best you can.").

Within reason, it's important for supervisors to be readily available to employees. An open door policy communicates a genuine interest and willingness to help. This is especially important for new employees or employees beginning a new job. It's a secure feeling for employees to know that there is a safety net beneath them if things become too difficult.

Supervisors who communicate the message, "Let me know if you have a problem but I've got enough problems right now, so I won't appreciate being handed one more," convey the attitude that they are not really interested in the employee and that employees are generally a nuisance. Invariably, these same supervisors remonstrate at employees for not bringing problems to them before they reach the crisis stage, because the supervisors are unaware of the double messages they send.

Supervisors who treat their employees fairly—that is, in ways that they themselves want to be treated—contribute a good deal to a positive motivational milieu. They give fair evaluations, follow through on promises, refuse to overload their employees with work, do not apply inordinate pressure, do not harbor unrealistic expectations, and don't blame employees for problems not of their making.

Supervisors who assign workloads on the basis of "the work has to get done," who apply inordinate pressure because it is being applied to them, and whose expectations are unrealistic ("I know it's a lousy textbook, but it's your job to sell it") do a good deal to subvert the possibility of a positive motivational milieu.

CHANGES FOR THE BETTER

Supervisors who are open—that is, who invite suggestions, and are amenable to constructive criticism—are likely to make changes that accommodate employees. Moreover, by virtue of their openness, they convey a genuine respect for the employee. Supervisors who are close and defensive treat employees as children and cannot validly complain that their employees' motivation is similar to that of children.

Supervisors who honestly evaluate themselves (their needs, motives, goals, strengths, shortcomings) will be in a good position to react in helpful ways. Some of the questions they ask themselves are:

1) Would I want to have my employee's job? If not, why not, and how can I make the job better?

2) Do I tend to accept too much responsibility and, in turn, pass down too much responsibility to my employees?

3) What are my strengths as a person and as a supervisor, and do I utilize these strengths as fully as possible?

4) Since everyone has biases, what are some of mine that may interfere with my supervisory ability?

5) What kind of person or situation threatens me the most at work, and why?

6) Do I operate on the principle that I won't say anything about an employee that I wouldn't say if he were present, or do I tend to gossip behind the backs of my employees?

7) Do I allow the poor performance or personal problems of employees to go unaddressed for too long because I'm afraid to confront them, or do I tend to nip problems in the bud?

Motivating supervisors ask these and other questions and modify their behavior according to the answers. Non-motivation supervisors compulsively avoid looking into themselves. Consequently, their stagnation and rigidity infect the overall motivational environment.

GENERATE INTEREST

Supervisors who are at least interested in their employees as workers, if not as people, generate interest from employees. These supervisors solicit feedback through interviews and signed or unsigned questionnaires. Examples of information they are interested in are outlined in the following questions:

1) What are the two most and two least satisfying parts of your work?

2) If you were your own supervisor, how would you supervise yourself differently than as currently done?

3) If you were to quit the company in the next six months, what would be your honest reasons for doing so?

4) You've chosen to stay with the company. What are the main reasons for this choice?

5) What are your career goals with the company? What job would you like to have in two years, five years, or 10 years?

6) How can I help you reach your goals?

Supervisors who are interested in employees only in so far as the work gets done will have employees who are interested in the company only in so far as they get a paycheck every two weeks.

THE COMPANY PHILOSOPHY

Every company (and department) has an articulated philosophy, even if this fact is not realized. This is true even when the philosophy of the company is unclear to employees. This simply means that the company philosophy is also unclear to the people who manage the company. The company philosophy is comprised of the traditions, values, beliefs, motives, and goals of the company.

Often companies have two philosophies: the formal one that is printed in a company brochure and the functional one that is unwritten and often unspoken, but which is the one upon which company operations are predicated. The following are some examples of company philosophy that will increase the motivational levels of employees.

The company should treat its employees with respect, both as persons and as employees. "Our employees are our greatest asset" is not just a slogan to be mouthed at company dinners, but a credo that should be put into action. The company should pay fair salaries, arbitrate issues in a just fashion, reward dedication and loyalty that is beyond the call of duty, take the suggestions of employees seriously, and immediately rectify all legitimate grievances.

A SPIRIT OF HELPFULNESS

The best effort should be made to retain employees who have given good service. When employees experience work difficulties or personal problems, the company must do everything in its power to help them. Competent supervisors and counselors must be provided, as well as access to anyone else in the company who can be helpful. Provide comprehensive insurance that covers both medical and psychological problems, and extend leaves of absence when a period of treatment and rehabilitation is necessary. Don't terminate an employee before every possible means of being helpful has been exhausted.

A positive spirit helps employees feel they belong to a good group of people and not just to a functional organization. This spirit can be fostered by company-sponsored social events, athletic activities, discussion groups, and workshops in which employees can learn to know and appreciate each other as people and not just as fellow workers. Then employees will hate to leave the company, not necessarily because the salary and benefits are outstanding, but because the people are.

A company must be sufficiently flexible to change with the times and the needs of the employees, yet be consistent in that basic values and beliefs remain the same. A company must be willing to change when sameness will breed stagnation and willing to maintain the status quo when people need some consistency and reliability. Keep employees well informed of marketing and personnel decisions that will directly or indirectly affect their lives. An excellent attitude is, "This is your company, as well as ours, and you have the right to know what we're doing with it and in turn with you."

A MOTIVATIONAL GOAL

When each of the four dimensions of internal motivation are fully present and are complementing each other, a sound motivational matrix is formed. This represents an ideal situation which, by definition, does not exist in reality. However, it is a model toward which to work.

When there is a deficit in one dimension, sometimes it can be compensated for by an overabundance in another. For example, a poor supervisor may be compensated for by very high job satisfaction and a very positive company philosophy. However, if there is a significant deficit in the supervisory dimension and the other dimensions remain the same, a serious decrease in motivation results.

If there are significant deficits in two dimensions (for example, supervision and philosophy), grave and possibly irreversible motivational symptoms may be created, unless a major reorganization takes place immediately. Unfortunately for both the employee and the company, the question usually asked in such a case is, "What's wrong with this employee?" instead of "What's wrong with the job, the supervisor, or the company philosophy?"

EARN EMPLOYEE MOTIVATION

High motivational levels in employees are the result of a good job, done by the right person, working for a competent supervisor, under the banner of a positive company philosophy. Low motivational levels are not problems in themselves, but they are symptoms of a deficit in one or more motivational dimensions.

There are no shortcuts to motivating employees. There is no consultant who can inject employees with a motivation serum.

There are no workshops, company newsletters, or bonuses that will increase motivation to an extent that is substantial or durable. The company that has internally-motivated employees is in a good position to answer the question, "How do we motivate our people?" Their answer would be, "We earn their motivation."

48.
HOW GOOD IS VALUES ANALYSIS?

Niles Howard

To help them cope with a changing work force, a number of companies are using this novel psychological technique in hiring and motivating employees. But there are problems.

It has become something of a truism that employees these days are harder to manage than were their counterparts of a generation ago. They are said to be far less predictable in their attitudes toward pay, supervision, and other work-related factors, which makes it harder for companies to assess job applicants and complicates the task of directing and motivating those who are hired. Some managers go so far as to blame this so-called decline of the work ethic for contributing to the slowdown in U.S. industrial productivity.

To help them cope with the changing work force, a number of large companies are experimenting with a psychological theory called "values analysis": a technique that attempts to identify the underlying values on which an individual's behavior is based. By classifying employees according to different value systems, the theorists contend, it is possible for managers to predict how they will react to a given situation, and this knowledge can be used to make them happier and more productive on the job.

Needless to say, values analysis is not being universally welcomed into the corporate world. To some people, it smacks of psychological manipulation, and labor leaders in particular charge that it is being used to forestall organizing efforts. Even some skeptical psychologists regard it as just another expensive, transient management fad à la transactional analysis, encounter groups, and sensitivity training.

Nevertheless, hundreds of companies are said to be experimenting with values analysis to some extent, including such major ones as American Telephone & Telegraph, Standard Oil of Indiana, United Airlines, and American Airlines. And most of them have nothing but praise for the technique. "It's extremely powerful and extremely easy to understand and apply without having a degree in psychology," says psychologist Diane Carter, management development representative for United Airlines, which has been using values analysis for the past two years. "I think it is the most useful way to look at behavior and organization that I have seen."

Another advocate is Irving Margol, personnel vice president at Los Angeles Security Pacific Bank, where values analysis is being used in selecting, training, motivating, and counseling employees. "We recognize that people who come to work for the bank today are different from those who started 20 years ago, and also that people are different from each other," Margol says. "Values analysis is a good tool to help management understand and comprehend this."

Values analysis is largely the invention of a little-known scholar named Clare Graves, who was for years a professor of developmental psychology at Union College in Schenectady, New York. Drawing on the psychological theories of human development formulated by Brandeis University's Abraham Maslow and Germany's Eduard Sprunger, in 1952 Graves undertook an ambitious academic project to pin down society's definition of human maturity. After administering personality and intelligence tests to more than 1,000 students and trying to fit the results into a single behavioral model, Graves finally threw up his hands. Such a definition apparently did not exist.

SEVEN PATTERNS

However, Graves noticed that the results of his work seemed to show there were distinctive patterns in the way people define maturity. After 14 years of testing dozens of concepts to explain patterns, he came up with his answers in a unique theory of human development.

Graves found seven patterns, each involving a complex web of commonly held values. These value systems are both hierarchical and evolving. Primitive man had only one value—staying alive—but as the human species evolved, other value systems emerged in response to changing environmental conditions and human needs. So far, said Graves, mankind has produced only seven systems because that is all his development has required. But others will surely evolve in the future.

As a person matures, Graves theorized, he progresses from one value system to another, more or less duplicating the progress made by the species. For one reason or another, few people get to stage seven; most make it to four or five. However, people do not reside in one category, like a pigeon occupies a nook, he cautioned. Most exhibit values of several systems at the same time, although one usually dominates.

To describe each value system, and explain when and why it emerged historically, Graves devoted thousands of words and dozens of esoteric psychological concepts. Highly simplified, the seven can be described as follows:

Subsistence. People at this level of existence seek only to stay alive. They react to warmth, pain and hunger but not to other humans as individuals. It is now characteristic only of infants and some brain-damaged people.

Tribalistic. This value system, which evolved 40,000 years ago, holds that basic needs can be met by submission to a strong authority figure. Myth, tradition, magic, and superstition are common. Today, it is mostly found under conditions of extreme poverty.

Egocentric. This system began to emerge 10,000 years ago as a reaction against tribal values. It eschews authority, norms, rules, and standards, and its adherents are often brash, rough, and brazen. It is still common in this country, according to Graves, its strongest adherents being found among laborers, truck drivers, and certain executives.

Absolutistic. First seen 4,000 years ago, it is characterized by the conviction that there is an underlying rationale to life, a reason why there are "haves" and "have-nots." The system puts a great deal of stock in absolute moral laws and in order, structure, sacrifice, and discipline. According to Graves, people who adhere to these values have been the mainstay of the hourly work force in America since the beginning of the Industrial Revolution.

Achievist. This set of values, which first appeared around the fifth century A.D., is distinguished by a desire to conquer the world through knowledge, rather than through brute force. It puts a high premium on aggression and competition. Politicians, salesmen, and marketing executives often cling strongly to these values, Graves says.

Sociocentric. This value system first emerged about the beginning of this century, Graves says. Reflecting aggression, it puts a premium on belonging. Adherents value goodwill more than free enterprise, social approval more than individual fame. They work on behalf of social causes, are opposed to the manipulation of people, and eschew rigid conformity.

Individualistic. A value system that emerged after World War II, it stresses oneself over others but lacks the hostility of the egocentric system. Adherents respond to reason, not rules. They are tolerant of ambiguity in people and situations, but expect top performance in themselves and others.

Graves' hypothesis fell on the psychological community like a feather. The major academic journals rejected his articles; every psychologist, it seems, has a theory about how the world works. So Graves recast his concept toward a practical business slant and sold it to the *Harvard Business Review,* which published it under the title, "Deterioration of Work Standards," in October 1966. Only after four more years, during which he was in and out of hospitals with a heart ailment, did Graves achieve the professional recognition he had long sought. In the fall of 1970, his "Levels of Existence: An Open System Theory of Values," was published in the *Journal of Humanistic Psychology.*

By then, word of Graves' novel concept was circulating among industrial psychologists, mainly in the relatively new and controversial field of organizational development. At the time, O.D. experts were in great demand by companies seeking to keep the countercultural revolution in the streets from sweeping through their factories. Applying humanistic psychology, the experts developed dozens of techniques. Two favorites of industry were transactional analysis, which defined human relationships in terms of three roles (parent, child, and adult) and taught managers to play those roles; and The Organizational Grid, which identified companies according to their concern with people versus production.

EARLY EXPERIMENT

One corporate psychologist who became interested in the Graves theory was Scott Myers, manager of personnel and management resources at Texas Instruments Inc. In 1971, while on leave as a visiting professor at the Massachusetts Institute of Technology's Sloan School of Management, Myers attended a seminar where he heard a presentation of values analysis by Graves himself. Though skeptical ("It seemed a little too pat," he recalls), Myers returned to MIT and, together with his wife Susan, began work on a questionnaire to identify values in individuals. The test included questions like, "To me, company loyalty means . . . " and "Money is important to me because. . . . " Each was followed by six possible answers, corresponding to six of the seven Graves value systems. ("Subsistence" was excluded on the assumption that individuals at that level couldn't take a written test.)

On returning to his job at Texas Instruments later that year, Myers explained the theory to his boss, personnel director Charles Hughes, and company assistant comptroller Vincent Flowers, who were wrestling with the problem of high employee turnover on the assembly lines. Reasoning that the values approach could be used to identify in advance employees who wouldn't fit in, they administered the test to applicants without the knowledge of company management, and then tracked them for a year.

They had suspected that assembly line work was best suited to employees with tribal values and unsuited to those with egocentric values. Their predictions proved accurate. After a year, individuals who had shown a strong degree of tribal values in the test turned out to be good, stable workers, while the egocentrics seemed to dislike the work, caused trouble, and eventually left. By this time, however, both Hughes and Myers, who were beginning to be regarded as eccentrics by other Texas Instruments managers, were on their way out of the company, and Flowers had quit to become associate dean of business at North Texas State University in Denton.

Since then, the values theory has spread fast in industry. Shortly before leaving Texas Instruments, Flowers and Hughes described their work at the company in a *Harvard Business Review* article and in a booklet for the American Management Association. Two years later they collaborated with Scott and Susan Myers in an ambitious survey and report for the AMA in which they administered the values quiz to 1,707 managers across the country.

By now, Flowers and Hughes, who run their own Dallas management consulting firm, Center for Values Research, claim to have introduced the concept to hundreds of companies. So do Scott and Susan Myers, who run the Center for Applied Management in Santa Barbara, California.

Of the dozens of other consultants who have set up firms to develop selection, training, and motivational procedures based on the Graves' theory, one of the most active is psychologist Donald Beck, a former professor who now runs a consulting firm outside Dallas called the National Values Center.

RECOGNIZING VALUES

Beck uses values analysis in training programs for executives and other supervisors. Like other practitioners, he operates on the theory that most personnel problems occur because managers tend to have different values from their employees. At the upper levels of management this imbalance can't be corrected, he says, nor should it be, since different values are needed in a corporation. But what one can do is teach managers to recognize the various value systems or, in Beck's phrase, the various positions on "the psychological map."

For instance, employees with tribalistic values respond best to a benevolently autocratic management style, he believes, while egocentrics would view such an approach as so weak and indecisive as to invite disobedience. Absolutist employees, on the other hand, expect to be treated in a dignified, business-like manner and take comfort in clear-cut rules and procedures. Achievists will chafe under those same rules; they value the end, not the means, and respond to material rewards for achieving goals. Such incentives, however, would mean little to a sociocentric person, who would much rather have a harmonious and mutually supportive relationship with his co-workers. Finally, the individualist takes pride in achievement—not so much for reward but for the feeling of being a part of a dynamic and successful enterprise.

Of course, experienced managers often recognize these types of people instinctively and discover through trial and error how to deal with them. But values consultants contend that a systematic framework enables organizations to avoid some of the problems that arise with hit-and-miss methods.

Take the case of Dallas's Republic National Bank, which asked Beck to help drum up employee enthusiasm for a new marketing drive. In past drives, the bank had offered prizes for bringing in the most new accounts, but those incentives had not worked.

To find out what would motivate employees, Beck interviewed a number of them to determine their values and found three dominant systems: tribalistic, absolutistic, and sociocentric. Using that information, he designed a sound-and-slide presentation to appeal to each group. For the tribalistic employees, he emphasized the idea of the bank as a family; for the absolutists, he emphasized tradition, with pictures of the bank in its early days; for the sociocentrics, he used scenes of employees helping customers. "The bank officers tended to be achievists, and we warned them that they probably wouldn't understand the presentation," Beck says. "We were right; it made no sense to them."

In quite a different application, Beck was called in by Standard Oil Company (Indiana) to teach values analysis to supervisors of professional employees, such as geologists and engineers, who, the company felt, could not be managed like regular rank-and-file workers. "Some people can't operate with a lot of rules and regulations and have to be treated differently," says James Glennon, Indiana Standard's director of training. "We've had a lot of supervisors go through this Beck thing, and they're mightily impressed."

Beck was also asked to help Southern Bell, a subsidiary of American Telephone & Telegraph, explain to its 45,000 employees the rationale behind the major restructuring of the parent corporation and its units two years ago. Employees seemed to respond as the company had hoped, according to Lane Talburt, public relations manager, although he admits that there is no way of knowing whether the approach was more effective than any other he might have used. "It's the kind of thing you just can't measure," he says.

But advocates claim that is not the point. Values analysis, they say, is not an absolute but a guide. "It doesn't give you skill," says United Airlines' Diane Carter, "but gives you direction in determining in what style to approach employees—what you should emphasize in your facts or how you should present your case."

Carter says that teaching supervisors how to use the system has proven very successful. She has also had good results applying it for team building among staffs that work together. "I will go in and work with, say, a comptroller, a supervisor, and an office manager; give everybody the instrument and then tell them what each one's value system is and what the implications are in terms of the way in which they ought to work with that particular person. It's more than just positive," she adds. "They tend to get very excited about it."

Nevertheless, values analysis has evoked criticism on several fronts. Most vocal are labor unions, which contend that some companies are using it as a way to weed out potential organizers and otherwise foil attempts to unionize factories.

A POTENT WEAPON?

Consultants Hughes and Flowers have earned the particular enmity of labor leaders for their efforts in this area. The two do not deny that values analysis can be turned into a potent anti-union weapon and, in fact, admit that such applications are the largest part of their business. But they contend that their techniques are aboveboard.

Their usual method is to go into a factory where management fears union organization and administer two anonymous tests to each employee: one to detect their value system, another to gauge their attitude toward the company. They take the results to management, explain what workers are dissatisfied about and profile the predominant value systems. Then they design a communications program based on those values to show employees why it would not be as good to organize. "We also use the values model to determine who the company should be hiring, how they should be placed, how they should be paid and how they should be led, according to what their value systems may be," says Hughes.

Labor, however, is not assuaged. Union members have picketed Hughes and Flowers seminars in Los Angeles, Seattle and Chicago, and were out in force when the two spoke to a group of managers at Denver's Fairmont Hotel.

The most controversial aspect of values analysis, however, may turn out to be its use as a personnel selection device (controversial in the same way that psychological and aptitude tests to screen out troublemakers and incompetents have long been under fire). So far, its use in hiring has not generated much controversy because it has only been applied in an informal way. But some values analysts fear that companies may begin to use a formal values questionnaire. Even Scott Myers, who was most responsible for introducing values analysis to business, warns that its use in hiring is dangerous. "There are very serious ethical questions involved here," he says.

What most experts in the field are coming to realize, then, is that values analysis should not be thought of as a specific tool but as a kind of mental aid to help managers deal with people of varying backgrounds and attitudes. "I don't think it's magic, and I don't think it's the most wonderful thing that ever happened," says Robert Archibald, a pyschologist at Ohio State University and authority on the values theory. "But it is a useful approach to many different areas of human behavior. My guess is that anybody who has ever been exposed to it uses it in some way and thinks about it."

49.
GETTING DOWN TO THE BRASS TACKS ON EMPLOYEE MOTIVATION

Martin J. Kilduff
Douglas D. Baker

Some widely praised theories on how to improve employee motivation offer valuable insights into employee needs, but are not proven productivity raisers. Some methods, however, are tried-and-true —especially the five described here.

Managers seeking answers to the riddle of how to improve employee performance are likely to be overwhelmed by the vast number of theories. Unfortunately, many of these notions on employee motivation have very limited application. The surprising truth is that such widely disseminated theories as Maslow's need hierarchy and Herzberg's motivation/hygiene theory are unproven in the critical area of predicting employee performance. As shorthand guides to human motivation, both theories offer the manager insights into employee needs. But there is little research evidence to indicate that either quality or quantity of output will be increased through their implementation.

Where, then, should managers turn for ideas on how to improve productivity? We will focus on five theories that are research-supported in the area of employee performance improvement: achievement motivation theory, goal-setting expectancy theory, equity theory, and organizational behavior modification. The thrust of these theories is that high performance is a function of having motivated employees, setting high goals for them, and rewarding goal attainment.

ACHIEVEMENT MOTIVATION THEORY

One of the easiest ways to have high performance from your employees is to hire individuals with a high need for achievement. For these people, challenging tasks and their successful completion elicits feelings of pleasure. Given the right circumstances, those with a high need for achievement will outperform those with low achievement needs. On the face of it, hiring high achievers sounds like a simple panacea for solving the motivation problems in organizations. However, there are some potentially serious pitfalls to this strategy. A relatively small portion of the population has a high need for achievement (about 10 percent). These individuals are relatively difficult to identify, and if put into inappropriate organizational settings, they may actually be low performers.

What makes these high achievers tick? David McClelland, the main proponent of achievement theory (see David C. McClelland and David S. Winter's *Motivating Economic Achievement*, Free Press, 1969), has found that entrepreneurs and others with strong achievement needs prefer situations characterized by these five conditions:

- Success is possible through individual effort.
- Task difficulty levels are intermediate.
- Feedback on degree of success is clear and unambiguous.
- Innovative and novel solutions are permitted.
- A distinct future orientation is required.

McClelland's theory allows managers to structure work situations to fully utilize the talents of high need for achievement individuals. Profit centers and other semi-autonomous entrepreneurial units within the larger business offer the prospects of achievement satisfaction so vital to increasing the performance of high achievers. Money, in McClelland's view, operates in such contexts chiefly as a source of feedback on how well the achiever is performing.

What about low need for achievement people? McClelland's theory emphasizes that under certain circumstances individuals can "learn" to be achievers through achievement motivation training. There is conclusive evidence that McClelland's training techniques do increase the need to achieve and do result in expanded entrepreneurial behavior, but a word of caution: Training someone to be an entrepreneur and then assigning that person to an environment that does not permit satisfaction of the need for achievement can be disastrous. The chances are that the person will either leave the job or attempt to drastically alter the work environment. Training a warehouse worker to be an entrepreneur, for example, will not result in an increase in performance unless he or she is placed in an achievement-oriented role, such as salesperson, where achievement needs can be satisfied.

How is the manager to maintain the intermediate levels of difficulty and risk demanded by high achievement? Edwin Locke's goal-setting theory stresses the importance of setting difficult goals to maintain the motivation of all employees. And although Locke's theory works particularly well with high achievers, it can also be successfully employed to motivate low need for achievement individuals.

GOAL-SETTING THEORY

Goal-setting theory presents an attractive and well-supported idea that managers can immediately implement in many diverse areas. That is, by setting specific, hard goals for employees, performance will increase. The trick is to choose goals that the employees will accept as attainable. These goals can either be assigned or arrived at through employee participation, depending upon organizational norms. Although goal setting alone will increase performance, research indicates that by providing feedback in goal accomplishment, managers can further enhance employee productivity.

Managers tempted to use goal setting should recognize that company-wide goal setting is likely to be less effective than individualized goal setting between particular managers and their subordinates. A comprehensive top-down management by objective (MBO) program, for example, may not challenge individuals with the specific, hard goals necessary to motivate increased performance. Further, MBO programs are difficult to maintain in organizations because of their time-consuming nature, the difficulty of administering them, and the frequent employee resistance.

Goal setting has been shown to be particularly useful in achieving increases in performance for employees of self-contained work units. For example, at one logging company a goal of 94 percent of the legal weight limit was established to encourage truck drivers to haul heavier loads to the mill. Average truck loads rose rapidly from 60 percent utilization and stabilized after nine months at over 90 percent, saving the company an estimated quarter of a million dollars that would have been spent for the purchase of additional trucks had truck loads not increased.

According to Locke's theory, the appeal of the specific hard goal itself will generate increased employee performance. That is, the intrinsic feedback of a job well done or a goal attained will reinforce the behavior. Hence, extrinsic rewards, such as money, are not always necessary to reinforce performance. However, feedback has been shown to be important in maintaining and enhancing long-run performance in some situations. Expectancy theory takes a different position, emphasizing the importance of rewarding performance.

EXPECTANCY THEORY

Expectancy theory states that if a worker sees high productivity as a path leading to the attainment of one or more of his personal goals, he will tend to be a high producer. Conversely, if he sees low productivity as a path to the achievement of his goals, he will tend to be a low producer. In essence, the theory states that people attempt to maximize pleasure and minimize pain. On the job, individuals determine the paths of behavior that will result in the highest expected pleasure or lowest level of pain and act accordingly. More specifically, expectancy theory defines three determinates of motivation that managers may invoke to apply the theory: the effort-performance link, the performance-reward link, and the value of rewards.

The effort-performance link suggests that employees will work harder only if they expect increased effort to result in increased performance. That is, they have to expect that by working harder they will be better able to meet the performance standard set by the organization. In turn, by meeting these performance standards, they must expect that their pleasure will be maximized or their pain minimized. This is referred to as the performance-outcome expectancy. Further, to increase the level of motivation the outcomes or rewards should have high value to the employee.

The implication is that managers need to set performance goals that are attainable in order to motivate effort. If the performance standards are too high then there will be no expectancy by the subordinate that increased effort will result in goal attainment and subsequent rewards. Hence no increases in effort or performance will occur. Further, managers need to communicate unambiguously to workers exactly what is expected of them, that is, the performance goal. Vague goals will only work to muddy perceptions of the effort-performance link and thereby lessen motivation.

One other note on the effort-performance link is that at times an employee may perceive that he or she does not have the requisite skills to perform at the organization's defined performance levels. If this is true, then the employee needs to be trained or replaced for performance to increase. In some cases the employee will have the appropriate skills and merely lack the confidence that he or she can do the job. In such incidences, coaching or encouraging the individual to model himself on successful employees' behavior can work to bring his effort-performance expectancy into line and increase motivation.

While making performance expectancy clear to employees, managers who wish to increase performance need to make the performance-outcome expectancy clear. Workers must believe that increased performance will lead to increased rewards. If this expectancy is low, there will be little motivation to perform at high levels. Ways to establish a strong performance-reward link include pay increases targeted to high performers rather than across-the-board increases and an open pay policy so that employees can observe that high performers receive high rewards.

One final component of expectancy theory deals with the value for (or valence of) the expected rewards. The theory emphasizes that different people prefer different outcomes. A worker will not be motivated to increase performance if the rewards offered by management are irrelevant to his or her needs. Managers need to determine what type of outcomes individuals value, or use relatively universally desired outcomes such as money. There are, of course, some difficulties with implementing this notion. Some individuals have a low valence for money. Additionally, it may be difficult to identify the types of outcome individuals desire.

One way to provide each individual with specially tailored incentives without having to analyze exhaustively the needs of each individual is to implement a cafeteria compensation system, which allows employees to design their own pay and benefit packages. Edward Lawler has suggested, in *Pay and Organization Development* (Addison-Wesley, 1981) that cafeteria benefit programs allow management to increase the perceived value of fringe benefits for all individuals in a company without necessarily increasing the total cost to the company of fringe benefits. Again, in many companies, especially small ones, cafeteria compensation plans may not be feasible. In such situations managers may have to rely on money as a reward or merely ask the employees what type of compensation they desire.

Expectancy theory focuses on the individual and the rewards he or she expects to receive. The theory depicts the individual as striving to maximize expected pleasure and minimize pain. In contrast, equity theory emphasizes the importance of social comparison in determining motivation. According to equity theory, people seek not to maximize rewards but to maintain equity between themselves and others.

EQUITY THEORY

Outcomes from a job (such as pay, prestige, and fringe benefits) and inputs to a job (such as effort, educational level, and experience) form a ratio for each individual, according to the equity theory formulations of J. Stacy Adams. The individual compares his or her ratio to that of a reference source, such as a neighbor or co-worker, in order to determine the equity of the situation. For example, Sarah may believe she works twice as hard as Tom but perceive that she gets twice as many benefits. All other things being equal, the ratios are balanced and Sarah feels equitably treated.

According to equity theory, individuals can perceive themselves to be in one of three conditions as a result of comparing outcome/input ratios with reference sources. These three conditions are overreward inequity, underreward inequity, and equity.

Overreward inequity exists when the person perceives himself or herself to be receiving more benefits for the job relative to inputs than the other person. In such a situation guilt will be induced and the individual will try to rectify the rates. To do this the person will either rationalize away the perceived inequity (for example, by choosing a different reference source with which to compare him or herself), or seek to adjust the outcome/input ratio. If piece-rate workers believe they are being paid at too generous a rate, for example, they could reduce their rate of work so as to reduce the wages they are to receive. Or, similarly, they could increase the quality of work to justify the high wages.

Underreward inequity exists when the individual perceives himself or herself to be receiving fewer outcomes versus inputs from the job than is the reference source. In such a situation, the individual tries to reestablish equity by increasing outcome or reducing input. For example, under piece-rate conditions, research suggests that underrewarded individuals tend to increase the total quantity of work being produced while skimping on quality.

Equity exists when the outcome/input ratio of the reference source is perceived to be the same as the individual's. In such a situation no behavioral change is expected since the ratios are in balance.

What can a manager who wishes to increase employee performances learn from equity theory?

First, equity theory, like expectancy theory, suggests that managers need to provide outcomes that are perceived by individuals as relevant. Different groups and individuals value different things. For example, a study of public utility employees showed that for clerical workers, job security was the most important outcome the company had to offer, while production workers valued pay above all other outcomes. The opportunity for advancement was second only to pay in importance for production workers but was relatively unimportant for clerical workers.

Second, managers need to design compensation systems to avoid the performance-destroying effects of underreward inequity. Increases in absenteeism, turnover, and disruptive behavior can represent attempts to eliminate perceived underrewards inequities.

Third, managers need to bear in mind that overrewarding does not necessarily produce more or better performance. Individuals are able to rationalize away substantial amounts of overrewards. Even if managers do succeed in creating overreward inequity, the employees may soon adjust themselves to the high reward level. This is especially likely in situations where workers are unclear about the performance levels, prior qualifications, and compensation levels of possible reference sources.

Equity theory, like all the theories discussed so far, offers the manager insights into employee motivation. The equity notion suggests that individuals examine the maximum expected outcomes from a job and, in addition, compare those outcomes to referents in gauging their satisfaction and future performance. Organizational behavior modification theory (O. B. Mod.) avoids speculation about the internal feelings, needs, and cognitions of employees. O. B. Mod. focuses solely on the behavior of the employees and suggests that performance can be increased solely through the use of reinforcement and punishment.

ORGANIZATIONAL BEHAVIOR MODIFICATION

Behavior is a function of its consequences, according to the noted behavioral scientist B. F. Skinner. In other words, people learn to behave in ways that help them to avoid unpleasant outcomes (punishment) and attain pleasant ends (reinforcement). Fred Luthans and his colleagues have used

Skinner's ideas to develop a five-step organizational behavior modification program (see Fred Luthans and Robert Kreitner's *Organizational Behavior Modification*, Scott, Foresman, 1975). Since this approach focuses specifically on observable behavior, it is of considerable value to managers interested in increasing employee performance.

The first step a manager must follow is to identify critical behaviors, those that are crucial for effective performance. Managers should concentrate on observable actions that can be specified exactly so that an independent observer would have no difficulty in counting how often each behavior occurs.

Next, the rate at which these critical behaviors are occurring must be measured to establish a baseline frequency. Third, the manager must determine the conditions then triggering the critical behaviors and the subsequent reinforcements and punishments. Fourth, the manager must develop an intervention strategy, which generally involves reinforcing desired behaviors and letting undesired behaviors disappear through lack of reinforcement or punishment.

Last, the overall performance effects of the O. B. Mod. program must be evaluated. To do this, the frequency of critical behaviors at the start and finish of the program can be compared to see if the desired level of performance has been achieved.

An example from the research literature will help to clarify how these steps can be carried out in practice. Luthans and two associates, Robert Paul and Douglas Baker, sought to improve the performance of retail clerks in a large department store. The critical behaviors were identified as selling, stock work, idle time, and absence from the work station. Clerks were carefully observed to determine the frequencies of each of these behaviors. After considerable observation, desirable performance was further specified in terms of whether the salesperson remained within three feet of displayed merchandise, whether customers were offered assistance within five seconds, and whether the display shelf was filled to at least 70 percent of its capacity.

An analysis of the events preceding and the consequences following desired and undesired behavior was conducted. The researchers found that whereas supervisors usually scolded (punished) undesired behavior, they generally said nothing when performance standards were met. Desired behavior was not being positively reinforced.

An intervention program was implemented that offered salespersons time off with pay and the chance to win a company-paid vacation for attaining performance standards. On the first day the reinforcements were offered, performance improved dramatically, and undesireable behaviors decreased to minimum levels. Clerks in a control group who were not offered positive reinforcers showed no significant changes in performance levels. The positive reinforcers were dropped after 20 days, but the clerks who had been reinforced continued to perform at the new high level.

O. B. Mod.'s emphasis on measurable behavior is both its greatest strength and greatest weakness. On the one hand, the theory frees managers from the need to assess subordinate need states or cognitions. In a straightforward manner it suggests that behavior can be changed solely through the manipulation of reinforcement contingencies. But on the other hand, O. B. Mod.'s relevance for improving managerial performance may be limited because of its emphasis on precisely measured performance. The theory may be most applicable to lower-level jobs where tasks are relatively simple and where reinforcements can be easily controlled to increase desired behaviors.

SUMMARY

What can a manager conclude from this discussion of organizational behavior theories?

First, high achievers can be expected to perform at higher levels than low achievers, possibly because they set higher goals for themselves. If individuals are not high achievers, high performance can be induced by managers setting difficult but attainable goals.

Second, feedback to employees is helpful in maintaining high performance. Goal-setting theory argues that this feedback will be provided by the task or by the individuals themselves upon successful completion of the job. Both expectancy theory and O. B. Mod. suggest that this is not always the case, and it is up to the manager to provide a salient link between performance and subsequent outcome in order to increase performance.

Third, in order to maintain and encourage higher performance, managers must be wary not to create inequitable reinforcement contingencies. As equity theory points out, dissatisfaction will occur if a person's outcome/input ratio is not in balance with the reference sources. Such inequity may result in dissatisfaction and reduced performance.

A manager faced with the task of increasing employee performance has a variety of options. Achievement motivation training could be initiated, but this would only be applicable if the job called for entrepreneurial skills. An alternative would be to clearly link and explicitly tie rewards to performance.

Concurrently, the manager could set high goals, reinforce high goal attainment, or do both. In order to avoid the potentially disastrous consequences of inequity, the manager should also attempt to ensure that employee outcome/input ratios are balanced.

Each of these theories has considerable scientific research support. How the theories are applied in practice, either alone or in combination with one another, is part of the difficult art of managment.

Martin J. Kilduff is a doctoral candidate in organizational behavior at Cornell University, and Douglas D. Baker is assistant professor in the department of management and systems at Washington State University.

50.
HELP EMPLOYEES MOTIVATE THEMSELVES

Leonard Ackerman
Joseph P. Grunenwald

> Nothing will motivate employees if they aren't meeting their own goals. Use this
> model to satisfy both employees and management.

Motivation isn't necessarily an issue of organizational climate, managerial strategy, counseling, job satisfaction, or any of the other standard behavioral terms. Instead, it depends on the objectives of the employee.

Consequently, management should look at motivation from the employee's perspective: What's the return on their personal investment of time and energy?

What we are proposing is an investment model of motivation in which the employee is the investor and the manager is the broker or investment adviser for the employee.

The objectives of the investor are defined by: (1) the nature and size of the investment; (2) the quality of the investment; (3) the time to realize the investment objectives; and (4) the return on investment.

THE INVESTMENT MODEL OF MOTIVATION

To establish an investment model of motivation, the employee and the manager need to answer the following questions.

Objective of the Investment:
What does the individual want to achieve (*e.g.*, promotion, pay, security)?
Nature of the Investment:
What does the individual have to invest (*e.g.*, time, effort, involvement, commitment)?

Size of the Investment:
   How much is the individual willing to invest in time, effort, involvement, commitment?
Quality of the Investment:
   How much risk is involved? What are the chances of reaching the objective?
Time Frame of the Investment:
   How long will it take to achieve the objective?
Return on Investment:
   What is the return to the individual employee?

Of course, the individual assigns his or her values to these questions. The managers can help by pointing out the organizational and managerial perspectives on these questions, but the investment decisions rest with the employee.

If the employee perceives that the objectives can be met, the result is a situation in which the individual decides to invest, and the manager receives a commission in the form of the employee's performance.

As in the real world of investment, there are no guarantees. Not everyone who aspires achieves.

The model focuses on objectives, such as the next promotion or eventual career goals. The assumption is that once an individual decides to invest, her day-to-day behavior will be relatively consistent with that desire.

As investors should, the employee will, periodically, have to reevaluate his position.

He may find that the objective is no longer attainable, that he doesn't have the resources, or that the risk has become too high. The employee may then cut his losses and look for other investment opportunities.

For the manager, it is far easier to deal with this general approach than to worry about satisfiers and dissatisfiers; where a person is in a hierarchy; how attractive a particular outcome might be or its psychological connotations; and their accompanying emotional impact. Most managers do not have the necessary organizational flexibility to respond to the ever-changing needs of their employees.

On a more holistic level, the investment model allows the manager to provide advice, guidance, support, and help in furthering the employee's efforts to achieve his or her objectives.

In short, this model does not attempt to explain why people behave in particular ways. Instead, it accepts, at face value, what an individual is attempting to achieve and gives the manager a pragmatic operating base.

There is one factor that is crucial to the application of the investment model of motivation, or any other motivational model for that matter. The organization must be able to deal with employees who do not want more money, more challenge, more responsibility or more advancement.

The organization must recognize that not wanting more does not necessarily indicate a lack of initiative or ambition, but may be the employee's judgment of the position of work in his or her way of life.

Surely, no organization wants a major portion of its work force, particularly at the professional and managerial levels, to regard the job as relatively unimportant. By the same token, no organization wants everyone scrambling to be the chief executive officer.

FROM THEORY TO PRACTICE

Converting the investment model of motivation from a theoretical concept into a plan of action is not particularly difficult.

It does, however, involve three steps.

The individual investor (*i.e.*, employee) must identify his or her investment objectives.

Identification of individual objectives may well be the most complex part of this investment-motivation plan. Essentially, the employee must identify the short- and long-range objectives to be accomplished within the organizational framework.

Objectives outside the organization, such as family and recreation, play a critical role in how much of the individual's total resources will be invested in the organization.

For example, a young worker with limited commitments to interests outside the organization might choose challenging and demanding work leading to rapid advancement.

In contrast, a more mature worker with commitments to family and community might emphasize continuing in his present position or retirement security.

Second, the investor must specify the components of his or her investment portfolio.

With the help of the manager, the employee should put together an investment portfolio specifically designed to accomplish her objectives.

This portfolio will identify how the individual is willing to invest in the organization.

Given a particular set of individual objectives, there are several portfolios that will satisfy individual expectations.

If an employee wishes to achieve a top management position, then he or she should be willing to make a heavy personal investment in terms of long hours, the development of requisite skills, and a high level of involvement with, and commitment to, the organization.

In this instance, there is a high degree of risk: the probability of not reaching the goal is high and the investment is large over a long period; however, the long-term dividends can be substantial.

If, on the other hand, an employee is more concerned with maintaining a current position and perpetuating job security, then his or her involvement will be sufficient to maintain competency in the present position.

In this case, the risk is considerably less and the investment is relatively small. The rewards may be just as meaningful for him as the other rewards are for the ambitious employee since the employees are allowed to direct their energies in personally rewarding directions.

Third, the investment advisor (*i.e.*, manager or supervisor) must play an active role.

As an advisor, the manager first helps the individual establish realistic objectives. It is unlikely that many employees have considered their employment objectives from an investment perspective. In addition, this process may well generate the employee's first formal statement of his or her objectives. Also, as the individual states his personal objectives, the organization develops a clearer understanding of what it will take to satisfy the needs of its employees.

A second responsibility of the manager investment advisor is to help the employee select investments for his or her portfolio. An individual probably needs assistance when it comes to the trade-off required in this step.

For example, an individual might choose both a high-risk career and job security. The manager must then carefully explain how the two objectives may conflict. The analysis of this conflict can then be compared with other options and other outcomes.

In addition, the manager can help assess the objectives. The manager may say, "You have a lot of investment and a moderate chance to achieve your objectives. This risk is high, but so is the return on investment."

What the manager must determine and then communicate to the employee is whether the type of investment that the employee is willing to make is acceptable to the organization.

If an employee's objectives cannot be met, the employee is faced with either adjusting his or her objectives to organizational reality or looking to other organizations where he or she can achieve those objectives.

The organization, of course, retains its ability to promote, demote, reassign, and separate. If there is an individual in the organization who is not willing to make the type of commitment required by the organization, then the organization must decide if the employee is of such value that it is willing to make the necessary accommodations.

THE INVESTMENT NEEDS MONITORING AND REVIEW

For the investment model to function well, the employee must periodically reassess his or her objectives.

As personal situations and professional environment change, the employee's objectives will also change.

For instance, early in their employment individuals may be most concerned about current salary. As employees broaden their financial bases, their goals change to reflect concern about job advancement or retirement.

The modification of objectives is not precipitous or arbitrary. It is the manifestation of the incremental changes an individual faces in life.

The work objectives themselves are not arbitrary either, although they may seem so to the employee if they are designed without his or her input. If an employee's job performance is his responsibility, it is only logical that the strategy behind that performance should be under his control. The safest way to hedge an investment gamble, for both the employee and the employer, is to set the odds.

Leonard Ackerman is professor of administrative science, Clarion University of Pennsylvania. He holds an Ed. D. in employee development from George Washington University and was professor of behavioral science at the Industrial College of the Armed Forces. Joseph P. Grunenwald is professor of marketing, Clarion University of Pennsylvania. He has an M.B.A. and D.B.A. from Kent State University.

51.
INTEGRATING MAJOR
MOTIVATIONAL THEORIES

Brian H. Kleiner

> Understanding motivational problems in organizations involves the ability to answer effectively four interrelated questions.

One topic that managers have tended to find of great interest for many decades is "motivation." Because of this many theories and research studies pertaining to motivation have been published. Yet, the interest in understanding how to deal with motivational problems at work does not seem to slacken. It's as if each new motivational theory that is introduced leaves managers at best only partially fulfilled in dealing with questions that they seek to answer.

The purpose of this article is not to propose another theory for motivating employees. Rather, the basic idea behind this article is to suggest that there is no single motivational theory available today that will fully satisfy the frequently stated problem of managers: "How can I motivate my employees?" Instead, it is suggested that the popular motivational theories today only answer their favorite part of the motivational problem while essentially de-emphasizing the remaining parts. And for managers to understand the motivational problem in its fullest dimensions, it will be necessary for managers to effectively answer four interrelated questions concerning all parts of the dilemma. Accordingly, what this article hopes to accomplish is to integrate the most popular theories that attempt to provide the answer to the motivational problem of managers, under these four basic questions. When a manager can answer these four questions well, that manager is likely to have the necessary theoretical knowledge to handle nearly any motivational problem well.

QUESTION 1. WHAT INTERNALLY STIMULATES EMPLOYEES' BEHAVIOR?

Probably the most widely known theory of motivation that seeks to answer this question is Maslow's Hierarchy of Needs theory. This theory states that there are five needs that all people have. They are:

1. Physiological: the need to fulfill basic needs of the body such as hunger and thirst
2. Security: the need to feel safe from threat
3. Social: the need to belong and have warm, friendly relations with others
4. Self esteem: the need to feel important and worthwhile
5. Self actualization: the need to fulfill one's entire potential

These needs are arranged for all people in the hierarchy described above. For instance, all people initially seek to fulfill their physiological needs. When these are fulfilled, they will then seek to fulfill their security needs. When these are fulfilled, they will then seek to fulfill their social needs, etc. Only one level of need tends to motivate a person at any given time. So, in answer to the question "What internally stimulates employee behavior?" Maslow would say the lowest level of need that is unmet.

While Maslow's theory continues to be very popular, it has several limitations that are worth understanding before one uses it. The most important is the fact that although this theory seems to have much face validity to many, it has yet to be empirically verified. Reasons for this include the facts that it is difficult to isolate and measure these needs, that this specific hierarchical arrangement may not be the same for all, that it does not sufficiently describe when a need is adequately fulfilled, and that there may be several needs that are dominant at the same time within a person.

A man who has done much empirical research in the business community to answer the question, "What internally stimulates employee behavior?" is David McClelland. He proposes that there are three main motives, which are as follows:

1. Affiliation: essentially the same as Maslow's social need
2. Power: the desire to influence and control others
3. Achievement: the desire to accomplish a worthwhile activity

He does not propose that these are arranged in the same hierarchy in all people. He does suggest that more than one can be dominant at the same time. To determine which motives are dominant, he has developed fine measuring instruments for that purpose.

QUESTION 2. WHAT EXTERNAL REWARDS DOES A MANAGER HAVE AVAILABLE TO SATISGY THE INTERNAL NEEDS OF EMPLOYEES?

McClelland's own research has done much to answer this question with regard to his own model. He would suggest the following three rewards:

1. For those who have a high affiliative motive, give them the opportunity to perform tasks within a self-selected group and develop a financial

compensation program based on group rather than individual productivity.

2. For those who have a high power motive, give them authority over others tempered to the degree of their own apparent skill.

3. For those with a high achievement motive, establish with them moderately difficult goals, give them the responsibility to accomplish these goals and the freedom to do it their way, and be sure that they have adequate knowledge of their progress through a good feedback system.

Another theory that answers this question and has enjoyed many years of popularity among managers is Herzberg's Two Factor Theory. In essence, this theory suggests that the conditions that create the greatest dissatisfaction at work contribute relatively little to motivation when they are improved. Among these "dissatisfiers" are company policy and administration; relations with one's boss, peers and subordinates; pay; job security; and physical conditions such as lighting, heating and ventilation. Rather, the key conditions that motivate employees pertain to the job itself. These include opportunities for meaningful responsibility and accomplishment, recognition, and advancement.

Subsequent research on Herzberg using different methodologies, however, has not supported the notion that his "dissatisfiers" (particularly pay) do little to motivate employees. Rather, improvement in all of the above work conditions described can be viewed as rewards that motivate people. In attempting to resolve practically the controversy surrounding this theory, managers should correct if possible any working conditions causing a lot of dissatisfaction, because dissatisfaction can reduce the level of energy needed to do the task at hand. However, in general, the second set of working conditions mentioned holds the key for major improvements in motivation among most employees, possibly because they tend to be so neglected among the employees where the greatest motivational problems tend to occur: lower level employees.

What makes this theory appealing to many managers is that it relieves them from the burden of having to "psycho-analyze" their employees to motivate them. Rather, it says just seek to improve these five motivators: the job itself and opportunities for responsibility, accomplishment, recognition, and advancement. The other aspect that makes this theory interesting is that it answers Question 2 in a manner that nearly perfectly complements Maslow's theory, even though it was developed quite independent of it. Specifically, the rewards that managers can use to satisfy an employee's physiological, security, and social needs are Herzberg's "dissatisfiers"—physical conditions, pay, job security, company policy and administration, and relations with one's boss, peers, and subordinates. The rewards that managers can use to satisfy an employee's self-esteem and self-actualization needs would be the above-mentioned motivators.

QUESTION 3. HOW CAN INTERNAL NEEDS OF EMPLOYEES AND EXTERNAL REWARDS BE APPROPRIATELY MATCHED?

One method that seeks to answer this question was popularized by Herzberg himself as the logical extension of his theory: job enrichment. While the strategy of how one enriches the job of another can be elaborate, there is only one important principle that needs to be understood. This is: Ask the employee whose job is to be enriched, what management functions is that employee's immediate boss doing that that employee would like to do and would be capable of doing. Then, delegate those functions to him. Accordingly, job enrichment involves doing additional responsible work and not simply giving, for instance, to a dishwasher the opportunity to now wash silverware and glasses as well!

Another method that has enjoyed great popularity in answering this question is management by objectives (MBO). This method can be quite complicated when applied to entire organization. However, most managers do not have the authority to implement this program on an organization-wide basis. They are mainly interested in seeing how the method has usefulness in helping them to manage their own departments. For this method, four steps will be outlined that a manager can follow and get great value from.

Goal Setting. A manager after first explaining the MBO concept requests each employee to identify the goals he wishes to accomplish during a specified time period and sets up a time to discuss these goals. The manager independently identifies goals he wishes the individual employee to accomplish. When he gets together with each, he attempts to work collaboratively to develop a joint list. Thus, the first characteristic of effective goal setting is that it be done collaboratively. Additional characteristics are that the joint goals should ideally stretch the employee to new limits yet also be realistic; and they should be measurable, and the means for their measurement agreed upon. Care should be taken not to neglect areas that are more difficult to pin down, such as longer-term payoff opportunities.

Action Planning. This step is usually taken during the same interview and involves developing a joint strategy of how the goals are to be accomplished. Thus, after the joint list of goals is established, the manager then asks the employee how he envisions these goals will get accomplished. Most of what the employee will express is likely to be quite appropriate. However, there are usually a few ideas that a manager can add that can make the goals' accomplishment a bit easier; and employees are usually eager to receive these ideas as long as there is no coercion to force the ideas upon them. If the underlying spirit should change to one of "Those in favor say 'aye.' Those not in favor say 'I resign.'" people will feel insecure and preserve their energy defensively to fend off attacks. When people feel secure and adequate, they have lots of energy to do the job. Security comes from functioning in an environment that seems predictable, understandable, trustworthy, and friendly. Adequacy comes from the feeling of being able to make a difference and influence the environment and not feeling totally pushed around. In the end it is the positive spirit that will determine the effectiveness of an MBO program, not its paperwork.

Implementation. This step merely involves carrying out the action steps to achieve the goals that have been agreed upon. Self-direction and self-control for the employee are the keys to this step. However, this step may involve some periodic reviews. Care should be taken to encourage employees not to lock into goals that may need to be changed.

Evaluation. At the end of the time period, get together with the employee and compare the goals with the actual results. When goals have been reached, reward him or her appropriately. When goals have not been reached, it is important to understand why. Many times it is due to external factors beyond the employee's control such as an unexpected increase in the price of oil, a raw material, thus reducing overall profits. In this case, goals in that area for the next time period would have to be more restrained. However, it is also possible that goals are not met because of factors within the employee's control. Perhaps both overestimated the employee's skill in a certain area. If this should be the case, then again goals in that area would have to be scaled down and perhaps a new goal might later be established—training and development in that area of weakness. After a few days of reflection on the performance appraisal discussion, a new meeting occurs to begin the MBO cycle again with goal setting and action planning.

In conclusion, MBO represents a philosophy of management based upon the assumption that there is real power in people setting their own goals. The major power lies in the goals, not the bosses. This is a vehicle for implementing this philosophy.

QUESTION 4. HOW CAN DESIRED EMPLOYEE BEHAVIOR BE MADE TO LAST?

Reinforcement theory, which has developed into a strategy termed behavior modification, has become increasingly popular among managers because it is simple yet effective. Essentially, there are three major steps for a manager to take in this system, which integrates in a most obvious way with MBO. They are:

Goal setting. As was discussed, this is the first step in using MBO. Reinforcement theory particularly emphasizes that the goals should be measurable.

Giving feedback. This step and the one following are actions a manager can effectively take during the implementation step of MBO. It emphasizes that employees should be able to know how they are progressing towards their goals whenever they want so that needed self-correcting action can be taken as soon as possible. Employees with a high motive for achievement, as has already been noted, find this step very motivating along with the whole MBO strategy in general.

Giving rewards in a timely manner. While reinforcement theory would be open to using all rewards identified by Herzberg, the reward that in practice has been shown to be the most important, and the most underutilized by managers, is that of recognition. It is a common complaint by employees that frequently, when they do a particularly good job, the boss appears not to notice. Yet, the first time they make a mistake, the boss is right there criticizing. This situation can demotivate even the best employees. Accordingly, when performance is meeting or exceeding the goal set, taking the time to perceive this fact and say a few sincere words of praise can be an excellent investment in the sustained motivation of employees. However, even when performance is not meeting goals it can still be quite effective to praise employees if there appear to be improvements in comparison with previous days.

Punishment can be an effective motivator in the short term, but it tends to have a number of dysfunctional consequences for the organization in the long term. Generally, it should be used much less than as typically exercised by most managers.

Reinforcement theory has traditionally viewed motivation from an external point of view, seeing it as essentially determined by reward and punishment from the environment. Thus, it can be criticized for neglecting the internal characteristics of the person.

One characteristic that has much power in affecting motivation is the employee's own expectancy that if he makes the effort asked, he will be rewarded in a desirable manner. From this has developed the expectancy theory of motivation, which states that not only is the value of the reward important in determining motivation but also the expectancy (probability) that the employee holds in his mind that he will get the reward if he makes the required effort. From this has developed the path-goal theory of leadership, which emphasizes that leaders should help employees select highly rewarding goals and find high probability paths for achieving these goals. This idea complements well the spirit behind the first two steps of MBO.

Before leaving the topic of the power of expectations and leadership behavior, there is one additional idea that managers can utilize to help sustain the motivation of employees: the notion that a manager's own expectations of his employees can strongly affect their motivation. Specifically, if managers expect their employees to dislike working for them and thus seek to avoid all responsibility and to work as little as possible, the very coercive and controlling leadership pattern that they are likely to use will probably create a self-fulfilling prophecy in which workers will be motivated to do the least amount of work possible. Conversely, if managers have an expectation towards their employees that they are quite willing to seek responsibility and are quite capable of skillful self-direction towards rewarding goals, that too can create a self-fulfilling prophecy. This is the notion of Theory X and Theory Y as developed by McGregor. The latter set of expectations, Theory Y, was originally developed from Maslow's Hierarchy of Needs theory and underlies significantly the ideas of job enrichment and MBO.

CONCLUSION

This article has attempted to show that understanding motivational problems in organizations involves the ability to answer effectively four inter-related questions. The major motivational theories that exist today tend to specialize in certain questions while ignoring the others. For managers to have the necessary theoretical foundation for dealing with all types of motivational problems that they are likely to experience, this article has provided an easily comprehensible framework for integrating the major motivational theories to achieve that purpose.

Brian H. Kleiner is a consultant in the management of change for various organizations in southern California. In addition, he is an associate professor of management at California State University, Fullerton, where he has been nominated for the Outstanding Professor award in the School of Business Administration and Economics on numerous occasions.

52.
HOW TO UNCOVER
A HIDDEN CORPORATE ASSET

Carlton P. McNamara

Many companies still calibrate management productivity solely in terms of financial criteria. But focusing on numbers is usually of little practical use. What's needed is more strategic positioning of key management resources.

The theme is sounded over and over again in business literature, industry conferences, government studies—every forum devoted to the discussion of Business. There has to be an increase in American productivity.

Peter Drucker has suggested in his book, *Management,* that "the greatest opportunities for increasing productivity are surely to be found in knowledge work itself, and especially in management." After all, who is entrusted with the responsibility for overall corporate performance? Who is most influential in shaping a company's future? Obviously, the answer is management. Yet, non-management productivity has received the lion's share of attention.

Why, in the furor over productivity, has so little concern been directed at managers? There are at least three traditional obstacles impeding proper analysis of, and improvement in, managerial productivity.

KEY OBSTACLES

The first is the difficulty inherent in trying to define managerial performance. The executive job is filled with so many elusively qualitative and intangible nuances that it is virtually impossible to isolate the key performance ingredients of an effective manager. Some firms understandably have been hesitant to face the challenge of improving productivity in the absence of a precise yardstick with which to measure individual performance.

A second obstacle to improving managerial productivity is the traditional emphasis on administrative skills and practical experience. The underlying rationale is that when managers gain competence and exposure in these specific areas, they become more productive. The problem with applying this rationale to top management is that if high level executives did not already possess technical capability, they likely would not have been promoted in the first place.

This approach relies on providing management with the most up-to-date techniques and concepts. But given similar technical skills, why does one executive plan better than another? Or design a more functional organizational structure? The Achilles heel of this approach is that it does not isolate those critical areas that can benefit most from the application of such techniques.

The third bottleneck can be described as the "success syndrome." Most top managers run a challenging obstacle course as they progress through their careers. The odyssey from functional manager and division president to group executive and senior management is usually fraught with competition, high stress, and substantial personal sacrifice. Not unreasonably, these managers possess a high degree of confidence in their ability, and their lofty positions confirm the perception of each that "I must have been doing something right or I wouldn't be here now." This self-assurance, working in combination with the awe accorded American management worldwide, hardly fosters self-analysis or examination.

In the late 1960s, a report entitled "The Technology Gap" focused on why America led Europe in industrial productivity. The answer lay not in a better labor force or more capital investment, but in the quality of top management. Today, the all-important question is: Could it be better? The answer, in my opinion, is an unqualified yes.

ALLOCATION OF RESOURCES

The Italian economist, Pareto, postulated a law stating that the significant items in a given group normally constitute a relatively small portion of the total items in that group. Thus, most of the items, even in the aggregate, are of relatively minor importance. His concept has direct relevance to improving managerial productivity.

Long-standing habits lead many executives to indiscriminately allocate their resources between high and low impact areas. Here are some typical manifestations of the organizational phenomenon of treating all tasks and activities alike.

- Management control systems (especially inventory) tend to establish uniform control, resulting inevitably in over-control of the insignificant items and under-control of the important items.
- The organization of marketing and field sales forces often results in equal coverage of high and low profit regions, districts, and accounts.
- Financial control systems produce a voluminous amount of computer printouts concerning operating data. But only a small percentage of it is

really necessary to monitor performance accurately and take corrective action.

- Many purchasing and accounts payable departments devote the same degree of time and effort to performing their respective functions—regardless of volume, cost, or dollar obligations.

The frequently heard management lament that there just isn't enough time to perform a demanding work load seems to spur executives on to simply work longer and harder. This response, popularly known as the "myth of the overworked executive," actually inhibits productivity in many cases. Others pursue the "myth of efficiency" by placing more emphasis on doing a task right than on performing the right task.

These instances indicate that significant improvement in management productivity is often inhibited by a misallocation of available managerial resources. This is caused by an overemphasis on activity at the expense of value.

Companies have recently begun to do a much better job of allocating corporate resources on a macro basis. This is underscored by the plethora of strategic business planning systems being implemented. But the evidence is less satisfactory at the micro level of the resources available to individual managers and their organizational entities. Even the more popular and heavily publicized planning systems, such as zero-based budgeting which requires an overall reexamination and justification of the need for resources, still focus on the actual level of resources.

STRATEGIC RESOURCE MANAGEMENT

They do not emphasize the strategic position of those resources—where major productivity improvements can be obtained. If managerial resources are going to be allocated in a more strategic manner and the desired gains in productivity are to be achieved, seven specific steps should be followed.

Value and activity analysis. All levels of management should identify their most pressing concerns. What really encourages effective performance? What is high impact? High value? Specific criteria may include such variables as dollar impact, schedule, performance, quality, historical experience, perceived results of a significant error, and common sense. The purpose of this exercise is to delineate those activities that are critical to the successful performance of a specific department or function, and to determine which activities are less important.

Executive and managerial consensus. Agreement among the various levels of management should be obtained so that there is a clear understanding of what is most important and what is less important. Unless a manager really knows what is important to his or her boss and agrees with those priorities, it will be difficult to refocus, and the shifting of resources won't be effected in a timely, effective manner.

Historical resources mix. Operating budgets provide the key indicator for examining the level and mix of previous managerial resource allocations. Who has received the financial support, highly skilled manpower, managerial concern, time, and other resources? Managers who stressed high value or those who focused on high activity? This overview usually reveals a significant mismatch, with the high activity/low impact areas given most of the resources.

Strategic reallocation. Given the preceding steps, the appropriate modifications in resource mix can be made. Actual implementation usually requires both structural and personnel changes. This is not an exercise in window dressing; it requires a major commitment to matching the best resources with the most important tasks. A parallel reduction in resources for the less important activities may include fewer personnel or less skilled manpower; more simplified procedures and systems; elimination of some tasks; and organizational restructuring.

Expected results. Agreement concerning the desired outcomes in both the high and low impact/value areas should also be obtained to ensure meaningful performance evaluation. An existing MBO program is an excellent vehicle for providing consensus.

Risk acceptance. An important corollary of this overall program is the agreement among all levels of management to accept a certain degree of risk concerning unsatisfactory performance in the low-impact areas. As one executive remarked, "If you want to achieve significant improvement in management productivity, you have to be willing to accept some shortfall in the noncritical areas without overreacting. This requires strong discipline or you revert to overcontrolling the less important areas. A periodic audit of the low value activities is the appropriate management tool in terms of both effectiveness and effort to minimize an out-of-scope situation."

Management follow-up. Finally, there has to be an ongoing effort, at all levels of management, to monitor this program so that it becomes a way of life. Although the basic concept is simple and easily understood, the implementation phase is extremely difficult because major changes have to be achieved in long established managerial habits and operational tendencies.

TIME MANAGEMENT ISN'T ENOUGH

There have been different responses to the challenge of resource allocation and increasing managerial work loads. The most common has been that of IBM, Hewlett-Packard, 3M, Bank of America, Kimberly-Clark, Saga Corporation, and a host of other companies that have exposed their managers to formal time management courses and seminars. A proliferation of time-saving tricks (dos and don'ts concerning how to conduct meetings, use idle time, save unnecessary report writing, handle unplanned visitors, and make best use of the telephone) have been generated by these sessions. Although these programs attempt to instill such worthy values as self-discipline and common sense, there is considerable doubt about their practical impact on management productivity since time represents only one of the manager's available resources.

Aerojet General Corporation's program represents a more sophisticated and concentrated attack on the priorities of resource allocation and the management of time. Following the strong sponsorship of its chief executive officer, all operating divisions undertook a comprehensive review of their customary pattern of managerial resource allocation. A primary objective was to refocus most of the manager's efforts on performing those tasks that were essential to effective performance.

Aerojet has achieved major success in converting its business by implementing specific changes in its financial and manpower resource allocations, organizational structure, functional work charters, financial reporting system, inventory control policy, strategic assignment of sales forces, and performance evaluations. Managers are more productive because their energy, time, and resources are allocated to the high impact, important areas.

PRACTICAL VIEWPOINT

A review of corporate practice, public statements, and empirical research confirms the existence of a growing interest in productivity. However, many companies still calibrate management productivity solely in terms of financial criteria.

From a practical viewpoint, whether corporate executives operating groups or P&L divisions "hit the numbers" has little relevance to productivity. Perpetuating misconceptions about management productivity merely impedes progress toward a sounder and more effective approach.

Carlton P. McNamara is the president of McNamara and Company, a management consulting firm. He has an M.B.A. degree from Columbia University and a Ph.D. from the University of Illinois.

Part VII
MOTIVATION AND JOB FOCUS

53.
MOTIVATE THE OLDER EMPLOYEE

Richard F. Tyler

> The aging population trend has been widely documented, but its specific im-
> plications for the management of people in the workplace are less well defined.

The work force in America is aging. The end of the baby boom, extensions of the mandatory retirement age, and increases in life expectancy are all important contributors to the phenomenon. While this aging trend has been widely documented, its specific implications for the management of people in the workplace are less well defined.

Certainly there will be important consequences of a functional nature. Management will need to review a broad range of issues, from modifications of hiring practices to the funding and format of retirement programs. Of more subtle and even greater significance, however, will be the impact of alterations in the social and psychological profiles of the work force as it matures.

These changes will reflect an evolving transformation of the need and value systems, the perspectives, and the aspirations of an ever-increasing segment of the working population. At issue is the manager-subordinate relationship and its effect on productivity.

A CHANGING FOCUS

For the most part, the focus has been on the younger and more aggressive employees who were seen as having the potential for growth up through the managerial hierarchy. Far less attention has been devoted to the older worker, whose major life goals have either been attained or are now seen as un-attainable. The zest for accomplishment and growth on the job may be waning, especially so in an environment in which the cultural and organizational emphasis on youth, newness, and rapid change tends to discount accumulated experience and wisdom. At the same time, the workplace emphasis is on in-creased effort in order to remain competitive and needed.

A heightened sense of insecurity is not without foundation. Family life, which for so long may have provided stability and meaning, may have long since taken on a new form. The number of friends and peer-age associates may be declining. Carefree attitudes about retirement, which once seemed light-years away, have given way to what has become a more immediate and uncertain future. Adverse economic news not only amplifies concern, but justifies it. In sum, the world of the older worker may be seen as one in which the anxieties that are the companion of change are intensified.

It would be misleading to suggest that such a composite of the older worker is universally applicable in its entirety. The focus here is on those who may only partially fit the mold. The intent is to emphasize that the perceptions and motivational patterns of the older worker may be considerably at variance with those of individuals who still look eagerly to the promises of the future and its potential for fulfillment.

The problem surfaces in the older worker who appears to lack interest, who is nonparticipative, or who may even be reclusive. The terms negative, argumentative, stubborn, or cynical are frequently applied to such individuals. A younger manager, bounded by the time-honored tradition of respect for elders, may shy away from criticizing work or procedures, evaluating performance directly and objectively, or otherwise counseling those with a more traditional and seemingly outmoded value system. Faced with the task of obtaining the commitment of such an employee, the leader is understandably troubled.

MOTIVATION PRESCRIPTIONS

With other issues demanding more immediate attention, there is a tendency to simply tolerate the situation and put the older employee out to pasture. The result is the assignment of tasks that are innocuous, routine, and unchallenging, with a resulting widening of the breach. For the manager who seeks a more constructive resolution, the answer lies in understanding and acting on the causes of the inappropriate behavior, not in reacting to its symptoms. The following motivational "prescriptions" can help.

Be alert to opportunities to provide positive self-image reinforcement through recognition. We all like compliments, and especially so older workers, who may feel that their efforts are undervalued. Give special recognition for their accomplishments, skills, and learning. This doesn't mean contriving artificial situations that lend themselves to equally artificial kudos. It does mean going a bit out of the way to offer a legitimate compliment.

Make a conscious effort to refer to the older employee any questions you may receive that fall within his or her area of competence. You may already know the answer, but treating the employee as the authority on the subject will certainly convey the notion that the accumulation of a lifetime of learning is valued. It could well be that the individual is, in fact, the expert.

When you attend meetings, bring along an older employee as an advisor in a particular subject area or on a specific issue. Such tangible evidence of the value you place on his or her opinions fosters a strong sense of self-worth. However, any such arrangement falsely conceived will be quickly recognized and will prove embarrassing all around.

Consult older workers for advice or confirmation of your thinking, or to get their reaction to your ideas or plans. As a senior in the work group, they may have helpful insights about employee reactions to changes you are considering or plans to be implemented. As devil's advocate, they may just force you to sharpen your thinking or your presentation. At the very least they will have been heard, and they will bask in the confidence you have shown.

MOTIVATIONAL METHODS

Practice the art of "satisficing." Satisficing means settling for something that is workable, but less than what you consider optimal. An employee's recommendation, suggestion, or solution proposal may be very workable, but may not be the optimal answer to a situation as you view it. However, the employee is allowed to carry the day because the employee will see that his or her suggestions really do matter. The employee's self-confidence is enhanced, and he or she will be more willing to step forward another time. The employee will experience immense satisfaction from having his or her knowledge recognized and valued. And the employee will derive positive benefits from being an important member of the team who has significant contributions to make.

Involve the older employee in a work-oriented study group. It would be unusual to find a work situation in which all problems have been resolved. Often there are nagging, low-priority, long-standing areas of difficulty, and the formation of a task force may have beneficial results that go beyond any final recommendations offered. Being called upon to serve generates self-confidence and a feeling of involvement. If the problem is real and the leader is sincere, the older employee cannot help but feel needed.

Keep older employees well informed about what's going on in the group, department, or company. Keep in mind that anxiety stems from fear of the unknown, and credible information eases tension and promotes a sense of stability. It must be remembered that any change will create some degree of anxiety. Younger workers tend to view change more positively, as a sign of progress. The older worker may see it negatively, as a threat to ability and perhaps even as criticism, or as a negation of a lifetime of values and learning.

SHOW REAL CONCERN

When change is necessary and the situation permits, use a trial period approach. Assure older employees that if, after an appropriate trial period, the change proves to be too unsettling, a return to the old, familiar ways will be permitted. Initial reluctance to adopt that which is new is often overcome through such a safety-valve technique. Once involved in the new trial, its strangeness fades and, coupled with the pressures for group conformity, acceptance follows. The process has the advantages of defusing the finality of any perceived threat and of conveying respect for the feelings of those who will be affected.

Find time to discuss with the older employee his or her success on the job, and help him or her analyze why things went so well on such occasions. This approach accentuates the positive and thereby reinforces the notion that the individual does have skills and abilities that are meaningful. Pinpointing the reasons for success may provide insight as to the type of assignment at which the individual will do well, and from which he or she will derive satisfaction.

In a similar vein, explore the employee's activities, interests, and satisfactions away from the job to uncover talents and skills that may be transferred to the workplace. Possibilities for job enrichment or job enlargement may come to light. It may be that the older employee's present position doesn't permit the application of such talents.

It is in the organization's interest that the employee's energies and satisfactions be job-centered, rather than diluted through outside activities. Even if such discussions fail to provide useful clues, if they are conducted in a sincere manner, they will be appreciated by the older employee as a mark of the manager's interest and concern.

Richard F. Tyler is currently assistant professor of management, School of Business, Fairfield University. He holds a master's degree in business administration from New York University and a master's degree in education from Boston College Graduate School.

54.
MID-CAREER BLOCK

Richard A. Payne

Facing up to (and solving) the nation's largest drain on productivity.

Many large corporations today find themselves facing a dilemma with their mid-career employees.

The performance of these employees with 12 to 20 years of service just hasn't measured up to the performance achieved earlier in their careers. However, it hasn't declined sufficiently to warrant warning or dismissal; still, it is obvious to everyone who works with these individuals that they aren't delivering as they once were.

To help motivate mid-career employees out of the doldrums, it is first necessary to find out why these employees need a "battery recharging." Discussions with longer-term employees usually reveal four common demotivating sources.

Boredom. Some employees have been doing the same job for so long, they could do it by rote. Their jobs are just no longer interesting or meaningful, and performance has slipped as a result.

Lack of challenge. Along with boredom, many employees have learned their jobs so well that they could perform them almost effortlessly. Without a challenge to stimulate these employees mentally, they find their jobs no longer need the involvement necessary to achieve the results management expects of them.

Poor managers. There are, of course, mid-career employees who aren't living up to their potential simply because their managers fail to inspire them, or because these managers fail to provide them with the kinds of direction and support needed in order to do superior work.

Success Backlash. Mid-career employees are also faced with "success backlash."

UNDERSTANDING SUCCESS BACKLASH

To understand Success Backlash we have to understand that the opportunity to become a success has been motivating these mid-career employees since childhood. Their parents stressed the desire to achieve success early in their lives, and encouraged them to work hard in school so that their grades and achievements in extracurricular activities would enable them to win admission to good colleges (the first rung on the ladder to success).

The desire to achieve success continued to influence their lives in college as they worked for better grades in order to get into better graduate schools, or to secure job offers from the better companies which recruited on campus.

As these people began careers with large companies, they continued to be encouraged by managers to strive for future success: to work hard, long, and smart in order to move further up the corporate ladder and to get closer to the future success which parents, teachers, and bosses promised them.

Unfortunately, for all of the mid-career professionals whose performance has declined, their quest for success turned out to be their nemesis. How is this possible?

In almost every case these employees have come to realize after 10 to 15 years with their companies that their careers are stymied. For one reason or another, each of these employees is no longer being considered for further promotion. They have, to coin a word, plateaued.

With this plateauing, the opportunity for rewards of future success ceases to exist. Once these mid-career employees realize that further growth is impossible, this fact actually becomes a demotivating force. And the organizations they serve are faced with the consequences of success backlash.

BLOCKED OPPORTUNITY CAN SOUR A GOOD EMPLOYEE

Demotivation of the stalled mid-career employee has been termed a "blocked opportunity" syndrome. This blocked opportunity manifests itself in a number of different ways, and every one of them can hurt the organization in which the employee works.

Let's consider four typical reactions of mid-career employees to blocked opportunity.

1. *Employees blame themselves for the situation.* Some loyal individuals accept responsibility for their stalled careers, figuring that for one reason or another they just don't measure up to current competition.

In response to this situation, these blocked opportunity employees are likely to try to hide in the shadows in order to keep their jobs and/or to perform their work by the numbers to avoid less than satisfactory performance evaluations. In either case, these employees are unlikely to show any real initiative since they fear standing out at a time when they are unsure of their own competence.

2. *Employees blame misuse of their organization's success system for the situation they find themselves in.* These blocked opportunity employees convince themselves that favoritism and politics have thwarted their career growth and that if skills, experience, training, etc., were the determining factors in selecting people for promotion, they would not be blocked in pursuit of further success.

Such employees are likely to resent the "undeserved" success of other employees and, if nothing else, are likely to provide their employers with minimally acceptable performance. They have determined in their own minds that extra effort on their part simply doesn't pay off.

3. *Employees become disenchanted with the success system.* Some blocked opportunity employees conclude that their organization's success system works only to a point, that it holds out hope of rising up the corporate ladder based on competence and contributions for almost 10 years—and thereafter the system falls apart.

Like the employees who blame misuse of the system for their stalled careers, this group of employees is likely to demonstrate their frustrations in a number of ways. They may do only the minimum necessary to get by in their jobs.

Their reaction is usually even more negative. They are likely to abandon any self-development programs recommended by their bosses or by the company. (Why put out the effort when they don't believe the system will reward them for it?)

These employees are likely, too, to seek recognition outside of their organizations. This need for recognition may lead them to moonlight to prove themselves in consulting assignments or in small companies of their own.

Their desire for recognition may lead them to spend time and effort on the golf course trying to secure trophies or low scores. It could lead to pursuing extramarital love affairs. In each case, they are seeking the success they do not believe it is possible to secure within their own organizations.

These employees are also likely to do things on the job the easiest way possible, even though the easy way may not be the approved or right way. After all, these blocked opportunity employees have opted to secure recognition outside of the confines of the company they work for, and since success is blocked at work, why not bend the rules to make life more pleasant?

These employees know that there is no opportunity for growth within their companies. Walking the straight and narrow path no longer has the meaning that it did when they were pursuing success within their own organizations.

These blocked opportunity employees may opt to express their dissatisfaction with their company's success system in two other ways, both of which hurt the organization which employs them.

They may seek positions with other companies which they hope will provide further opportunities to pursue success. If they do this, the company which they leave loses their job knowledge and experience.

Worse still, these employees may "retire" on the job. If these employees have families who, for one reason or another, do not wish to leave the locale, they may just go into a holding pattern until they retire formally—enjoying alternate sources of recognition while expecting none and receiving none from the organization which provides their weekly paycheck.

4. *Employees attack the company, the perceived source of the failed success system.* Embittered employees may sabotage company goals by pursuing their own interests instead of what the boss wants done. Or they may bad-mouth the company to potential customers and employees, as "I wouldn't join ABC if I were you. They forget loyal employees, believe me!"

The anger and frustration over stalled careers can take its toll not only on the performance of the blocked opportunity employee, but also on the performances of those who work with them.

VALUE OF MID-CAREER EMPLOYEES

At this point you may well ask: "Why keep mid-career employees with the blocked opportunity syndrome?" A very good question! After all, the manifestations of blocked opportunity work against the organization. Rather than letting them go, there are four reasons for trying to correct the negative attitudes of mid-career employees with this syndrome.

Job knowledge. Mid career employees have, perhaps, the greatest concentration of technical expertise about your business of any single group of employees. After all, they have 12 to 20 years of service, and many have worked in the same positions for five years or so.

They are an important skills resource even if they are operating at the C-level (70 percent effectiveness) rather than A-level (90 percent effectiveness), the way they had in the past.

Organizational knowledge. This group of employees not only knows how to perform their jobs; they also know how your organization works. Experience has taught them whom to call upon within your organization for assistance and how to secure the cooperation of their own groups.

They know your organization's style, including the way written documents should look and the way presentations should sound. This knowledge of organizational style can have a very positive impact on your organization's success, if only these employees could be motivated to perform as they had in the past.

Loyalty. Those mid-career employees with almost 20 years with your company have usually demonstrated enormous loyalty in the past with their willingness to relocate, to take on lateral assignments, and to remain in positions for years on end.

They aren't the job hoppers who have left your organization for greener pastures. You can count on them in the future if there is a way to get them going again.

Concern for the well-being of mid-career employees. If your organization were to routinely terminate all mid-career employees with this syndrome, it would have a disastrous effect on the attitudes of every employee who approaches the mid-point in his or her career.

Every such employee would be fearful that careers with the company could be short-lived, and good employees (as well as those with blocked opportunity syndrome) would seek alternative organizations *before* the axe got them.

CORRECTING DEMOTIVATION

It would be both impractical and imprudent to terminate mid-career employees with the blocked opportunity syndrome. There are too many of them. They are too valuable to the organization despite their current performance; and their loss would hurt the morale of others in the organization.

The only alternative, then, is to try to correct the demotivation and the negative attitudes which this demotivation brings about. But how?

Five points for consideration are:

- provide alternative means recognition to mid-career employees
- develop new ways to make their current jobs more satisfying
- effect revitalization through reassignment
- utilize "reality-based" self-development programs
- change managerial attitudes towards mid-career employees

PROVIDING RECOGNITION

There are at least five alternative ways to provide recognition to the mid-career employee who can no longer hope for recognition via promotion to a more responsible, better-paying job. These include:

Task force assignments. It's not always necessary to assign the up-and-coming member of a subsection to a section level task force. Task force assignments provide a unique opportunity to recognize the contributions of blocked opportunity employees, and if they are competent to serve on task forces, there should be no reason not to consider them.

Participation in brainstorming/decision-making meetings. The employees with blocked opportunity syndrome often feel like second-class citizens because they are left out of "greenlight" sessions and major plans reviews. Even if meeting size is a factor, surely there is room to include one or several of these employees in any group to demonstrate their creative thinking.

Representation of the organization to others. It is a fact of life that people on the way up tend to be the ones who are selected to attend symposia, conventions, and industry workshops. But they don't necessarily have to be the ones selected for this type of prestigious assignment. Loyal blocked opportunity employees often have sufficient job and organizational knowledge to function successfully at such meetings.

And the thrill of being selected occasionally to represent their organizations may be the source of motivation for significantly improved performance.

Training and development of new people. Just because an employee is no longer in the running for promotions doesn't automatically exclude him or her from being able to train newcomers to the organization. The challenge of so doing can enrich an employee's otherwise drab existence.

Being asked to train new people tells blocked opportunity employees that their knowledge is valued and important to the organization—a fact that these employees have come to doubt. It is precisely because employees feel needed by the organization in such instances, that they rise to the challenge and perform better as trainers than anyone in management imagined they would.

Meaningful management response to employee efforts. Typically, blocked opportunity employee effort is just average, and it is all too easy to take these employees for granted. Occasionally these employees surprise everyone with exceptional work. This work could be recognized not just by immediate bosses but by far more senior people in the organization, if only such outstanding performance were called to their attention. Typically top management interfaces with these employees down the line only to present 15- or 20-year pins or 25-year watches.

To be meaningful, top management's approbation of employees should occur when it is least expected, and that should be when outstanding performance deserves such recognition. There is nothing that tells blocked opportunity employees they are needed by their organization more than a phone call or note from a senior person recognizing the significance of a specific, noteworthy contribution.

BRINGING BACK THE CHALLENGE

The more employees can be motivated by the fun and challenge of *existing* jobs, the less need there is for motivation related to possible future opportunities. How can supervisors rekindle mid-career employees' interest in their positions?

Supervisors can relate employees' performance more to total company goals. This can be done by something as trivial as inviting these employees to departmental or section level meetings at which objectives and plans are discussed.

Attendance at such meetings can help these employees better understand the big picture and how they fit into it. When these employees realize how important their cog is to the total wheel, it can make their jobs more mean-ingful, and thus increase work motivation.

If it isn't possible to invite these employees to such meetings, it would pay at the very least to keep them informed of the results of such gatherings.

As a case in point, we recently out-placed a financial analyst. During the course of working with him, we asked what resulted from the financial studies he had conducted for management. He told us no one had bothered to advise him how the analyses were used, or what decisions were reached as a result of them! Agreed, the employee wasn't at the decision-making level. But surely he would have been more involved in his work if he were kept apprised of the next step in the analytical process. This individual's situation is, unfortunately, not atypical.

Some individuals function in one corner of an operation for years and are never invited to tour the total operation. Lack of involvement in the goals of an organization can demotivate any employee, but for the blocked opportunity employee who has no hope for future rewards from the organization, it is particularly demoralizing.

Supervisors can create competition in the job. Creating competition is appropriate to blocked opportunity employees because their circumstances are similar to that of salespersons who: have been passed over for promotion to sales management; have very routine positions, calling on the same customers and selling the same products year after year; and work by themselves in isolated markets where there is little or no opportunity for recognition except on those few occasions when the sales manager comes to town.

In circumstances like these, managers maintain salespersons' performance by challenging them to beat their own (and peers') records: this month vs. last; this year vs. last; this salesperson vs. others in the sales unit; and this sales unit vs. others in the region. The fact is that many long-term salespersons who might otherwise just get by thrive on this type of management-induced competition.

Can non-selling supervisors utilize competition to rekindle job interest, satisfaction and, hence, performance of mid-career employees who don't sell for a living? Perhaps not as easily as their selling counterparts, but it is possible.

One way is to ask employees to write up their specific contributions to sales, production output, quality improvements, and cost savings. Such descriptions should not be recitations of functional responsibilities. Rather, these descriptions should be of tangible actions, recommendations, suggestions which can be translated into actual (or hypothetical) dollar contributions.

ENCOURAGE COMPETITION

These employees could also be encouraged to compete in the number of recommendations and suggestions which are made. Blocked employees could also measure functional output as precisely as possible.

For example, how many days does it usually take for a scheduler to produce factory projections for next month or next year? How accurate are such forecasts? How large are negative and/or positive variances for a particular assembly line each month? Quarter? Year?

Determining precise output criteria will take some thinking on the part of the supervisor and those employees who are asked to assist in establishing specific functional output criteria. But such measurements can be made, and with the help of today's personal computers, can be maintained. The secret of getting functional output measurements to create greater job involvement and satisfaction is to use them only in a positive way.

The manager should not use competitive losses ("This month is lower than last") to reprimand, but should instead offer praise and congratulation each time superior performance is achieved.

These types of competitive measurements can be the basis for telephone calls and memos from management several levels above the employee—the kind of unexpected personal praise that can show employees that they are loved and needed by the organizations they serve. This type of recognition can do much to remotivate employees who are no longer motivated by the hope (or promise) of future success within the organization.

If senior management recognition cannot be secured, the employee's own supervisors can still promote these successes to fellow workers and to the employees themselves, each time they beat their own records. To do this, supervisors will, of course, need to be on the lookout continually for instances of competitively superior performance by the employees who report to them (greater output this month vs. last; fewer errors than others in the department in the past year, etc.). It will take work, but its impact on performance will be worth it.

SYSTEMATIC JOB SWITCHING

Another motivational tool is systematic job switching to positions at the same level which require many, but not necessary all of the skills and experience of the jobs which the blocked employees are vacating.

The advantages of reassignment of mid-career employees who have been in the same job for five years or more are probably obvious. Still, they deserve brief mention here.

Blocked employees who are moved into new positions are forced to utilize all of their skills and resources because they are confronted with new and different job challenges. Rote performance of jobs is no longer possible. As a result, there is likely to be a spontaneous reawakening of mental and physical capabilities that have not been needed or utilized for years.

Blocked employees must also work with new people. They have to establish new working relationships and learn to work effectively with individuals with different personalities and backgrounds.

Employees are provided with an opportunity to be evaluated by new evaluators. The blocked employees now have an opportunity to convince new evaluators that perhaps they may be capable of further growth. Employees who haven't put forth their best efforts for years (because they believe those who evaluate them have already concluded they have no potential for growth) may improve performance remarkably just knowing that they have, in fact, a fighting chance of convincing new evaluators they should be considered for promotion.

Critics of job transfer programs can and do point to obvious potential drawbacks of such programs. Each job transfer can cost the organization $30,000 to $50,000 if physical relocation is required. That's a lot of money to spend on employees with just adequate performance.

Fortunately, there are many organizations that have enough employees at any one location so that transfers might not require physical moves. To be sure, there are other organizations in which relocation is a necessity, and there is no getting around such costs. It could still pay to relocate blocked employees in these instances. Keep in mind that most blocked employees are operating at 70 percent efficiency. Improving performance to 90 percent efficiency could easily result in paying back the cost of relocation over a three- to five-year period.

Moving employees into new positions obviously involves short-term inefficiencies since there is a learning curve inherent in any job transfer. While this is true, over time the higher level of performance from blocked employees should offset this short-term disadvantage.

There is also the potential for blocked employees to misunderstand the meaning of such transfer, to infer, perhaps, that their careers are "on track" to future success again. This criticism can be nullified if management advises all employees that it intends to increase the total number of transfers between positions as a means of enhancing performance and job knowledge.

There is always the question of whether it might not be better for an organization to fill openings with up-and-coming employees who might be expected to perform better than blocked employees.

SELF-DEVELOPMENT PROGRAMS

Another way to improve mid-career motivation relates to an organization's self-development programs. When employees plateau in their careers, despite having previously participated aggressively in self-development programs designed to move them ahead, they are likely to feel that they were misled about the value of such programs. They can be bitter about the wasted effort of such participation. In cases like this, it is probable that blocked employees have been advised by supervisors to take technical and business management programs—none of which led to the anticipated promotions.

The fact is in some organizations managers are reluctant to advise subordinates of critical weaknesses that are likely to block future growth. Instead, they recommend additional formal education ("Why don't you get an MBA, Mary?") or suggest broadening of job knowledge ("George, you ought to get some marketing experience under your belt.") as ways of fostering growth.

In actuality, blocked opportunity is often linked to weaknesses in *people skills* (with peers, subordinates, and most often with superiors); *organizational skills* (the management of time, projects, and people); *communications skills* (both written skills and oral presentation); and to the image blocked employees project to superiors.

Some blocked employees might not have found their progress stymied had bosses only been more honest with them earlier in their careers about development needs in these personal skills areas. The organization which teaches its supervisors to be open about concerns in these areas, and fosters self-development programs addressing them, might well reduce the number of demotivated mid-career employees in the future.

But what about today's crop of blocked employees? Can self-development programs improve their performance? Some blocked employees might be interested in pursuing self-development programs (when they are suggested) to add challenge to their routine work lives, or to improve their chances of beating their own past performance.

Whenever programs are suggested to these employees, common sense suggests that supervisors recommend ones that can help these employees do a better job in their present positions. It would be misleading to suggest they might impact on further growth when, in fact, that is simply not the case.

SUPERVISORY ATTITUDES

An important factor in motivating blocked employees is supervisory attitudes. Blocked employees point to the amount of time supervisors spend with them versus up-and-coming peers; to inequalities in intra-department assignments; and to the level of direction and assistance which they receive from managers versus others in their organization.

A concerted effort to get supervisors to demonstrate positive attitudes toward this group of employees could have significant impact on both motivation and performance. This, of course, requires top management to recognize the importance of blocked employees to the organization's success, and to commit the organization to the motivation of this human resource.

NO MEAN TASK

Once management support is obtained, it is necessary to focus everyone in the organization who manages mid-career professionals on the need to make employees with blocked opportunity syndrome feel needed by the organization;

to make them feel a sense of equal treatment with peers on fast tracks; to create challenges that make the job itself worth the doing since there is no future reward to goad employees to greater effort; and finally to make all supervisors aware of the importance of making mid-career employees feel accepted and valued by the boss.

This is no mean task. Without management commitment it won't happen; without a comprehensive awareness and training program it is unlikely to happen. But it would pay any organization to seriously address this issue.

Richard A. Payne is an honor graduate of Princeton and the Harvard Business School. He has taught search strategy and career management for New York University and was retained by the Pentagon to make television-taped programs on search techniques. He is author of How to Get a Better Job Quicker.

55.
MOTIVATING THE MODERN EMPLOYEE

Robert W. Goddard

As management by authority fades, these techniques will help you profit from your employees' emerging values.

If someone asked you to name the most serious management challenge of the next decade, what would your answer be?

- Increasing the productivity of employees?
- Reducing waste and operating expenses?
- Improving the knowledge and skill of people?
- Raising worker morale?

It is doubtful that anyone would mention motivating a modern workforce as the most serious challenge. Ironically, this is one of the most difficult tasks that managers will face in the years ahead.

Today a new breed of employee is arriving in increasing numbers on the North American business scene. Compared to workers of 10 to 20 years ago, these employees are better educated, more interested in achieving objectives than in following orders and procedures, more loyal to their disciplines and professions than to their employers, and much more concerned about the quality of their worklife and the self-fulling aspects of their jobs.

Studies have revealed some characteristics which are typical of this emerging new breed in the workplace—the "new values" workers.

- They want meaningful work.
- More energy and attention is devoted to leisure-time activities.
- They display a combination of super confidence and fear.
- They are indifferent to traditional penalties for poor performance.
- They have an intense need for personalized feedback and recognition.
- They exhibit a stepped-up sense of time which translates into an unwillingness to wait for career success.

- They show a desire for autonomy, the authority to get the job done, and input into decision making.
- They possess a strong interest in informality and in less rigid authority in organizational structure.
- They are involved in a wide array of lifestyles.

The complicating factor in this shift from self-subordination to self-absorption is a measurable drop in long-term optimism. New values workers, for the most part under 35 years of age, look at the unstable economy, inflation, and shortages, and can see the pie shrinking. They know that the number of applicants for mid-career promotions will double, possibly triple, during the next two decades as the prime-age workforce (25-54) swells to more than 75 percent of the working population. It is no longer a certainty that, simply by sitting in one place and waiting to be recognized, they will wind up with the piece of the pie they envision for themselves—or that they will get any at all.

Thus today's new values workers are hard to motivate. A cushy, across-the-board benefit plan, job security, and regular wage increases won't work because what were once regarded as rewards are now considered entitlements and, in some cases, entrapments. The current brisk pace of replacement hiring underscores this point.

"The old values of loyalty, allegiance, and the intrinsic benefit of hard work are eroding fast," says Florence Skelly, president of Yankelovich, Skelly and White, Inc., one of the world's foremost public opinion firms. "What we see developing now is a self-centered, 'What's in it for me?' culture—a culture of narcissism."

What, then, can be done to turn these new values to positive and productive advantage?

According to Ted Mills, chairman of the American Center for the Quality of Work Life in Washington, D.C., managers must first pull themselves out of the trap of equating productivity with efficiency, as the two are not the same. "In none of the definitions of productivity is the word 'quality,' whether of product or service, even mentioned. The term as it is being used is totally lacking in precision. In plain fact, the decline of productivity has little if anything to do with the worker. The fault lies with the financial community. Capital productivity is at a disgracefully low level."

The problem, as Mills and others see it, is worker dissatisfaction—not worker performance—and a growing mismatch between incentives and motivations. Daniel Yankelovich, chairman of Yankelovich, Skelly and White, Inc., says, "Formerly management had the tools for motivating people adequately enough to ensure ever-increasing productivity. This is no longer true. People's values and attitudes have changed faster than the incentive system . . . The tools we rely upon to give people incentive to work hard and effectively have become blunted."

One of the most pressing tasks facing corporate leadership today is to develop and maintain a working climate that will stimulate rather than stifle employees. Over the past 10 years, most of the studies undertaken on the subject of turnover indicate that there is a large gap between what top management thinks workers want and what they actually desire.

One survey, conducted in 1969 by the Research Center of the University of Michigan, reported that 1,533 workers from a variety of occupational levels *all* ranked interesting work and the authority to get the job done far ahead of good pay and job security. These findings have been confirmed in more recent studies in 1973 and 1978. Although today's high unemployment certainly has increased the motivational value of job security, any benefit will be fleeting as labor surplus gives way to labor scarcity during the next decade.

WHAT YOU CAN DO

Managers can do much to motivate and retain valuable employees, especially the new values variety.

Assume the role of "results" leader. Unlike past managerial approaches, which were based on management as a system of authority, present managerial styles tend to be based on management as a resource. The growing use of management by objective incorporates this philosophy. So do most performance appraisal programs which stress goal-setting and the achievement of results. Today, in more and more organizations around the world, the subordinate and the manager together work toward mutual objectives by using the skills, knowledge, and aptitudes of both to solve problems and achieve results. It is an approach of power through people, not over them.

This philosophy is based on the growing recognition that results management, which is the process of motivating and assisting people to achieve specific, realistic objectives that they have helped set, is the most productive way of managing a modern workforce.

Always define a person's job and the expected results. Survey after survey reveals that unfulfilled expectations are a leading cause of turnover, and that employees who are given an accurate picture of their jobs are less prone to quit and also tend to be more satisfied.

Individuals should receive realistic and complete information about the job, including any negative aspects. Given the facts, people are able to determine with some precision whether particular job situations will fit their needs and abilities. Further, they develop realistic expectations about the nature of the work, and disappointment is minimized. To forestall any problems, responsibilities, authority, and methods to be followed should be defined and agreed upon at the outset.

Treat each employee as an individual. Since contemporary employees value good personal relationships and personal recognition, they work best for managers who create an environment where people work because they want to, rather than need to; where personal feelings contribute to, rather then detract from task accomplishments; and where rewards, rather than punishments, get the job done.

Research evidence reveals that no one management style is better than another in creating the proper environment—it all depends on the individuals being managed. Managers must be able to diagnose specific situations, recognize individual differences, and alter their behavior accordingly.

Provide opportunities for employee input in planning and decision making. Today's young people want to be involved in the decision-making process. They have spent much time making decisions about their lives and careers, and resent being governed for 40 hours a week by corporate rules which were not of their making and which they lack the power to change. What they seem to be saying is, "The boss should talk it out with me before he makes a decision. Don't treat me like a number. Treat me like a person. Listen to me."

One of the most positive steps a manager can take is to involve each subordinate in setting his or her own work and career goals. In many performance appraisal, productivity management, and management by objectives programs, organizations are attempting to involve employees in this process by focusing on two equally important targets: fostering commitment to company objectives and cultivating the personal growth of each employee.

Encourage self-development and point out opportunities for advancement. Projections indicate that the rising demand for more highly educated workers during the next two decades will intensify employer involvement in the total education of employees. Subordinates must be psychologically prepared to take repeated and continuous training and to think hard about the logical career paths within the organization.

The rapid changes now occurring in every field of endeavor cause many individuals to feel insecure in their work and unprepared to face new and difficult work challenges. People need faith in their abilities to face these changes, and managers need to encourage and support their efforts to grow and develop in a job specialty or profession, to take on assignments that will enhance career development, and to assume greater responsibilities when ready.

Encourage creativity and keep jobs as challenging as possible. Leisure activities such as skiing, hang gliding, scuba diving, and mountain climbing have become run-of-the-mill activities for today's youth. To reach these new workers, managers must appeal to this sense of adventure and provide opportunity for them to take risks and grow in their day-to-day jobs.

One way is to increase job redesign and job reassignments to better use skills, knowledge, and experience. Another is more effective delegation.

Subordinates should be allowed to take on as much responsibility as they feel comfortable with. The ideal climate for new values workers is one which encourages and supports innovation, examines existing procedures and practices, and experiments with new behavior. In this environment, employees can develop creative ways to solve new or recurring problems, adopt challenging standards of excellence, and try newly developed techniques.

Set up effective channels of communication. An open-door policy and ongoing dialog are essential to today's workers. This means providing employees with the information they need to do their jobs, discussing work-related problems with those seeking advice and counsel, criticizing and correcting, and listening. Feedback is particularly important because many professional and technical jobs aren't clearly defined, and feedback doesn't come automatically from the job itself. People need information on how they are doing in order to grow and develop.

Give praise and credit when due. Praise is one of the major psychological considerations of leadership and an intense personal need of the new values worker. Recognition for a job well done reinforces an individual's self-image and self-satisfaction and increases the desire to make a greater contribution in the future. The most effective praise is that given in quantitative terms. Not just, "You're doing fine," but, "You did a good job on the ABC project. Your results are consistently above standard, and when I see how you do your work, I know why."

Be aware of changing values. Take the time to learn how contemporary workers think and what turns them on to opportunities in private enterprise.

According to behavioral scientist Frederick Herzberg, "Finding out what employees want and need today is like listening to a schizophrenic word salad for hidden meanings in such code words as tradition, work ethic, career rights, participation, and quality of worklife." In order to understand and motivate the new values worker, we will all have to sharpen our human relations skills, and learn some new ones.

In summary, we can no longer rely on old incentives to stimulate people. We are in the midst of transition. Pressures to improve human productivity are increasing. The attitudes, ideals, and goals of employees are shifting. Management by authority is giving way to management by motivation, objectives, and teamwork. How managers adapt to these changes will have enormous impact on the work results of their people and on their own managerial success.

Robert W. Goddard is director of publication in the personnel development department of Liberty Mutual Insurance Companies, Boston, Massachusetts.

56.
BORING JOBS?
REDESIGN THEM!

Roy W. Walters

New technology presents management with the opportunity to eliminate or significantly reduce the segmented nature of most jobs.

When Charley started his new job, he was very enthusiastic and productive. His company had just spent a huge sum of money for additional computer mainframe capacity, new software packages and beautiful furniture and fixtures.

Charley's job was to read data information sheets and to input data into the computer. He sat in front of a well-designed, adequately lighted and engineered microprocessor. He was trained and became very proficient at the keyboard. This was quite a change from his previous job as a card sorter.

The first six weeks on the new job were interesting, and he enjoyed the work. The machines was programmed to take the data in only one way—the right way. Once he discovered a mistake, he corrected it and rarely repeated the error. But work soon became boring. He performed the same tasks over and over. He felt he had little responsibility and did not know what the figures he used represented or who used the information.

This is a classic example of the problem organizations face when installing new office equipment. The almost unlimited potential of new office technology causes management to lose sight of the critical need to better utilize its human resources. It is not surprising that workers often resent the introduction of new technology into the workplace because they believe the equipment threatens their security and diminishes their value to the company. These perceptions have a disastrous impact on productivity.

There will be more of these problems cropping up because few organizations understand these human issues, let alone act on them before they create a host of disgruntled "Charleys."

HUMAN FACTOR

If today's "gee whiz" machinery is to result in the productivity increases touted in sales appeals, manufacturers, as they mold the office technology of the future, must work with customers in thinking through how the jobs of the people who will operate their machines will be affected.

To accomplish this, technical experts must understand the principles of well-designed work. A worker who is truly motivated to do his or her job well must: perceive work to be meaningful as he defines it, not as management defines it; experience real responsibility for the results of his work; and have knowledge of these results.

To be meaningful, jobs must contain skill variety, task identity, and task significance.

Skill variety is the degree to which a job requires workers to use a number of talents and abilities and, ideally, to keep developing and acquiring new ones. A job that includes task identity enables the worker to do a "whole job" from beginning to end with an identifiable outcome. Task significance is the degree to which the workers can recognize that their work has meaning to others, whether inside or outside the organization.

For workers to experience responsibility for the results of their efforts, jobs must contain a significant degree of autonomy. The quality and quantity of work in highly autonomous jobs depends more on the worker's own initiative and effort than on job descriptions and close supervision.

WORK RESULTS MATTER

For workers to have knowledge of the results of their work, feedback must be established. Jobs that include feedback provide workers with relevant information about the effectiveness of their work. Feedback is most powerful when it comes from the work itself.

Jobs should be interesting and motivating. For example, a job like Charley's can be restructured to include these characteristics by allowing for:

- responsibility for handling the input from a group of "internal clients" rather than a random assignment of work
- a say in redesigning input format so that it sails through more easily
- an opportunity to learn and acquire more advanced computer skills
- an opportunity for workers to see the results of their work and learn from "clients" how the output data is used

By broadening Charley's responsibilities, management is preparing him for a new position as he becomes a more valuable and productive member of the organization. This takes time, but the process reduces Charley's boredom and continued underutilization.

JOB DESIGN

New technology presents management with the opportunity to eliminate or significantly reduce the segmented nature of most jobs. When built into properly designed jobs, new technology can help workers successfully handle new and greater responsibilities beyond management's most optimistic expectations. When human resources are fully used, productivity increases, the quality of work improves, and costs are reduced.

The human factor in the productivity equation is as important in its way as the hardware/software considerations of the technical experts. Until engineers understand the principles of well-designed work and build these principles into the work of equipment operators, people like Charley will continue to be bored and unproductive.

57.
MOTIVATING YOUR R&D STAFF

George E. Manners, Jr.
Joseph A. Steger
Thomas W. Zimmerer

Ten basic tenets form a body of practical knowledge for generating the excitement
that is the essence of motivation for technical people.

Over the years, we have found that research managers list "motivation" as
the most perplexing requirement of the managerial role. This observation is
true in many management situations. Motivation is one of the most critical
ingredients in work performance as well as the most difficult to understand.
There is a voluminous amount of literature on the topic, some of it quite
valuable to the manager. However, this enormity of information lacks focus
and, shall we say, a common body of practical knowledge.

We conceive of motivation simply as excitement—an energizer that is
reflected as excitement or arousal. This definition makes the concept of
motivation more understandable and applicable. Most managers tend to conceive of motivation as a complex set of dimensions that in fact are not
encompassed in our definition. Thus, performance is not motivation. Satisfaction is not motivation. Behaviors are not motivation. Results are not motivation. Too often these are, in some confusing and ambiguous fashion,
encompassed in the concept of motivation when discussed by managers.

Another point: Because people are excited about work and are exhibiting
lots of activity does not mean they are productively active. That is, the group
could be highly motivated and running amok because it is not managed to
optimize the motivational spirit.

While the presence of motivation does not guarantee performance, the
absence of motivation guarantees long-term performance problems. Obviously, a lack of arousal begets no effort and the precursor to effort is excitement or
arousal. Edison's famous quote about genius being 99 percent perspiration and
one percent inspiration is the essence of what motivation yields in our conception.

Thus, as long as one does not over-define motivation, we think that a focus, or common body of knowledge, is available to the practicing manager. This focus is contained in 10 basic tenets which yield useful insight into how to generate work-group excitement without requiring the vocabulary of a clinical psychologist.

A tenet is an opinion which is held to be true—our opinion. These opinions, however, have been slowly articulated over a 10-year period by carefully observing successful motivational practices through our interactions with industrial and government R&D laboratories. We have come to view these tenets as fundamental truths of work excitement. We have found that the extent to which these tenets—and their prescriptions for managerial action—are understood by the practicing manager is the extent to which the capacity to motivate is understood. Some of these tenets may be viewed as simple platitudes, some not. Taken as a whole, however, they do form a common body of practical knowledge. The tenets follow.

Difficulty. The first tenet of motivation is, quite simply, that generating incremental excitement about work is very difficult. On the other hand, most managers have observed that destroying excitement is relatively easy. Many young project managers find that the old excitement created by technical interactions while on the bench no longer works when they assume power. Or, they agonize over how to rekindle work excitement in a bench scientist many years their elder.

It is interesting how many of these befuddled research managers blame "the corporation" for their motivational difficulties. Meanwhile, the effective motivators understand a fact of managerial existence: Do not expect much help from the larger organization. Many of the reasons why the larger organization (the laboratory or the corporation) will not necessarily aid the individual manager in his day-to-day motivations of researchers will become more clear once the other basic tenets are offered.

Difficult though this business is, the prize is worth the chase. We offer this advice, *Never give up.* The motivated work group is too important an antecedent to research success to stop trying. One can feel its effects simply by walking in the door of research offices. As the sage football scout once said: "I don't know what it is, but I know it when I see it."

Fat Happy Rats. Since so much of the literature on motivation emanates from experimental psychology, we should offer the observation that fat, happy rats never run mazes. They sit there. Now, this tenet should not lead to the conclusion that research managers should keep researchers deprived. On the contrary, keep the rewards coming to those who perform. And as the Japanese have so effectively pointed out, one must maintain a "positive tension." That is, an excitement that is directed toward answering, "How do we do it better?" Thus, no resting on one's laurels is allowed.

The other facet of the "fat happy rat" tenet is that most "positive tension" is generated within the individual. Thus, selection of talents that are generators of their own excitement is critical and yet often neglected by R&D managers who focus on credentials.

The literature on achievement motivation reinforces this fact by concluding that those possessing the motivation to achieve (which is terribly difficult to "train"—thus the focus on selection) tend to maintain that motivation to the extent that the desire to excel is given a climate to operationalize the desire. Thus, hungry researchers tend to stay hungry, given the manager's understanding of other basic tenets.

An anecdote may serve to make the point about achievers: We once asked a research manager what he looked for in a young scientist or engineer. His response was, "I will tell you what *not* to look for: 'Soft Suburbanites.' They are never hungry enough!" While we all can observe some exceptions to this manager's rule, the work excitement of the hungry researchers in his laboratory was truly exceptional.

The observation of the achiever during the employment interview takes no special skill on the part of the manager. Thus, we are amused at how many R&D labs have dropped the practice of having prospective researchers make a presentation on their dissertation or other current research because "we do not learn much." Technically, this is probably true. But if a young researcher has just spent several years on a scientific/engineering problem and cannot communicate some excitement about it, that really tells you something about that candidate. We would argue that you reinstitute the presentation if you do not have one and consider the motivation impact of the candidate as well as his/her technical content.

Low Intellectual Content. A very interesting facet of motivation is the fact that emotion has almost no intellectual content. This creates problems for the research community because it is staffed by people of high intellect who believe you can intellectualize all motivational problems away. Thus, you will hear the argument that if so-and-so only understood he would act differently. The research manager has missed the motivational point: intellectualizing doesn't handle emotion. And so-and-so acts the way he does not because of lack of understanding but in spite of understanding. The act makes him feel good regardless of the content.

The manager must understand that every managerial act has two principle components, namely, information and affect (or emotion). We observe that there is rarely much intellectual content in emotion but, where motivation is concerned, there is also very little intellectual content in information. A manager must be intellectually aware of his motivational objectives, but should not necessarily try to communicate them. Emotion gets in the way.

Even if a research manager possesses a Ph.D., he is rarely a clinical psychologist. Thus: *if it feels good, do not ask why; do it again.* We once had a manager say that you could not motivate adult researchers by sticking stars on poster paper the way they did in grade school. Meanwhile, his staff was falling all over themselves to get their names listed on the "patent award" plaque in the office foyer.

Hedonism. As a fundamental determinant of motivation, we must observe that all individuals "seek pleasure and avoid pain." Although this may appear to be a worthless platitude, managers must first understand this to be absolutely true, because its implications for managerial thought and action are substantive.

First, hedonism implies getting to *know your people.* What is pleasurable to person A may be quite unpleasant to person B. Especially where delegation is concerned, research managers tend to assume that a researcher will enjoy a task because the manager himself would enjoy it and yet it may threaten the researcher who is assigned the task.

All individuals are different in what they like and what they fear. Thus, one of the most critical errors a manager can commit is to make broad generalizations about what people like—or what motivates them. This is extremely important if for no other reason than the fact that formal reward systems do imply such broad generalizations. Pay systems have become very standardized, even in the unlikely event that they are based only on performance. The individual manager in his day-to-day interactions has very little control over formal reward systems. He does, however, have considerable control over many informal rewards and these should be applied to specific individuals in terms of their specific likes and dislikes. Thus, for example, the manager can use job assignments, travel, equipment, and his time as important elements in his system to motivate his employees. The key to hedonism as a tenet of motivation begins with the recognition of individual differences.

Second, hedonism requires the manager to *maintain control over (informal) rewards.* We find it interesting how many managers give up control over obvious rewards because they are an administrative headache. If the manager loses control over what a researcher likes (or may like), he may lose the capacity to excite that individual about work. He must then rely on the employee's self motivation—which may be fine in some cases but we do not suggest that one rely solely on it.

Protection of Self. All individuals have a certain desire for protection of self. Particularly in research work, the basic tenet of protection typically means protection from the possibility and consequences of failure. People who have spent their lives building self-esteem based upon technical competence will go to great lengths to avoid losing that fragile base. It is surprising how many managers cannot see through apathy, defensiveness, and aggression as a manifestation of the fear of failure.

In order to keep work excitement and openness high, the manager must communicate that "you take some risks and I will protect you if you fail." This is an imperative step in a good motivational program. We once worked with an R&D manager who gave great inspirational speeches, always ending with: "You people must take more risks. The future of the company and the country depends on it!" The people who then took risks and failed were handed their heads. Needless to say, risk taking and research performance in that company are very low.

Protection also implies a desire to "save face," a concept which American managers continuously ignore. This tenet simply requires that we *treat people with dignity.* Any researchers who tour an operating division—particularly blue-collar situations—have observed the pervasive attacks on simple human dignity and have commented, "no wonder the union is hostile." But some of the same researchers will return to the lab and exhibit the same attacks on the dignity of a technician. *Respect* and *dignity* are precursors to the generation of work excitement.

Given the contemporary economic climate, even well-educated employees work in a world of extreme uncertainty. This uncertainty is magnified by managers who feel that keeping subordinates "off-guard" keeps them "on their toes." These attacks can be quite subtle and when the desire for protection is aroused, the defenses can be very subtle. People find it difficult to respond openly to an injury to their self-esteem although the damage, in fact, may be crippling to their capacity to perform.

Enhancement of Self. Managers must recognize the inherent conflict between the desire for protection and the desire for enhancement. By enhancement of self, we mean that all individuals seek some symbols of status. But in work, symbols of status should be associated with taking some risks and succeeding. Thus, while a manager should communicate some protection from failure, he must also communicate that *incremental rewards should only be associated with success.* This is a difficult balancing act requiring a significant amount of self-discipline and consistency on the part of the manager. (It also assumes some control over rewards.)

Aside from the distribution of rewards, an extremely simple corollary to this tenet is: everybody wants to solo. A researcher likes to be seen as making an identifiable, perhaps singular, contribution to the group, however trivial this contribution may seem to an external observer. The emerging field of organization design seems to base its theory on this desire to solo.

We should also emphasize that soloing is not at all incompatible with teamwork. Our observation is that where effective team building has taken place, this tenet receives prime consideration. At one laboratory, a team-building exercise left us very impressed with the ability of each team to enhance its members, particularly the older professionals.

Social Relativity. When a manager recognizes the first six tenets of motivation (*i.e.*, he works hard at it, selects achievers, views excitement for excitement's sake, understands individual differences, provides a climate of dignity and protection, rewards incremental performance), he can still be perplexed at the level of dissatisfaction. Why? Because this tenet implies that all consequences in work are relative—relative to what other people are getting. This is one of the principal reasons why motivation, especially maintaining motivation, is so frustrating to many managers.

But satisfaction, as we have noted, is *not* motivation. Achievers are rarely satisfied. They want more. We have observed many managers who have gotten so tired of this "ingratitude" that they begin to believe that the only way to manage is to treat everybody absolutely equally. What the frustrated manager must realize is that *managing to motivate is incompatible with managing to minimize dissatisfaction.* The worst mistake a manager can make regarding motivation is to adopt a strategy to minimize dissatisfaction and yield a satisfied, complacent work group. Positive tension (by definition, lack of satisfaction) is a necessity.

Social relativity is also important as an input into how a manager allocates his time spent with those reporting to him. One must learn to distinguish between time spent on supervision and time spent on motivation. In general, low performers require disproportionate amounts of supervisory time. You have to give them that time. Their excuse of not understanding the role requirements just might be true. But do not spend motivational time on low performers, "invest" it on the higher performers. One moves the group's mean performance to a new plateau by further motivating the high performers, not by rescuing the low performers.

This tenet also requires that the manager *make the recognition of performance very visible* to as many people as possible. Many have heard and agree with the principle of not publicly punishing a subordinate. But rewarding a high performer should be as public as possible. Not only does this prescription work on the show-off phenomenon (*i.e.*, enhancement), but it also communicates what constitutes performance to other group members. Everybody likes to have their work displayed for others to see. How many artists create a piece of work and hide it? This tenet, more than any other, forces the manager to recognize both the information and emotion of a motivational act.

Satiation vs. Variability. We earlier defined motivation as excitement, the managerial act being the proper mix of information and emotion. Nowhere is this act more perplexing than in the trade-off between constancy and variability in work. Research managers may understand this concept somewhat better than most, but it is nevertheless perplexing. Consider the following three conclusions from Pelz and Andrews' *Scientists in Organizations* (New York: John Wiley and Sons, Inc., 1966):

1. In both research and development, the more effective men undertook several specialties or technical functions.
2. Effective scientists reported good opportunities for professional growth.
3. As age increased, performance was sustained with periodic change in project.

In work, satiation on the job has a pejorative effect on motivation. Change is exciting. Change is developmental. Change shapes expectations about the future. As one R&D director related: "I reorganize my lab periodically whether it needs it or not."

Thus, this tenet implies that a manager should create change, but not too fast. In this regard, the time-honored principle that there should not be change for change's sake is simply incorrect. We might even suggest that managers should engage in a form of "limited Trotskyism," implying a small dose of permanent revolution (or evolution). Continuous small change sensitizes researchers to the fact of change, and this in itself is exciting. (But not too fast, the protection tenet, or too equally as regards specific individuals, the hedonism tenet.) Small, continuous change prevents the necessity of huge change which is too threatening.

The satiation versus variability tenet also implies that a manager should *vary the delivery of rewards*, meaning, of course, that no manager should reward incremental performance every time or use the same reward every time. Even if managers had an infinite pool of resources, a 100 percent reinforcement schedule has little information (it's redundant) and little emotion (it's boring).

Finally, this tenet implies that career planning is not just for the young. The aging technical specialist has too often been allowed to become obsolete. In this regard, dual-track systems have been a dismal failure. (We will readdress this question shortly). Hard work at team building is extremely important in this area. The research manager who can provide a work climate where coworkers are willing to provide others with growth support will find that he has a valuable motivational tool. The *Zeitgeist* of teamwork and mutual respect for the growth of others is what every manager, whatever his level in the organization, should seek to establish.

Juxtaposition. One of the facts of organizational life that any manager must come to accept if he is to be an effective motivator is that most formal systems of rewards are inherently not motivational. We are not saying that money is not motivational, we are saying the *system* of delivering money is not motivational. This is because the basic tenet of the juxtaposition of act and consequence is invariably violated by pay systems. In essence the effectiveness of a reward is largely predicated upon the reward being tied to the act (to be rewarded) in time and space.

Rewards should be delivered in a timely manner. Although human beings have a greater capacity for memory than primates, it is surprising how short that memory span is where excitement about rewards and its association with appropriate behaviors is concerned. This is not an idle behavioral science concept, but too many managers treat it that way. One reason for this is that the juxtaposition concept requires a compulsion to observe the day-to-day performance of subordinates and provide something, anything, in the way of positive reinforcement to performers.

This returns us to an unavoidable conclusion: a manager's motivational resources are rarely formal. This is because the vast majority of managers have no control over the timely delivery of formal rewards. Ineffective managers translate this fact into the assumption that they have no power. Effective managers do not worry about it, and employ a continual stream of informal rewards to generate employee excitement. Moreover, we have observed how effective managers must keep coming up with new types of reward schemes, not only because resources are quickly exhausted but also because "higher" management will see a certain approach working, take control of it, routinize it, standardize it, and destroy it.

One of the more pleasing implications of this tenet is that performance *per se* is immediately exciting. In other words, if the manager can get the performance up, the excitement should go up ("Eureka, I did it!"). Nevertheless, the rapid recognition must still be there. A beautiful golf shot may be exciting, but much less so if no one sees it.

Expectations. As a final tenet of employee motivation, this is the most pervasive. Expectations are the essence of motivation. As such, this tenet is highly correlated with the other tenets.

First, this tenet implies that the capacity to motivate is dependent upon managerial credibility. If a manager has little credibility relative to his willingness or ability to deliver rewards, employees are not likely to be excited about the manager's requests for incremental effort. Credibility is hard to establish; easy to lose. If the subordinate does not believe in you, you cannot motivate him or her.

The demise of dual track systems in many research laboratories classically illustrates the role of expectations. In terms of the tenets of motivation, such systems are imperative. Over the years, however, the administration of the dual career path was such that the management track was perceived, usually correctly, as the only path to personal and professional growth. The director of research will say the system works, but the researcher knows better—he just saw an ineffective manager moved from the management track to high-up on the technical track to save his face because he was actually fired and then ended up better than many on the technical track. The expectations are then changed and become very difficult to reverse.

Where expectations are concerned, establishing an *image of objectivity* requires a balance between information and emotion. A good research manager must draw a distinction between having a reputation for objectivity about research goals and having a reputation for objectivity about people. Effective research managers are often viewed as somewhat lacking in objectivity in goal setting (they set very high goals, then orchestrate the motivation to achieve them), but are typically viewed as very objective (by high performers) in their evaluation of people.

In other words, the manager creates motivations about work goals by holding great expectations. He pushes for the three-minute mile and is seen as somewhat non-objective in his expectations. Yet his target is motivation and the ventilation by the researchers about such targets is in fact a reflection of excitement, be it a bit frightening.

The expectations tenet certainly implies that rewards are vastly superior to punishments as a motivational device. Obviously we are not saying that ineffective research managers run around punishing technical professionals.

What they resort to, however, are threats, subtle attacks on self-esteem, and so forth. These approaches have plenty of emotion, but little information. They only tell you what not to do. They generate minimal compliance and a desire to escape. Effective motivators recognize that attention to rewards provides both information and emotion. In short, they tell you what to do—and make you feel great doing it.

In summary, effective research managers long ago learned that the recipe for success in motivating in a technical environment requires the careful formulation of an approach tailored to each individual. Successful motivation of employees begins with an in-depth understanding of the person in question. Blending these ten tenets into a conscious managerial style requires thoughtful consideration of the needs and expectations of the persons involved and the circumstances of the specific situation. It is obvious that if the manager cannot offer what the individual wants he cannot motivate that individual. This is an axiom that managers should never forget. The manager should strive to control rewards or access to those rewards and not let the rewards get lost in a bureaucratic system.

Employees' trust and confidence in you as their manager will go a long way in forgiving a lack of skill in delivery, but a perception by subordinates of deceit and false manipulation will emasculate any plan. Never forget the emotional component of motivation. Blend these tenets of motivation with an honest and straightforward managerial delivery and we feel you will reap the rewards of your time and effort.

George E. Manners, Jr., is professor of management at Clemson University. He received his Ph.D. from Georgia State University and has also taught at Atlanta University, Notre Dame University and Rensselaer Polytechnic Institute. Joseph A. Steger is executive vice president and provost at the University of Cincinnati. He also served as director of human resources at Colt Industries and dean of management at Rensselear Polytechnic Institute. Thomas W. Zimmerer has worked in both business and academia. Since completing his doctorate in 1971, he has published five books and over 45 articles in various national journals. Dr. Zimmerer has been twice recognized as the outstanding teacher in his college and in 1974 was elected to Outstanding Educators in America.

58.
FINDING OUT WHY A GOOD PERFORMER WENT BAD

Steve Buckman

Instead of relying on management through fear to turn the situation around—try a
better approach.

It had been a long and difficult week for Al Miller. Besides the myriad tasks
that he had had to perform, earlier in the week he had spent several uncomfortable minutes with his boss as his boss explained in no uncertain terms why
he would no longer tolerate excuses from Al for missed deadlines on an important weekly sales report. Al headed up the data processing department, and
for several weeks the overall sales report used by several company departments
for decision making had been late. The heads of these departments had
complained not to Al or Al's boss but to the head of the division.

Al was considering the impact that the complaints might have on his
performance appraisal, due in a few weeks' time, as he walked down the hallway
to Judy Kennedy's desk.

"Judy, are those printouts ready for distribution now?" he asked.

"I'm sorry, Mr. Miller, they're not finished. It's going to take me about two
hours to complete the work."

Part of Al's problem over the last several weeks had been caused by Judy's
inability to have her work completed on time. Miller couldn't understand what
was behind the problem, for in the past Judy's work had been good. One thing
was certain: He was not going to allow the situation to continue for another
week. "Judy, I'd like to see you in my office right now!" he demanded.

Once in his office, Al exploded. "Judy, I've been taking a lot of heat for these
late reports of yours, and it's not going to continue. I want that report in one
hour, and next week it had better be done on time. Do you understand? What's
more, I'm going to have to give you a written warning. Next week, there had
better be some improvement!"

Judy didn't know what to say. Al had never talked to her that way before. At
the end of the meeting, she left feeling very hurt and angry and not knowing
exactly what "getting a written warning" meant.

348

A BETTER APPROACH

Given the way he handled the situation, it's unlikely that there will be any improvement in the situation next week. Al forgot some very basic rules about counseling in his handling of Judy, relying instead on management through fear to turn the situation around. In this respect, he's not unlike many supervisors. While it's true that the club sometimes must be used, it's much better for both the supervisor and his or her organization if an attempt is made first to identify the cause of an employee's performance problem and then develop a plan to resolve the situation. This is particularly the case when the employee involved is someone like Judy, a long-time good performer whose performance for one reason or another is slipping.

Let's assume that you as a manager find yourself in a situation like Al's. How would you handle the interview with the problem performer?

In a nonthreatening manner, describe what you have observed and why that behavior is important. Avoid being emotional and stick to the specifics. Don't talk about intangibles like attitude or work ethics. As a manager, you should focus on the specific behavior that is creating a problem. You're not qualified to judge the individual's value system. If the work is not getting done on time, then that's the subject for discussion. Don't go beyond that to suggest that the work is not completed because the employee is "lazy" or "not interested."

Simply and succinctly state the facts as you have observed them, then discuss the implications in terms of the department's objectives. In some instances, the new employee may simply not understand the priority that is placed on a particular task. Simply discussing your concern may be enough to bring about an improvement in performance.

Review prior meetings. If appropriate, discuss previous meetings that have been held with the employee. Perhaps this is the third time in three months that it has been necessary to discuss the problem with the employee. If it is, then it will be helpful to review what was discussed and what the employee said that he or she would do about the problem.

Listen attentively. Ask the employee if there is any reason for the continued unacceptable performance. In some cases, there may be an acceptable explanation. In Judy's case, for instance, if Al had taken the time to probe, he would have found that because of staff reductions Judy had become responsible for several other reports. The demands of the user departments on her time had grown, creating a work bottleneck.

Keep in mind that active listening requires more than simply opening your ears (although that may be the most difficult part of the job). To be an effective listener, one has to hear not only what is said but also what is not said.

With the employee's input, identify problem solving techniques to be used. Guide the employee to resolve the problem on his or her own. Often, by simply talking it out, the employee will be able to determine on his or her own where the weakness is and what must be done to correct it. The need for supervisory input into this process depends on the employee. Clearly a new employee who is not familiar with the job will need more help than a five-year veteran in the position. Perhaps you can describe some similar situations you have observed and discuss some possible solutions, allowing the employee to review each alternative.

It would also be appropriate at this point for you to explain what action you expect to take. For example, if you plan to document the meeting in the form of a disciplinary memo, make that clear. Explain the intent of the memorandum and what it means to the employee.

Wrap up, restating your position. After you have gone through the steps above, restate the course of action that you have agreed on with the employee and repeat your concern about the problem. Make it clear to the employee that resolution of the problem is his or her responsibility. Assure the individual that you will, of course, be there to help, but point out that you do not intend to do the work for the employee.

Set the time for follow up. Always schedule a follow-up meeting. The interval between the two meetings will depend on the gravity of the situation. In Judy's case, one week would be appropriate. But in some cases you may want to hold a follow-up meeting several months later.

Document the meeting. If you plan to document the meeting, do so immediately after it has taken place while the conversation is still fresh in your mind. Your documentation should be short and to the point. Include the employee's comments about the meeting whenever they are relevant. Note the reason why the meeting was called, what exactly was discussed, what the employee said that he or she would do to correct the situation, and when the next meeting will be held with the employee to discuss any positive changes in performance. The documentation should include the date of the meeting, the dates of any related prior meetings, and a list of those who will receive a copy of the documentation.

AL AND JUDY

Let's go back and see how Al could more effectively have handled the problem-solving session with Judy.

"Judy, I would like to see you before you leave today. Give me a call when you are ready."

At the end of the day, Judy enters Al's office. "Judy, I asked to see you this afternoon to discuss a problem that I have observed. Over the last several weeks, you have been at least two or three hours late with the overall sales report Friday afternoons. I think you understand how important it is that the work be processsed on time so that printouts are available to the heads of the user departments Monday mornings. Many of the decisions that will affect our company are based on the information that you provide. Is there any special reason why you have been unable to complete the work on time?"

"I know it's been late, Mr. Miller, but really I have been trying. The cutback on employees certainly hasn't helped. Also, it seems that more and more I'm being asked by the user departments to generate additional reports."

"We have discussed the work force reductions before, and I know that you understand why we had to transfer some of your former co-workers to other work areas. But I wasn't aware that the user departments were giving you additional work. Who assigned the work?"

"It comes primarily from sales and distribution. I don't mind getting the information they ask for, but it puts me behind on the overall sales report."

"How much time is involved in this additional work?"

"Probably several hours each week. If someone else could take over the work or at least some of it, I'm sure that I could get the overall sales report done on time."

"Well, I think that some of the work on these additional reports could be reassigned. I also want to talk to these managers to find out if they really need all this paperwork. In the meantime, I want you to focus on meeting our deadline on Friday. Also, because of the seriousness of the problem, I am going to have to document our discussion so that we are clear on what was discussed. I'll give you a copy of the note when it is finished.

"Let's meet again one week from this Monday to talk about the progress that has made. If you have any questions before then, let me know. Is there anything else that you would like to discuss?"

CONCLUSION

This time Al did a good job of explaining what the problem was. By discussing the situation, Al and Judy were able to identify the cause, and in all likelihood they will be much closer to resolving the problem the next time they meet. Judy now understands how important meeting the deadline is, and Al has a better picture of what is happening.

Steve Buckman is personnel manager, Insalaco's Supermarkets, Pittston, Pennsylvania.

59.

TO IMPROVE PERFORMANCE, TRY A LITTLE "PSYCHOLOGICAL TOUCHING"

Herbert E. Brown
Thomas D. Dovel

> To sum it all up, motivation is still one of the most potentially productive, yet perplexing, functions challenging sales managers today.

"O.K.," you say, "so what can I do to motivate my people?"

If you really just said that, you have just made your first mistake. What you really should have said is, "If I'm going to motivate my people, I first have to understand what motivation is." No need to really worry about a definition of the term. "That which gets someone to take action," will do for now. The crux is to understand what underlies the process. But that's not so easy because motivation wears many faces.

A nonproductive situation is not necessarily caused by a lack of motivation. On the contrary, the employees involved are usually quite motivated, but are just not producing the desired results.

Your question might then be, "O.K., so what can I do to motivate my people to do what management wants?" The answer is simple and yet complex for the "want lists" of management and salesperson are seldom similar. One way to get desired results, however, is to give proper recognition.

ACCENTUATE THE POSITIVE

Recognition can be positive or negative, but there is little doubt that we all need it. A newborn infant needs recognition (especially through physical contact). As one matures, a substitution process begins which features nonphysical "psychological touching" or recognition. Sustained psychological touching is strongly desired by most individuals throughout their lifetime.

The answer to your question, then, is that psychological touching (or recognition) on the job is the best way to motivate your sales force to work toward your managerial objectives. There are, moreover, two basic types of recognition: negative and positive.

The Andrews Sisters weren't highly regarded behaviorists (except, perhaps, by Bing Crosby), but they hit the nail on the sales manager's head when they suggested that "you've gotta accentuate the positive and eliminate the negative." Even at that, the positive sometimes needs a little smoothing out, too. What do we mean? Let's take a look.

Ed Pennyson, sales manager for Bradley Shovels, thought that he had a great format for positive recognition. Anyone who exceeded quota by five percent was singled out for praise at the annual sales meeting. This time Peter Baynanham, who had hit 109 percent of quota and Bob Barrelhead (115 percent) were going to receive honors.

Sounds pretty reasonable doesn't it? Well, it is O.K. The trouble is that this type of positive reinforcement is usually given to the superior performers. How, then, is the "good" salesperson (e.g., one who misses his annual quota but, during the course of a year, has an overall average of 95 percent) to know that he is appreciated? The answer is that he usually doesn't. Consequently, such an individual will tend to do one or both of the following:

1. Seek outside recognition; someone else gives him what he wants.
2. Seek inside recognition—by wittingly or unwittingly committing mistakes.

Either way you can lose volume and valuable personnel. Moral: Recognize the "good" performance as well as the exceptional.

We might pause here to inject a "Skinnerism" in that while positive recognition is usually something good, positive reinforcement (a behavior strengthener) can be either a reward or a punishment. The key here is to add something new to a given situation.

For example, the salesperson who is lovingly greeted by his spouse each time that he brings home a bonus check is receiving strong positive reinforcement for his goal-meeting efforts. Conversely, a nagging spouse at the door on Friday night and no loving care over the weekend as a result of not meeting one's goal by working late in the territory each week night is similarly positively reinforcing.

The thing for the sales manager to remember is that the simple act of adding something good or bad to either a desired or undesired form of behavior is extremely effective in bringing about desired performance.

Does this seem to be a bit too simple a solution at first glance? Perhaps, but give it some thought or even a try and we think that you'll be convinced of its basic merits.

Negative recognition is another matter all together. Typically, it will lead to salespeople doing exactly what the sales manager doesn't want them to do. This philosophy is usually articulated as, "I leave my sales force pretty much alone, unless they foul something up. Then I jump all over them—hard." Similar problems crop up here as they did with the improper use of positive recognition. For under this premise the sales force will tend not to see the sales manager as a major source of need fulfillment. Here, too, they will look outside of the territory for desired recognition or, even worse, will attempt to obtain it internally through nonperformance. Ironically enough, by not giving recognition for acceptable performance, the sales manager is actually encouraging foul-ups.

For example, what happens when call reports are late? Right again: everything. You see, the salespeople did get your attention after all. Maybe not in a positive way, but they did get the recognition that they needed.

Just as positive recognition is complemented by positive reinforcement, so is negative recognition aided by an understanding of negative reinforcement. Negative reinforcement is *subtracting* something from a given situation. It may or may not be something bad.

Take, for example, the sales-person who falls behind in his monthly sales quotas and is royally chewed-out each time this happens. If he finds this unpleasant, he may work to attain quota simply to avoid this unpleasant consequence. Conversely, and perhaps more likely, he will continue to miss quota in order to obtain the recognition he is seeking.

On the other hand, suppose a salesperson thoroughly enjoys the peer recognition and admiration he receives for constantly making or exceeding quota. If he consistently misses his quota he will lose peer recognition and admiration and may work hard to regain them. In either example, negative reinforcement has effected an increase in desired behavior. So, in a nut shell, recognition through reinforcement basically involves only the following terms:

- Reinforcement: the consequence(s) of behavior
- Positive reinforcement: where something is added to the situation
- Negative reinforcement: where something is subtracted from the situation

ADDITIONAL DIMENSIONS

Before wrapping things up, we should probably take a quick look at two additional dimensions of motivation: extinction and punishment.

The former says that you can change unwanted behavior by eliminating any reinforcement of that activity because if an action has no consequence, it will eventually disappear from one's repertoire. Be careful, though, because sometimes you can eliminate desirable habits through the inadvertent removal of reinforcements.

Suppose, for example, that you want your salespeople to attend more professional meetings related either to their profession or to their customers' because this type of fraternization pays off in increased professionalism, possible leads, and general competitive intelligence feedback. Initially you openly praise those salespeople who do this but, over a period of time, you forget to reinforce. The most probable response will be for your people to either diminish significantly or eliminate altogether this type of activity with a "Why should we do it, it doesn't matter to anyone" attitude.

Punishment is usually just the opposite of reinforcement. In this instance, immediately following behavior, something good stops happening or, conversely, something bad begins to happen. This is not nearly as good a method as is extinction, however, because it merely suppresses rather than removes the unwanted behavior. Consequently, it will probably have to be consistently reapplied as the bad behavior reemerges.

HOW TO START MOTIVATING

So what does a sales manager do to start doling out authentic recognition? Well, getting in touch with yourself is a good start. Just ask yourself:

- What do I want to do (feel)?
- Am I doing (feeling) what I want to do (feel)?
- If not, why not?
- How can I do (feel) what I want to do (feel)?

"Feel" has been added in parentheses because the end results of our actions with others depend more upon what we feel than upon what we do. The sales manager, then, must feel O.K. about himself and what he wants his people to do before he can effectively communicate his requests to them. Moreover, it is difficult to give recognition if one cannot give it in a genuine straightforward sense. Authentic motivation requires it. Ambiguity and ulterior motives must be eliminated.

If you say, for example, that a female sales representative shouldn't be given a major account responsibility because "she's just not ready yet," when, in reality, you feel that you don't want a woman receiving more possible attention from top management (if she succeeds) than you do—admit it. Then look for the basic root cause of your insecurity and get your recognition in some other way than at the expense of an innocent party. Remember, effective recognition is both immediate and related to the desired behavior.

To sum it all up, motivation is still one of the most potentially productive, yet perplexing, functions challenging sales managers today. To be an effective motivator, however, involves not only understanding what it is but also being aware of the essential elements available to help you play the game.

We're suggesting that both positive and negative recognition, coupled with the concepts of reinforcement, extinction, and punishment, can help you to become a good, solid motivator: a sales manager who realizes that positive psychological touching (recognition) is requisite to motivation and improved performance of his sales force.

Try it. Give someone a *proper* dose of recognition at your next sales meeting. Psychologically speaking, we're convinced that you'll both be "O.K."

MOTIVATION BIBLIOGRAPHY

Adler, P., *Momentum: A Theory of Social Action* (New York: Russell Sage Foundation, 1981).

Aldag, R.J. and Brief, A.P., *Task Design & Employee Motivation* (Glenview, Ill.: Scott, Foresman & Co., 1979).

AMA Reprint Collection Series, *Making Yourself Promotable* (New York: American Management Association, 1975).

Apter, M., *The Experience of Motivation: The Theory of Psychological Reversals* (New York: Academic Press, 1982).

Argyris, C., *Integrating the Individual and the Organization* (New York: John Wiley & Sons, 1984).

Arkes, H.R. and Garske, J.P., *Psychological Theories of Motivation* (Monterey, Calif.: Brooks/Cole Publishing, 1981).

Arnold, W.J., *Nebraska Symposium on Motivation*, multi-volume series (Lincoln, Neb.: University of Nebraska Press, 1968).

Atkinson, J.W., *Introduction to Motivation* (New York: Van Nostrand Reinhold, 1978).

Atkinson, J.W. and Raynor, J.O., *Personality, Motivation, and Achievement* (New York: John Wiley & Sons, 1974).

Barry, R. and Wolf, B., *Motives, Values & Realities: A Framework for Counseling* (Westport, Conn.: Greenwood Press, 1965).

Beck, R.C., *Motivation: Theories & Principles* (Englewood Cliffs, N.J.: Prentice-Hall, 1978).

Bennis, W.G., *Leadership and Motivation: Essays of Douglas McGregor* (Cambridge, Mass.: MIT Press, 1966).

Bolles, R.C., *Theory of Motivation* (New York: Harper & Row, 1975).

Brody, N., *Motivation* (New York: Academic Press, 1983).

Bruno, F.J., *Human Adjustment and Personal Growth: Seven Pathways* (New York: John Wiley & Sons, 1977).

Buck, R.W., *Human Motivation & Emotion* (New York: John Wiley & Sons, 1976).

Cattell, R.B. and Child, D., *Motivation and Dynamic Structure* (New York: John Wiley & Sons, 1974).

Christie, L.G., *Human Resources: A Hidden Profit Center* (Englewood Cliffs, N.J.: Prentice-Hall, 1983).

Chung, K.H., *Motivational Theories & Practices* (Columbus, Ohio: Grid Publishing, 1977).

Coe, G.A., *The Motives of Men* (New York: AMS Press, 1928).

Cofer, C.N. and Appley, M.H., *Motivation: O.S.I. Theory & Research* (New York: John Wiley & Sons, 1964).

Cofer, C.N., *Human Motivation: A Guide to Information Sources* (Detroit, Mich.: Gale Research, 1980).

Cooper, R., *Motivation & Job Design* (New York: International Publishers Service, 1977).

Couger, J.D. and Zawacki, R.A., *Motivation and Managing Computer Personnel* (New York: John Wiley & Sons, 1980).

Day, H.I., *Intrinsic Motivation* (New York: Holt Rinehart & Winston, 1971).

Day, H.I., *Advances in Intrinsic Motivation & Aesthetics* (New York: Plenum Publishing Corp., 1981).

Deci, E.L., *Intrinsic Motivation* (New York: Plenum, 1975).

Deci, E.L., *The Psychology of Self-Determination* (Lexington, Mass.: Lexington Books, 1980).

Dichter, E., *Getting Motivated: The Secret Behind Individual Motivations by the Man Who Was Not Afraid to Ask "Why?"* (New York: Pergamon, 1979).

Dichter, E., *Motivating Human Behavior* (New York: McGraw-Hill, 1971).

Eims, L., *Be a Motivational Leader* (Wheaton, Ill.: Victor Books, 1981).

Evans, P., *Motivation* (New York: Methuen, Inc., 1975).

Ferguson, E.D., *Motivation* (Melbourne, Fla.: Robert E. Krieger Publishing Co., 1982).

Fiegehen, G.C., *Companies, Incentives and Senior Managers* (New York: Oxford University Press, 1981).

Franken, R.E., *Human Motivation* (Monterey, Calif.: Brooks/Cole Publishing, 1981).

Gellerman, S.W., *Management by Motivation* (New York: American Management Association, 1968).

Gellerman, S.W., *Motivation & Productivity* (New York: American Management Association, 1963).

George, J.L., *Prescription for Effective Communication and Motivation* (Miami: Symposia Specialists, 1978).

Gilbert, T.F., *Human Competence* (New York: McGraw-Hill, 1978).

Green, R.G., *Human Motivation* (Boston: Allyn & Bacon, 1984).

Hacker, W. et al., *Cognitive and Motivational Aspects of Action* (New York: Elsevier, 1983).

Hanks, K. *Motivating People* (Allen, Tex.: Argus Communications, 1982).

Heckhausen, Heinz et al., *Achievement Motivation in Perspective* (New York: Academic Press, 1986).

Herzberg, F., *Work and the Nature of Man* (Cleveland: World Publishing, 1966).

Herzberg, F., Mausner, B. and Synderman, B.B., *The Motivation to Work* (New York: John Wiley & Sons, 1959).

Hinrichs, J.R., *The Motivation Crisis* (New York: American Management Association, 1974).

Houston, J.P., *Motivation* (New York: Macmillan, 1985).

Johnson, S. and Johnson, A.D., *Value of Dedication* (Racine, Wis.: Western Publishing, 1979).

Johnson, S. and Johnson, A.D., *Value of Determination* (Racine, Wis.: Western Publishing, 1979).

Jung, J., *Understanding Human Motivation: A Cognitive Approach* (New York: Macmillan, 1978).

Kaiser, A., *Motivation Techniques* (Claremont, Calif.: Hunter House, Inc., n.d.).

Klein, S.B., *Motivation: Biosocial Approaches* (New York: McGraw-Hill, 1982).

Kolesnik, W.B., *Motivation Understanding & Influencing Human Behavior* (Newton, Mass.: Allyn & Bacon, 1978).

Korman, A.K., *The Psychology of Motivation* (Englewood Cliffs, N.J.: Prentice-Hall, 1974).

Lawler, E.E., *Motivation in Work Organizations* (Monterey, Calif.: Brooks/Cole Publishing, 1973).

Lawler, E., *Pay and Organization Development* (Boston: Addison-Wesley, 1981).

LeClaire, E.J., *Profit Sharing: A Natural for Today's Changing Work Force/ Economy* (Evanston, Ill.: Profit Sharing Research Foundation, 1982).

Leff, H.L., *Experience, Environment and Human Potentials* (New York: Oxford University Press, 1978).

Levine, F.M., *Theoretical Readings in Motivation* (Chicago: Rand McNally, 1976).

Levinson, H., *The Great Jackass Fallacy* (Boston: Harvard University, Division of Research, 1973).

Lidstone, J., *Motivating Your Sales Force* (Westmead, Farnborough, Hampshire, England: Teakfield Ltd., 1978).

Litwin, G.H. and Stringer, R.A., *Motivation & Organizational Climate* (Boston, Mass.: Harvard University Press, 1968).

Luthans, F. and Kreitner, R., *Organizational Behavior Modification* (Glenview, Ill.: Scott, Foresman & Co., 1985).

Macrov, D., *Incentives to Work* (Ann Arbor, Mich.: UMI Research Press, 1970).

Madsen, K.B., *Modern Theories of Motivation* (New York: John Wiley & Sons, 1974).

Maier, N.R.F., *Psychology in Industrial Organizations* (Boston: Houghton Mifflin, 1982).

McAshan, H.H., *The Goals Approach to Performance Objectives* (Philadelphia: Saunders, 1974).

McCay, J.T., *Beyond Motivation* (New York: Jeffery Norton Publishers, 1973).

McClelland, D.C., *Human Motivation* (Glenview, Ill.: Scott, Foresman & Co., 1973).

McClelland, D. and Winters, D.S., *Motivating Economic Achievement* (New York: Free Press, 1971).

McDonough, R., *Keys to Effective Motivation* (Nashville, Tenn.: Broadman Press, 1979).

Marting, E., *Invitation to Achievement* (New York: American Management Association, 1972).

Maslow, A.H., *Toward a Psychology of Being* (New York: Van Nostrand Reinhold, 1968).

Maslow, A.H., *Motivation & Personality* (New York: Harper & Row, 1970).

Montapert, A.A., *Inspiration & Motivation* (Englewood Cliffs, N.J.: Prentice-Hall, 1982).

Murrell, H., *Motivation at Work* (New York: Methuen Inc., 1976).

Nevin, J.A., *The Study of Behavior: Learning, Motivation, Emotion, and Instinct* (Glenview, Ill.: Scott, Foresman & Co., 1973).

Perti, H., *Motivation: Theory & Research* (Belmont, Calif.: Wadsworth Publishing, 1981).

Phillips, E.L., *Day to Day Anxiety Management* (Melbourne, Fla.: R.E. Krieger Publishing Co., 1977).

Quick, T.I., *The Quick Motivation Method* (New York: St. Martin's Press, 1980).

Raynor, J.O. and Entin, E.E., *Motivation, Career Striving, & Aging* (New York: Hemisphere Publishing, 1982).

Rosenbaum, B.L., *How to Motivate Today's Workers: Motivational Models for Managers & Supervisors* (New York: McGraw-Hill, 1981).

Roy, W. Walters & Associates, *Job Enrichment for Results* (Boston: Addison-Wesley, 1975).

Ryan, T.A., *Intentional Behavior: An Approach to Human Motivation* (New York: Ronald Press, 1970).

Samzotta, D., *Motivational Theories & Applications for Managers* (New York: American Management Association, 1977).

Schaefer, S.D., *The Motivation Process* (Boston: Little, Brown & Co., 1977).

Shaw, M.E., *Making It Assertively* (Englewood Cliffs, N.J.: Prentice-Hall, 1980).

Steers, R.M., and Porter, L.W., *Motivation & Work Behavior* (New York: McGraw-Hill, 1983).

Stein, D.G. and Rosen, J.J., *Motivation and Emotion* (New York: Macmillan, 1974).

Stogdill, R.M., *Team Achievement Under High Motivation* (Columbus, Ohio: Ohio State University Press, 1963).

Toates, F. and Halliday, T., *Analysis of Motivational Processes* (New York: Academic Press, 1981).

Turner, H.M., *The People Motivators* (New York: McGraw-Hill, 1973).

Ulrich, R., *Motivation Methods That Work* (Englewood Cliffs, N.J.: Prentice-Hall, 1981).

Valle, F.P., *Motivation* (Monterey, Calif.: Brooks/Cole Publishing, 1975).

Van Houten, R., *How to Motivate Others Through Feedback* (Lawrence, Kan.: H & H Enterprises, 1980).

Vernon, M.D., *Human Motivation* (New York: Cambridge University Press, 1969).

Vroom, V.H., *Work and Motivation* (New York: John Wiley & Sons, 1982).

Weiner, B., *Human Motivation* (New York: Holt, Rinehart & Winston, 1980).

Weiner, B., *Cognitive Views of Human Motivation* (New York: Academic Press, 1974).

Weiner, B., *Theories of Motivation: From Mechanism to Cognation* (Chicago: Rand McNally, 1972).

Wenzel, W.J., *Motivation Training Manual* (New York: CBI Publishing, 1970).

INDEX

Abarbanel, Jerome, 140
Achievement motivation
    theory, 290-291
Activation theory, 229-234
Adams, J. Stacy, 294
Aerojet General
    Corporation, 314
Alderfer, Clayton P., 184
American Management
    Association, 57
American Telephone and
    Telegraph Company, 37-38
Andrews, Frank M., 344
Andrews Sisters, The, 353
Archibald, Robert, 289
Argyris, Chris, 98
Arousal theories, 184-185
Arthur Young & Co., 138
Attitude towards work,
    101-102
        importance of, 83-84
Automated offices, 259-260

Babb, Hugh W., 186
Badin, I.J., 178
Baker, Douglas D., 296, 297
Baumeister, R.R., 162
Beck, Donald, 287-288
Beehr, T.A., 184
Behling, O., 186
Bell, Cecil H., 187
Bem, Daryl J., 162
Benefits, 58-63, 67
    government impact on,
        60
Berdy, Michele, 38

Bethlehem Steel
    Corporation, 39, 107
Bias, 86-87
"Blocked opportunity"
    syndrome, 321-330
Boring jobs, redesign of,
    336-338
Bray, Douglas, 37-38, 150
Brousseau, K.R., 149
Burdick, W.E., 39
Bureau of Labor Statistics,
    36
Byrd, Richard E., 129

Cabrera, James, 36
Cafeteria style benefits,
    67
Campbell, John P., 149,
    150, 178, 182, 207
Career motivation theory,
    149-170
        interactive model,
            162-167
        variables of, 154-161
Carrell, M.R., 186
Carter, Diane, 283-284, 288
Centerre Bank of Branson,
    41-48
Challenge, 24-26, 325-326
Chaplin, Charlie, 259
Choice, theories of,
    185-187
Chrysler, 137
Coaching: see Performance
    coaching
Communication, 23

Communications techniques,
47-48
Compensation, inequitable,
117
Compensation program,
55-56, 58-63
Competency, 90-91
Competition, 326-327
Connolly, T., 186
Constraints to effective
motivation, 83-87
Cooper, Michael, Dr., 38,
106, 107

Davis, Keith, 186
Deci, Edward L., 162
Decline of employee
motivation, 262-268
Defining motivation,
206-207, 229-230
Delegation of duties, 17-20
Delta Air Lines, 39-40
Demma, Tim, 107, 108
Demotivation, correcting,
324
"Deterioration of Work
Standards," 285
Dittrich, John E., 186
Dossett, D.L., 178
Drake Beam Morin Inc., 36
Drucker, Peter, 67-68, 257,
310
Dual factor theory: see
Two-factor theory
Dubin, Richard, 149
Dugan, Richard, 138
Dunnette, Marvin D., 182,
207

Edison, Thomas A., 339
Employee involvement
program, 32-34

Employee needs, 114-115
survey to gauge,
216-220
Employee performance: see
Performance
Employment, 21-22
Environmental factors, 87,
91-92
Equity theory, 294-295
Ewing, James, 40
Expectancy theory, 292-294
Expectations, 93-95
realistic, 221-224

Factors affecting
motivation, 275-282
Farr, J.L., 181
Feedback, 92
Ferris, G.R., 184
Fisher, C.D., 189
Flowers, Vincent, 286,
288-289
Ford Motor Co.
Louisville assembly
plant, 33
Foreign competition, 97

Geers Gross, 38
General Electric Co., 76
Credit Corp., 140
Gilkey, Roderick, 39
Gilmore, D.C., 184
Glennon, James, 288
Goals, individuality of,
80-82
Goal-setting theory, 292
Goodman, P.S., 186
Government impact on
benefits, 60
Grant, Philip C., 150, 269
Graves, Clare, 284-286
Greenhaus, J.H., 178
Guide to Personal Risk
Taking, 129

Hackman, J. Richard, 183, 184
Hart, David K., 181
Hay Group, 38, 106, 107
Heneman, Herbert G., 186
Herzberg, Frederick, 10, 13, 14, 15, 66, 81, 98, 230, 270-271, 308
    see also Two-factor theory
Hewlett-Packard Company, 39
Hierarchy of needs theory, 230, 303-304
High-morale groups, 27-31
Holland, W., 122
Holmes, Sherlock, 147
How to Get a Better Job Quicker, 330
Hughes, Charles, 286, 288-289
Human behavior, importance of understanding, 241-249
Human Resources: A Hidden Profit Center, 71
Human resources manager, roles of, 225-228

Iacocca, Lee A., 39, 137
Ilgan, Daniel R., 189
International Business Machines Corporation, 38-39
Introduction to Management, 57
Investment model, 298-302

Japanese approach, 66
Japanese auto industry, 97
Job enrichment, 67
Job evaluation interviews, 116
Job loyalty, 35-40
Job modeling, 43-44

Job redesign, 65-69
Job satisfaction, importance of, 236-237
Job switching, systematic, 327-328

Kane, J.S., 181
Kanter, Rosabeth Moss, 35
Katz, R., 189
Kavanagh, M.J., 181
Keller, Pat, 88
Kennedy, Marilyn Moats, 139
Kopp, D.G., 186
Korman, Abraham K., 178, 184
Kreitner, Robert, 296

Landy, Frank J., 181
Latham, Gary P., 178, 185
Lawler, Edward, 181, 182, 183, 186, 207, 294
Leadership, styles of, 102-103
LeClaire, Edmond Jean, 73-74
Lefton, Robert, 138-140
"Levels of Existence: An Open System Theory of Values," 285
Likert, Rensis, 98
Likert Scale, 217-219
Livingston, J. Sterling, 93-94
Locke, Edwin, 185, 187, 291, 292
Lorsch, J.W., Professor, 146
Los Angeles Security Pacific Bank, 284
Luthans, Fred, 186, 295-296

Macromotivation, 125, 126-127
Maier, Norman R.F., 27

Malaise
    managerial, 2-8
    worker, 106-108
Management, 310
Management basics, validity
    of, 104
Management by Objectives
    (MBO), 67-68, 306-309
Management training, 22
*The Manager's Guide to
    Equal Employment
    Opportunity
    Requirements*, 105
Margol, Irving, 284
Martin, Thomas, 39
Maslow, Abraham H., 10, 13,
    14, 65-67, 81, 98, 113,
    178, 184, 230, 270-273,
    284
    see also Need
        hierarchy theory
Massachusetts Institute of
    Technology, 286
Mawhinney, T.C., 186
Mayo, Elton, 76
McClelland, David, 76, 291,
    304-305
McGinnon, Peter, 37
McGregor, Douglas, 65-66,
    98, 116-117, 184
Merit Report, 107
Methods of motivating,
    290-297
Metzger, Bert, 72, 73
Micromotivation, 125
Mid-career block, 320-330
Mills, Ted, 332
Miner, John B., 149
Mischel, Walter, 162
Misconceptions, 238-240
Mitchell, Terence R., 178,
    186, 187
"Modern Times," 259
Modern workforce, 331-335

Money, 117
    as motivator, 50-53,
        54-57
Monsanto Co., 139
Morale
    employee, 75-77
    problems, solutions
        for, 107-108
    see also Worker
        malaise
*Motivating Economic
    Achievement*, 291
Murray, H.A., 150
Myers, Scott, 286, 287, 289
Myers, Susan, 286, 287

Nadler, David A., 189
Need hierarchy theory, 10,
    113-114
Nightingale, Donald, 72, 73

Office design, 118-124
Older employees, 316-319
Oldham, Greg R., 184
Oliver, C., 122
Open-office landscape,
    118-121
    related issues,
        121-122
    steps to follow,
        122-123
Organization behavior
    modification, 295-297
*Organizational Behavior
    Modification*, 296
Outside conditions, 125-127

Pareto, Vilfredo, 311
Participative management,
    41-48, 116-117
Path-goal framework, 10
Paul, Robert, 296
*Pay and Organization
    Development*, 294

Payne, Richard A., 330
Pelz, Donald C., 344
Pennyson, Ed, 353
Performance
    factors influencing,
        182-183
    improvement of, 194-
        199
    problems, 88-92
    techniques for
        improving, 348-351,
        352-356
Performance appraisal,
    181-182
Performance coaching,
    221-224, 250-258
"Performance Equals Ability
    and What," 182
Performance evaluation,
    138-140
Performance motivation
    conditions, 50-52
Personality, effect of,
    144-146
Pfeffer, Jeffrey, 162, 178,
    184
Planning process, 32-34
Porter, Lyman W., 182, 185
Positive management,
    advantages of, 75-77
Pritchard, R.D., 149, 178,
    182
Productivity, 96-105,
    310-314
    improvement of, 21-23
    increased, 202-215
Profit sharing, 72-74
Profit Sharing: A Natural
    for Today's Changing
    Work Force/Economy, 74
Profit Sharing Council of
    America, 72
Psychological Associates,
    Inc., 138-140

Psychological touching,
    352-356
Public Agenda Foundation,
    94, 172
Putting the Work Ethic to
    Work, 177
"Pygmalion in Management,"
    93-94

Raynor, Joel O., 149
Reality-Centered People
    Management: Key to
    Improved Productivity,
    105
Reass, Bob, 139, 140
Recognition, means of
    providing, 324-325
Reinforcement theory,
    307-309
Republic National Bank,
    287-288
Research and development
    staff, 339-347
Risk taking, 128-134
Robbins, Bob, 38
Rohrer, Hibler & Replogle,
    35, 37
Ropes for Management
    Success: Climb Higher,
    Faster, 8

Salancik, Gerald R., 162,
    178, 184
Salary practices, 70-71
Sauer, John, 35
Schwab, Donald P., 66, 186
Scientists in
    Organizations, 344
Scott, William G., 181
Self-development programs,
    328-329
Silicon Valley, 32
Skelly, Florence, 332
Skills, 94

Skinner, B.F., 295, 296,
    353
Sloan School of Management,
    286
Smith, Michael, 199
Southern Bell, 288
Sprunger, Eduard, 284
Standard Oil Company
    (Indiana), 288
Standards, importance of
    defining, 89-90
Staw, B.M., 162, 178
Steel mills, 33
Steers, Richard M., 185
Strategy, 142-148
Style of motivating,
    113-117
Success backlash, 320-321
*Successful Personnel
    Recruiting and
    Selection*, 105
Surveys to gauge employee
    needs, 216-220
Szilagyi, Andrew D., 121,
    122

Talburt, Lane, 288
Taylor, Frederick, 76
Taylor, M.S., 189
"The Technology Gap," 311
Technology, new, 336-338
Teets, John, 36
Terkel, Studs, 95
Texas Instruments, Inc.,
    286
Thatcher, Margaret, Prime
    Minister, 145
Theories, 65-67, 98-100,
    113-114, 135-137, 149-
    170, 178-189, 229-234,
    270-273, 290-297, 298-
    302
    application of, 9-16

    integration of, 303-
        309
    see also specific
        theories
Tower, Perrin, Forster &
    Crosby, 107
Treadmill constraint, 84-85
Trickle down theory,
    135-137
Two-factor theory, 10-11,
    230, 305

United Airlines, 283-284,
    288
University of Michigan
    Research Center, survey
    conducted by, 333

Values
    employees', 50-53
    individuality of,
        80-82
Values analysis, 283-289,
    312
Vroom, Victor H., 182, 189

Wage and salary
    administration, 22-23
Wage compression, 57
Wages: *see* Compensation;
    Money; Salary
Walker, James W., Dr., 107
Wallop, Don, 88
Wang, An, 39
Wang Laboratories, 39
Watson, John H., M.D., 147
Weick, Karl E., 207
Weiner, Bernard, 184
White, Robert, 187, 231
Wible, J. Richard, 108
Wilson, Lord, former Prime
    Minister, 145
Winter, David S., 291
Wisckol, Kim, 39

Wofford, Jerry C., 187
"Women and Work, An
    In-Depth Survey," 107
Work climate, positive
    rules for providing,
    109-112
Work content, enrichment
    of, 15, 65-69
Work environment: *see*
    Environmental factors
Work ethics, 100-101
    implementation of,
        171-177

Worker malaise, 106-108

Yankelovich, Daniel, 72-73,
    332
Yankelovich, Skelly & White
    Inc., 72, 332
Yetton, Philip W., 189
Yukl, Gary A., 185

Zaleznik, Abraham,
    Professor, 144
Zenger-Miller, Inc., 95